MAT®

STRATEGIES, PRACTICE, AND REVIEW

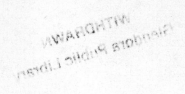

ALSO FROM KAPLAN PUBLISHING

GRE® Strategies, Practice, and Review with 4 Practice Tests
GRE® Premier with 6 Practice Tests
GRE® Vocabulary Flashcards + App
GRE® Math Workbook
GRE® Verbal Workbook

MAT®

STRATEGIES, PRACTICE, AND REVIEW

Sixth Edition

KAPLAN

PUBLISHING

New York

This publication is designed to provide accurate and authoritative information in regard to the subject matter covered. It is sold with the understanding that the publisher is not engaged in rendering legal, accounting, or other professional service. If legal advice or other expert assistance is required, the services of a competent professional should be sought.

© 2016 by Kaplan, Inc.

Published by Kaplan Publishing
750 Third Avenue
New York, NY 10017

10 9 8 7 6 5 4 3 2 1

ISBN: 978-1-5062-1112-1

Contents

How to Use This Book

If you picked up this book, you're probably preparing to take the Miller Analogies Test® in the near future. While the MAT may seem like a huge hurdle that could prevent you from getting into the grad school of your dreams, everything you need to get yourself over this hurdle is right in your hands. Like so many things, the MAT gets less and less intimidating with familiarity. As the test prep adage goes, **familiarity breeds success.**

Here are some suggestions as to how you can most effectively use this book in your exam preparation:

1. Read **Section One: The Basics** to set the stage for your training and testing success. In this section, we'll introduce you to the mysteries of the MAT and show you how to take control of the test-taking experience.

2. Take the full-length **Diagnostic Test** under strictly timed conditions. Then review your Diagnostic Test. Be sure to check the answer explanations for **all** the questions, not just those you answered incorrectly. Take note of the types of questions you found difficult so you can concentrate on those areas when reading through the content chapters and Kaplan Study Lists.

3. Read **Section Three: MAT Content Areas** to get a better idea of how to tackle the breadth of topics that are covered on the MAT. After learning from the example problems, try the short quiz at the end of each chapter.

4. Spend the bulk of your study time going through **Section Four: Kaplan Study Lists** for help with vocabulary and important names, terms, and concepts in a wide variety of subjects.

5. Take **Practice Test 1** under strictly timed conditions. Review your test, reading carefully through all the answer explanations. Find out where you need help, and then review the appropriate chapters and/or Kaplan Study Lists. Repeat this process with **Practice Tests 2 through 6**.

6. Keep reviewing the terms and study lists in this book the week before your test date. Then give yourself a day of rest right before the real exam.

The Basics

CHAPTER ONE

An Overview of the MAT

If you're reading this, you are probably considering applying to graduate school and have been informed that the program you're interested in weighs scores from the **Miller Analogies Test** (commonly known as the **MAT**) as part of its application process. And before you heard this news, you were probably blissfully ignorant of the very existence of the MAT.

Just what is the MAT? **The MAT is a 60-minute test of 120 analogies** (that's 30 seconds per question!) testing far-ranging knowledge in areas as diverse as vocabulary, history, literature, fine arts, mathematics, science, general knowledge, and even anagrams. One hundred of the analogies count toward your score, while 20 are experimental and do not affect your score. Unfortunately, it is impossible to tell while taking the MAT which questions are experimental and which ones count.

In some ways, the MAT is a trivia test, and as such, it would seem more appropriate as a qualifying test for *Jeopardy*™ contestants than as an admissions test for grad school applicants. But no matter: If you need to take the MAT, the good news is that you can learn how to get a great score on this test. That's what we're here for.

If you haven't done so already, check out the MAT website: **http://milleranalogies.com**. There you'll find what the test maker has to say about the test.

HOW TO APPROACH THE MAT

There are two ways you can look at the MAT: as fun or intimidating. We would prefer that you look upon the MAT as fun—it will help you score higher. But we can also understand why it can seem intimidating, and we want to explain why it shouldn't be.

Why the MAT Seems Intimidating

- The subject matter covered is incredibly broad, covering math and science as well as art, literature, and history, with a few truly wacky questions added in just to spice up the mix.
- The format is confusing. Before you can even try to pick an answer, you have to figure out which words go with which.
- No matter how hard you study for the MAT, there's no way in the world that you will be able to answer every question with complete confidence (at least we've never heard of it being done yet).
- It's a bizarre exam that barely survived into the 21st century, and yet somehow, for some reason, your graduate program still makes you take it!

Why the MAT Is Actually Fun

- It's so weird that you really can't take it too seriously.
- It's like being a contestant on *Jeopardy*™, without having to suffer through the tryouts.
- By the time you're done with this book, you're bound to get a higher score than you would have originally (and doing well is always fun).

So—let the fun begin!

MANAGING STRESS

The countdown has begun. Your date with the test is looming on the horizon. Anxiety is on the rise. The butterflies in your stomach have gone ballistic, and your thinking is getting cloudy. Maybe you think you won't be ready. Maybe you already know your stuff, but you're going into panic mode anyway. Don't worry. It's possible to tame that anxiety and stress—before and during the test.

Quick Tips for the Days Just Before the Exam

Taper off your study schedule and take it easy on yourself. The best test takers do less and less as the test approaches. You want to be relaxed and ready on the day of the test. Give yourself time off, especially the evening before the exam. By then, if you've studied well, everything you need to know is firmly stored in your memory banks.

Build your confidence through self-affirmations. Positive self-talk can be extremely liberating and invigorating, especially as the test looms closer. Tell yourself things such as, "I choose to take this test," rather than "I have to"; "I will do well," rather than "I hope things go well"; "I can," rather than "I cannot." Be aware of negative, self-defeating thoughts and images and immediately replace them with affirming statements that encourage your self-esteem and confidence.

Get your act together sooner rather than later. Have everything (pencils, ID, admission ticket, etc.) laid out days in advance. Most important, know where the test will be held and the easiest, quickest way to get there. You will gain great peace of mind if you know that all the little details are firmly in your control before the day of the test.

Handling Stress During the Test

The biggest stress monster will be the test itself. Fear not; there are methods of quelling your stress during the test.

Keep moving forward instead of getting bogged down in a difficult question. You don't have to get everything right to achieve a good score. The best test takers skip difficult material temporarily in search of the easier stuff. Note the questions that require extra time and thought. This strategy buys time and builds confidence so you can handle the tough stuff later.

Don't be thrown if other test takers seem to be plowing through the test faster than you. Continue to spend your time patiently thinking through your answers; it's going to lead to better results. Don't mistake other people's sheer activity as a sign of progress and higher scores.

Keep breathing! Weak test takers tend to forget to breathe properly as the test proceeds. They start holding their breath without realizing it, or they breathe erratically or arrhythmically. Improper breathing interferes with clear thinking.

Some quick isometrics during the test—especially if concentration is wandering or energy is waning—can help. Try this: Put your palms together and press intensely for a few seconds. Concentrate on the tension you feel through your palms, wrists, forearms, and up into your biceps and shoulders. Then, quickly release the pressure. Feel the difference as you let go. Focus on the warm relaxation that floods through the muscles. Now you're ready to return to the task. Another isometric that will relieve tension in both your neck and eye muscles: Slowly rotate your head from side to side, turning your head and eyes to look as far back over each shoulder as you can. Feel the muscles stretch on one side of your neck as they contract on the other. Repeat five times in each direction.

With what you've learned in this book, you're armed and ready to do battle with the test. You also know how to deal with any excess tension that might come along, both when you're studying for and taking the exam. You've learned everything you need to tame your anxiety and stress. You're going to get a great score.

SAMPLE ANALOGIES

Let's take a quick look at some sample Miller Analogies.

Directions: For each of the following questions, you will find three capitalized terms and, in parentheses, four answer choices designated *a*, *b*, *c*, and *d*. Select the one answer choice that best completes the analogy with the three capitalized terms.

1. PENURIOUS : OBSEQUIOUS :: FRUGAL : (a. compliant, b. economical, c. supercilious, d. retiring)

2. ANDERSON : (a. Ford/Carter, b. Reagan/Carter, c. Reagan/Mondale, d. Bush/Dukakis) :: PEROT : BUSH/CLINTON

3. ODE TO A NIGHTINGALE : THE RAVEN :: (a. Byron, b. Keats, c. Shelley, d. Yeats) : POE

4. RENOIR : SEURAT :: IMPRESSIONISM : (a. cubism, b. fauvism, c. pointalism, d. naturalism)

5. $\frac{1}{3} : \frac{5}{6}$ :: 6 : (a. 10, b. 12, c. 15, d. 20)

6. (a. Bacon, b. Galileo, c. Kepler, d. Ptolomy) : COPERNICUS :: GEOCENTRIC : HELIOCENTRIC

7. NORWAY: (a. Denmark, b. Scotland, c. Finland, d. Wales) :: LUTEFISK : HAGGIS

8. STRAP : SPOOL :: (a. part, b. reel, c. trap, d. tars) : LOOP

Answer Explanations

1. PENURIOUS : OBSEQUIOUS :: FRUGAL : (**a. compliant**, b. economical, c. supercilious, d. retiring)

   (**a**) Someone who is penurious is extremely frugal, and someone who is obsequious is extremely compliant.

2. ANDERSON : (a. Ford/Carter, **b. Reagan/Carter**, c. Reagan/Mondale, d. Bush/Dukakis) :: PEROT : BUSH/CLINTON

   (**b**) Third-party candidate John Anderson ran in the Reagan/Carter election of 1980, and third-party candidate Ross Perot ran in the Bush/Clinton election of 1992.

3. ODE TO A NIGHTINGALE : THE RAVEN :: (a. Byron, **b. Keats**, c. Shelley, d. Yeats) : POE

   (**b**) Keats wrote the poem "Ode to a Nightingale," and Poe wrote the poem "The Raven."

4. RENOIR : SEURAT :: IMPRESSIONISM : (a. cubism, b. fauvism, **c. pointalism**, d. naturalism)

   (**c**) August Renoir was one of the founders of the art movement known as impressionism, and Georges Seurat was one of the founders of the art movement known as pointalism.

5. $\frac{1}{3} : \frac{5}{6} : 6 : $ (a. 10, b. 12, **c. 15**, d. 20)

   (**c**) The ratio of $\frac{1}{3}$ to $\frac{5}{6}$ is 2 to 5, and the ratio of 6 to 15 is also 2 to 5.

6. (a. Bacon, b. Galileo, c. Kepler, **d. Ptolomy**) : COPERNICUS :: GEOCENTRIC : HELIOCENTRIC

   (**d**) Ptolomy proposed the geocentric theory of the solar system (that the earth was the center of the solar system), and Copernicus proposed the heliocentric theory of the solar system (that the sun was the center of the solar system).

7. NORWAY: (a. Denmark, **b. Scotland**, c. Finland, d. Wales) :: LUTEFISK : HAGGIS

   (**b**) The national dish of Norway is lutefisk, and the national dish of Scotland is haggis.

8. STRAP : SPOOL :: (**a. part**, b. reel, c. trap, d. tars) : LOOP

   (**a**) If you reverse the letters in the word *strap* and remove the *s*, you get the word *part*, and if you reverse *spool* and remove the *s*, you get the word *loop*.

MAT TOPICS

Now let's take a look at the topics that could appear on the MAT. Subsequent chapters will examine these subject areas in greater detail. Try to answer the following questions, but don't worry about whether you get them right or wrong.

Directions: For each of the following questions, you will find three capitalized terms and, in parentheses, four answer choices designated *a*, *b*, *c*, and *d*. Select the one answer choice that best completes the analogy with the three capitalized terms.

Language (Vocabulary, Word Meanings, Grammar, Usage)

1. ARCADIAN : ARCANE :: IDYLLIC : (a. pastoral, b. worshipful, c. mysterious, d. popular)

2. IRASCIBLE : PLACID :: GULLIBLE : (a. impetuous, b. impecunious, c. incredulous, d. indelible)

3. MEGA : META :: LARGE : (a. beyond, b. before, c. between, d. beneath)

4. SODDEN : (a. dirty, b. sober, c. impassive, d. moist) :: MAUDLIN : EMOTIONAL

5. BE : SEE :: REFLEXIVE : (a. imperative, b. indicative, c. subjunctive, d. transitive)

6. OVUM : STIMULUS :: (a. ova, b. ovi, c. ovula, d. ovums) : STIMULI

7. SAUSAGE : NECTARINES :: ASSUAGE : (a. transience, b. cantinas, c. entrances, d. renascent)

8. REWARD : TIME :: DRAWER : (a. clock, b. shelf, c. emit, d. smite)

9. TOUGH : THOUGH :: STUFF : (a. tough, b. tow, c. true, d. trough)

Answers

1. **(c)** *Arcadian* is a synonym for *idyllic* or *peaceful*, and *arcane* is a synonym for *mysterious.*

2. **(c)** An *irascible* person is the opposite of *placid*, just as a *gullible* person is the opposite of *incredulous*, meaning "skeptical."

3. **(a)** *Mega* is a prefix meaning "large," and *meta* is a prefix meaning "beyond."

4. **(d)** *Sodden* means "overly moist," and *maudlin* means "overly emotional."

5. **(d)** *To be* is a reflexive verb, and *to see* is a transitive verb.

6. **(a)** The plural of *ovum* is *ova*, just as the plural of *stimulus* is *stimuli*.

7. **(a)** Rearrange the letters in *sausage* and get the word *assuage*, and rearrange the letters in the word *nectarines* and get the word *transience*.

8. **(c)** Reverse the word *reward* and get the word *drawer*, just as you reverse the word *time* and get the word *emit*.

9. **(b)** *Tough* rhymes with *stuff*, and *though* rhymes with *tow*.

Humanities (Fine Art, Literature, History, Philosophy, Religion, Music)

1. (a. Bosch, b. Botticelli, c. Durer, d.Michelangelo) : DA VINCI :: THE GARDEN OF EARTHLY DELIGHTS : THE LAST SUPPER

2. CHRYSLER BUILDING : (a. gothic, b. art deco, c. baroque, d. postmodern) :: SEARS TOWER : MODERNIST

3. MARLOWE : SHAKESPEARE :: MELVILLE : (a. Hawthorne, b. Hamlet, c. Hugo, d. Hart)

4. VIRGIL : (a. Aeneid, b. Iliad, c. Media, d. Metamorphosis) :: DVORAK : NEW WORLD SYMPHONY

5. THE BLACK DEATH : 14th :: THE REFORMATION : (a. 15th, b. 16th, c. 17th, d. 18th)

6. D-DAY : (a. World War I, b. Hundred Years' War, c. World War II, d. Vietnam) :: GETTYSBURG : CIVIL WAR

7. MUHAMMAD : (a. Lao-tzu, b. Siddhartha, c. Confucius, d. Wang-Wei) :: ISLAM : TAOISM

Answers

1. **(a)** Hieronymus Bosch painted *The Garden of Earthly Delights*, and Leonardo Da Vinci painted *The Last Supper*.

2. **(b)** The Chrysler Building in New York City is an example of art deco architecture, while the Sears Tower in Chicago is an example of modernist architecture.

3. **(a)** The writer Christopher Marlowe was a contemporary of Shakespeare, and author Herman Melville was a contemporary of Nathaniel Hawthorne.

4. **(a)** Virgil wrote the *Aeneid*, and Anton Dvorak wrote the *New World Symphony*.

5. **(b)** The Black Death took place in the 14th century, and the Reformation took place in the 16th century.

6. **(c)** D-Day was a major battle during World War II, and Gettysburg was a major battle in the Civil War.

7. **(a)** Muhammad is the founder of the religion Islam, just as Lao-Tzu is the founder of the religion Taoism.

Social Sciences (Psychology, Sociology, Anthropology, Political Science, Economics)

1. DURKHEIM : (a. Adler, b. Erickson, c. Jung, d. Piaget) :: COLLECTIVE EFFERVESCENCE : COLLECTIVE UNCONSCIOUS

2. DAS KAPITAL : MARX :: DEMOCRACY IN AMERICA : (a. Paine, b. Veblen, c. Tocqueville, d. James)

3. CEYLON : (a. Burma, b. Malaysia, c. Indonesia, d. Sri Lanka) :: SIAM :: THAILAND

4. JEFFERSON : ADAMS :: (a. Roosevelt, b. Nixon, c. MacArthur, d. Eisenhower) : TRUMAN

5. STATES' RIGHTS : (a. VII, b. VIII, c. IX, d. X) :: FREE SPEECH : I

Answers

1. **(c)** Sociologist Emile Durkheim created the theory of collective effervescence, and psychologist Carl Jung created the theory of the collective unconscious.

2. **(c)** *Das Kapital* is a seminal political treatise by Karl Marx, just as *Democracy in America* is a seminal political treatise by Alexis de Toqueville.

3. **(d)** Ceylon is the former name of Sri Lanka, and Siam is the former name of Thailand.

4. **(d)** Thomas Jefferson was elected president immediately after John Adams, and Dwight Eisenhower was elected president after Harry S. Truman.

5. **(d)** States' rights are the subject of the Tenth Amendment to the U.S. Constitution, represented by Roman numeral X, just as free speech is the subject of the First Amendment to the U.S. Constitution, represented by Roman numeral I.

Natural Sciences (Biology, Chemistry, Physics, Ecology)

1. MARSUPIAL : OPOSSUM :: PLACENTAL : (a. platypus, b. penguin, c. crocodile, d. whale)

2. NA : NE :: (a. naphtha, b. silver, c. sodium, d. tungsten) : NEON

3. EINSTEIN : (a. chaos, b. entropy, c. quantum mechanics, d. relativity) :: DARWIN : EVOLUTION

4. JUPITER : MARS :: GREAT RED SPOT : (a. Sea of Tranquility, b. Europa, c. Olympus Mons, d. rings)

Answers

1. **(d)** An opossum is a marsupial mammal, and a whale is a placental mammal.

2. **(c)** The periodic symbol for sodium is *Na*, just as the periodic symbol for neon is *Ne*.

3. **(d)** Albert Einstein originated the theory of relativity, and Charles Darwin originated the theory of evolution.

4. **(c)** Jupiter is known for its Great Red Spot, and Mars is known for its Olympus Mons.

Mathematics (Ratios, Terms and Definitions, Roman Numerals, Units of Measurement)

1. V : X :: (a. XXV, b. C, c. CCL, d. M) : D

2. 90 : 180 :: COMPLEMENTARY : (a. scalene, b. perpendicular, c. obtuse, d. supplementary)

3. POUND : STONE :: 1 : (a. 6, b. 10, c. 14, d. 20)

Answers

1. **(c)** Five, or Roman numeral V, is half of 10, or Roman numeral X, just as 250, Roman numeral CCL, is half of 500, Roman numeral D.

2. **(d)** Two angles are known as complementary if their sum total equals 90 degrees, and two angles are known as supplementary if their sum total equals 180 degrees.

3. **(c)** One stone equals 14 pounds.

General Knowledge (Culture, Work, Business, Life Experience)

1. TWILIGHT ZONE : STAR TREK :: (a. Bova, b. Clarke, c. Odets, d. Serling) : RODDENBERRY

2. ARMY : NAVY :: GENERAL : (a. admiral, b. captain, c. commodore, d. commander)

3. CHARTREUSE : (a. brown, b. green, c. red, d. maize) :: AZURE : BLUE

4. BILL RUSSELL : (a. Lakers, b. Sonics, c. Celtics, d. Astros) :: MICKEY MANTLE : YANKEES

Answers

1. **(d)** Rod Serling was the creator of the television show *Twilight Zone*, and Gene Roddenberry was the creator of the television show *Star Trek*.

2. **(a)** A general is the highest rank in the Army, just as an admiral is the highest rank in the Navy.

3. **(b)** Chartreuse is a shade of green, and azure is a shade of blue.

4. **(c)** Center Bill Russell played his entire career for the Boston Celtics, and Mickey Mantle played his entire career with the New York Yankees.

MAT SCORING

About two weeks after you take the MAT, you'll receive a score report containing three pieces of information:

- Your scaled score, between 200 and 600, computed from the number of questions you got right
- Your percentile rank within your intended major
- Your percentile rank among all test takers

Here are the most important things to understand about MAT scoring:

- Your score is based only on **the number of questions you get right**. That means there's **no wrong-answer penalty**. So **you should always guess** on questions you can't answer or don't get to.

- Your percentile rank among all test takers doesn't matter. **What does matter is your percentile rank within your intended major and, even more importantly, your percentile rank within the specific school and program to which you are applying.** Call the admissions office of whichever program you want to know about and ask them what score they are looking for and how important the MAT is to their admissions process. You may well find that you have less to worry about than you think.

- The testmaker has not released an updated raw score to scaled score conversion table in several years. The average MAT scaled score is about a 400, and if scoring has not changed much over the years, a raw score in the low 40s will likely produce this average score. Remember that your raw score is the number you get right out of 100 scored questions; 20 of the 120 questions you see on Test Day will be experimental and will not count toward your score in any way.

The No-Score Option

When you take the MAT, you will be given a "no-score" option at the end of the exam. If you choose the no-score option, your test will not be scored, and you won't find out how well you did on the exam. Given the difficult nature of the MAT, you could easily be persuaded to choose the no-score option. Here's why you **shouldn't**.

- You're likely to feel you did poorly right after you take the MAT. Even the best test takers can't be expected to answer every MAT question with confidence.

- Do you really want to take the test again if you don't have to? Even if you think you bombed the test, you may well get the baseline score you need for the program you're considering.

- If you find out you really did do worse than you wanted to on the test, you can always take the test again. Many schools only look at your highest score on the MAT.

WHERE, WHEN, AND HOW TO TAKE THE MAT

Unlike many other standardized tests, the MAT is not offered at set times during the year, and the same test is not administered to everyone at a given test site at a given time.

Instead, the MAT is administered at hundreds of Controlled Testing Centers (CTCs) in the United States, Canada, and overseas, and each CTC determines its own test schedule and test fees. While the MAT is administered throughout the year, it is administered most frequently in the fall. To determine where and when to take the MAT, you should look through the list of CTCs, which you can get by contacting Pearson.

Pearson
MAT Customer Relations
19500 Bulverde Road
San Antonio, Texas 78259
Telephone: 800-622-3231 or (210) 339-8710
Monday–Friday, 8:30 A.M.–5:00 P.M. Central Standard Time
Fax: 888-211-8276
Email: MATscoring.services@pearson.com
Web: milleranalogies.com

If you call, you can also ask for the phone numbers of CTCs in your area. You must call the CTC directly to find out the dates and times the MAT will be offered and other relevant information. The cost to take the test is also determined by the CTC. At the time of publication, the cost is generally around $85.00.

CHAPTER TWO

Kaplan's Method for Miller Analogies

Miller Analogies can be tricky. To do well on them, you need to be able to avoid answer choice traps. And you need to use a single approach that will allow you to handle all the different types of analogies that can appear on the exam.

Fortunately, Kaplan's 4-Step Method for Miller Analogies can help you to accomplish all of these things. With no further ado, here are the steps:

KAPLAN'S 4-STEP METHOD

Step 1. Determine whether the relationship is 1:2—3:4 or 1:3—2:4.

Step 2. Build a bridge between the complete pair.

Step 3. Use your bridge on the incomplete pair and choose the answer that fits the bridge.

Step 4. Work backwards when you have to.

Now let's see how this method works in practice.

STEP 1. DETERMINE THE RELATIONSHIP

One annoying thing about MAT analogies is that you have to figure out for yourself which two of the three given stem words form a proper relationship. Luckily, we know the relationship must be either **1:2—3:4** or **1:3—2:4**.

Here's a typical 1:2—3:4 analogy:

BOLOGNA : COLD CUT :: PARFAIT : (a. banana, b. dessert, c. pastrami, d. entrée)

The first two words in this analogy fit easily together: BOLOGNA is a type of COLD CUT. (If you try to fit BOLOGNA and PARFAIT together, you get nothing that anyone would want to eat.)

Answer: Just as BOLOGNA is a type of COLD CUT, a PARFAIT is a type of DESSERT, so the answer is **(b)**.

Now take a look at a 1:3—2:4 analogy:

RENEGADE : INTROVERT :: LOYAL : (a. gregarious, b. steadfast, c. treacherous, d. withdrawn)

Go ahead and try to find a relationship between RENEGADE and INTROVERT. It can't be done. A RENEGADE *may or may not be* an INTROVERT, so try to find a relationship between RENEGADE and LOYAL instead. These two words do fit together: a RENEGADE is *not* LOYAL. Now answer the question:

Answer: A RENEGADE is not LOYAL, just as an INTROVERT is not GREGARIOUS, so the answer is **(a)**.

In both the cases we looked at, the missing word was in position 4, but what happens when it occurs elsewhere? We're glad you asked! **The missing word can appear in any position**—but it still should be easy (most of the time) to determine whether the analogy has a 1:2—3:4 or a 1:3—2:4 arrangement:

FRAGILE : (a. brittle, b. spoiled, c. sturdy, d. malleable) :: BREAK : MOLD

You should start by seeing whether you could have a 1:3—2:4 relationship. Is there a clear relationship between FRAGILE and BREAK? Sure there is. Something that's FRAGILE is easy to BREAK. Now pick an answer.

Answer: Just as something FRAGILE is easy to BREAK, something MALLEABLE is easy to MOLD, so the answer is **(d)**.

And, of course, if a 1:2 or 1:3 relationship can't be determined, you can always check out the 2:4 or 3:4 relationship:

CHAPTER : (a. conductor, b. novel, c. orchestra, b. paragraph) :: MOVEMENT : SYMPHONY

Here, there's no easily defined relationship between relationship between CHAPTER and MOVEMENT (and you should never spend more than a few seconds trying to come up with a relationship).

So what about MOVEMENT and SYMPHONY? Now there's a relationship that makes sense. A SYMPHONY is composed of MOVEMENTS. (Tip: You can always start with the second word first, as long as you do the same thing with the other pair of words.) Now find the answer.

Answer: As a SYMPHONY is composed of MOVEMENTS, likewise a NOVEL is composed of CHAPTERS, so the answer is **(b)**.

Finally, you should always try this approach when the missing word is in position 1. Try the following:

> (a. etymology, b. ontology, c. pedagogy, d. philosophy) : ENTOMOLOGY ::
> EDUCATION : INSECTS

Answer: Just as the study of INSECTS is called ENTOMOLOGY, the study of EDUCATION is called PEDAGOGY. The correct answer is **(c)**.

STEP 2. BUILD A BRIDGE BETWEEN THE COMPLETE PAIR

A **bridge** is the sentence you come up with to relate one word to another after you've determined that two words go together. For instance, if your analogy pair is GOOSE : GANDER, your bridge might be this: A male GOOSE is called a GANDER.

Keys to Building Good Bridges

- Build a sentence that makes the relationship between the two words clear.
- Keep the sentence short and to the point.
- Avoid qualifying phrases such as *could*, *sometimes*, *may or may not*, etc.

Now try building your own bridges and see how they compare to ours. Write your bridges into the spaces provided.

1. THOMAS JEFFERSON _____ DECLARATION OF INDEPENDENCE.
2. LETHARGY _____ ENERGY.
3. FOAL _____ HORSE.
4. POTTER _____ CLAY.
5. SCHOOL _____ FISH.

Here are the bridges we came up with. Yours might be worded somewhat differently.

1. THOMAS JEFFERSON wrote the DECLARATION OF INDEPENDENCE.
2. LETHARGY is a lack of ENERGY.
3. A FOAL is a baby HORSE.
4. A POTTER works with CLAY.
5. A SCHOOL is a group of FISH.

STEP 3. CHOOSE THE ANSWER THAT FITS THE BRIDGE

After you have determined which stem word goes with which and have made a bridge with the two complete stem words, you're ready to try out your bridge on the incomplete pair.

You should, in fact, be able to predict the missing word if you've built a good bridge—maybe not an exact word but a word that could complete the analogy. Before we give you the answer choices, let's see if you can finish the analogies for the following questions.

Directions: Come up with words to complete the following analogies and write those words in the blanks provided.

1. DEFLATE : BALLOON :: ABRIDGE : _____

2. _____ : AUTHENTICITY :: ELABORATE : COUNTERFEIT

3. CENSUS : POPULATION :: _____ : MERCHANDISE

4. BELL : _____ :: MARCONI : RADIO

5. MAPLE : DECIDUOUS :: SPRUCE : _____

Now we've provided the answer choices, so that you can pick the answer choice that comes closest to your prediction.

Choose **a**, **b**, **c**, or **d** for each of the following questions:

1. DEFLATE : BALLOON :: ABRIDGE : (a. canal, b. inner tube, c. novel, d. party)

2. (a. explanation, b. simplicity, c. idle, c. sophisticated) : AUTHENTICITY :: ELABORATE : COUNTERFEIT

3. CENSUS : POPULATION :: (a. commodity, b. poll, c. inventory. d. market) : MERCHANDISE

4. BELL : (a. television, b. air conditioner, c. alarm, d. telephone) :: MARCONI : RADIO

5. MAPLE : DECIDUOUS :: SPRUCE : (a. coniferous, b. tropical, c. perennial, d. verdant)

Answers:

1. **(c)** Deflating a balloon makes it smaller, and abridging a novel makes it smaller.

2. **(b)** Something that's elaborate lacks simplicity, and something that's counterfeit lacks authenticity.

3. **(c)** A census counts population, and an inventory counts merchandise.

4. **(d)** Alexander Graham Bell was the inventor of the telephone, and Guglielmo Marconi was the inventor of the radio.

5. **(a)** A maple is a deciduous tree, and a spruce is a coniferous tree.

STEP 4. WORK BACKWARDS WHEN YOU HAVE TO

So far, everything has gone smoothly (we hope), but what do you do when the going gets tough? What if you can't build a bridge between the stem words? Or you don't know some of the stem words? Or you know you understand one half of the analogy, but you don't know how to complete it?

When the going gets tough, the tough work backwards.

Let's see how this is done.

The first thing to remember when you hit a hard question is to skip it until you've answered all the questions that don't give you trouble. If you do have the time to go back to it, here are our tips for working backwards.

Tips for Working Backwards

1. If you can't build a bridge, pay attention to the parts of speech of the stem words. Consider different ways to build a bridge.
2. Look for trap answer choices and eliminate them.
3. Try out the remaining answer choices and see if one of them makes sense.
4. If you're stuck, guess.

Let's take a look at each of these strategies.

Pay Attention to Parts of Speech

If an analogy confuses you, you should take a look at the **parts of speech** in the question—that is, whether the words are **nouns**, **verbs**, **adjectives**, etc. With very few exceptions, parts of speech are always consistent within an analogy. In other words, if the first word of one word pair is an adjective and the second word is a noun, then the same is true for the other word pair. You can use this information to determine whether the analogy is 1:2—3:4 or 1:3—2:4.

For instance, if you see

ADJECTIVE : (a. adjective, b. adjective, c. adjective, d. adjective) :: NOUN : NOUN

you would know that the analogy is 1:3—2:4:

ADJECTIVE : (a. adjective, b. adjective, c. adjective, d. adjective) :: NOUN : NOUN

Moreover, because it's not always clear whether a word is being used as a noun, verb, or adjective, referring to the parts of speech of the other words in the analogy can help you get a fix on how the word is being used.

For instance, check out the following analogy.

TABLE : MOTION :: (a. incur, b. defer, c. disburse, d. repay) : PAYMENT

By looking at the other words in this analogy, how would you predict that TABLE is being used here? As a noun? A verb? An adjective?

Answer: MOTION and PAYMENT are both nouns. The answer choices—*incur*, *defer*, *disburse*, and *grant*—are all verbs. Thus TABLE here is being used as a verb.

Once you've identified the parts of speech for all the words in your analogy, you can usually determine whether the analogy is 1:2—3:4 or 1:3—2:4. For instance, you now know you have

VERB : NOUN :: (a. verb, b. verb, c. verb, d. verb) : NOUN

Because the parts of speech are consistent within an analogy, you would predict that this analogy is 1:2—3:4.

Now that you know that you have a 1:2—3:4 analogy and that TABLE here is being used as a verb, you should try to build a bridge between TABLE and MOTION and choose the answer choice that best fits the bridge.

TABLE : MOTION :: (a. incur, b. defer, c. disburse, d. repay) : PAYMENT

Answer: **(b)** To table a motion is to postpone it, just as to defer a payment is to postpone it.

Eliminate Trap Answer Choices

You can use what you know about parts of speech to eliminate answer choices that exhibit the wrong parts of speech.

Directions: Cross out any answer choice that you can eliminate because it is the wrong part of speech.

ADJECTIVE : NOUN :: (a. waft, b. temperate, c. ferocious, d. obliterate) : NOUN

Answer: You should have eliminated choices (a) and (d) because neither *waft* nor *obliterate* is an adjective, as we require.

Now here's the entire question.

Directions: Pick the best answer.

GENTLE : BREEZE :: (a. waft, b. temperate, c. ferocious, d. obliterate) : SQUALL

Answer: **(c)** A breeze is a gentle wind, just as a squall is a ferocious wind.

You can also use what you know about the order of difficulty to be on the lookout for answer choice traps. If you're on an early question, you can usually assume that your first instincts will be correct and that the most common usage of a word is being tested. However, by the time you get to the tough questions, answer choice traps abound, and your initial instincts cannot be trusted. Here the test maker often tests obscure meanings to common words. Answer choices that contain obvious associations with your stem words are often traps.

So for instance, which answer choices do you think might be traps in the following question, if it were question 119 in the 120-question test?

Directions: Eliminate trap answer choices and pick the best answer.

119. NAPOLEON : (a. pastry, b. Waterloo, c. shoe, d. Josephine) :: STETSON : HAT

Answer: **(a)** is correct. When most people see NAPOLEON, they think first of the French emperor and thus are tempted by choices such as (b) Waterloo and (d) Josephine, which makes these answers suspect, at best. Since we're late in the set, you should ask yourself: Can NAPOLEON mean anything else? Can a bridge be built between STETSON and HAT? Yes and yes! A Napoleon is a type of pastry, just as a Stetson is a type of hat.

Try Out the Answer Choices

Working backwards can be especially helpful when you don't know the meaning of one of the stem words or if you suspect that an uncommon meaning of a common word is being tested. If you don't know how a word is being used, ignore it and see what the other words can reveal. For instance, with one word obscured, what do you know about the following analogy?

(a. puzzle, b. anticoagulant, c. confusion, d. tourniquet) : XXXXXX :: BLEEDING : NOISE

Question: Does this analogy have a 1:2—3:4 arrangement or a 1:3—2:4 arrangement?

Answer: There's no way to make a logical bridge between BLEEDING and NOISE, so this analogy must have a 1:3—2:4 arrangement.

Question: What part of speech is the obscured word? A noun? A verb? An adjective? Something else?

Answer: All the answer choices are nouns, so the obscured word, which corresponds to the correct answer choice in the analogy, must also be a noun.

Now try working backward from the answer choices.

(a. puzzle, b. anticoagulant, c. confusion, d. tourniquet) : XXXXXX :: BLEEDING : NOISE

Question: From which of the following can you make a bridge?

    a. PUZZLE : BLEEDING
    b. ANTICOAGULANT : BLEEDING
    c. CONFUSION : BLEEDING
    d. TOURNIQUET : BLEEDING

Answer: There is no way to make a bridge between choices (a) and (c), so these choices can be eliminated. You should be able to make a bridge between ANTICOAGULANT and BLEEDING (an anticoagulant encourages bleeding) and between TOURNIQUET and BLEEDING (a tourniquet reduces bleeding), so you should keep those answer choices.

Now we'll reveal the other stem word, so you can pick the correct answer.

    (a. puzzle, b. anticoagulant, c. confusion, d. tourniquet) : BAFFLE :: BLEEDING : NOISE

Answer: (**d**) A tourniquet is used to impede bleeding, and a baffle is used to impede noise.

KAPLAN'S TEST-TAKING AND PACING STRATEGIES

In addition to Kaplan's 4-Step Method for Miller Analogies, you need to know Kaplan's Test-Taking and Pacing Strategies in order to maximize your score.

- Be prepared to handle the early questions fairly quickly—but don't be in such a rush that you get them wrong. An easy question is worth just as much as a hard one.
- Take note of the questions you guessed on by writing the question numbers on scratch paper (which will be provided for you). You can go back to these questions after you've answered all the remaining questions in the test.
- Don't waste time on questions that give you trouble when you first go through the test. Either skip them or make a guess and take note of the question, as mentioned above.
- Difficult questions call for different approaches. On questions that contain terms or vocabulary you haven't seen before, use strategies and eliminate answer choice traps.
- Don't worry about trying to give every question your fullest effort. If you don't get around to some of the questions that you skipped on your first time through the test, just be sure to make a guess on these questions.
- Bring a watch and pay attention to the time. When there are just two minutes left, make sure to fill in answers for all the remaining questions. The quickest method: Pick one letter (*a*, *b*, *c*, or *d*) and fill in that letter for all the unanswered questions.

CHAPTER QUIZ: STRATEGIES FOR TACKLING MILLER ANALOGIES

Now try answering the following analogy questions, using the strategies you've just learned.

1. ADVANCE : FLOW :: (a. creep, b. gush, c. drip, d. decline) : TRICKLE

2. INVIDIOUS : OFFEND :: EVANESCENT : (a. shock, b. disappear, c. grow, d. rubbish)

3. IAGO : SHAKESPEARE :: (a. Othello, b. Fagan, c. Romulus, d. Milton) : DICKENS

4. XX : (a. L, b. C, c. CC, d. D) :: C : D

5. CANBERRA : (a. Melbourne, b. Iberia, c. Madeira, d. Lisbon) :: AUSTRALIA : PORTUGAL

6. PRECARIOUS : FALL :: (a. immutable, b. volatile, c. insecure, d. hesitant) : CHANGE

7. FILTH : CLEANSE :: (a. dirt, b. lift, c. preempt, d. faith) : LANCES

8. IODINE : GOITER :: VITAMIN C : (a. beriberi, b. maleria, c. scurvy, d. psoriosis)

9. PROTO : PSEUDO :: (a. genuine, b. intelligent, c. forerunner, d. good) : IMITATION

10. ALUMNA : (a. alumna, b. alumnus, c. alumnas, d. alumnae) :: CURRICULUM : CURRICULA

Answers

1. **(a)** To advance very slowly is to creep, and to flow very slowly is to trickle. (This is a 1:3—2:4 relationship.)

2. **(b)** An invidious person will likely offend, just as something evanescent will likely disappear. (This is a 1:2—3:4 relationship.)

3. **(b)** Iago is a villainous character created by Williams Shakespeare in *Othello*, and Fagan is a villainous character created by Charles Dickens in *Oliver Twist*. (This is a 1:2—3:4 relationship.)

4. **(b)** Twenty (Roman numeral XX) is one-fifth of 100 (Roman numeral C), and 100 (Roman numeral C) is one-fifth of 500 (Roman numeral D). (This is a 1:2—3:4 relationship.)

5. **(d)** Canberra is the capital city of Australia, just as Lisbon is the capital city of Portugal. (This is a 1:3—2:4 relationship.)

6. **(b)** Something precarious is in danger of falling, and something volatile is in danger of changing. (This is a 1:2—3:4 relationship.)

7. **(b)** Removing the final letter of *filth* and rearranging the letters gives you the word *lift*, and removing the final letter of *cleanse* and rearranging the letters gives you the word *lances*. (This is a 1:3—2:4 relationship.)

8. **(c)** Iodine is taken to prevent a goiter, and vitamin C is taken to prevent scurvy. (This is a 1:2—3:4 relationship.)

9. **(c)** *Proto-* is a prefix meaning *forerunner*, and *pseudo-* is a prefix meaning *imitation*. (This is a 1:3—2:4 relationship.)

10. **(d)** The plural of *alumna* (meaning a female graduate) is *alumnae*, and the plural of *curriculum* is *curricula*. (This is a 1:2—3:4 relationship.)

Diagnostic Test

ANSWER SHEET FOR DIAGNOSTIC TEST

1. a b c d	41. a b c d	81. a b c d
2. a b c d	42. a b c d	82. a b c d
3. a b c d	43. a b c d	83. a b c d
4. a b c d	44. a b c d	84. a b c d
5. a b c d	45. a b c d	85. a b c d
6. a b c d	46. a b c d	86. a b c d
7. a b c d	47. a b c d	87. a b c d
8. a b c d	48. a b c d	88. a b c d
9. a b c d	49. a b c d	89. a b c d
10. a b c d	50. a b c d	90. a b c d
11. a b c d	51. a b c d	91. a b c d
12. a b c d	52. a b c d	92. a b c d
13. a b c d	53. a b c d	93. a b c d
14. a b c d	54. a b c d	94. a b c d
15. a b c d	55. a b c d	95. a b c d
16. a b c d	56. a b c d	96. a b c d
17. a b c d	57. a b c d	97. a b c d
18. a b c d	58. a b c d	98. a b c d
19. a b c d	59. a b c d	99. a b c d
20. a b c d	60. a b c d	100. a b c d
21. a b c d	61. a b c d	101. a b c d
22. a b c d	62. a b c d	102. a b c d
23. a b c d	63. a b c d	103. a b c d
24. a b c d	64. a b c d	104. a b c d
25. a b c d	65. a b c d	105. a b c d
26. a b c d	66. a b c d	106. a b c d
27. a b c d	67. a b c d	107. a b c d
28. a b c d	68. a b c d	108. a b c d
29. a b c d	69. a b c d	109. a b c d
30. a b c d	70. a b c d	110. a b c d
31. a b c d	71. a b c d	111. a b c d
32. a b c d	72. a b c d	112. a b c d
33. a b c d	73. a b c d	113. a b c d
34. a b c d	74. a b c d	114. a b c d
35. a b c d	75. a b c d	115. a b c d
36. a b c d	76. a b c d	116. a b c d
37. a b c d	77. a b c d	117. a b c d
38. a b c d	78. a b c d	118. a b c d
39. a b c d	79. a b c d	119. a b c d
40. a b c d	80. a b c d	120. a b c d

FULL-LENGTH DIAGNOSTIC TEST

Time: 60 minutes
Length of Test: 120 Questions

Directions: For each of the following questions, you will find three capitalized terms and, in parentheses, four answer choices designated *a*, *b*, *c*, and *d*. Select the one answer choice that best completes the analogy with the three capitalized terms. (To record your answers, use the answer sheet that precedes this test.)

1. WHISTLE : REFEREE :: (a. motion, b. verdict, c. gavel, d. chamber) : JUDGE

2. 32° : FREEZE :: (a. 100°, b. 180°, c. 212°, d. 320°) : BOIL

3. SCHOLAR : (a. science, b. erudition, c. decency, d. publication) :: PARTISAN : BIAS

4. PIG : GOOSE :: BOAR : (a. gaggle, b. gander, c. gosling, d. cygnet)

5. NIBBLE : (a. whet, b. quench, c. sip, d. guzzle) :: HUNGER : THIRST

6. (a. Samurai, b. Cossack, c. Geisha, d. Mandarin) : PAGODA :: WARRIOR : TOWER

7. THE BIG APPLE : THE BIG EASY :: NY : (a. NB, b. NO, c. NV, d. NZ)

8. CRAB : SEED :: (a. arthropod, b. carapace, c. gill, d. ocean) : HULL

9. SYBARITE : (a. wealth, b. ease, c. power, d. pleasure) :: AESTHETE : BEAUTY

10. HAIRY : (a. slippery, b. shaggy, c. scaly, d. soggy) :: HIRSUTE : SQUAMOUS

11. PLANE : SPHERE :: 2 : (a. 1, b. 2, c. 3, d. 4)

12. MOVIE : (a. celluloid, b. outtakes, c. documentary, d. cinema) :: MEAT : OFFAL

13. GIRDER : FACADE :: BONE : (a. building, b. skeleton, c. pediment, d. skin)

14. (a. referendum, b. election, c. democracy, d. certificate) : DIRECT :: LEGISLATION : REPRESENTATIVE

15. FLASHLIGHT : (a. uniform, b. illuminating, c. mobile, d. direct) :: REFRIGERATOR : ALTERNATING

16. URN : FLAGON :: ASHES : (a. wine, b. dust, c. coffee, d. meat)

17. THROUGH : TOUGH :: BLUE : (a. beau, b. bough, c. boo, d. buff)

18. EMBARRASS : (a. overindulge, b. discomfit, c. feed, d. starve) :: MORTIFY : GLUT

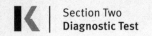

19. ALCHEMY : CHEMISTRY :: ASTROLOGY : (a. astronomy, b. zodiac, c. casuistry, d. clairvoyance)

20. COOPER : CASK :: (a. brim, b. haberdasher, c. fedora, d. milliner) : HAT

21. MISO : ISO :: HATRED : (a. complex, b. equal, c. fluid, d. multiple)

22. MORSE : (a. air conditioner, b. television, c. thermometer, d. telegraph) :: BELL : TELEPHONE

23. JUNIPER : (a. berry, b. peat, c. brandy, d. licorice) :: GIN : SCOTCH

24. FLOCK : (a. herd, b. sheep, c. school, d. walk) :: FLY : SWIM

25. (a. colossus, b. corpus, c. publicus, d. prima) : AMICUS :: DELICTI : CURIAE

26. WITH : BUT :: PREPOSITION : (a. predicate, b. conjunction, c. interrogative, d. adverb)

27. JULIENNE : (a. vegetable, b. square, c. dice, d. cut) :: STRIP : CUBE

28. JANUS : 1 :: (a. Flavius, b. Augustus, c. Odysseus, d. Julius) : 8

29. COLLEGE : (a. wardrobe, b. wine, c. perfume, d. cigar) :: GUIDANCE COUNSELOR : SOMMELIER

30. WWI : WWII :: (a. Versailles, b. Ghent, c. Warsaw, d. Paris) : YALTA

31. m^3 : cm^3 :: 1 : (a. 1, b. 10, c. 1,000, d. 1,000,000)

32. TOP : BOTTOM :: SOUP : (a. kettle, b. base, c. nuts. c. spoon)

33. SPHYGMOMANOMETER : (a. body fat, b. respiration, c. bone density, d. blood pressure) :: ODOMETER : DISTANCE

34. WHO : WHOSE :: SUBJECTIVE : (a. objective, b. dative, c. possessive, d. conditional)

35. NUCLEI : NUCLEAR :: MEN : (a. man, b. manly, c. males, d. people)

36. (a. mushroom, b. pipe, c. jacket, d. hat) : MEERSCHAUM :: FABRIC : SEERSUCKER

37. CHORDATE : PHYLUM :: HOMO : (a. class, b. order, c. family, d. genus)

38. UNDERWRITER : (a. contract, b. signature, c. insurance, d. liability) :: BORROWER : DEBT

39. DESERT : SERE :: VELDT : (a. range, b. grassy, c. tropical, d. woods)

40. $1 : (a.\ 2,\ b.\ 4,\ c.\ 6,\ d.\ 8) :: \sqrt{4} : 2^4$

41. (a. Chaucer, b. Poe, c. Trollope, d. Amis) : FLAUBERT :: DICKENS : ZOLA

42. BISMARCK : GARIBALDI :: GERMANY : (a. Argentina, b. Brazil, c. Italy, d. Portugal)

43. (a. confined spaces, b. public places, c. being alone, d. heights) : AGORAPHOBIA :: STRANGERS : XENOPHOBIA

44. (a. zither, b. ocarina, c. bassoon, d. tabla) : HARMONICA :: STRING : WIND

45. HEPATIC : OTIC :: LIVER : (a. stomach, b. ear, c. throat, d. bone)

46. GRANIVOROUS : PISCIVOROUS :: (a. antelope, b. baboon, c. penguin, d. squirrel) : SEAL

47. CIRCLE : CONE :: POLYGON : (a. cylinder, b. tetrahedron, c. face, d. pyramid)

48. CORNER : (a. room, b. ceiling, c. edge, d. line) :: POINT : PLANE

49. ORANGE : ANGER :: GRAPE : (a. reap, b. range, c. gripe, d. ogre)

50. APIAN : LUPINE :: (a. primate, b. bird, c. rabbit, d. bee) : WOLF

51. JASON : (a. Sacred Covenant, b. Golden Fleece, c. Argonaut, d. Cretan Bull) :: PERCEVAL : HOLY GRAIL

52. MATISSE : FAUVISM :: DE KOONING : (a. futurism, b. cubism, c. abstract expressionism, d. surrealism)

53. NON SEQUITUR : (a. tenet, b. zealot, c. heresy, d. disciple) :: LOGIC : FAITH

54. CABALIST : JUDAISM :: SUFI : (a. Buddhism, b. Islam, c. Hinduism, d. Shintoism)

55. LOMAN : MILLER :: (a. Gabler, b. Ionesco, c. Kowalski, d. Ivanov) : IBSEN

56. (a. Eskimo, b. Siamese, c. Bedouin, d. Persian) : INUIT :: TENT : IGLOO

57. PLATO : ARISTOTLE :: SOCRATES : (a. Alexander, b. Parmenides, c. Plato, d. Protagoras)

58. CORPUS : STIMULUS :: (a. corpi, b. corpus, c. corpora, d. corpuses) : stimuli

59. (a. furnish, b. plethora, c. fester, d. sufficiency) : SURFEIT :: CEASE : SURCEASE

60. ENCOMIUM : SERMON :: (a. comprehensive, b. praiseful, c. discursive, d. disapproving) : MORALISTIC

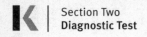

61. INCULCATE : INCULPATE :: (a. instill, b. insure, c. invest, d. incur) : INCRIMINATE

62. STREP : BACTERIA :: MONOTREME : (a. virus, b. reptile, c. mammal, d. fish)

63. AVOGADRO : PLANCK :: (a. 5.434×10^8, b. 3.144×10^{13}, c. 6.023×10^{23}, d. 8.087×10^{27}) : 6.626×10^{-34}

64. SIMILAR : SAME :: SIMILE : (a. hyperbole, b. semaphore, c. allegory, d. metaphor)

65. (a. pyre, b. phoenix, c. dust, d. sphinx) : ASHES :: LAZARUS : DEAD

66. COPLAND : FANFARE FOR THE COMMON MAN :: (a. Bernstein, b. Ellington, c. Gershwin, d. Miller) : RHAPSODY IN BLUE

67. ONEIRIC : (a. myths, b. ethics, c. obligations, d. dreams) :: FLUVIAL : RIVERS

68. TIC : GNAT :: ENTICE : (a. magnate, b. gigantic, c. grants, d. tangerine)

69. SUMERIANS : IRAQ :: PICTS : (a. Greece, b. France, c. Russia, d. Scotland)

70. CICATRIX : (a. mole, b. scar, c. cross, d. joint) :: PATELLA : KNEECAP

71. BAHAMAS : COLUMBUS :: HAWAII : (a. Cook, b. Franklin, c. Magellan, d. Shackleton)

72. ETIOLATE : (a. soft, b. dry, c. pale, d. long) :: OSSIFY : RIGID

73. ORPHEUS : (a. Circe, b. Eurydice, c. Phaedra, d. Electra) :: TRISTAN : ISOLDE

74. NOSTRUM : (a. insult, b. adage, c. remedy, d. consensus) :: APOCRYPHA : STATEMENTS

75. CARBOHYDRATE : (a. lipid, b. energy, c. protein, d. sugar) :: STARCH : LACTOSE

76. DONUT : RACETRACK :: TORUS : (a. ellipse, b. rhombus, c. athlete, d. sprint)

77. PRIME : COMPOSITE :: 2 : (a. 1, b. 3, c. 4, d. 5)

78. ERG : WORK :: AMPERE : (a. resistance, b. energy, c. illumination, d. electrical current)

79. CLEMENS : DODGSON :: TWAIN : (a. Charles, b. Eliot, c. Carroll, d. Sinclair)

80. HALOGEN : NOBLE GAS :: (a. iodine, b. sodium, c. silicon, d. nitrogen) : ARGON

81. (a. Rasputin, b. Lenin, c. Pushkin, d. Bukharin) : CROMWELL :: NICHOLAS II : CHARLES I

82. (a. Kronos, b. Ares, c. Poseidon, d. Hermes) : ZEUS :: SATURN : JUPITER

83. DARWIN : EVOLUTION :: WEGENER : (a. quantum mechanics, b. plate tectonics, c. electromagnetism, d. photography)

84. (a. coral, b. flotsam, c. krill, d. kelp) : ALGAE :: PLANTAE : MONERAN

85. SYMMETRICAL : ISOSCELES :: ASSYMETRICAL : (a. scalene, b. equilateral, c. rectangular, d. rhomboid)

86. EMIGRANT : IMMIGRANT :: APOSTATE : (a. proselyte, b. missionary, c. layman, d. seminarian)

87. ~ : TILDE :: (a. ?, b. ˘, c. ˋ, d. ¨) : DIAERESIS

88. (a. Lang, b. Murnau, c. Pabst, d. Weine) : M :: WELLES : CITIZEN KANE

89. HAWKING : A BRIEF HISTORY OF TIME :: (a. Brodie, b. Dawkins, c. Fortie, d. Gould) : THE SELFISH GENE

90. MASTICATE : CHEW :: MACERATE : (a. cogitate. b. criticize, c. sharpen, d. soften)

91. III : XV :: CXII : (a. MCV, b. DCX, c. DLX, d. CDL)

92. BEGINNING : END :: ALLITERATION : (a. consonance, b. coda, c. termination, d. euphony)

93. VEXILLOLOGY : FLAGS :: (a. monetarism, b. numerology, c. philately, d. numismatology) : MONEY

94. PLUTOCRACY : AUTOCRACY :: (a. elderly, b. scholarly, c. worthy, d. wealthy) : DICTATOR

95. (a. epistemology, b. axiology, c. deontology, d. pedagogy) : TELEOLOGY :: DUTY : ENDS

96. SUPERCILIOUS : CONTUMELIOUS :: (a. scornful, b. pithy, c. verbose, d. impassive) : PROLIX

97. SCIMITAR : SWORD :: TRUNCHEON : (a. gun, b. barricade, c. sling, d. stick)

98. (a. Constable, b. Eakins, c. Gainsborough, d. Hals) : DUCHAMP :: BLUE BOY : NUDE DESCENDING A STAIRCASE

99. HEGEL : KIERKEGAARD :: (a. rationalist, b. empiricist, c. idealist, d. materialist) : EXISTENTIALIST

100. DOUBLE JEOPARDY : (a. IV, b. V, c. VI, d. VII) :: CRUEL AND UNUSUAL PUNISHMENT : VIII

101. GEORGES LEFÈVRE : TOUR DE FRANCE :: MERIWETHER LEWIS CLARK JR. : (a. Indianapolis 500, b. Boston Marathon, c. Kentucky Derby, d. U.S. Tennis Open)

102. SYCOPHANT : (a. nemesis, b. flatterer, c. nadir, d. sedative) :: REACTIONARY : ULTRACONSERVATIVE

103. MAGNA CARTA : 13TH :: NINETY-FIVE THESES : (a. 14th, b. 15th, c. 16th, d. 17th)

104. SUMERIANS : (a. temple, b. tomb, c. ziggurat, d. citadel) :: EGYPTIANS : PYRAMID

105. BERRY : HOLLY :: (a. pine nut, b. pineapple, c. acorn, d. pinecone) : CONIFER

106. LONDON : (a. Rome, b. Baghdad, c. Cairo, d. Paris) :: THAMES : TIBER

107. CAIN : ABEL :: JACOB : (a. Esau, b. Daniel, c. Joseph, d. Ezekiel)

108. 100°C : 212°F :: (a. –72°C, b. –40°C, a. –32°C, d. 8°C) : –40°F

109. (a. pursuing, b. slept, c. usury, d. fling) : GERUND :: ARISEN : PAST PARTICIPLE

110. SOUND : AMPLIFIER :: DNA : (a. electrolysis, b. chromatography, c. PCR, d. AQN)

111. IMPERIALISM : TOTALITARIANISM :: (a. Catherine the Great, b. Queen Victoria, c. Henry IV, d. Alexander the Great) : JOSEF STALIN

112. I. M. PEI : JORN UTZON :: (a. Paris, b. Hong Kong, c. Le Corbusier, d. Gehry) : SYDNEY

113. STRAUSS : THE BLUE DANUBE :: (a. Rossini, b. Puccini, c. Ravel, d. Caruso) : THE BARBER OF SEVILLE

114. RICHTER : (a. Fujita, b. Quentin, c. Hamashu, d. Smith-Samson) :: EARTHQUAKE : TORNADO

115. ISTANBUL: CONSTANTINOPLE :: ST. PETERSBURG : (a. Leningrad, b. Stalingrad, c. Minsk, d. Kiev)

116. WHALE : CROW :: POD : (a. fleet, b. murder, c. jury, d. cabal)

117. ORCHESTRA : LICENSE :: CARTHORSE : (a. censors, b. lenitive, c. silence, d. scenery)

118. MANET : MODERNISM :: (a. Dalí, b. Duchamp, c. Picasso, d. Pollock) : POSTMODERNISM

119. BALFOUR DECLARATION : (a. Turkey, b. Palestine, c. Iran, d. Iraq) :: YALTA : GERMANY

120. MITIGATE : (a. accept, b. dissent, c. except, d. diatribe) :: EXACERBATE : DEMUR

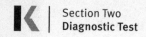

ANSWERS AND EXPLANATIONS

1. WHISTLE : REFEREE :: (a. motion, b. verdict, **c. gavel**, d. chamber) : JUDGE
   (c) A referee uses a whistle to gain attention, and a judge uses a gavel to gain attention.

2. 32° : FREEZE :: (a. 100°, b. 180°, **c. 212°**, d. 320°) : BOIL
   (c) 32° Fahrenheit is the freezing point of water, and 212° Fahrenheit is the boiling point of water.

3. SCHOLAR : (a. science, **b. erudition**, c. decency, d. publication) :: PARTISAN : BIAS
   (b) A scholar has erudition, and a partisan has bias.

4. PIG : GOOSE :: BOAR : (a. gaggle, **b. gander**, c. gosling, d. cygnet)
   (b) A male pig is called a boar, and a male goose is called a gander.

5. NIBBLE : (a. whet, b. quench, **c. sip**, d. guzzle) :: HUNGER : THIRST
   (c) To nibble is to eat lightly, and one eats to stop a hunger; likewise, to sip is to drink lightly, and one drinks to stop a thirst.

6. (**a. Samurai**, b. Cossack, c. Geisha, d. Mandarin) : PAGODA :: WARRIOR : TOWER
   (a) A Samurai is a type of Japanese warrior, and a pagoda is a type of Japanese (or Chinese) tower.

7. THE BIG APPLE : THE BIG EASY :: NY : (a. NB, **b. NO**, c. NV, d. NZ)
   (b) NY, or New York, is known as the Big Apple, and NO, or New Orleans, is known as the Big Easy.

8. CRAB : SEED : (a. arthropod, **b. carapace**, c. gill, d. ocean) : HULL
   (b) The shell of a crab is called a carapace, and the shell of a seed is called a hull.

9. SYBARITE : (a. wealth, b. ease, c. power, **d. pleasure**) :: AESTHETE : BEAUTY
   (d) A sybarite is a devotee of pleasure, and an aesthete is a devotee of beauty.

10. HAIRY : (a. slippery, b. shaggy, **c. scaly**, d. soggy) :: HIRSUTE : SQUAMOUS
    (c) A fancy word for hairy is *hirsute*, and a fancy word for scaly is *squamous*.

11. PLANE : SPHERE :: 2 : (a. 1, b. 2, **c. 3**, d. 4)
    (c) A plane has 2 dimensions, and a sphere has 3 dimensions.

12. MOVIE : (a. celluloid, **b. outtakes**, c. documentary, d. cinema) :: MEAT : OFFAL
    (b) The unused parts in the production of a movie are called outtakes, and the unused parts in the production of meat are called offal.

13. GIRDER : FACADE :: BONE : (a. building, b. skeleton, c. pediment, **d. skin**)
    (**d**) The girder provides structural support for a building, and the facade is the outer layer of a building; likewise, a bone provides structural support for a human, and the skin is the outer layer of a human.

14. (**a. referendum**, b. election, c. democracy, d. certificate) : DIRECT :: LEGISLATION : REPRESENTATIVE
    (**a**) A referendum is an example of direct democracy, and legislation is an example of representative democracy.

15. FLASHLIGHT : (a. uniform, b. illuminating, c. mobile, **d. direct**) :: REFRIGERATOR : ALTERNATING
    (**d**) A flashlight uses direct current (battery), and a refrigerator uses alternating current (electrical outlet).

16. URN : FLAGON :: ASHES : (**a. wine**, b. dust, c. coffee, d. meat)
    (**a**) An urn is designed to hold ashes, and a flagon is designed to hold wine.

17. THROUGH : TOUGH :: BLUE : (a. beau, b. bough, c. boo, **d. buff**)
    (**d**) *Through* rhymes with *blue*, and *tough* rhymes with *buff*.

18. EMBARRASS : (a. overindulge, b. discomfit, **c. feed**, d. starve) :: MORTIFY : GLUT
    (**c**) To mortify is to embarrass excessively, and to glut is to feed excessively.

19. ALCHEMY : CHEMISTRY :: ASTROLOGY : (**a. astronomy**, b. zodiac, c. casuistry, d. clairvoyance)
    (**a**) Alchemy is a pseudoscience that predates the scientific study of chemistry, and astrology is a pseudoscience that predates the scientific study of astronomy.

20. COOPER : CASK :: (a. brim, b. haberdasher, c. fedora, **d. milliner**) : HAT
    (**d**) A cooper makes casks, and a milliner makes hats.

21. MISO : ISO :: HATRED : (a. complex, **b. equal**, c. fluid, d. multiple)
    (**b**) *Miso-* is a prefix meaning "hatred" (as in *misogyny*), and *iso-* is a prefix meaning "equal" (as in *isosceles*).

22. MORSE : (a. air conditioner, b. television, c. thermometer, **d. telegraph**) :: BELL : TELEPHONE
    (**d**) Samuel Morse is credited in America with inventing the telegraph, just as Alexander Bell is credited with inventing the telephone.

23. JUNIPER : (a. berry, **b. peat**, c. brandy, d. licorice) :: GIN : SCOTCH
    (**b**) Juniper is used to flavor gin, and peat is used to flavor scotch.

24. FLOCK : (a. herd, b. sheep, **c. school**, d. walk) :: FLY : SWIM
    (**c**) A flock (of birds) moves about by flying, and a school (of fish) moves about by swimming.

25. (a. colossus, **b. corpus**, c. publicus, d. prima) : AMICUS :: DELICTI : CURIAE
    (**b**) *Corpus delicti* is a legal phrase (meaning "material substance of a crime"), and *amicus curiae* is a legal phrase (meaning "friend of the court").

26. WITH : BUT :: PREPOSITION : (a. predicate, **b. conjunction**, c. interrogative, d. adverb)
    (**b**) *With* is an example of a preposition, and *but* is an example of a conjunction.

27. JULIENNE : (a. vegetable, b. square, **c. dice**, d. cut) :: STRIP : CUBE
    (**c**) In cooking, to julienne is to cut into strips, and to dice is to cut into cubes.

28. JANUS : 1 :: (a. Flavius, **b. Augustus**, c. Odysseus, d. Julius) : 8
    (**b**) January, the 1st month, was named after Janus, and August, the 8th month, was named after Augustus.

29. COLLEGE : (a. wardrobe, **b. wine**, c. perfume, d. cigar) :: GUIDANCE COUNSELOR : SOMMELIER
    (**b**) A guidance counselor recommends a good or appropriate college, and a sommelier in a restaurant recommends a good or appropriate wine.

30. WWI : WWII :: (**a. Versailles**, b. Ghent, c. Warsaw, d. Paris) : YALTA
    (**a**) The treaty formally ending border disputes after WWI was signed in Versailles, and the treaty formally ending border disputes after WWII was signed in Yalta.

31. cm^3 : m^3 :: 1 : (a. 1, b. 10, c. 1,000, **d. 1,000,000**)
    (**d**) One cubic meter (m^3) equals 1,000,000 cubic centimeters (cm^3).

32. TOP : BOTTOM :: SOUP : (a. kettle, b. base, **c. nuts**. c. spoon)
    (**c**) The expression *from top to bottom* means "covering the whole spectrum," as does the expression *from soup to nuts*.

33. SPHYGMOMANOMETER : (a. body fat, b. respiration, c. bone density, **d. blood pressure**) :: ODOMETER : DISTANCE
    (**d**) A sphygmomanometer measures blood pressure, and an odometer measures distance.

34. WHO : WHOSE :: SUBJECTIVE : (a. objective, b. dative, **c. possessive**, d. conditional)
    (**c**) *Who* is the subjective form of the indefinite pronoun for a person, and *whose* is the possessive form of the same.

35. NUCLEI : NUCLEAR :: MEN : (a. man, **b. manly**, c. males, d. people)
    (**b**) *Nuclei* is the plural form of *nucleus*, and *nuclear* is the adjectival form of the same; likewise, *men* is the plural form of *man*, and *manly* is the adjectival form of the same.

36. (a. mushroom, **b. pipe**, c. jacket, d. hat) : MEERSCHAUM :: FABRIC : SEERSUCKER
    (**b**) A meerschaum is a type of smoking pipe, and seersucker is a type of fabric.

37. CHORDATE : PHYLUM :: HOMO : (a. class, b. order, c. family, **d. genus**)
    (**d**) *Chordate* is the name for the phylum that includes man, and *homo* is the name for the genus that includes man.

38. UNDERWRITER : (a. contract, b. signature, c. insurance, **d. liability**) :: BORROWER : DEBT
    (**d**) An underwriter takes on a liability, and a borrower takes on a debt.

39. DESERT : SERE :: VELDT : (a. range, **b. grassy**, c. tropical, d. woods)
    (**b**) A desert is sere (meaning arid), and a veldt is grassy.

40. 1 : (a. 2, b. 4, c. 6, **d. 8**) :: $\sqrt{4} : 2^4$
    (**d**) The ratio of 1 to 8 is $\frac{1}{8}$, and the ratio of $\sqrt{4}$, or 2, to 2^4, or 16, is also $\frac{1}{8}$.

41. (a. Chaucer, b. Poe, **c. Trollope**, d. Amis) : FLAUBERT :: DICKENS : ZOLA
    (**c**) Gustave Flaubert and Emile Zola were literary contemporaries in France, and Anthony Trollope and Charles Dickens were literary contemporaries in England.

42. BISMARCK : GARIBALDI :: GERMANY : (a. Argentina, b. Brazil, **c. Italy**, d. Portugal)
    (**c**) Otto von Bismarck was a leader who sought to unify Germany in the 19th century, and Giuseppe Garibaldi was a leader who sought to unify Italy in the 19th century.

43. (a. confined spaces, **b. public places**, c. being alone, d. heights) : AGORAPHOBIA :: STRANGERS : XENOPHOBIA
    (**b**) The fear of public places is called agoraphobia, and the fear of strangers is called xenophobia.

44. (**a. zither**, b. ocarina, c. bassoon, d. tabla) : HARMONICA :: STRING : WIND
    (**a**) The zither is a string instrument, and the harmonica is a wind instrument.

45. HEPATIC : OTIC :: LIVER : (a. stomach, **b. ear**, c. throat, d. bone)
    (**b**) *Hepatic* means having to do with the liver, and *otic* means having to do with the ear.

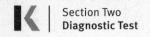
46. GRANIVOROUS : PISCIVOROUS :: (a. antelope, b. baboon, c. penguin, **d. squirrel**) : SEAL
    (**d**) The seal is an example of a piscivorous animal (primary diet is fish), and a squirrel is an example of a granivorous animal (primary diet is seeds, grain, or nuts).

47. CIRCLE : CONE :: POLYGON : (a. cylinder, b. tetrahedron, c. face, **d. pyramid**)
    (**d**) A circle forms the base of a cone, and a polygon forms the base of a pyramid.

48. CORNER : (a. room, **b. ceiling**, c. edge, d. line) :: POINT : PLANE
    (**b**) A corner is a point in a room, and a ceiling is a plane in a room.

49. ORANGE : ANGER :: GRAPE : (**a. reap**, b. range, c. gripe, d. ogre)
    (**a**) If you take *orange*, remove the first letter, and rearrange the others, you get *anger*; if you take *grape*, remove the first letter, and rearrange the others, you get *reap*.

50. APIAN : LUPINE :: (a. primate, b. bird, c. rabbit, **d. bee**) : WOLF
    (**d**) *Apian* means referring to bees, and *lupine* means referring to wolves.

51. JASON : (a. Sacred Covenant, **b. Golden Fleece**, c. Argonaut, d. Cretan Bull) :: PERCEVAL : HOLY GRAIL
    (**b**) In mythology, Jason embarked on a quest to find the Golden Fleece, and Perceval embarked on a quest to find the Holy Grail.

52. MATISSE : FAUVISM :: DE KOONING : (a. futurism, b. cubism, **c. abstract expressionism**, d. surrealism)
    (**c**) Henri Matisse painted in the school of art known as fauvism, and Willem DeKooning painted in the school of art known as abstract expressionism.

53. NON SEQUITUR : (a. tenet, b. zealot, **c. heresy**, d. disciple) :: LOGIC : FAITH
    (**c**) A non sequitur deviates from logic, and a heresy deviates from faith.

54. CABALIST : JUDAISM :: SUFI : (a. Buddhism, **b. Islam**, c. Hinduism, d. Shintoism)
    (**b**) A Cabalist practices a mystical branch of Judaism, and a Sufi practices a mystical branch of Islam.

55. LOMAN : MILLER :: (**a. Gabler**, b. Ionesco, c. Kowalski, d. Ivanov) : IBSEN
    (**a**) Arthur Miller created the character of Willy Loman, and Henrik Ibsen created the character of Hedda Gabler.

56. (a. Eskimo, b. Siamese, **c. Bedouin**, d. Persian) : INUIT :: TENT : IGLOO
    (**c**) A Bedouin traditionally lives in a tent, and an Inuit traditionally lives in an igloo.

57. PLATO : ARISTOTLE :: SOCRATES : (a. Alexander, b. Parmenides, **c. Plato**, d. Protagoras)
(**c**) Plato taught Aristotle, and Socrates taught Plato (alternatively, Plato was a student of Socrates, and Aristotle was a student of Plato).

58. CORPUS : STIMULUS :: (a. corpi, b. corpus, **c. corpora**, d. corpuses) : stimuli
(**c**) The plural form of *corpus* is *corpora*, and the plural form of *stimulus* is *stimuli*.

59. (a. furnish, **b. plethora**, c. fester, d. sufficiency) : SURFEIT :: CEASE : SURCEASE
(**b**) *Plethora* is a synonym for *surfeit*, and *surcease* is a synonym for *cease*.

60. ENCOMIUM : SERMON :: (a. comprehensive, **b. praiseful**, c. discursive, d. disapproving) : MORALISTIC
(**b**) An encomium is by definition praiseful, and a sermon is by definition moralistic.

61. INCULCATE : INCULPATE :: (**a. instill**, b. insure, c. investigate, d. incur) : INCRIMINATE
(**a**) To inculcate means to instill, and to inculpate means to incriminate.

62. STREP : BACTERIA :: MONOTREME : (a. virus, b. reptile, **c. mammal**, d. fish)
(**c**) Strep is a type of bacteria, and a monotreme is a type of mammal.

63. AVOGADRO : PLANCK :: (a. 5.434×10^8, b. 3.144×10^{13}, **c. 6.023×10^{23}**, d. 8.087×10^{27}) : 6.626×10^{-34}
(**c**) Avogadro's number is 6.023×10^{23}, and Plank's constant is 6.626×10^{-34}.

64. SIMILAR : SAME :: SIMILE : (a. hyperbole, b. semaphore, c. allegory, **d. metaphor**)
(**d**) Simile is a figure of speech that states that two things are similar ("My love **is like** a red, red rose…"), and a metaphor is a figure of speech that states that two things are the same ("The heart **is** a lonely hunter…").

65. (a. pyre, **b. phoenix**, c. dust, d. sphinx) : ASHES :: LAZARUS : DEAD
(**b**) The phoenix was said to rise from the ashes, and Lazarus was said to rise from the dead.

66. COPLAND : FANFARE FOR THE COMMON MAN :: (a. Bernstein, b. Ellington, **c. Gershwin**, d. Miller) : RHAPSODY IN BLUE
(**c**) Aaron Copland wrote the musical piece *Fanfare for the Common Man*, and George Gershwin wrote the musical piece *Rhapsody in Blue*.

67. ONEIRIC : (a. myths, b. ethics, c. obligations, **d. dreams**) :: FLUVIAL : RIVERS
(**d**) Oneiric means having to do with dreams, and fluvial means having to do with rivers.

68. TIC : GNAT :: ENTICE : (**a. magnate**, b. gigantic, c. grants, d. tangerine)
(**a**) If you take away the first two letters and the last letter of the word *entice*, you're left with the word *tic*; if you take away the first two letters and the last letter of the word *magnate*, you're left with the word *gnat*.

69. SUMERIANS : IRAQ :: PICTS : (a. Greece, b. France, c. Russia, **d. Scotland**)
(**d**) The Sumerians were an ancient people who lived in what is now Iraq, and the Picts were an ancient people who lived in what is now Scotland.

70. CICATRIX : (a. mole, **b. scar**, c. cross, d. joint) :: PATELLA : KNEECAP
(**b**) A cicatrix is a scar, and a patella is a kneecap.

71. BAHAMAS : COLUMBUS :: HAWAII : (**a. Cook**, b Franklin, c. Magellan, d. Shackleton)
(**a**) Christopher Columbus was the first Westerner to discover the Bahamas, and Captain James Cook was the first Westerner to discover Hawaii.

72. ETIOLATE : (a. soft, b. dry, **c. pale**, d. long) :: OSSIFY : RIGID
(**c**) To etiolate is to become pale, and to ossify is to become rigid.

73. ORPHEUS : (a. Circe, **b. Eurydice**, c. Phaedra, d. Electra) :: TRISTAN : ISOLDE
(**b**) Orpheus and Eurydice were mythological lovers, as were Tristan and Isolde.

74. NOSTRUM : (a. insult, b. adage, **c. remedy**, d. consensus) :: APOCRYPHA : STATEMENTS
(**c**) A nostrum is a false or dubious remedy, and apocrypha are false or dubious statements.

75. CARBOHYDRATE : (a. lipid, b. energy, c. protein, **d. sugar**) :: STARCH : LACTOSE
(**d**) Starch is a type of carbohydrate, and lactose is a type of sugar.

76. DONUT : RACETRACK :: TORUS : (**a. ellipse**, b. rhombus, c. athlete, d. sprint)
(**a**) A donut is shaped like a torus, and a racetrack is shaped like an ellipse.

77. PRIME : COMPOSITE :: 2 : (a. 1, b. 3, **c. 4**, d. 5)
(**c**) 2 is a prime number, and 4 is a composite number (i.e., it has more factors than 1 and itself). The other choices—1, 3, and 5—are all prime numbers.

78. ERG : WORK :: AMPERE : (a. resistance, b. energy, c. illumination, **d. electrical current**)
(**d**) An erg measures work, and an ampere measures electrical current.

79. CLEMENS : DODGSON :: TWAIN : (a. Charles, b. Eliot, **c. Carroll**, d. Sinclair)
(**c**) The pen name of Samuel Clemens was Mark Twain, and the pen name of Charles Dodgson was Lewis Carroll.

80. HALOGEN : NOBLE GAS :: (**a. iodine**, b. sodium, c. silicon, d. nitrogen) : ARGON
(**a**) Iodine is a halogen (the other halogens are fluorine, chlorine, bromine, and astatine). Argon is a noble gas (the other noble gases are helium, neon, krypton, xenon, and radon).

81. (a. Rasputin, **b. Lenin**, c. Pushkin, d. Bukharin) : CROMWELL :: NICHOLAS II : CHARLES I
(**b**) Oliver Cromwell ruled after toppling the reign of Charles I, and Vladimir Lenin ruled after toppling the reign of Nicholas II.

82. (**a. Kronos**, b. Ares, c. Poseidon, d. Hermes) : ZEUS :: SATURN : JUPITER
(**a**) Kronos and Saturn are the Greek and Roman names for the same deity, and Zeus and Jupiter are the Greek and Roman names for the same deity.

83. DARWIN : EVOLUTION :: WEGENER : (a. quantum mechanics, **b. plate tectonics**, c. electromagnetism, d. photography)
(**b**) Charles Darwin came up with the theory of evolution, and Alfred Wegener came up with the theory of plate tectonics.

84. (a. coral, b. flotsam, c. krill, **d. kelp**) : ALGAE :: PLANTAE : MONERAN
(**d**) Taxonomically, kelp belongs to the Plantae (or just plain Plant) kingdom, and algae belongs to the Moneran kingdom.

85. SYMMETRICAL : ISOSCELES :: ASYMETRICAL : (**a. scalene**, b. equilateral, c. rectangular, d. rhomboid)
(**a**) An isosceles triangle is symmetrical, and a scalene triangle is asymmetrical.

86. EMIGRANT : IMMIGRANT :: APOSTATE : (**a. proselyte**, b. missionary, c. layman, d. seminarian)
(**a**) An emigrant is one who leaves a country, and an immigrant is one who enters a country; likewise, an apostate is one who leaves a religion, and a proselyte is one who enters a religion.

87. ~ : TILDE :: (a. ?, b. ˘, c. ˋ, **d. ¨**) : DIAERESIS
(**d**) ~ is the symbol for the diacritical mark called a tilde, and ¨ is the symbol for the diacritical mark called a diaeresis.

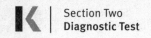
88. (**a. Lang**, b. Murnau, c. Pabst, d. Weine) : M :: WELLES : CITIZEN KANE
    (**a**) Fritz Lang directed *M*, and Orson Welles directed *Citizen Kane*.

89. HAWKING : A BRIEF HISTORY OF TIME :: (a. Brodie, **b. Dawkins**, c. Fortie,
    d. Gould) : THE SELFISH GENE
    (**b**) Stephen Hawking wrote *A Brief History of Time*, and Richard Dawkins wrote *The Selfish Gene*.

90. MASTICATE : CHEW :: MACERATE : (a. cogitate. b. criticize, c. sharpen, **d. soften**)
    (**d**) To masticate means to chew, and to macerate means to soften.

91. III : XV :: CXII : (a. MCV, b. DCX, **c. DLX**, d. CDL)

    (**c**) The ratio of III (3) to XV (15) is $\frac{1}{5}$, and the ratio of CXII (112) to DLX (660)
    is also $\frac{1}{5}$.

92. BEGINNING : END :: ALLITERATION : (**a. consonance**, b. coda, c. termination,
    d. euphony)
    (**a**) Alliteration is the repetition of the same sounds at the beginning of words, and
    consonance is the repetition of the same sounds at the end of words.

93. VEXILLOLOGY : FLAGS :: (a. monetarism, b. numerology, c. philately,
    d. numismatology) : MONEY
    (**d**) Vexillology is the study of flags, and numismatology is the study of money.

94. PLUTOCRACY : AUTOCRACY :: (a. elderly, b. scholarly, c. worthy, **d. wealthy**) :
    DICTATOR
    (**d**) Plutocracy is rule by the wealthy, and autocracy is rule by a dictator.

95. (a. epistemology, b. axiology, **c. deontology**, d. pedagogy) : TELEOLOGY :: DUTY :
    ENDS
    (**c**) Deontology is the branch of philosophy that deals with duty, and teleology is the
    branch of philosophy that deals with ends.

96. SUPERCILIOUS : CONTUMELIOUS :: (a. scornful, b. pithy, **c. verbose**, d. impassive)
    :: PROLIX
    (**c**) *Supercilious* and *contumelious* are synonyms (both mean "arrogant") ; likewise,
    verbose and *prolix* are synonyms (both mean "talkative").

97. SCIMITAR : SWORD :: TRUNCHEON : (a. gun, b. barricade, c. sling, **d. stick**)
    (**d**) A scimitar is a type of sword, and a truncheon is a type of stick.

98. (a. Constable, b. Eakins, **c. Gainesborough**, d. Hals) : DUCHAMP :: BLUE BOY :
NUDE DESCENDING A STAIRCASE
(**c**) Thomas Gainesborough painted *Blue Boy*, and Marcel Duchamp painted *Nude Descending a Staircase*.

99. HEGEL : KIERKEGAARD :: (a. rationalist, b. empiricist, **c. idealist**, d. materialist) :
EXISTENTIALIST
(**c**) The philosopher Georg Hegel was an idealist, and the philosopher Søren Kierkegaard was an existentialist.

100. DOUBLE JEOPARDY : (a. IV, **b. V**, c. VI, d. VII) :: CRUEL AND UNUSUAL
PUNISHMENT : VIII
(**b**) US citizens are protected against double jeopardy by the Fifth Amendment (Amendment V), and they are protected against cruel and unusual punishment by the Eighth Amendment (Amendment VIII).

101. GEORGES LEFÈVRE : TOUR DE FRANCE :: MERIWETHER LEWIS CLARK JR. :
(a. Indianapolis 500, b. Boston Marathon, **c. Kentucky Derby**, d. U.S. Tennis Open)
(**c**) Georges Lefèvre is credited with devising the concept of the Tour de France, and Meriwether Lewis Clark Jr. is credited with devising the concept of the Kentucky Derby.

102. SYCOPHANT : (a. nemesis, **b. flatterer**, c. nadir, d. sedative) :: REACTIONARY :
ULTRACONSERVATIVE
(**b**) A sycophant is a flatterer, and a reactionary is an ultraconservative.

103. MAGNA CARTA : 13TH :: NINETY-FIVE THESES : (a. 14th, b. 15th, **c. 16th**,
d. 17th)
(**c**) The Magna Carta was written in the 13th century, and the Ninety-Five Theses were written in the 16th century.

104. SUMERIANS : (a. temple, b. tomb, **c. ziggurat**, d. citadel) :: EGYPTIANS : PYRAMID
(**c**) The Sumerians built ziggurats, and the Egyptians built pyramids.

105. BERRY : HOLLY :: (a. pine nut, b. pineapple, c. acorn, **d. pinecone**) : CONIFER
(**d**) Holly plants produce berries, while the pine tree, a member of the conifer family, produces seed-bearing pinecones.

106. LONDON : (**a. Rome**, b. Baghdad, c. Cairo, d. Paris) :: THAMES : TIBER
(**a**) The Thames River runs through London, and the Tiber River runs through Rome.

107. CAIN : ABEL :: JACOB : (**a. Esau**, b. Daniel, c. Joseph, d. Ezekiel)
(**a**) Jacob and Esau were Old Testament brothers, as were Cain and Abel.

108. 100°C : 212°F :: (a. –72°C, **b. –40°C**, a. –32°C, d. 8°C) : –40°F
     (**b**) 100°C is the equivalent of 212°F, and -40°C is the equivalent of -40°F.

109. (**a. pursuing**, b. slept, c. usury, d. fling) : GERUND :: ARISEN : PAST PARTICIPLE
     (**a**) *Pursuing* is an example of a gerund, just as *arisen* is an example of a past participle.

110. SOUND : AMPLIFIER :: DNA : (a. electrolysis, b. chromatography, **c. PCR**, d. AQN)
     (**c**) An amplifier magnifies sound, and PCR multiplies DNA.

111. IMPERIALISM : TOTALITARIANISM :: (a. Catherine the Great, **b. Queen Victoria**, c. Henry IV, d. Alexander the Great) : JOSEF STALIN
     (**b**) Queen Victoria was an imperial queen, and Josef Stalin was a totalitarian leader.

112. I. M. PEI : JORN UTZON :: (**a. Paris**, b. Hong Kong, c. Le Corbusier, d. Gehry) : SYDNEY
     (**a**) The architect I. M. Pei is renowned for his pyramid at the Louvre in Paris, as Jorn Utzon is famed for the iconic opera house in Sydney, Australia.

113. STRAUSS : THE BLUE DANUBE :: (**a. Rossini**, b. Puccini, c. Ravel, d. Caruso) : THE BARBER OF SEVILLE
     (**a**) Austrian composer Johann Strauss composed *The Blue Danube,* and Italian composer Gioacchino Rossini composed *The Barber of Seville.*

114. RICHTER : (**a. Fujita**, b. Quentin, c. Hamashu, d. Smith-Samson) :: EARTHQUAKE : TORNADO
     (**a**) The Richter scale measures the size of earthquakes, and the Fujita scale measures the size of tornadoes.

115. ISTANBUL: CONSTANTINOPLE :: a. ST. PETERSBURG : (**a. Leningrad**, b. Stalingrad, c. Minsk, d. Kiev)
     (**a**) St. Petersburg was known as Leningrad during the Soviet Era; Istanbul is the former Byzantine capital Constantinople.

116. WHALE : CROW :: POD : (a. fleet, **b. murder**, c. jury, d. cabal)
     (**b**) A group of whales is called a pod, and a group of crows is called a murder.

117. ORCHESTRA : LICENSE :: CARTHORSE : (a. censors, b. lenitive, **c. silence**, d. scenery)
     (**c**) Rearrange the letters in *orchestra* and get the word *carthorse,* and rearrange the letters in *license* and get the word *silence.*

118. MANET : MODERNISM :: (a. Dalí, **b. Duchamp**, c. Picasso, d. Pollock) : POSTMODERNISM
   (**b**) Edouard Manet's painting heralded the dawn of Modernist painting, while Marcel Duchamp is considered a progenitor of Postmodernism in art.

119. BALFOUR DECLARATION : (a. Turkey, **b. Palestine**, c. Iran, d. Iraq) :: YALTA : GERMANY
   (**b**) The Balfour Declaration called for the partition of Palestine into the Jewish homeland and Palestine, and the Yalta Agreement called for the partition of Germany.

120. MITIGATE : (**a. accept**, b. dissent, c. except, d. diatribe) :: EXACERBATE : DEMUR
   (**a**) *Mitigate* is the opposite of *exacerbate,* and *accept* is the opposite of *demur.*

SCORING YOUR DIAGNOSTIC TEST

The MAT will have 120 questions, but only 100 of them will count toward your score. After you finish any of the practice tests in this book, you will have completed 120 questions. In order to approximate your raw score, give yourself 1 point for every correct answer, divide that number by 120, and multiply by 100. A raw score in the low 40s will produce a scaled score of about 400, which is the average scaled score on the MAT.

MAT Content Areas

CHAPTER THREE

MAT Language Strategies

A WORD ABOUT WORDS ON THE MAT

You must have noticed that the MAT likes to trot out some pretty obscure vocabulary words. Obviously, the MAT is not purely a test of vocabulary, but the majority of the questions on the test involve words you don't hear every day. Let's face it: The MAT test writers could never come up with such a difficult test if they didn't use lots of words that most people don't know.

This needn't be a cause for despair. This chapter will teach you how to cope with MAT vocabulary. We'll begin by taking a look at the vocabulary bridges that appear most often on the MAT. Next we'll examine MAT analogies that involve wordplay, grammar terms, and other wacky verbal relationships. Finally, we'll review some techniques that will help you build your vocabulary quickly, as well as deal with unfamiliar words on Test Day. All this before we even get to our study lists in the next section of the book, which contains, among other goodies, 700 obscure vocabulary words that could appear on your MAT, along with definitions and all-important synonyms.

So cheer up, and let's get started.

CLASSIC VOCABULARY BRIDGES

Fortunately for you, the MAT writers aren't very creative in the types of bridges they use to connect obscure vocabulary words. In fact, some bridges appear over and over again on every test. This is great for two reasons. First, knowing what to expect will help you to recognize these bridges more quickly when you take the test. Second, knowing these classic bridges will allow you to make educated guesses when you get to questions that contain unfamiliar vocabulary.

Of course, the following classic bridges don't cover every type of vocabulary relationship that you're likely to see on the test, but they do account for a solid majority of them. Let's take a look.

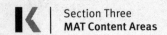
Classic Bridge #1: Synonyms

The most common type of bridge on the MAT is also the easiest. A **synonym**, or a word that means the same thing as another word, is usually an easy connection to make. Take, for example, the following:

> TRUCULENT : FEROCIOUS
>
> ABASH : DISCONCERT
>
> IMPECUNIOUS : POOR
>
> RENEGADE : MUTINEER

It's nice to know that the most common bridge on the MAT is also the most straightforward. *Truculent* means *ferocious*, and so on. Expect several analogies on the test you take to contain pure and simple synonyms.

Now that you've seen the way a synonym bridge works, let's see what a question might look like on the MAT:

> MALEVOLENT : HATEFUL :: HERMETIC: (a. lonely, b. immune, c. airtight, d. callous)

Answer: (**c**) *Malevolent* means "hateful," and *hermetic* means "airtight."

Now that we've covered how to handle words with the same meaning, it's time to move on to bridges where the word pairs have opposite meanings.

Classic Bridge #2: Antonyms

A common bridge on the MAT involves two words that are opposites, or **antonyms**, of each other. Here are a few examples:

> TACITURN : VOLUBLE
>
> APEX : NADIR
>
> AMBIGUOUS : CLEAR-CUT

Once again, the bridge here is not difficult to comprehend. *Taciturn* means "disinclined to talk." That's the opposite of *voluble*, which means "talkative." Another way to phrase this bridge is: Someone who is taciturn is NOT voluble. The key here is to build bridges that work for you. Likewise, an *apex*, or high point, is the opposite of a *nadir*, or low point. You get the idea.

Strategy tip: If you can't come up with an exact bridge between two tough vocabulary words, ask yourself: Are these words more like synonyms or antonyms? Often, just answering this simple question can lead you to the correct answer.

Here's a look at how an antonym bridge might appear on the MAT:

> RANDOM : SIMPLE :: (a. de facto, b. planned, c. ad hoc, d. tricky) : COMPLEX

Answer: (**b**) Something random is the opposite of something planned or done with a purpose, and something simple is the opposite of something complex.

Now that you've seen the two easiest bridges to make, let's see what happens when the connections between words get a little trickier.

Classic Bridge #3: Characteristic Qualities (or Lack Thereof)

The next classic bridge can take a number of forms. See if you can formulate your own bridge for each of the following word pairs. Write it in the blank provided.

1. SCHOLAR _____ ERUDITION

2. CHARLATAN _____ SINCERITY

3. LIBERTINE _____ LICENTIOUS

4. DASTARD _____ COURAGEOUS

5. SEDATIVE _____ SLEEPINESS

6. HAZE _____ VISIBILITY

Answers:

1. A scholar has erudition.

2. A charlatan lacks sincerity.

3. A libertine is licentious.

4. A dastard is not courageous.

5. A sedative causes sleepiness.

6. A haze reduces visibility.

How did you do? This is a fairly broad category, but it's usually not too hard to come up with an appropriate bridge once you see that one word is a characteristic that is used define the other word.

Since this type of MAT question pops up fairly frequently, try the following questions that involve these kinds of bridges:

1. RACONTEUR : (a. hunt, b. ego, c. wit, d. cold) :: OPTIMIST : HOPE

2. STRANGER : MYSTERY :: (a. kin, b. renegade, c. conformist, d. scapegoat) : DEFIANCE

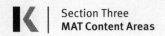
Answers:

1. **(c)** A raconteur has wit, just as an optimist has hope.

2. **(b)** A stranger has an air of mystery, and a renegade has an air of defiance.

Now we're ready for our next type of bridge, where the relationship is exemplary rather than simply characteristic.

Classic Bridge #4: Types and Examples

In this fairly straightforward bridge, one word is a direct example or type of another. Check out the following examples:

WOMBAT : MARSUPIAL

SEERSUCKER : FABRIC

CLOUD : CUMULUS

DAGGUERREOTYPE : PHOTOGRAPH

A wombat is an example of a marsupial. Seersucker is a type of fabric. Cumulus is a type of cloud. The fourth example is a slight variant that is particularly beloved by those crusty old MAT writers; namely, a dagguerreotype is a *primitive* type of photograph.

Now try one on your own:

(a. camarilla, b. guide, c. elementary, d. politician) : ELEPHANT :: ENTOURAGE : PACHYDERM

Answer: **(a)** A camarilla is a type of entourage, just as an elephant is a type of pachyderm.

Classic Bridge #5: Degrees

Let's see if you can discern the nature of these bridges. Come up with your own bridge for the analogy below.

DISLIKE : ABHOR

Answer: To abhor is to dislike intensely.

This is just one example of what we call an **extreme** bridge—that is, one word is an extreme version of the other. Here are some other examples:

FLURRY : BLIZZARD

Answer: A blizzard is an extreme form of a flurry.

ADMIRATION : ADULATE

Answer: To adulate is to have extreme admiration.

FLAGON : BOTTLE

Answer: A flagon is a large bottle.

Other Classic Bridges

Here are a few miscellaneous examples to consider as well. Write your bridges in the blanks:

1. STONE _____ WEIGHT

2. THESAURUS _____ SYNONYMS

3. POTTER _____ CLAY

4. METEOROLOGY _____ WEATHER

Answers:

1. A stone is a unit of weight.

2. A thesaurus is a collection of synonyms.

3. A potter works with clay.

4. Meteorology is the study of weather.

Now that you've seen the classic types of vocabulary bridges, it's time to take a close look at the other major type of word analogy you're likely to see.

WORDPLAY BRIDGES

The other major type of vocabulary analogy you're likely to see on the MAT doesn't involve meanings of words at all. Instead, the MAT plays with the **spelling** or **sounds** of the words themselves. Some of these will take you off guard because unlike with direct synonyms or antonyms, the relationship between the words is not one of meaning but of the words as objects.

Take a shot at a few examples of this type of bridge:

1. BANTER : BREACH :: RANT : (a. invert, b. cross, c. char, d. teach)

2. NADIR : RECANT :: DRAIN : (a. recall, b. nectar, c. lowest, d. sap)

Answers:

1. **(c)** Removing the *b* and *e* from the word *banter* and jumbling the letters gives you the word *rant*, while removing the *b* and *e* and jumbling the word *breach* gives you the word *char*.

2. **(b)** Rearrange the letters in *nadir* to get *drain*, and rearrange the letters in *recant* to get *nectar*.

GRAMMAR BRIDGES

Some linguistic bridges involve the basic grammar of the words themselves. These analogies will simply involve parts of speech or plural forms. These will be more easily recognizable, perhaps, but not as easily discerned, unless you are a plurals whiz! Let's see what a few of these might look like:

1. NOUN : FREEDOM :: VERB : (a. freed, b. from, c. deem, d. boredom)

2. ELF : ELVES :: GENUS : (a. genera, b. genus, c. geni, d. genii)

Answers:
1. **(c)** *Freedom* is a noun, and *deem* is a verb. (And *freed* is an adjective, *from* is a preposition, and *boredom* is a noun.)

2. **(a)** The plural of *elf* is *elves*, and the plural of *genus* is *genera*.

We're almost through our look at Vocabulary and Wordplay Analogies for the MAT. Next we'll review some ways to boost your MAT vocabulary.

VOCABULARY BUILDING

At first glance, increasing your vocabulary might seem like a difficult task. Where to begin?

Well, you should **start with your vocabulary and wordplay study lists,** found in the next section of this book. They provide you with more than 700 MAT-friendly words, many of which have appeared on recent versions of the test. But there are other things you can do as well:

- **Make a vocabulary workbook.** Keep track of the new words you encounter (especially new words you encounter on MAT practice tests and quizzes).

- **Get to know word roots** that will allow you to decipher tough unfamiliar words.

- And last, but not least, learn to **think like a thesaurus.**

Thinking Like a Thesaurus

For the purposes of learning words for the MAT, it's better to think like a thesaurus than like a dictionary. By this, we mean that you will increase the bank of words that you know "close enough" for success on the MAT by **learning words in groups.**

Compare how a dictionary might define a MAT vocabulary word with how a thesaurus defines the same word:

> **Dictionary:** ASSUAGE (v.): to make something less intense or severe; to satisfy or appease.
>
> **Thesaurus:** ASSUAGE (v.): lessen, relieve, alleviate, ameliorate, appease, mitigate, mollify, propitiate, palliate, satiate, placate, pacify, slake, quench. CALMING WORDS

If you think like a dictionary, you will know a lot about this one word. If you think like a thesaurus, you will know a little about 15 words. Since all you need to handle most analogies on the MAT is a general sense of a word's meaning, thinking like a thesaurus puts you on the fast track to a score improvement on the MAT.

Lists of synonyms are much easier to learn than many words in isolation. So don't learn words with a dictionary; learn them with a thesaurus. Make synonym index cards based on the common families of words and look through those lists periodically. It's like weight lifting for vocabulary. Pretty soon you will start to see results.

Dealing with Unfamiliar Words: Using Word Roots

Roots are the most basic elements of meaning into which you can divide words. Because MAT words are often drawn from Latin and Greek, familiarizing yourself with roots can be extremely useful, both in deciphering words with obscure meanings and in guessing intelligently. Once you know, for example, that the root PLAC means "to please," you have a hook for remembering the meanings of several words: *placate*, *implacable*, *placid*, *placebo*, and *complacent*.

Sometimes you can use roots to figure out the meaning of an unfamiliar word. Suppose, for example, you come across the word *circumnavigate* and don't know what it means. If you know that the root CIRCUM means "around" and that the root NAV means "ship, sail," then you can guess that *circumnavigate* means "to sail around," as in "circumnavigate the globe."

But don't get too excited. Roots offer the common heritage of words thousands of years old—but things have changed a lot. Roots don't always point to the right way to go.

Example: Affinity is of the root FIN, meaning end. But *affinity* means "a kinship" or "attractive force."

Sometimes, the meaning is close, but the spelling has gone haywire.

Example: Cogent is actually of the root ACT/AG (to do, to drive to lead). *Cogent* means "convincing" or "having the power to compel." These two are somewhat close in meaning, but you can see what we mean about the spelling.

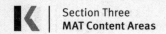

As it turns out, the etymology of a word is merely a good trick. It can help you to figure out and remember the meaning of a word. But it won't work every time, and it certainly can't provide the basic definition of a word. It may even put you on the wrong track.

So why bother? Because if you don't have a clue what a word means, you have to start somewhere. Roots are an efFICacious place to begin (FIC: to do, to make).

Use Kaplan's Root List in the next section of this book to pick up the most valuable roots. Target these words in your vocabulary prep. Learn a few new roots a day, familiarizing yourself with their meanings.

TYING IT ALL TOGETHER

The MAT will ask you a lot of questions relating to your knowledge of language and your ability to recognize the connections (however obscure) between words. The best way for you to approach the vocabulary questions on the MAT is to be aware of the different types of connections that are likely to appear.

Whether it's a synonym, an antonym, a part of speech, or a word jumble, figuring out how the words in front of you relate to each other is the first step to mastering MAT vocabulary analogies. Now that you've completed this stage of the review, it's time for you to immerse yourself in some of the more in-depth content that we have provided in the next section of this book in the form of our vocabulary and wordplay study lists. But first, practice answering MAT vocabulary and wordplay questions in the following quiz.

CHAPTER QUIZ: LANGUAGE

Try answering the following analogy questions, using the strategies you've just learned.

1. MILLENNIUM : NEBULA :: MILLENNIA : (a. nebulous, b. nebular, c. nebulic, d. nebulae)

2. MYCOLOGY : FUNGI :: (a. paleontology, b. pathology, c. teleology, d. apiology) : DISEASES

3. SUI GENERA : (a. pro forma, b. carpe diem, c. de jura, d. alter ego) :: ONE OF A KIND : SECOND SELF

4. TANTRUM : RANT :: BANTER : (a. ten, b. term, c. talk, d. ant)

5. ASYLUM : HERMETIC :: SANCTUARY : (a. lonely, b. immune, c. tight, d. callous)

6. INIMICAL : (a. telling, b. sappy, c. meticulous, d. flashy) :: HOSTILE : MAWKISH

7. SERBIA : (a. country, b. rabies, c. independent, d. Croatia) :: CREATIVE : REACTIVE

8. KAYAK : COUGH :: PALINDROME : (a. simile, b. conjunction, c. onomatopoeia, d. sick)

9. MOOSE : MOOSE :: OPUS : (a. opulent, b. open, c. opera, d. song)

10. GENERIC : SPECIFIC :: (a. cleave, b. chain, c. cleaver, d. mix) : SPLIT

11. ONEIRIC : DREAMLIKE :: AUSTERE : (a. headstrong, b. outmoded, c. dour, d. sweet)

12. CLOUDS : EXISTENCE :: NEPHOLOGY : (a. ornithology, b. ontology, c. cytology, d. spelology)

13. GROUSE : (a. berate, b. pheasant, c. advise, d. strata) :: SOUR : TART

14. NOUN : IMPUNITY :: VERB : (a. noun, b. exemption, c. allow, d. freedom)

15. (a. assuage, b. colic, c. penitent, d. pithy) : PRESAGE :: ALLEVIATE : AUGUR

16. NIGHT : APEX :: DAY : (a. output, b. callous, c. nadir, d. climax)

17. LOQUACIOUS : NOISOME :: GARRULOUS : (a. putrid, b. loud, c. collapsed, d. naïve)

18. DILETTANTE : (a. artsy, b. superficial, c. simple, d. angry) :: PESSIMIST : NEGATIVE

Answers

1. **(d)** The plural of the word *millennium* is *millennia*, and the plural of *nebula* is *nebulae*.

2. **(b)** Mycology is the study of fungi, just as pathology is the study of diseases.

3. **(d)** *Sui genera* is Latin for "one of a kind," and *alter ego* is Latin for "second self."

4. **(a)** Removing three letters from *tantrum* and rearranging the remaining letters, you get *rant*. Removing three letters from *banter* and rearranging the letters, you get *ten*.

5. **(c)** An asylum is a sanctuary, and *hermetic* means tight: a classic synonym bridge.

6. **(b)** *Inimical* means hostile, just as *mawkish* means sappy: another synonym bridge.

7. **(b)** Since *creative* and *reactive* are anagrams, the same letters spelling a different word, the answer is *rabies*, an anagram of *Serbia*.

8. **(c)** *Kayak* is an example of a palindrome (a word spelled the same backwards or forwards), and *cough* is an example of onomatopoeia (a word that mimics a natural sound).

9. **(c)** The plural of *moose* is *moose*, and the plural of *opus* is *opera*.

10. **(a)** *Generic* and *specific* are opposites. *Cleave* and *split* are also opposites.

11. **(c)** *Oneiric* means to be dreamlike, just as *austere* means to be dour.

12. **(b)** Nephology is the study of clouds, and ontology is the study of existence.

13. **(d)** Remove the first and last letter of *grouse* and then reverse the word to get *sour*, and remove the first and last letter of *strata* and reverse the word to get *tart*.

14. **(c)** *Impunity* is a noun, and *allow* is a verb.

15. **(a)** *Assuage* is a synonym for *alleviate*, just as *presage* is a synonym for *augur*.

16. **(c)** Night is the opposite of day, and apex is the opposite of nadir.

17. **(a)** *Loquacious* and *garrulous* both mean talkative, and *noisome* and *putrid* both mean to have a foul odor.

18. **(b)** A dilettante is superficial, and a pessimist is negative.

CHAPTER FOUR

MAT Humanities Strategies

WHAT TO EXPECT FROM MAT HUMANITIES

As we've seen already, it is most important to understand the **relationship** between the various elements of any particular analogy, whether they refer to people, places, or things. The Humanities questions on the MAT are no different.

The best way to prepare for the Humanities component of the MAT is to familiarize yourself with the literary, artistic, and musical superstars throughout history: those individuals and groups that helped shape modern creative life with their art, words, and songs.

You don't need to know all that much about the artist, book, or song in question. All that is really necessary for the MAT is a working knowledge of the **who**, **what**, **when**, and, on some occasions, **where** of the artist or artwork. For instance, you may never have read James Joyce's colossal novel *Ulysses*. (The person writing the MAT probably hasn't either.) But if asked about it, you'd at least want to know that Joyce, an Irishman, wrote *Ulysses*, which was first published in 1922, in a **stream-of-consciousness** narrative style. This information would help you to make connections between, say, Joyce and other Irish novelists or between *Ulysses* and the works of Virginia Woolf, another writer who often wrote in stream-of-consciousness style, and so on.

In the study lists in the next section of this book, we've done our best to show you the links between artists and movements, between writers and their mentors, and between composers and their symphonies. What follows is an overview of the sort of cultural knowledge that the MAT will expect you to know.

LITERARY FIGURES AND THEIR WORKS

As we noted, one of the MAT writers' favorite pastimes is coming up with analogies on the **who** and **what** of canonical literature. Don't expect to find many writers of popular fiction or comic books here (alas). Instead, prepare to be tested on the major works and writers that have been accepted into the literary canon.

The questions in this genre will most likely ask you to recognize the following:
- a major work or works of a prominent novelist or poet
- the writing contemporaries of a prominent novelist or poet
- the literary movement or period with which a writer is primarily associated

Note that none of these requires you to understand who or what the works of these artists, most of which are generally acknowledged to be among the greatest works in (primarily English) literary history, are actually about. This is a small victory for you, even if it is unfortunate for your intellectual development. Consequently, your job is to review who wrote what and when.

Literary Terminology

In addition to, and certainly in concert with, asking you to recognize writers and their works, the MAT expects you to have a fundamental knowledge of prominent literary terms and styles. This is a useful method of testing a deeper knowledge of the works and writers that have shaped the modern literary landscape.

You should also brush up on literary movements and genres. It would be wise to learn not only when the movements occurred but also which writers are considered most representative of them and what the basic tenets of each might be. For instance, **Ezra Pound** was a poet and editor who is often linked with the **Modernist** movement, prominent in the late teens and early 1920s in Europe.

Lastly, while many of the other terms the MAT tests are words you may know from other disciplines, it would behoove you to review their specific relationships to literature. Let's look at a couple of examples.

1. FAULKNER : AS I LAY DYING :: (a. Tolstoy, b. Woolf, c. Dostoevsky, d. Hesse) : THE IDIOT

2. STREAM OF CONSCIOUSNESS : JOYCE :: (a. monologue, b. pentameter, c. denouement, d. noir) : HAMMETT

Answers:
1. (**c**) William Faulkner wrote the novel *As I Lay Dying*, and Fyodor Dostoevsky wrote the novel *The Idiot*.

2. (d) James Joyce often used a stream-of-consciousness narration in his novels, including *Ulysses*, while Dashiell Hammett used a noir narration in his novels, including *The Thin Man*.

MYTHOLOGY

Rather than begin at the Dawn of Time and inch our way through human history, we've chosen instead to highlight those aspects that seem to pique the interest of MAT test makers. One of their favorite topics is Greek, Roman, and Norse mythology, much of which has oozed into Western culture in the years since the Renaissance. Among other things, many of the planets in our solar system share names with Roman gods, and several days of the week are derived from Norse mythology. Certain key items tend to appear again and again on the MAT. We'll cover these ideas in the next few pages.

Greek and Roman Mythology

One of the most basic ways the MAT tests Greek and Roman mythology is by connecting Greek gods to their Roman counterparts or by connecting Greek or Roman gods to what they were gods of. The table below covers the basics:

GREEK NAME	ROMAN NAME	WHAT YOU SHOULD KNOW ABOUT THEM
Zeus	Jupiter	Supreme god
Hera	Juno	Goddess of marriage and maternity
Apollo	Apollo	God of the sun
Athena	Minerva	Goddess of wisdom and war
Aphrodite	Venus	Goddess of love
Dionysus	Bacchus	God of pleasure and drink
Hermes	Mercury	Messenger of the gods
Poseidon	Neptune	God of the sea
Ares	Mars	God of war
Artemis	Diana	Goddess of the moon
Hades	Pluto	God of the underworld

Let's look at how these concepts might be tested on your exam. Take a shot at the following sample MAT question.

ARES : (a. war, b. sun, c. underworld, d. sea) :: APHRODITE : LOVE

Answer: (a) Ares is the Greek god of war, and Aphrodite is the Greek goddess of love.

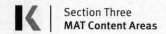

Norse Mythology

Occasionally, the MAT analogies require a rudimentary knowledge of Norse gods and mythology. Aside from relating the god or goddess to his or her domain, some analogies will connect the god to the day of the week associated with his or her name.

GOD	DOMAIN	DAY OF THE WEEK
Odin	Supreme god	Wednesday
Thor	Thunder	Thursday
Tiw (Tyr)	War	Tuesday
Frigg (Frija)	Love and marriage	Friday
Loki	Mischief	_____

That's all we're looking at as far as mythology goes. Be sure to review these concepts heading into your test. The next stop on our tour of Humanities focuses on world religions.

RELIGION

On the MAT, you may encounter a few questions that require basic knowledge of world religions. Frequently these questions will simply involve connecting the founder to the religion or understanding basic religious vocabulary.

Here's an example of a typical religion-based question:

CONFUCIUS : CONFUCIANISM : (a. Lao-tzu, b. Siddhartha. c. Khan, d. Shinto) : TAOISM

Answer: (**a**) Confucius was the founder of Confucianism, and Lao-tzu was the founder of Taoism.

PHILOSOPHY

Philosophy may remind you of all-night discussions you had when you were in college. For the MAT, it's mostly about schools of thought, basic terms, and famous philosophers. So if you know that Locke, empiricism, and *tabula rasa* all go together, you're ready to handle any Locke questions you might see on Test Day. Let's take a look at a sample question.

SARTRE : EXISTENTIALISM :: HUSSERL : (a. transcendentalism, b. empiricism, c. phenomenology, d. rationalism)

Answer: (**c**) Sartre is a philosopher linked to existentialism. Husserl is a philosopher linked to phenomenology.

VISUAL ARTISTS AND THEIR WORKS

The MAT test writers also love to ask about major visual artists—painters, sculptors, and architects—and their most prominent works. This type of question is most often a direct one, asking you, for instance, to choose from a list of famous works the one that correctly corresponds to the artist in question. Rarely will a question reference a controversial or contemporary artist—the MAT prefers to focus on artists already well established and displayed in museums around the world.

Don't worry if you encounter an artist on the MAT whose works you have not actually seen, as the content of the painting or sculpture referenced is far less likely to appear on the test than the name or the genre of the piece.

Art Terminology

As with literature, the MAT also tests on a variety of art terms and movements. The trick here is to be able to recognize the major players in each movement and when the movement took place, not the subtle nuances and philosophical stances that distinguish one movement from another.

Most of the terms you can expect will most likely be about types of art and the ways in which they relate to artistic movements. Let's look at a couple of sample questions.

1. DA VINCI : MICHELANGELO :: (a. *The Thinker*, b. *Sunflowers*, c. *Mona Lisa*, d. *Guernica*) : DAVID

2. ABSTRACT EXPRESSIONISM : BAUHAUS :: (a. Warhol, b. O'Keeffe, c. Klimt, d. Pollock) : KLEE

Answers:

1. (**c**) Leonardo Da Vinci created the *Mona Lisa*, and Michelangelo created *David*.

2. (**d**) Jackson Pollock is considered a founder of the Abstract Expressionist movement, and Paul Klee is considered a founder of the Bauhaus movement.

MUSICIANS, COMPOSERS, AND THEIR WORKS

Don't expect Elvis, Madonna, or the Beatles in this type of question, as the MAT writers seem to have stopped listening to music around 1955. No matter. Rename this section "Classical Music," and you'd pretty much get the point. While many young adults today are not as familiar with classical pieces as their counterparts might have been in 1902, the MAT will still ask questions about the classical repertoire.

Remember that classical music is primarily a study in history; in this case, the musical movements that dominated much of the world (although primarily Europe and the United States) in the 17th through 19th centuries. Also note that occasionally nonclassical musicians

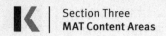

and composers of the 20th century, such as Charlie Parker, George Gershwin, and other early jazz and pop composers, may appear on a MAT exam.

Musical Terms

MAT writers have a fondness for musical terminology, especially those Italian terms used on music scores to inform musicians how fast, slow, sad, happy, etc. to play a particular section of a piece.

If you don't know these terms, you have two choices: (1) study to become a symphony-caliber musician, or (2) review the study lists in the next section of this book. Once again, the first approach may be the more worthwhile, but it's probably too time consuming for most students. Let's look at a couple of sample questions.

1. RAVEL : BOLÉRO :: (a. Beethoven, b. Brahms, c. Copland, d. Vivaldi) : THE FOUR SEASONS

2. ADAGIO : LARGO :: ALLEGRO : (a. andante, b. diminuendo, c. fortissimo, d. presto)

Answers:

1. (**d**) Maurice Ravel composed the orchestral piece *Boléro*, and Antonio Vivaldi composed the set of concertos *The Four Seasons*.

2. (**d**) *Adagio* means slow, and *largo* means very slow; likewise, *allegro* means fast, and *presto* means very fast.

TYING IT ALL TOGETHER

Thus ends our brief look at the humanities portion of the MAT exam. As we've seen throughout this book, the key to maximizing your score on these questions is your ability to recognize the connections that exist between any two terms.

Try to remember that it's not how much you know about the topics we've covered but rather how much you can associate with them. Now it's time for you to steep yourself in as much humanities content as you can in preparation for the test by using our study lists in the next section of this book. But first, test your knowledge with our humanities chapter quiz. You'll be "culturally literate" before you know it!

CHAPTER QUIZ: HUMANITIES

Try answering the following analogy questions, using the strategies you've just learned.

1. SOPHOCLES : EURIPIDES :: WOOLF: (a. Beckett, b. Dickens, c. Kafka, d. Aeschylus)

2. JOYCE : (a. Shakespeare, b. Milton, c. Woolf, d. Flaubert) :: ULYSSES : PARADISE REGAIN'D

3. HUMBERT HUMBERT : HEATHCLIFF :: (a. Catch-22, b. Huckleberry Finn, c. Lolita, d. Madame Bovary) : WUTHERING HEIGHTS

4. SATIRE : HISTORICAL NOVEL :: SWIFT : (a. Plath, b. Eliot, c. Orwell, d. Scott)

5. (a. coda, b. commencement, c. couplet, d. climax) : MURDER :: DENOUEMENT : SOLUTION

6. JOHNS : WARHOL :: (a. mobile, b. American flag, c. splatter-paint, d. abstract expressionism) : SOUP CANS

7. (a. *The Scream*, b. *Water Lilies*, c. *American Gothic*, d. *Bather*) : MUNCH :: STARRY NIGHT : VAN GOGH

8. CUBISM : IMPRESSIONISM :: NEOCLASSICISM : (a. Bauhaus, b. futurism, c. Victorian, d. rococo)

9. PARIS : NEW YORK :: (a. Hagia Sophia, b. Prado, c. Louvre, d. Rijks) : THE MET

10. PABLO CASALS : (a. harp, b. cello, c. guitar, d. violin) :: CHARLIE PARKER : SAXOPHONE

11. RODIN : MICHELANGELO :: (a. *The Thinker*, b. *Sunflowers*, c. *Mona Lisa*, d. *Guernica*) : DAVID

12. HAIKU : THREE :: SONNET : (a. 4, b. 12, c. 14, d. 6)

13. STEIN : FLAUBERT :: LOST GENERATION : (a. enlightenment, b. le mot juste, c. romantics, d. classicism)

14. CRANE : RED BADGE OF COURAGE :: (a. Tolstoy, b. Woolf, c. Dostoevsky, d. Hesse) : CRIME AND PUNISHMENT

15. SNAIL : HARE :: LARGO : (a. presto, b. lento, c. rondo, d. fortissimo)

16. ROSSINI : (a. *Bolero*, b. *The Barber of Seville*, c. *Romeo and Juliet*, d. *Rodeo*) :: PUCCINI : LA BOHÈME

17. GERSHWIN : BERNSTEIN :: (a. Beethoven, b. Shostakovich, c. Debussy, d. Vivaldi) : RAVEL

18. ABSTRACT EXPRESSIONISM : BAUHAUS :: POLLOCK : (a. Warhol, b. O'Keeffe, c. Klimt, d. Kandinsky) :

19. GEHRY : GUGGENHEIM BILBAO :: WRIGHT : (a. Tate, b. Whitney, c. Prado, d. Guggenheim New York)

20. (a. Dürer, b. Rothko, c. Manet, d. Dali) : WEBER :: PLATO : SOCRATES

21. SOLILOQUY: SHAKESPEARE :: (a. monologue, b. pentameter, c. denouement, d. noir) : CHANDLER

22. RENAISSANCE : (a. Dickens, b. Rabelais, c. Conrad, d. Dante) :: REFORMATION : MILTON

23. ODYSSEY : HOMER :: METAMORPHOSES : (a. Dante, b. Ovid, c. Sappho, d. Euripides)

24. DEGAS : FRANCE :: CHRISTO : (a. Russia, b. Monaco, c. Bulgaria, d. Spain)

25. DADA : SURREALISM :: (a. pop art, b. classicism, c. naturism, d. rococo) : MINIMAL ART

26. PERSEUS : THESEUS :: (a. Pegasus, b. Urania, c. Medusa, d. Prometheus) : MINOTAUR

27. ARMSTRONG : MOON :: GAGARIN : (a. Mars, b. space, c. international space station, d. cosmonaut)

28. UNION : (a. Grant, b. Lincoln, c. Booth, d. Davis) :: CONFEDERATE : LEE

29. DOUGLASS : ABOLITIONIST :: NATION : (a. temperance, b. suffrage, c. alcohol, d. prohibition)

30. (a. Loki, b. Hera, c. Zeus, d. Odin) : WEDNESDAY :: THOR : THURSDAY

31. SUFFRAGE : PROHIBITION :: XIX : (a. XV, b. XVI, c. XVII, d. XVIII)

32. VERSAILLES : LOUIS XIV :: (a. White House, b. Watergate, c. impeachment, d. Congress) : NIXON

33. JUPITER : ZEUS :: MINERVA : (a. Diana, b. Demeter, c. Hera, d. Athena)

Answers

1. **(a)** Sophocles was a contemporary of Euripides, just as Virginia Woolf was a contemporary of Samuel Beckett.

2. **(b)** James Joyce wrote *Ulysses*, and John Milton wrote *Paradise Regain'd*.

3. **(c)** Humbert Humbert is the male protagonist in Nabokov's *Lolita*, and Heathcliff is the male protagonist in Brontë's *Wuthering Heights*.

4. **(d)** Jonathan Swift was a noted master of satire, and Sir Walter Scott was a noted master of the historical novel.

5. **(b)** In a mystery story, the commencement, or opening, is the likely time for a murder to occur, and the denouement, or resolution, is when the solution to the murder is shared with the reader.

6. **(b)** Jasper Johns created art using the American flag as a motif, and Andy Warhol created art using soup cans as a motif.

7. **(a)** Norwegian artist Edvard Munch painted *The Scream*, and Dutch painter Vincent Van Gogh painted *Starry Night*.

8. **(d)** Cubism was an artistic movement that came after impressionism, and neo-classicism was an artistic movement that came after the rococo movement.

9. **(c)** The Louvre is a world famous art museum in Paris, while the Metropolitan Museum ("The Met") is a world famous art museum in New York.

10. **(b)** Pablo Casals was a master of the cello, and Charlie Parker was a master of the saxophone.

11. **(a)** Auguste Rodin created *The Thinker*, and Michelangelo created *David*.

12. **(c)** A haiku is a type of poem that consists of 3 lines, and a sonnet is a type of poem that consists of 14 lines.

13. **(b)** Gertrude Stein coined the phrase *lost generation*, and Gustave Flaubert coined the phrase *le mot juste*.

14. **(c)** Stephen Crane wrote the novel *Red Badge of Courage*, and Fyodor Dostoevsky wrote the novel *Crime and Punishment*.

15. **(a)** A snail is a very slow animal, and *largo* means a very slow pace, just as a hare is a very fast animal, and *presto* means a very fast pace.

16. **(b)** Gioacchino Rossini composed the opera *The Barber of Seville*, and Giacomo Puccini composed the opera *La Bohème*.

17. **(c)** George Gershwin and Leonard Bernstein were both American composers of the mid–20th century, and Claude Debussy and Maurice Ravel were both French composers of the late 19th century.

18. **(d)** Jackson Pollock is considered a founder of the Abstract Expressionist movement, and Vasily Kandinsky is considered a founder of the Bauhaus movement.

19. **(d)** Architect Frank Gehry designed the Guggenheim museum in Bilbao, Spain, and Frank Lloyd Wright designed the Guggenheim museum in New York City.

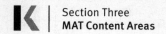

20. **(b)** Artist Mark Rothko was a disciple of artist Max Weber, just as the philosopher Plato was a disciple of philosopher Socrates.

21. **(d)** Shakespeare used soliloquies in his plays, and Raymond Chandler used noir in his novels.

22. **(d)** Dante Aligheri (usually referred to as "Dante") was one of the foremost writers of the Italian Renaissance, and John Milton was one of the foremost writers of the English Reformation.

23. **(b)** Homer wrote the classic *Odyssey*, and Ovid wrote the classic *Metamorphoses*.

24. **(c)** Edgar Degas was a French artist, and Christo Javacheff (usually referred to as "Christo") is a Bulgarian artist.

25. **(a)** Surrealism emerged from the dadaist movement, just as minimalism emerged from the pop art movement.

26. **(c)** According to Greek mythology, Perseus is the Greek hero who slayed Medusa, and Theseus is the Greek hero who slayed the Minotaur.

27. **(b)** Neil Armstrong was the first human on the moon, and Yuri Gagarin was the first human in space.

28. **(a)** In the U.S. Civil War, Grant led the Union Army, and Lee led the Confederate Army.

29. **(a)** Frederick Douglass was an important leader of the abolitionist movement, and Carry Nation was an important leader of the temperance movement.

30. **(d)** Odin is the Norse god whose name is the basis for Wednesday, and Thor is the Norse god whose name is the basis for Thursday.

31. **(d)** Suffrage (the right to vote) was the subject of the 19th (XIX = 19) amendment to the Constitution. Prohibition (banning alcohol) was the subject of the 18th (XVIII = 18) amendment to the Constitution.

32. **(a)** Versailles was the seat of power for Louis XIV, and the White House is the seat of power for U.S. presidents, such as Richard Nixon.

33. **(d)** Jupiter is the Roman name for the Greek god Zeus. Minerva is the Roman name for the Greek god Athena.

CHAPTER FIVE

MAT Social Sciences Strategies

WHAT TO EXPECT FROM MAT SOCIAL SCIENCES

The analogies on the MAT cover a panoply of topics loosely associated with social science. Social science covers a lot of ground, and so will we in this chapter and in the study lists in the next section of this book. The key to handling the wide range of social science covered on the MAT is to review as many names and concepts as you can and then let them gradually seep in. You won't be expected to know a whole lot about the names, dates, and terms that appear in this section for your exam, but a few such terms, names, and dates will appear on your MAT, so working through this section will give you the head start you need to get the score you're aiming for. Remember: Breadth, not depth, is the key to studying for the MAT. While there might be a gap or two here or there, we're giving you the basic content you'll need to prepare for the test.

EXPLORERS AND DISCOVERERS

Explorers and discoverers, like inventors and scientists, are bread and butter for an MAT test maker. As deadlines approach, they can grab a list of explorers, pair them with what they discovered, and voilà, they've got scads of analogies ready to go.

Here's an example of this type of question:

CORTEZ : AZTEC :: PIZARRO : (a. Inca, b. Mayan, c. Conquistador, d. Mexico)

Answer: (**a**) Cortez is the conquistador who conquered the Aztec empire, and Pizarro is the conquistador who conquered the Inca empire.

GEOGRAPHY

Geography and geographical terms pop up from time to time on the MAT. They can be handled like every other subject area we've covered thus far. Connect the basic concepts

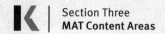

without delving too deeply into the details, and you're good to go. Also note that the MAT writers have a fondness for questions that ask about former names of places on the map.

Take a crack at the following sample geography questions:
1. WATER : LAND :: (a. archipelago, b. peninsula, c. strait, d. shore) : ISTHMUS
2. BRITISH HONDURAS : (a. Belize, b. Guatemala, c. Honduras, d. Trinidad) :: FRENCH INDO-CHINA : LAOS

Answers:
1. (**c**) A strait is a narrow link of water between two larger bodies of water, and an isthmus is a narrow strip of land between two larger land masses.
2. (**a**) The former name for Belize was British Honduras, and the former name for Laos was French Indo-China.

POLITICAL SCIENCE

The MAT will require you to link political leaders and figures to the movements they headed. While a nuanced and detailed understanding of early Byzantine culture might (or actually might not) wow your friends at your next dinner party, it won't translate into points on the MAT. Remember, the MAT rewards breadth, not depth, of political knowledge.

For instance, you need to associate Lenin with the Russian Revolution and Communism and Robespierre with the French Revolution. You should recognize that Carrie Nation was a leader of the temperance movement (the movement to ban alcohol) and Frederick Douglass was a leader of the abolitionist movement (the movement to ban slavery). Any additional knowledge about these figures or terms might help you on the MAT, but it might also get in the way. Armed with the surface knowledge that gets tested, you'll crush the political questions that come your way.

Take a crack at the questions that follow:
1. AXIS : ALLIES :: ITALY : (a. Germany, b. England, c. Japan, d. Europe)
2. CZECH REPUBLIC : (a. Capek, b. Hasek, c. Havel, d. Mucha) :: INDIA : NEHRU

Answers:
1. (**b**) Italy was a member of the Axis alliance during World War II, and England was a member of the Allies during World War II.
2. (**c**) The first democratically elected leader of the Czech Republic was Vaclav Havel, and the first democratically elected leader of India was Jawaharlal Nehru.

That wasn't so bad was it? Be ready for more questions like these on your exam, but don't expect them to require a deeper understanding. When it comes to MAT content knowledge, keep it simple and superficial.

With political science under control, it's time to move on to economics.

ECONOMICS

Economics is the social science that studies the production and consumption of goods and services. Microeconomics examines the economic behavior of individuals and firms. Macroeconomics addresses issues of unemployment, inflation, and monetary and fiscal policy for an entire economy or economic system. Here's a sample question:

KEYNES : REGULATION :: (a. Friedman, b. Krugman, c. Stockman, d. Samuels) : FREE MARKETS

Answer: (**a**) Milton Friedman's theories focused on the power of free markets, while John Maynard Keynes believed that market regulation would lead to better economic outcomes.

PSYCHOLOGY

You may have leaned about psychology watching daytime talk shows, but there is still hope. A cursory understanding is all you need to bank points on the MAT. Psychology is known for its schools of thought, key practitioners, and key terms. So if you know that Freud is about ego, id, and superego and Skinner's work is about behaviorism, you're ready to handle the questions you might see on Test Day. Let's take a look at a sample question.

COGNITIVE : LAZARUS :: BEHAVIORISM : (a. Jung, b. Pavlov, c. Chomsky, d. dogs)

Answer: (**b**) Ivan Pavlov was one of the founders of behaviorism, and Richard Lazarus was one of the founders of cognitive psychology.

SOCIOLOGY

Sociology is the study of society. It uses empirical investigation and critical analysis to develop theories about human social activity. Historical figures like Alexis DeToqueville are good to know about, as well as more modern figures like Bruno Bettelheim and Max Weber. Following is a sample sociology question:

ORGANIZATION MAN : WHYTE :: DEMOCRACY IN AMERICA : (a. Bettelheim, b. Weber, c. Reagan, d. de Toqueville)

Answer: (**d**) Alexis de Toqueville wrote *Democracy in America*, which is considered his seminal work. William Whyte's seminal work was *The Organization Man.*

ANTHROPOLOGY

Anthropology is the study of humanity. What defines man? Answers include ancestors, physical traits, behavior, variation, evolution, and culture. Here's a sample anthropology question:

MARGARET MEAD : (a. United States, b. Spain, c. American Samoa, d. Guam) :: DIANE GOODALL : AFRICA

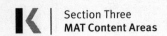

Answer: (**c**) American Samoa is where Margaret Mead did her seminal work. Diane Goodall did hers in Africa.

TYING IT ALL TOGETHER

As you can see, the key to mastering social science questions is getting comfortable making basic connections between terms. Now that you've been introduced to the basic kinds of topics you will see on your exam, it's time to expose yourself to as much content as you can. Once you can make a basic connection, lock it away and move on. Again, it's the number of your connections, not the depth, that will translate to a higher score.

To get a better handle on the social science content you might see on the MAT, see the study lists in the next section of this book. But first, see how much you already know by taking the following Social Science Quiz. Before you know it, you'll be an MAT social science star.

CHAPTER QUIZ: SOCIAL SCIENCES

Try answering the following analogy questions, using the strategies you've just learned.

1. PALEOLITHIC : NEOLITHIC :: (a. Mezozoic, b. Stone, c. Rock, d. Paleozoic) : BRONZE

2. MERTON : SCIENCE :: MILLS: (a. humanism, b. structuralism, c. tropism, d. positivism)

3. ID : THESIS :: (a. superego, b. ego, c. conscience, d. guilty) : ANTITHESIS

4. PRIME MERIDIAN : LONGITUDE :: (a. Tropic of Cancer, b. North Pole, c. South Pole, d. Equator) : LATITUDE

5. MERMAID : FISH :: CENTAUR : (a. dog, b. horse, c. lion, d. goat)

6. INDUSTRIALIZATION : URBANIZATION :: (a. factories, b. reason, c. objectivity, d. secularization) : RATIONALIZATION

7. (a. micro, b. mini, c. major, d. player) : MACRO :: INDIVIDUAL : SYSTEM

8. (a. Madison, b. Adams, c. Jefferson, d. Hamilton) : DECLARATION OF INDEPENDENCE :: MARX : COMMUNIST MANIFESTO

9. HAMILTON : MACHIAVELLI :: (a. Federalist Papers, b. Articles of Confederation, c. Common Sense, d. Declaration of Independence) : THE PRINCE

10. CASTRO : LENIN :: (a. Bolivia, b. Peru, c. Cuba, d. Argentina) : RUSSIA

11. BOAS : (a. Germany, b. England, c. United States, d. Hungary) :: DURKEIM : FRANCE

12. (a. proselyte, b. prophet, c. acolyte, d. apostate) : DISCIPLE :: TRAITOR : PATRIOT

13. SUPPLY : EXISTING :: DEMAND : (a. immediate, b. prolonged, c. desired, d. needed)

14. AMAZON : (a. river, b. South America, c. Brazil, d. jungle) :: NILE : AFRICA

15. ARCHAEOLOGICAL EVIDENCE : (a. physics, b. chemistry, c. geography, d. history) :: FIELD RESEARCH : SOCIOLOGY

16. AQUIFER : WATER :: LODE : (a. heavy, b. ore, c. wood, d. mountain)

17. (a. Asia, b. Africa, c. cape, d. Australia) : GOOD HOPE :: SOUTH AMERICA : HORN

18. SALTWATER : FRESHWATER :: (a. isolationist, b. interventionist, c. liquid, d. determinist) : LAISSEZ-FAIRE

Answers

1. **(b)** Stone and Bronze are ages. Paleolithic and Neolithic are eras.

2. **(a)** Robert K. Merton was a sociologist famous for focusing on science, while C. Wright Mills was a sociologist who focused on humanism.

3. **(a)** The id and superego are opposing forces that are synthesized into the ego in Freud's personality theory. The thesis and antithesis are opposing ideas that combine to form the synthesis in Hegel's dialectic.

4. **(d)** The Prime Meridian is zero degrees longitude, and the Equator is zero degrees latitude.

5. **(b)** A mermaid is a mythological creature that is part human and part fish, and a centaur is a mythological creature that is part human and part horse.

6. **(d)** Industrialization and urbanization are closely linked processes in sociology, as are secularization and rationalization.

7. **(a)** Microeconomics is the study of individuals; macroeconomics is the study of systems.

8. **(c)** Thomas Jefferson wrote the Declaration of Independence, and Karl Marx wrote the Communist Manifesto.

9. **(a)** Alexander Hamilton wrote most of the *Federalist Papers*, and Niccolò Machiavelli wrote *The Prince*.

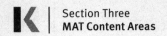

10. **(c)** Fidel Castro led the Communist revolution in Cuba, and Vladimir Lenin led the Communist revolution in Russia.

11. **(c)** Franz Boas was one of the founders of anthropology in the United States, and Émile Durkheim was one of the founders of anthropology in France.

12. **(d)** An apostate rejects loyalty to religious faith, while a disciple maintains loyalty to a religious faith. Likewise, a traitor rejects loyalty to the nation, while a patriot maintains loyalty to the nation.

13. **(c)** In economics, supply is the existing goods or services available, and demand is the amount of goods or services that are desired.

14. **(b)** The Amazon River is the longest river in South America, and the Nile is the longest river in Africa.

15. **(d)** Archaeological evidence is an important source of information in the field of history, just as field research is an important source of information in sociology.

16. **(b)** An aquifer is an underground reservoir of water, and a lode is an underground vein of mineral ore.

17. **(b)** The Cape of Good Hope is the southernmost tip of Africa. Cape Horn is the southernmost tip of South America.

18. **(b)** The Saltwater school of economics (Berkeley, Harvard, MIT Penn, Princeton, and Yale) is considered interventionist. The Freshwater school (University of Chicago, Carnegie Mellon, University of Minnesota, University of Rochester) is considered laissez-faire, or free-market driven.

CHAPTER SIX

MAT Natural Sciences and Mathematics Strategies

WHAT TO EXPECT FROM MAT NATURAL SCIENCES AND MATHEMATICS

About 10 or so MAT questions (or a few more or less, depending on how you classify them) deal with concepts from math and the natural sciences. As always, the name of the game on the MAT is breadth, not depth. Some concepts are almost certain to appear (Roman numerals, imaginary numbers), some are very likely to appear (names of animal groups and genders, taxonomy, temperature scales), and others may or may not appear (scientists and their contributions, geological terminology, etc.).

As in other areas you have reviewed so far, terminology plays a key role in the makeup of the MAT science questions. This is partially due to the very nature of analogies as word problems. And while you can't expect to know every term in the fields of biology, physics, chemistry, and ecology, it would be wise to review the science terminology favored by the test writers before you take the MAT.

Let's take a look at some of the concepts that the MAT writers favor when creating math and science questions.

BIOLOGY

One topic on the MAT that is far too vast to master on short notice is biology. Luckily, because of the breadth-over-depth philosophy of the MAT, you shouldn't need to know much more than the basics. But you will be expected to have a smattering of knowledge about the human organism and how it functions. What follows is a brief review of the sort of concepts and terms in medicine that you should know before you take the MAT.

Remember, it's not necessary to know all that much about biology for the MAT—which is lucky for you. It's only necessary to know the essentials.

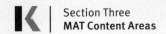
Human Biology: Bones

Know the names of these bones and where they are in the body:

Clavicle	Mandible	Scapula
Cranium	Patella	Sternum
Femur	Pelvis	Tibia
Fibula	Radius	Ulna
Humerus		

Human Biology: The Circulatory System

The human circulatory system is a closed system, with a chambered heart that pumps blood through a network of blood vessels. Blood is pumped from the heart through the aorta, which branches into smaller arterioles and then into capillaries. Capillaries are extremely small vessels where an exchange of material between the circulation and the tissues occurs. From the capillaries, blood travels through venules, or small veins, and then flows back to the heart through veins into the vena cava of the heart.

Human Biology: Muscles

You should know that there are three kinds of muscle:

- **Skeletal or striated**: includes all those used for voluntary movements such as walking, talking, etc. What we tend to think of when we talk about muscles.
- **Smooth**: muscles used in involuntary movements such as digestion, reproduction, etc.
- **Cardiac**: special muscles that exist only in the heart

Human Biology: The Nervous System

The nervous system is obviously complex. Consequently, there are only a few things you might need to know about such a complicated system for the MAT.

Parts of the Central Nervous System

- **Cerebrum:** the major part of the brain, thought to be the center of intelligence
- **Medulla:** connection between the brain and the spinal cord
- **Cerebellum:** big cluster of nerve tissue that forms the basis for the brain
- **Spinal cord:** carrier of impulses between all organs and the brain

Parts of the Peripheral Nervous System

- **Somatic nervous system:** consists of peripheral nerve fibers that send sensory information to the central nervous system and motor nerve fibers that project to skeletal muscle.

- **Autonomic nervous system:** regulates the organs of our body, such as the heart, stomach, and intestines.

Ready to take a stab at a few questions on your own? Here's what a few medical questions on the MAT might look like:

1. TIBIA : FIBULA :: (a. femur, b. ulna, c. humerus, d. clavicle) : RADIUS

2. HEART : (a. duct, b. valve, c. pump, d. ventricle) :: ELBOW :: HINGE

3. SMOOTH : INTESTINAL :: (a. articulated, b. flat, c. autonomous, d. striated) : ABDOMINAL

Answers:

1. **(b)** The tibia and fibula bones are paired in the lower leg, just as the radius and ulna bones are paired in the forearm.

2. **(c)** A heart works in the same way as a pump, and an elbow joint works in the same way as a hinge.

3. **(d)** Intestinal muscles are smooth, and abdominal muscles are striated.

Now that we've seen some basics in medicine, let's take a look at a similar question type: General Science.

GENERAL SCIENCE

The MAT loves to ask questions that require a basic knowledge of general science. No one expects you to know the weight of air on Jupiter or the number of butterfly species in the world, but you should be familiar with the kind of biology and chemistry that might appear on the MAT.

What follows is a brief introduction to the sort of basic, general science you could see on the MAT. While it's certainly not all-inclusive, it will give you a heads-up on what you need to brush up on.

Bear in mind that the science questions on the MAT often call on concepts that you probably haven't looked at since you were back in high school. That's why you may need to spend time with our study lists in the next section of this book.

Taxonomy (i.e., the Classification of Living Things)

You are probably aware that all living things fall into a careful classification scheme that goes from the most broad level of similarity (kingdom) to the most narrow (species).

Classifications from the broadest category to the most specific:

Kingdom / Phylum / Class / Order / Family / Genus / Species

And here's a handy mnemonic device to help you remember the classifications: "King Philip's Class Ordered the Family-sized Gino's Special."

Let's look at some examples of this naming scheme.

Kingdom	Animalia	Animalia	Animalia	Animalia	Plantae
Phylum	Chordata	Chordata	Arthropoda	Mollusca	Magnoliophyta
Class	Mammalia	Mammalia	Insecta	Cephalopoda	Magnoliopsida
Order	Primate	Carnivora	Diptera	Teuthida	Caryophyllidae
Family	Homidae	Felidae	Muscidae	Architeuthidae	Cactaceae
Genus	Homo	Felis	Musca	Architeuthis	Opuntia
Species	Sapiens	Domestica	Domestica	Dux	Phaeacantha
Also known as	Human	House cat	House fly	Giant squid	Prickly pear

You don't need to know how to break each category down, but you should at least familiarize yourself with the broadest category, the kingdoms.

The Kingdoms

- **Moneran**: bacteria, blue-green algae, and primitive pathogens. Considered the most primitive kingdom, it represents **prokaryotic** (as opposed to **eukariotic**) life forms—that is, the cells of Moneran organisms **do not have distinct nuclei**.
- **Protista**: primitive animal-like organisms, distinguished by method of locomotion
- **Fungi**: fungus
- **Plantae**: plants
- **Animalia**: animals

Animal Group and Baby/Male/Female Names

Did you know that a group of **ferrets** is called a **business**? Or that a **female kangaroo** is sometimes referred to as a **doe**? Or that a **baby swan** is called a **cygnet**? What all this has to do with science we don't know, but these terms are fun (or at least it helps to pretend they are when you are trying to memorize them), and they do pop up on the MAT from time to time. So go to the All About Animals list in chapter 12 of this book and familiarize yourself with as many of the terms as you can (and hopefully you'll remember what a **crocklet** is on Test Day).

Periodic Table of the Elements

Don't panic—you don't need to memorize the entire periodic table. Here are the elements and symbols that are most likely to appear on the MAT:

Hydrogen: H **Arsenic: As** **Mercury: Hg** **Potassium: K** **Radium: Ra**

Silver: Ag **Sodium: Na** **Tin: Sn** **Tungsten: W** **Copper: Cu**

Gold: Au **Iron: Fe** **Lead: Pb**

The following are two examples of man-made elements, as opposed to the above, which are naturally occurring:

Californium: Cf **Einsteinium: Es**

If you want a more thorough review of the periodic table, see the study lists in chapter 12 of this book.

Now let's take a look at a few general science questions as they might appear on the MAT.

1. WARREN : HIVE :: (a. fox, b. beaver, c. rabbit, d. otter) : BEE

2. AU : (a. Ag, b. As, c. Pl, d. Pb) :: GOLD : SILVER

3. CHORDATA : HOMO :: PHYLUM : (a. class, b. order, c. genus, d. species)

Answers:

1. **(c)** A group or home for rabbits is called a warren, and a group or home for bees is called a hive.

2. **(a)** Au is the chemical symbol for gold, and Ag is the chemical symbol for silver.

3. **(c)** The phylum that includes man is called Chordata, and the genus that includes man is called Homo.

INVENTORS, SCIENTISTS, AND MATHEMATICIANS

Another type of question that may appear on the MAT relates to figures of historical significance within the fields of science and mathematics. Some of the names are likely to be familiar to you, such as Einstein or Pythagoras. Others you will have never heard of before, though you probably use the items they invented or the math they discovered nearly every day.

Just a note: Take some time with our study lists in the next section of this book to refresh yourself on the major science and math figures of the last two thousand years. While this sounds daunting, you'll probably be surprised at how much you already know about them.

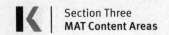

Let's try an example.

> ASTRONOMER : (a. anthropologist, b. molecular biologist, c. physicist, d. botanist) ::
> HALLEY : LEAKEY

Answer: **(a)** Edmond Halley was a prominent astronomer (he discovered Halley's comet), and Louis Leakey was a prominent anthropologist (he discovered some of the first fossils of early man).

UNITS OF MEASUREMENT

How many butts are in a hogshead? While this may seem like an irrelevant question, given that you have no interest in becoming an innkeeper in medieval England, the MAT may nonetheless test your familiarity with these and other obscure units of measurement. Sure, the metric system is easier to remember, but it's a testament to the mindset of the MAT that you will see some odd and even humorous measurements on the test. Fortunately, these terms shouldn't take too long to review. For a full recap of these terms, check out the study lists in chapter 12 of this book.

In the meantime, try your hand at a couple of examples:

1. 32 : (a. –273, b. 0, c. 100, d. 273) :: FAHRENHEIT : KELVIN

2. TROY POUND : POUND :: (a. 8, b. 10, c. 12, d. 32) : 16

Answers:
1. **(d)** Thirty-two degrees is the freezing point of water on the Fahrenheit scale, just as 273 degrees is the freezing point of water on the Kelvin scale.

2. **(c)** A troy pound has 12 ounces, and a (regular) pound has 16 ounces.

Now let's take a gander at some basic math concepts that you may well see when you take the MAT.

BASIC MATHEMATICS CONCEPTS AND TERMINOLOGY

The MAT dabbles in math terminology and basic math principles. Some of these terms you may remember from high school or even elementary school math classes:

- **Product:** the result of multiplication
- **Quotient:** the result of division
- **Dividend:** a number to be divided
- **Divisor:** a number that divides into another number
- **Integer:** any of the natural numbers ("whole numbers"), the negatives of these numbers, or zero
- **Right angle:** an angle measuring exactly 90°

As with other MAT subjects, it's better to know a little bit about a wide array of math concepts than to know the inner workings of any single one. And don't forget that the MAT often likes to focus on the fairly obscure and pedantic. To this end, you can expect to see some interesting analogies involving mathematics that may stray from simple arithmetic and algebra. So be sure to go over the basic math terminology and concepts in our study lists in chapter 12.

Here are some examples of MAT-style math questions:

1. (a. divisor, b. dividend, c. factor, d. quotient) : PRODUCT :: DIVISION : MULTIPLICATION

2. (a. sphere, b. torus, c. cylinder, d. cone) : PYRAMID :: CIRCLE : POLYGON

Answers:

1. (**d**) A quotient is the end result of division, and a product is the end result of multiplication.

2. (**d**) A cone has a circle as its base, and a pyramid has a polygon as its base.

ROMAN NUMERALS

One of the more predictable aspects of the MAT is its penchant for questions involving Roman numerals. While you have probably been exposed to Roman numerals in the past, in everything from school lessons to the credits of movies, you may be a bit fuzzy on them. Let's quickly review the basics of Roman numerals.

| I = 1 | V = 5 | X = 10 | L = 50 | C = 100 | D = 500 | M = 1,000 |

A smaller number placed **before** a larger number means you **subtract** the smaller number from the larger number. *Example:* **IV = 5 – 1 = 4**.

A smaller number placed **after** a larger number means you **add** the smaller number to the larger number. *Example:* **VI = 5 + 1 = 6**.

Directions: Translate the Roman numerals below into Arabic numbers.

1. XXXVII = _____

2. XCIV = _____

3. CDLXIV = _____

4. MCMXCIX = _____

Answers:

1. XXXVII = 37

2. XCIV = 94

3. CDLXIV = 464

4. MCMXCIX = 1,999

Now try a MAT-style Roman numeral question.

C : (a. M, b. I, c. D, d. L) : X : V

Answer: (**d**) 100 (Roman numeral C) is twice as much as 50 (Roman numeral L), and 10 (Roman numeral X) is twice as much as 5 (Roman numeral V).

We've reached the end of our look into MAT natural sciences and mathematics questions. Now try your hand at the chapter quiz on the next page.

CHAPTER QUIZ: NATURAL SCIENCES AND MATHEMATICS

Try answering the following analogy questions, using the strategies you've just learned.

1. PRIDE : (a. sounder, b. herd, c. business, d. warren) :: LION : PIG

2. BATTERY ACID : 0 :: PURE WATER : (a. 1, b. 4, c. 7, d. 10)

3. XXV : C :: LX : (a. DC, b. CCC, c. CCXL, d. CDX)

4. EAGLE : WOODPECKER :: CARNIVORE : (a. herbivore, b. insectivore, c. pescavore, d. omnivore)

5. CYGNET : SWAN :: (a. boar, b. shoat, c. sow, d. sty) : PIG

6. $\frac{1}{4}$: $\frac{7}{8}$ :: 4 : (a. 7, b. 8, c. 14, d. 16)

7. DIAGONAL : DIAMETER :: (a. slope, b. diamond, c. vertical, d. square) : CIRCLE

8. LAMARCK : (a. Galileo, b. Kepler, c. Ptolomy, d. Bohr) :: DARWIN : COPERNICUS

9. PENGUIN : VOLE :: PISCIVOROUS : (a. insectivorous, b. herbivorous, c. granivorous, d. carnivorous)

10. (a. Cenozoic, b. Mesozoic, c. Triassic, d. Jurassic) : CAMBRIAN :: 65,000,000 : 544,000,000

11. CUBIT : FATHOM :: (a. volume, b. length, c. density, d. area) : DEPTH

12. METATHERIA : PROTHERIA :: (a. bat, b. duck, c. kangaroo, d. elephant) : PLATYPUS

13. PITUITARY GLAND : GROWTH HORMONE :: PANCREAS : (a. insulin, b. bile, c. adrenaline, d. seratonin)

14. (a. decagon, b. decahedron, c. dodecagon, d. dodecahedron) : HEXAGON :: HEXAGON : TRIANGLE

15. MENDEL : GENETICS :: (a. Gauss, b. Kepler, d. Mendeleev, d. Newton) : OPTICS

16. K : NA :: (a. krypton, b. tungsten. c. mercury, d. potassium) : SODIUM

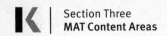
Answers

1. **(a)** A group of lions is known as a pride, just as a group of pigs is known as a sounder.

2. **(c)** Battery acid has a pH number of 0, and pure water has a pH number of 7.

3. **(c)** Twenty-five (Roman numeral XXV) is one-fourth of 100 (C), just as 60 (LX) is one fourth of 240 (CCXL).

4. **(b)** An eagle is a carnivore, or meat eater, and a woodpecker is an insectivore, or insect eater.

5. **(b)** A cygnet is a baby swan, just as a shoat is a baby pig.

6. **(c)** The fractions $\frac{1}{4}$ and $\frac{7}{8}$ have a ratio of 2 to 7, as do the integers 4 and 14.

7. **(d)** The longest line segment connecting two points on a square is called a diagonal, and the longest line segment connecting two points on a circle is called a diameter.

8. **(c)** Chevalier de Lamarck's theory of acquired traits was refuted by the evolutionary theory of Charles Darwin, and Ptolomy's theory of a geocentric solar system was refuted by the heliocentric theory of Nicholas Copernicus.

9. **(c)** A penguin is a piscivorous, or fish-eating, animal, while a vole is a granivorous, or grain-eating, animal.

10. **(a)** The Cenozoic Era was roughly 65,000,000 years ago, and the Cambrian Era was roughly 544,000,000 years ago.

11. **(b)** A cubit is a unit of length, while a fathom is a unit of depth.

12. **(c)** The kangaroo is a metatheric animal, or marsupial, and a platypus is a protheric mammal, or egg layer.

13. **(a)** The pituitary gland is responsible for producing growth hormone in the body, and the pancreas is responsible for producing insulin.

14. **(c)** A dodecagon, or 12-sided shape, has twice the number of sides as a hexagon, or 6-sided shape, and a hexagon has twice the number of sides as a triangle.

15. **(b)** Gregor Mendel pioneered the science of genetics, just as Johannes Kepler pioneered the science of optics.

16. **(d)** Potassium has a chemical symbol of K, while sodium has a chemical symbol of Na.

Kaplan Study Lists

CHAPTER SEVEN

Vocabulary Word List

TERM	DEFINITION	SYNONYMS
ABASH	to embarrass	disconcert, discomfit, faze, mortify
ABATE	to decrease, reduce	dwindle, ebb, recede, flag, wane
ABERRATION	something different from the usual	anomaly, irregularity, abnormality, deviation
ABET	to aid, act as accomplice	help, succor, assist
ABJECT	miserable, pitiful	pathetic, lamentable, sorry
ABRIDGE	to condense, shorten	abbreviate, cut, prune
ABSCOND	to depart secretly	flee, decamp, fly, bolt
ABSTEMIOUS	marked by restraint, especially in the consumption of food or alcohol	moderate, temperate, sparing
ABSTINENT	abstaining	forbearing, refraining, ascetic
ACCEDE	to express approval; agree to	assent, acquiesce, consent, concur
ACCOLADE	praise, distinction	praise, acclaim, approbation, commendation, kudos
ACCRETION	growth in size or increase in amount	buildup, accumulation, accrual
ACCRUE	to accumulate, grow by additions	augment, enlarge, expand, burgeon, wax
ACERBIC	bitter, sharp in taste or temper	tart, biting, caustic, cutting
ACME	highest point, summit	apex, crown, peak, pinnacle, zenith

ACQUIESCE	to agree, comply quietly	accede, consent, submit
ACRID	harsh, bitter	sharp, pungent, caustic
ACRIMONY	bitterness, animosity	choler, spleen, rancor, asperity, antipathy
ACUMEN	sharpness of insight	sagacity, discernment, shrewdness
ADAGE	old saying or proverb	apothem, aphorism, maxim
ADMONISH	to caution or reprimand	reprove, chide, upbraid, berate, rebuke
ADROIT	skillful, accomplished, highly competent	deft, dexterous, proficient, accomplished, adept
ADULATION	high praise	admiration, flattery, accolade
ADULTERATE	to corrupt or make impure	contaminate, dilute
AESTHETIC	pertaining to beauty or art	artistic, tasteful
ALACRITY	cheerful readiness, promptness in response	celerity, promptness, dispatch, enthusiasm
ALLUSION	indirect reference	intimation, suggestion
ALTERCATION	noisy dispute	argument, clash, fight, quarrel
ALTRUISM	unselfish concern for others' welfare	benevolence, generosity, kindness
AMALGAMATE	to mix, combine	integrate, assimilate, merge, incorporate, league
AMBIVALENCE	attitude of uncertainty, conflicting emotions	indecision, vacillation
AMBULATORY	of, relating to, or adapted to walking, moving about from place to place	itinerant, nomadic, peripatetic, roving, vagabond
AMELIORATE	to make better, improve	amend, better, reform
AMULET	ornament worn as a charm against evil spirits	talisman, fetish
ANACHRONISTIC	outdated	anomalous, inconsistent, inappropriate
ANATHEMA	ban, curse; something shunned or disliked	execration; horror, abomination
ANCILLARY	accessory, subordinate, helping	adjunct, additional, auxiliary, supplemental
ANECDOTE	short, usually funny account of an event	story, joke

ANOMALY	irregularity or deviation from the norm	oddity, aberration, deviance, peculiarity, abnormality
ANTEDILUVIAN	prehistoric, ancient beyond measure	old, archaic, antique
ANTIPATHY	dislike, hostility, extreme opposition or aversion	enmity, malice, antagonism
ANTITHESIS	exact opposite or direct contrast	contrary, reverse
APEX	highest point, summit	acme, crown, zenith, peak, crest
APHORISM	old saying or short, pithy statement	adage, apothegm, maxim, proverb
APOCRYPHAL	not genuine, fictional	erroneous, fictitious, fraudulent, false
APOSTATE	one who renounces a religious faith	renegade, turncoat, deserter
APPROPRIATE (v.)	to take possession of	usurp, arrogate, commandeer
AQUATIC	belonging or living in water	watery, maritime, pelagic
ARABLE	suitable for cultivation	farmable, fertile
ARCANE	secret, obscure, known only to a few	esoteric, mysterious
ARCH (adj.)	mischievous, roguish	impish, waggish, saucy, ironic
ARCHIPELAGO	large group of islands	cluster, scattering
ARROGATE	to demand, claim arrogantly	appropriate, usurp, seize, commandeer, assume
ASCETIC	self-denying, abstinent, austere	continent, temperate, abstemious
ASCRIBE	to attribute to, assign	accredit, impute, refer
ASHEN	resembling ashes; deathly pale	blanched, pallid, pasty, wan
ASPERSION	false rumor, damaging report, slander	allegation, insinuation, reproach
ASSIDUOUS	diligent, persistent, hard-working	industrious, steadfast, thorough
ASSONANCE	resemblance in sound, especially in vowel sounds; partial rhyme	repetition, similarity, echo
ASSUAGE	to make less severe, ease, relieve	mitigate, alleviate, ease, appease, mollify
ASTRINGENT	harsh, severe, stern	sharp, bitter, caustic
ASYLUM	refuge, sanctuary	haven, shelter

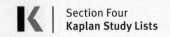

ATROCIOUS	monstrous, shockingly bad, wicked	horrible, appalling, deplorable, direful
ATROPHY	to waste away, wither from disuse	deteriorate, degenerate
ATTENUATE	to make thin or slender; weaken	reduce, rarefy, diminish
AUGURY	prophecy, prediction of events	omen, auspices, portent, harbinger, presage
AUGUST	dignified, awe-inspiring, venerable	grand, majestic, admirable, awesome
AUSPICIOUS	having favorable prospects, promising	encouraging, propitious, hopeful, positive
AUSTERE	stern, strict, unadorned	dour, bare, ascetic
AUTOCRAT	dictator	tyrant, authoritarian, despot, totalitarian
AUTONOMOUS	separate, independent	sovereign, self-governed, free
AVARICE	greed	cupidity, rapacity
AVER	to declare to be true, affirm	assert, attest
AVIARY	large enclosure housing birds	birdhouse, zoo
AWRY	crooked, askew, amiss	aslant, wrong
AXIOM	premise, postulate, self-evident truth	adage, apothegm, aphorism, maxim, rule
BALEFUL	harmful, with evil intentions	dark, sinister
BALK	to refuse, shirk; prevent	stop; check, thwart, frustrate
BANAL	trite, overly common	hackneyed, shopworn, inane
BANE	something causing death, destruction, or ruin	curse, scourge, poison
BANTER	playful conversation	chatter, palaver, prattle
BASTION	fortification, stronghold	bulwark, defense, haven
BAWDY	obscene, lewd	vulgar, risqué, rude, coarse
BAY (*v.*)	to bark, especially in a deep, prolonged way	howl, ululate, wail, keen
BEHEMOTH	huge creature	giant, titan, monster
BELABOR	to insist repeatedly or harp on	dwell upon, harp upon
BELLICOSE	warlike, aggressive	belligerent, hostile, combative, pugnacious
BELLIGERENT	hostile, tending to fight	bellicose, aggressive, combative, pugnacious
BENIGHTED	unenlightened	ignorant, unschooled, illiterate

BEST (*v.*)	to get the better of, beat	defeat, trounce, vanquish, rout, worst
BEVY	group	band, gang, bunch, pack, troop
BILK	to cheat, defraud	swindle, dupe, fleece
BIPEDAL	two-footed	upright, two-legged
BLANDISH	to coax with flattery	cajole, charm, seduce, wheedle
BLASPHEMOUS	cursing, profane, irreverent	sacrilegious, impious
BLITHE	joyful, cheerful, or without appropriate thought	glad, happy, carefree, insouciant
BOOR	crude person, one lacking manners or taste	lout, clod, oaf, vulgarian, yahoo
BOURGEOIS	middle-class	capitalist, conventional
BOVINE	cowlike, relating to cows	sluggish, dull, stolid
BRAZEN	bold, shameless, impudent; of or like brass	audacious, brash, contumelious, insolent
BREACH	act of breaking, violation	gap, lapse, rift, contravention, dereliction
BROACH (*v.*)	to mention or suggest for the first time	raise, introduce, propose
BRUSQUE	rough and abrupt in manner	blunt, curt, gruff, rude, tactless
BUCOLIC	pastoral, rural	rustic, country, agrarian
BURGEON	to sprout or flourish	blossom, thrive, expand, grow, proliferate
BURNISH	to polish, make smooth and bright	shine, buff
BUSTLE	commotion, energetic activity	flurry, ado, tumult
BUTTRESS (*v.*)	to reinforce or support	bolster, brace, prop, strengthen
CACHE (**pronounced "cash"**)	hiding place, stockpile	hoard, reserve, store
CACOPHONY	jarring, unpleasant noise	din, clatter, racket
CAJOLE	to flatter, coax, persuade	blandish, wheedle
CALLOW	immature, lacking sophistication	ingenuous, naïve, artless
CALUMNY	false and malicious accusation, misrepresentation, slander	libel, aspersion, defamation
CANNY	smart, founded on common sense	percipient, perspicacious, astute, shrewd
CANONIZE	to declare a person a saint, raise to highest honors	exult, elevate, ennoble, glorify

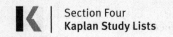
CAPRICIOUS	impulsive, whimsical, without much thought	erratic, fickle, flighty, inconstant, wayward
CARICATURE	exaggerated portrait, cartoon	burlesque, travesty, lampoon
CARNIVOROUS	meat-eating	predatory, flesh-eating
CARTOGRAPHY	science or art of making maps	charting, surveying, topography
CASTIGATE	to punish, chastise, criticize severely	discipline, lambaste
CATALYST	something causing change without being changed	stimulus, instigation, provocation
CATHARSIS	purification, cleansing	purgation, release
CATHOLIC	universal, broad and comprehensive	extensive, general
CELERITY	speed, swiftness, alacrity	dispatch, velocity, rapidity
CENSURE	to criticize, find fault	denounce, pillory, vilify, indict, condemn
CHAGRIN	shame, embarrassment, humiliation	mortification, discomfiture
CHAMPION (*v.*)	to defend or support	advocate, promote
CHARLATAN	quack, fake	imposter, fraud, humbug
CHARY	watchful, cautious, extremely shy	wary, careful, sparing
CHERUBIC	sweet, innocent, resembling a cherub	angelic, babyish
CHICANERY	trickery, fraud, deception	deceit, duplicity, dishonesty
CHIDE	to scold, express disapproval	chasten, chastise, admonish, reprimand, reprove
CHIMERICAL	fanciful, imaginary, visionary, impossible	illusory, unreal
CHOLERIC	easily angered, short-tempered	irritable, surly, wrathful, irate
CHORTLE	to chuckle	laugh, snort
CHURLISH	marked by a lack of civility or graciousness	boorish, cloddish, clodhopping, loutish, lowbred, rustic
CIRCUMVENT	to go around, avoid	evade, sidestep, dodge
CLAIRVOYANT (*adj.*)	having ESP, psychic	prophetic, oracular

CLANDESTINE	secretive, concealed for a darker purpose	covert, underground
CLOD	a chunk of earth or clay; a stupid person	lump, nugget; dolt, oaf, dullard
CLOISTER (*v.*)	to confine, seclude	isolate, sequester
CLOYING	sickly sweet, saccharine	excessive, fulsome
CODDLE	to baby, treat indulgently	pamper, spoil, cosset
COERCE	to compel by force or intimidation	domineer, constrain
COGENT	logically forceful, compelling, convincing	persuasive, winning
COLLOQUIAL	characteristic of informal speech	conversational, idiomatic, slangy
COLLUSION	collaboration, complicity, conspiracy	intrigue, machination, connivance
COMMUTE	to change a penalty to a less severe one	exchange, mitigate, palliate
CONJUGAL	pertaining to marriage	connubial, matrimonial, spousal, marital
CONNIVE	to conspire, scheme	collude, plot, contrive
CONSECRATE	to declare sacred; dedicate to a goal	sanctify; devote
CONSONANT (*adj.*)	consistent with, in agreement with	accordant, compatible, congruous
CONSUMMATE (*adj.*)	accomplished, complete, perfect	thorough, exhaustive, ideal, flawless
CONTEMPTUOUS	scornful	derisive, disdainful, supercilious
CONTENTIOUS	quarrelsome, disagreeable, belligerent	argumentative, fractious, quarrelsome, litigious
CONTRITE	deeply sorrowful and repentant for a wrong	regretful, apologetic, remorseful
CONTUMACIOUS	stubbornly disobedient	insubordinate, factious, insurgent, mutinous, rebellious, seditious
CONTUMELIOUS	insolently abusive and humiliating	impertinent, impudent, procacious, saucy
CONVOLUTED	twisted, complicated, involved	intricate, elaborate, baroque
COPIOUS	abundant, plentiful	ample, abounding

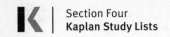

CORPOREAL	having to do with the body; tangible, material	somatic; concrete, physical
CORPULENCE	obesity, fatness, bulkiness	stoutness, rotundity, portliness, plumpness
COTERIE	small group of persons with a similar purpose	circle, clique, set
COUNTENANCE (*v.*)	to favor, support	condone, approve, tolerate
CRYPTIC	puzzling	mysterious, recondite, inscrutable, enigmatic
CUDGEL	a short, heavy club	baton, billy club, bludgeon, club, mace, nightstick, shillelagh
CUPIDITY	greed	avarice, rapacity, covetousness
CURMUDGEON	cranky person	grouch, crab, coot
CURSORY	hastily done, superficial	shallow, careless
DAUNT	to discourage, intimidate	demoralize, dishearten, consternate
DEARTH	lack, scarcity, insufficiency	absence, shortage, paucity
DEFERENTIAL	respectful and polite in a submissive way	courteous, obsequious
DEFUNCT	no longer existing, dead, extinct	gone, vanished, deceased, departed, extinguished
DELEGATE (*v.*)	to give powers to another	assign, entrust, commit, appoint, authorize
DELETERIOUS	harmful, often in a subtle or unexpected way	pernicious, harmful, detrimental, nocent, nocuous
DEMAGOGUE	leader, rabble-rouser, usually using appeals to emotion or prejudice	agitator, inciter, instigator, fomenter, firebrand
DEMUR	to express doubts or objections	protest, remonstrate, kick, expostulate, dissent
DENIGRATE	to slur or blacken someone's reputation	malign, belittle, disparage, vilify, slander
DEPRAVITY	sinfulness, moral corruption	decadence, debauchery, enormity, corruption, degradation
DEPRECATE	to belittle, disparage	minimize, denigrate, discount
DESPOT	tyrannical ruler	authoritarian, autocrat, dictator, totalitarian

DIAPHANOUS	allowing light to show through; delicate	sheer, transparent, gauzy, translucent; tenuous
DIATRIBE	bitter verbal attack	tirade, jeremiad, fulmination, harangue, philippic
DICHOTOMY	division into two parts	split, distinction, bifurcation, opposition
DICTUM	authoritative statement; popular saying	decree, edict; adage, apothegm, aphorism
DIDACTIC	excessively instructive	educational, improving, moralistic
DIFFIDENCE	shyness, lack of confidence	timidity, reticence
DIGRESS	to turn aside, to stray from the main point	diverge, deviate, wander
DILAPIDATED	in disrepair, run-down, neglected	decrepit, ramshackle, deteriorated, decayed
DILATORY	slow, tending to delay	sluggish, tardy, unhurried
DIRGE	funeral hymn	elegy, threnody, lament
DISCREPANCY	difference between	contradiction, divergence, incongruity, disparity, incompatibility
DISCRETIONARY	subject to one's own judgment	elective, optional, voluntary, unforced
DISCURSIVE	moving from topic to topic without order	digressive, rambling, unfocused
DISDAIN	to regard with scorn and contempt	spurn, slight
DISHEVELED	untidy, disarranged, unkempt	disordered, messy, rumpled
DISINTERESTED	fair-minded, unbiased	impartial, evenhanded, unprejudiced, dispassionate
DISPARAGE	to belittle, speak disrespectfully of	denigrate, derogate, ridicule, deride
DISPARITY	contrast, dissimilarity	discrepancy, contradiction, divergence, incongruity, incompatibility
DISPASSIONATE	free from emotion; impartial, unbiased	impassive, stolid; disinterested, evenhanded, unprejudiced
DISPEL	to drive out or scatter	disband, disperse
DISPERSE	to break up, scatter	dissipate, disintegrate, dispel
DISREPUTE	disgrace, dishonor	ignominy, infamy
DISSEMBLE	to pretend, disguise one's motives	feign, conceal, cloak, camouflage
DISSEMINATE	to spread far and wide	circulate, diffuse, disperse

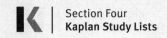

DISSIPATE	to scatter; to pursue pleasure to excess	squander, disperse, consume, dissolve; carouse
DISSONANT	harsh and unpleasant sounding	discordant, inharmonious
DISSUADE	to persuade someone to alter original intentions	discourage, deter
DIURNAL	daily	daylight, daytime
DOGGED	stubbornly persevering	tenacious, obstinate, pertinacious, determined, mulish
DOGMATIC	rigidly fixed in opinion, opinionated	inflexible, dictatorial, doctrinaire, authoritative, obstinate
DOLEFUL	sad, mournful	funereal, somber, lugubrious, dismal, woeful
DOUR	sullen and gloomy, stern and severe	austere, strict, grave, solemn, somber
DOWRY	money or property given by a bride to her husband	dower, hope chest
DRAW	pull, drag, attract	haul, tow, tug, lure, entice
DROLL	amusing in a wry, subtle way	witty, comic, funny, entertaining, risible
DULCET	pleasant sounding, soothing to the ear	melodious, agreeable, sweet, harmonious
DUPE (*v.*)	to deceive, trick; (*n.*) fool, pawn	(*v.*) hoodwink, cozen, beguile, gull
DUPLICITY	deception, dishonesty	perfidy, infidelity, disloyalty, treachery, guile
DYSPEPTIC	suffering from indigestion; gloomy and irritable	morose, solemn, melancholy, sour, acerb
EBB	to fade away, recede	retreat, subside, abate, wane, withdraw
ECLECTIC	selecting from various sources	catholic, selective, broad
EFFRONTERY	impudent boldness, audacity	presumption, brashness, temerity, nerve, gall
EGREGIOUS	conspicuously bad	blatant, flagrant, glaring, gross, rank
ELEGY	mournful poem, usually about the dead	dirge, lament, threnody
EMANCIPATE	to set free, liberate	deliver, manumit, release
EMBROIL	to involve in; cause to fall into disorder	implicate, ensnare; entangle

ENCOMIUM	enthusiastic praise	eulogy, panegyric, tribute
ENERVATE	to weaken, sap strength from	deplete, debilitate, drain, exhaust
ENGENDER	to produce, cause, bring about	procreate, propagate, originate, generate
ENIGMATIC	puzzling, inexplicable	mysterious, cryptic, baffling
ENJOIN	to urge, order, command; forbid or prohibit, as by judicial order	direct, instruct, charge; prohibit, proscribe
ENMITY	hostility, antagonism, ill will	animosity, antipathy, rancor, animus
ENNUI	boredom, lack of interest and energy	tedium, listlessness, world-weariness
ENORMITY	state of being gigantic or terrible	outrageousness, atrociousness
EPHEMERAL	momentary, transient, fleeting	transitory, fugitive, evanescent
EPICURE	person with refined taste in food and wine	gourmet, gourmand, connoisseur, gastronome
EPIGRAM	short, witty saying or poem	maxim, adage, aphorism
EPILOGUE	concluding section of a literary work	afterward, finale
EPITOME	representative of an entire group; summary	paragon, exemplar, prototype, quintessence; abstract
EQUINE	relating to horses	horsy, asinine, mulish
EQUIVOCAL	ambiguous, open to more than one interpretation	doubtful, misleading, uncertain
EQUIVOCATE	to use vague or ambiguous language intentionally	mislead, prevaricate
ERRATIC	inconsistent, irregular	eccentric, capricious, unstable, unpredictable
ERUDITE	learned, scholarly	knowledgeable, cultured, educated, well-read, literate
ESOTERIC	understood by only a learned few	mysterious, arcane, occult, recondite, secret
ESPOUSE	to support or advocate; to marry	champion, embrace, adopt
ESTRANGE	to alienate, keep at a distance	disaffect, separate, divorce
ETHEREAL	not earthly, spiritual, delicate	intangible, diaphanous, airy, gossamer, sheer

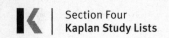

ETIOLATE	to bleach and alter the natural development of (a green plant) by excluding sunlight	blanch, decolorize
EULOGY	high praise, often in a public speech	tribute, commendation, encomium, panegyric, salute
EVANESCENT	momentary, transitory, short-lived	transient, ephemeral, fleeting, fugitive
EXACERBATE	to aggravate, deepen the bad qualities of	worsen, escalate, intensify
EXCRUCIATING	agonizing, intensely painful	torturous, acute, fierce
EXCULPATE	to clear of blame or fault, vindicate	exonerate, acquit
EXIGENT	urgent; excessively demanding	pressing, imperative, compelling, critical, crucial
EXORBITANT	extravagant, greater than reasonable	excessive, immoderate, inordinate, extreme
EXPIATE	to atone for, make amends for	answer, compensate, pay
EXPUNGE	to erase, eliminate completely	delete, cancel, efface, annul, obliterate
EXPURGATE	to censor	cut, bowdlerize, sanitize
EXTORT	to obtain something by threats	wring, coerce, blackmail, bludgeon, bully
EXTRANEOUS	irrelevant, unrelated, unnecessary	immaterial, impertinent, extrinsic, foreign, alien
EXTRICATE	to free from, disentangle	disengage, untangle, release, disencumber
FACADE	face, front; mask, superficial appearance	surface; pretense, cloak, guise, semblance
FACILE	easily done; simplistic; poised, assured	effortless; simple; nimble, fluent
FALLOW	uncultivated, unused	unseeded, inactive, idle
FANATICISM	extreme devotion to a cause	zeal, mania, obsession
FASTIDIOUS	careful with details	meticulous, painstaking, scrupulous, punctilious, precise
FATHOM (*v.*)	to measure the depth of, gauge	comprehend
FATUOUS	stupid, foolishly self-satisfied	silly, absurd, preposterous, ridiculous, ludicrous
FAWN (*v.*)	to flatter excessively, seek the favor of	kowtow, grovel, truckle

FAZE	to bother, upset, or disconcert	discomfit, rattle, chagrin
FECKLESS	ineffective, careless, irresponsible	aimless, shiftless, lazy
FECUND	fertile, fruitful, productive	prolific, flourishing
FERVID	passionate, intense, zealous	vehement, ardent, enthusiastic, avid, eager
FETID	foul-smelling, putrid	noisome, stinky, funky, malodorous, rank
FETTER	to bind, chain, confine	shackle, manacle, handcuff, curb, tether
FILIGREE	ornamental openwork of delicate or intricate design on metal	ornament, embellishment, decoration, latticework
FLAG (*v.*)	to decline in vigor, strength, or interest	wane, subside, ebb, dwindle, slacken
FLAGRANT	outrageous, shameless	glaring, egregious, blatant, gross, rank
FLAUNT	to show off	parade, flourish, vaunt, exhibit, display
FLORA	plants	vegetation, botany, verdure, herbage
FLORID	gaudy, extremely ornate; ruddy, flushed	ornate, flamboyant, ostentatious, loud, garish
FLOUNDER	to falter, waver, muddle, struggle	blunder, stumble, bumble, lurch, lumber
FLUVIAL	of, relating to, or living in a stream or river	flowing, alluvial
FOIBLE	minor weakness or character flaw	fault, failing, frailty, vice, blemish
FOIL (*v.*)	to defeat, frustrate	thwart, balk, check, baffle
FOMENT	to arouse or incite	instigate, abet, promote
FOOLHARDY	recklessly bold	reckless, rash, precipitate, temerarious
FOP	a man who is devoted to or vain about his appearance or dress	coxcomb, dandy
FORBEARANCE	patience, restraint, leniency	resignation, long-suffering, tolerance
FORD (*v.*)	to cross a body of water at a shallow place	traverse, wade
FORTE	strong point, something a person does well	métier, specialty
FORTUITOUS	happening by chance, fortunate	accidental, contingent, incidental
FOSTER	to nourish, cultivate, promote	nurture, nurse, advance, further
FOUNDER (*v.*)	to fall helplessly, sink	miscarry, immerse, plunge

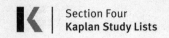

FRACAS	noisy dispute	brawl, broil, donnybrook, fray, melee
FRACTIOUS	unruly, rebellious	peevish, cranky, quarrelsome, contentious
FRENETIC	wildly frantic, frenzied, hectic	excited, active, bustling, feverish
FURTIVE	secret, stealthy	covert, clandestine, surreptitious, underhand, shifty
GALL (*n.*)	bitterness; careless nerve; (*v.*) to exasperate and irritate	rancor; temerity, audacity, effrontery
GARNER	to gather and store	reap, glean, harvest, amass, acquire
GARRULOUS	very talkative	loquacious, voluble, verbose, chatty, prolix
GLIB	fluent in an insincere manner; offhand, casual	superficial; easy
GLOWER	to glare, stare angrily and intensely	frown, lower, scowl
GRANDILO-QUENCE	pompous talk, fancy but meaningless speech	bombast, fustian, prolixity, verbiage
GRIMACE	facial expression showing pain or disgust	scowl, leer, glare
GROTTO	small cave	cavern, recess, burrow, den, pocket
GROVEL	to humble oneself in a demeaning way	cringe, fawn, kowtow
GUILE	trickery, deception	cunning, artifice, wiliness, duplicity
HACKNEYED	worn out by overuse	trite, shopworn, stale, banal
HALLOWED	holy, treated as sacred	sanctified, consecrated, venerated, sacrosanct, blessed
HAPLESS	unfortunate, having bad luck	ill-fated, ill-starred, luckless, unlucky, jinxed
HARBINGER	precursor, sign of something to come	forerunner, presage, omen, herald
HARDY	robust, vigorous, sturdy	healthy, hale, fit, strong, courageous
HAUGHTY	arrogant and condescending	proud, disdainful, supercilious, scornful, vainglorious
HEDONIST	one who pursues pleasure as a goal	sensualist, voluptuary, libertine
HEGEMONY	leadership, domination, usually by a country	influence, power, sway, rule

HEINOUS	shocking, wicked, terrible	reprehensible, abominable, monstrous, appalling, dreadful
HEMORRHAGE (*v.*)	to bleed heavily; (*n.*) heavy bleeding	seep, discharge, gush
HERETICAL	opposed to an established religious orthodoxy	heterodox, schismatic, dissident
HERMETIC	tightly sealed	airtight, watertight, impervious
HIATUS	break, interruption, vacation	gap, interruption, recess, interval, pause
HOARY	very old; whitish or gray from age	antediluvian, antique, vintage, ancient, venerable
HOMAGE	public honor and respect	acclaim, kudos, panegyric, tribute, encomium
HOMILY	sermonlike speech	lecture, admonition, oration
HUSBAND (*v.*)	to farm; manage carefully and thriftily	conserve, economize
HYPERBOLE	purposeful exaggeration for effect	inflation, magnification, embellishment
ICONOCLAST	one who attacks traditional beliefs	rebel, dissident, nonconformist
IGNOMINIOUS	disgraceful and dishonorable	despicable, degrading, debasing
ILK	type or kind	sort, nature, character, variety, class
ILLICIT	illegal, improper	unlawful, criminal, prohibited, forbidden
IMMUNE	exempt; protected from harm or disease; unresponsive to	impervious, shielded
IMMUTABLE	unchangeable, invariable	fixed, stationary, permanent, steady
IMPASSIVE	showing no emotion	expressionless, stolid, cold, indifferent, placid
IMPECUNIOUS	poor, having no money	indigent, needy, penniless, impoverished, destitute
IMPERIOUS	arrogantly self-assured, domineering, overbearing	dictatorial, authoritarian, despotic
IMPERTINENT	rude	improper, forward, bold, impolite, discourteous
IMPERVIOUS	impossible to penetrate, incapable of being affected	immune, callous
IMPIOUS	not devout in religion	irreverent, profane, immoral

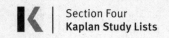
IMPLACABLE	inflexible, incapable of being pleased	obstinate, unyielding
IMPORTUNE	to ask repeatedly, beg	crave, beseech, entreat, implore, supplicate
IMPOVERISH	to make poor or bankrupt	beggar, ruin, pauperize, deplete, drain
IMPRECATION	curse	execration, anathema, malediction
IMPREGNABLE	totally safe from attack, able to resist defeat	unassailable, invincible, secure, inviolable, invulnerable
IMPUDENT	arrogant, audacious	shameless, insolent, impertinent, brazen
IMPUGN	to call into question, attack verbally	challenge, dispute, gainsay
IMPUTE	to attribute	ascribe, credit, assign, refer, charge
INADVERTENT	unintentional	accidental, involuntary
INCENSE (v.)	to infuriate, enrage	madden, exasperate, outrage
INCHOATE	imperfectly formed or formulated	incipient, undeveloped, undefined
INCIPIENT	beginning to exist or appear, in an initial stage	dawning, nascent, inchoate
INCONTRO-VERTIBLE	unquestionable, beyond dispute	irrefutable, indisputable
INCORRIGIBLE	incapable of being corrected	unrepentant, intractable, unmanageable, uncooperative, unchangeable
INCREDULOUS	skeptical, doubtful	disbelieving, suspicious
INCULCATE	to teach and impress by frequent repetitions or admonitions	instill, instruct, educate
INCULPATE	to incriminate	charge, impeach, indict
INDELIBLE	permanent, not erasable	ineffaceable, inexpugnable, permanent
INDIGENOUS	native, occurring naturally in an area	intrinsic, innate, endemic, autochthonous, aboriginal
INDIGENT	very poor	needy, impecunious, impoverished, destitute, penniless
INDIGNANT	angry, incensed, offended	furious, irate, mad, wrathful, ireful
INDOLENT	habitually lazy, idle	slothful, languid, lethargic, sluggish, fainéant
INEXORABLE	inflexible, unyielding	adamant, obdurate, relentless
INGENUOUS	straightforward, open, naive	simple, natural, unaffected, artless, candid, unsophisticated

INIMICAL	hostile, unfriendly	injurious, harmful, adverse, antagonistic
INIQUITY	sin, evil act	immorality, injustice, wickedness, vice, enormity
INSENSATE	lacking sensation, unconscious	inanimate, unfeeling, numb
INSINUATE	to suggest, say indirectly, imply	to hint, intimate
INSIPID	bland, lacking flavor, lacking excitement	lackluster, dull, flat, weak
INSOLENT	insulting and arrogant	audacious, rude, presumptuous, impertinent, audacious
INSUPERABLE	insurmountable, unconquerable	unbeatable, undefeatable, invincible
INTER	to bury	entomb, inhume
INTERROGATE	to question formally	examine, catechize
INTIMATION	clue, suggestion	implication, allusion, insinuation
INTRACTABLE	not easily managed	unruly, stubborn, refractory, recalcitrant, headstrong
INTRANSIGENT	uncompromising, refusing to be reconciled	obdurate, obstinate, adamant, unbending, unyielding
INUNDATE	to cover with water; overwhelm	flood, swamp, deluge, engulf
INURE	to harden; accustom, become used to	habituate, familiarize, condition
INVECTIVE	verbal abuse	vituperation, denunciation, revilement
INVETERATE	confirmed, long-standing, deeply rooted	habitual, chronic
INVIDIOUS	causing envy, obnoxious	causing resentment, discriminatory, insulting, jaundiced
ITINERANT	wandering from place to place, unsettled	nomadic, roving, traveling, vagabond, vagrant
ITINERARY	route of a traveler's journey	plan, record, guidebook
JADED	tired by excess or overuse, slightly cynical	wearied, jaundiced, sated, callous, blasé
JARGON	nonsensical talk, specialized language	dialect, cant, argot, idiom, slang
JETTISON	to cast off, throw cargo overboard	discard, toss
JINGOISM	belligerent support of one's country	chauvinism, nationalism

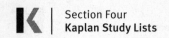

KINETIC	relating to motion, characterized by movement	mobile, active, dynamic
KNELL	sound of a funeral bell; omen of death or failure	toll, chime, peal
KUDOS	fame, glory, honor	acclaim, praise, encomium, accolade, homage
LABYRINTH	maze	entanglement, mesh, web
LACERATION	cut or wound	gash, tear
LACHRYMOSE	tearful	weeping, teary
LACKADAISICAL	idle, lazy, apathetic, indifferent	languorous, indolent, listless, blasé, fainéant
LACONIC	using few words	terse, concise, pithy, succinct
LAMPOON	to attack with satire, mock harshly	burlesque, travesty, caricature
LANGUID	lacking energy, indifferent, slow	weak, listless, lackadaisical, sluggish, fainéant
LARYNX	organ containing vocal cords	voice box, Adam's apple
LASSITUDE	lethargy, sluggishness	weariness, listlessness, torpor, stupor
LEVIATHAN	a biblical sea monster; something large and formidable	behemoth; mammoth; something cyclopean, elephantine, or gargantuan
LIBERTINE	one without moral restraint	hedonist, voluptuary, rogue, rake, roué
LICENTIOUS	immoral, unrestrained by society	wanton, dissolute, salacious, lewd, prurient
LIMPID	clear, transparent	lucid, pellucid, serene
LIONIZE	to treat as a celebrity	regale, honor, feast, ply
LISSOME	easily flexed, limber, agile	supple, lithe, graceful
LISTLESS	lacking energy and enthusiasm	lethargic, sluggish, languid, fainéant, indolent
LITHE	moving and bending with ease, graceful	lissome, limber, agile, supple
LIVID	discolored from a bruise; pale; reddened with anger	black-and-blue; ashen, pallid; furious
LOATHE	to abhor, despise, hate	abominate, execrate, detest, contemn
LOQUACIOUS	talkative	garrulous, verbose, voluble, prolix
LUGUBRIOUS	sorrowful, mournful, dismal	gloomy, funereal, somber, melancholy, woeful

LUMBER (*v.*)	to move slowly and awkwardly	stumble, lurch, hulk, galumph
MACABRE	ghoulish, gruesome	ghastly, grim, grisly, lurid, morbid
MACERATE	to waste away or to become soft, esp. by being steeped	soak, soften, deliquesce
MACHINATION	plot or scheme	conspiracy, intrigue, design, cabal
MACULATE	marked with spots	besmirched, impure
MAELSTROM	whirlpool; turmoil, agitated state of mind	eddy, vortex; pandemonium, uproar
MAGNATE	powerful or influential person	potentate, tycoon, nabob, dignitary, luminary
MALADROIT	clumsy, tactless	awkward, inept, gauche, ungainly
MALEDICTION	curse	execration, anathema, imprecation
MALEFACTOR	evildoer; culprit	criminal, offender, felon
MALINGER	to evade responsibility by pretending to be ill	shirk, fake
MALODOROUS	foul-smelling	fetid, noisome, stinky, funky, rank
MANDATORY	necessary, required	obligatory, compulsory, inevitable
MARITIME	relating to the sea or sailing	nautical, marine, naval
MARTIAL	warlike, pertaining to the military	soldierly, combative
MARTINET	strict disciplinarian, one who rigidly follows rules	tyrant, stickler, dictator
MAUDLIN	overly sentimental	mawkish, bathetic, saccharine, weepy
MAVERICK	nonconformist	dissident, rebel
MAWKISH	sickeningly sentimental	maudlin, insipid, bathetic, saccharine, weepy
MEANDER	to wander aimlessly	ramble, roam, rove, range, stray
MELANCHOLY	sadness, depression	dejection, despondency, woe, sorrow
MENDACIOUS	dishonest lying, untruthful	deceitful, false
MENDICANT	beggar	pauper, panhandler
MERCENARY (*n.*)	soldier for hire in foreign countries; (*adj.*) motivated only by greed	hireling; venal, materialistic, avaricious
MERCURIAL	quick, shrewd; unpredictable	clever, crafty; volatile, whimsical

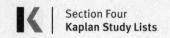

MERETRICIOUS	gaudy, falsely attractive	flashy, loud, tawdry, insincere, specious
METAPHOR	figure of speech comparing two different things	analogy, symbol, allegory, simile
METICULOUS	extremely careful, fastidious, fussy	scrupulous, punctilious, precise, finicky, painstaking
METTLE	courageousness; endurance	spirit, character; fortitude
MILITATE	to operate against, work against	influence, affect, change
MIMIC	to imitate or copy	ape, simulate, impersonate
MISNOMER	an incorrect name or designation	error, misapplication, deception
MISSIVE	note or letter	bulletin, dispatch, epistle, memorandum, message
MOLT (*v.*)	to shed hair, skin, or an outer layer periodically	cast, defoliate, desquamate
MONASTIC	extremely plain or secluded, as in a monastery	contemplative, disciplined, regimented, self-abnegating, austere
MOOT	debatable; purely academic, deprived of practical significance	arguable, open, inconclusive, doubtful
MORES	customs or manners	usages, attitudes, ways, traditions, practices
MUNDANE	worldly; commonplace	secular; ordinary
MUNIFICENT	generous	liberal, bountiful
MUTABILITY	changeability	inconstancy, impermanence
MYOPIC	nearsighted	shortsighted, sand-blind
MYRIAD	immense number, multitude	crowd, army, legion, mass
NADIR	lowest point	bottom, depth, pit
NAÏVE	innocent, lacking in worldly experience	ingenuous, unsophisticated, artless, credulous
NARCISSIST	someone who is completely self-absorbed	egotist, egomaniac
NASCENT	starting to develop, coming into existence	emerging, incipient, inchoate, embryonic
NEBULOUS	vague, cloudy	misty, hazy, fuzzy, undefined, unclear
NEFARIOUS	vicious, evil	wicked, fiendish, malevolent, sinister
NEOPHYTE	novice, beginner	apprentice, tyro, greenhorn

NETTLE (*v.*)	to irritate	vex, annoy
NICHE	recess in a wall; best position for something	alcove, cranny, crevice; place, station
NOISOME	stinking, putrid	foul, disgusting, malodorous
NOMADIC	moving from place to place	itinerant, vagabond, roving
NONCHALANT	appearing casual, detached, cool	composed, unruffled, cavalier, blasé
NOSTRUM	a questionable remedy or scheme	panacea, catholicon, cure-all
NUGATORY	of slight worth, trivial, insignificant	unimportant, impotent, null
OBDURATE	stubborn	inflexible, inexorable, adamant, impenitent, intractable
OBEISANCE	a movement of the body made in token of respect or submission; deference	bow, curtsy; homage, reverence
OBFUSCATE	to confuse, obscure	cloud, complicate, darken
OBSEQUIOUS	overly submissive, brownnosing	fawning, servile, compliant, groveling, unctuous
OBSOLETE	no longer in use	outmoded, passé, old-fashioned, antiquated, dated
OBSTINATE	stubborn	headstrong, stiff-necked, bullheaded, pigheaded, mulish
OBTUSE	insensitive, stupid, dull	slow, dense, blunt
OBVIATE	to make unnecessary, anticipate and prevent	preclude, avert, forestall, deter
OCCLUDE	to shut, block	close, obstruct
OFFICIOUS	overly helpful, meddlesome	eager, unwanted, intrusive
OPULENCE	wealth	affluence, abundance, prosperity, luxury, plenty
ORACLE	person who foresees the future and gives advice	seer, prophet, soothsayer, sibyl, fortune-teller
ORATION	lecture, formal speech	discourse, declamation, sermon, address, homily
ORNITHOLOGIST	scientist who studies birds	birder, bird-watcher
OSCILLATE	to move back and forth	swing, sway, fluctuate, vacillate, undulate
OSSIFY	to turn to bone; to become rigid	harden, set

OSTENSIBLE	apparent	represented, supposed, surface
OSTENTATIOUS	showy	pretentious, flamboyant, gaudy, ornate, fulsome
PALLIATE	to make less serious, ease	extenuate, mitigate, alleviate, assuage
PANACEA	cure-all elixir, miracle	drug, sovereign remedy
PANACHE	flamboyance, verve	dash, flair
PANEGYRIC	elaborate praise, formal hymn of praise	eulogy, compliment, laudation, encomium, homage
PARADIGM	ideal example, model	pattern, exemplar
PARAGON	model of excellence or perfection	ideal, nonpareil, paradigm, example
PARAMOUNT	supreme, dominant, primary	chief, commanding, primary
PARIAH	outcast	untouchable, leper, reject
PAROCHIAL	of limited scope or outlook, provincial	narrow, restricted, insular
PARODY	humorous imitation	caricature, burlesque, travesty, lampoon, satire
PARRY	to ward off or deflect	evade, avoid, repel, repulse
PARSIMONY	stinginess	frugality, economy, meanness, miserliness
PATENT (*adj.*)	obvious, unconcealed	apparent, clear, distinct, evident, manifest
PATRICIAN	aristocrat	noble, peer, blue-blood, nabob
PECCADILLO	minor sin or offense	fault, failing, lapse, misstep
PEDANT	uninspired, boring	academic scholar, schoolmaster, pedagogue
PEDESTRIAN (*adj.*)	commonplace	undistinguished, ordinary, dull, mediocre, lackluster
PEJORATIVE	having bad connotations, disparaging	belittling, dismissive, insulting
PENANCE	voluntary suffering to repent for a wrong	atonement, reparation, chastening, reconciliation
PENCHANT	inclination	predilection, bias, leaning, partiality, proclivity
PENITENT	expressing sorrow for sins or offenses, repentant	remorseful, contrite, apologetic
PENURY	extreme poverty	destitution, beggary, need, privation, want

PERFIDIOUS	faithless, disloyal, untrustworthy	treacherous, devious, deceitful
PERFUNCTORY	done in a routine way; indifferent	halfhearted, tepid, careless
PERIPATETIC	moving from place to place	itinerant, nomadic, vagabond
PERSPICACIOUS	shrewd, astute, keen-witted	sagacious, insightful, intelligent
PETULANCE	rudeness, peevishness	irritability, querulousness, testiness, fretfulness
PHALANX	massed group of soldiers, people, or things	body, infantry
PHILISTINE	narrow-minded person, someone lacking appreciation for art or culture	boor, barbarian, vulgarian, bourgeois
PHLEGMATIC	calm in temperament, sluggish	unemotional, placid
PHOBIA	exaggerated, illogical fear	dislike, aversion
PINNACLE	peak, highest point of development	summit, acme, apex, zenith, climax
PIOUS	dedicated, devout, extremely religious	observant, reverent, sanctimonious
PIQUE (*n.*)	fleeting feeling of hurt pride	vexation, resentment, indignation, dudgeon, umbrage
PITHY	profound, substantial; concise, succinct, to the point	brief, compact, terse, laconic
PLACATE	to soothe, pacify	mollify, conciliate, appease
PLACID	calm	tranquil, serene, peaceful, complacent
PLAINTIVE	sad, lamenting	mournful, melancholy
PLATITUDE	stale, overused expression	cliché, bromide, commonplace, truism
PLEBEIAN	crude, vulgar, low-class	unrefined, coarse, common
PLETHORA	excess, overabundance	superfluity, surplus, glut, surfeit
POIGNANT	emotionally moving	stirring, touching, pathetic, affecting, piquant
POLEMIC	controversy, argument; verbal attack	refutation, denunciation
POLITIC	discreet, tactful	prudent, artful, diplomatic, judicious, cunning
POLYMATH	a person of encyclopedic learning	savant, litterateur
PORTENT	omen	augury, harbinger, herald, token, prodigy

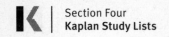

POSTERITY	future generations; all of a person's descendants	progeny, offspring, line, lineage, heritage
POTABLE	drinkable	harmless, nonpoisonous, comestible
POTENTATE	monarch or ruler with great power	leader, emperor, king, prince, czar
PRAGMATIC	practical, moved by facts rather than abstract ideals	prudent, wise, sensible, expedient, politic
PRATTLE *(n.)*	meaningless, foolish talk	chatter, babble, gibberish, drivel, blather
PRECARIOUS	uncertain	insecure, unstable, hazardous, perilous
PRECIPITATE *(adj.)*	sudden and unexpected	abrupt, impetuous, headlong, reckless, rash
PRECOCIOUS	unusually advanced at an early age	premature, developed
PRECURSOR	forerunner, predecessor	herald, vanguard
PREDATOR	one that preys on others, destroyer, plunderer	carnivore, pillager, attacker
PREPOSTEROUS	absurd, illogical	ridiculous, ludicrous, nonsensical, outlandish, incredible
PRESAGE	to foretell, indicate in advance	portend, forewarn, augur, divine, bode
PRESCIENT	having foresight	premonitory, augural, divinatory, mantic, oracular
PREVARICATE	to lie, evade the truth	equivocate, fib, palter, hedge, fabricate
PRIMEVAL	ancient, primitive	primordial, original, archaic, antediluvian
PRIMORDIAL	original, existing from the beginning	primeval, ancient, primitive, archaic, antediluvian
PRISTINE	untouched, uncorrupted	pure, clean
PRIVATION	lack of usual necessities or comforts	forfeiture, loss, deprivation, poverty
PRODIGAL *(adj.)*	wasteful, extravagant, lavish	riotous, luxurious, improvident, thriftless, profligate
PROFICIENT	expert, skilled in a certain subject	adept, skillful, deft, experienced, accomplished
PROFLIGATE	corrupt, degenerate	dissolute, wasteful, extravagant, improvident, prodigal
PROGENITOR	originator, forefather, ancestor in a direct line	forebear, precursor, founder, predecessor
PROGENY	offspring, children	heirs, issue, descendents, posterity

PROLIX	marked by or using an excess of words	verbose, loquacious, garrulous
PROPITIOUS	favorable, advantageous	auspicious, benign, conducive
PROSAIC	relating to prose; dull, commonplace	matter-of-fact, straightforward, unimaginative, pedestrian
PROSCRIBE	to condemn; to forbid, outlaw	denounce, prohibit, ban, banish, interdict
PROSELYTIZE	to convert to a particular belief or religion	missionize, preach, sway, move, convince
PRURIENT	lustful, exhibiting lewd desires	lascivious, lecherous, licentious, salacious, wanton
PSEUDONYM	fictitious or borrowed name	alias, sobriquet, pen name, nom de guerre
PUERILE	childish, immature, silly	juvenile, infantile, jejune
PULCHRITUDE	beauty	loveliness, prettiness, handsomeness, comeliness, gorgeousness
PURLOIN	to steal	filch, pilfer, embezzle, misappropriate, pirate
QUAGMIRE	marsh; difficult situation	swamp, bog, fen, mire, morass
QUANDARY	dilemma, difficulty	predicament, plight, jam, fix
QUARANTINE	isolate to prevent spread of disease	sequester, ostracize
QUELL	to crush or subdue	suppress, pacify, quiet, quash, stifle
QUERULOUS	inclined to complain, irritable	peevish, whiny, sniveling, puling
QUIBBLE	to argue about insignificant and irrelevant details	carp, cavil, nitpick, pettifog
QUIXOTIC	overly idealistic, impractical	romantic, unrealistic, capricious, impulsive
QUOTIDIAN	occurring daily, commonplace	everyday, normal, usual
RACONTEUR	witty, skillful storyteller	anecdotalist, monologist
RAMSHACKLE	likely to collapse	rickety, dilapidated, decrepit
RANT	to harangue, rave, forcefully scold	fulminate, thunder, yell, inveigh
RAREFY	to make thinner, purer, or more refined	attenuate, prune
RAVENOUS	extremely hungry	voracious, gluttonous, rapacious, predatory, famished

RAVINE	deep, narrow gorge	gully, canyon, gulch, arroyo
RAZE	to tear down, demolish	level, ruin, destroy, wreck, annihilate
REACTIONARY	marked by extreme conservatism	ultraconservative, right-wing, orthodox, antiprogress
REBUT	to refute by evidence or argument	counter, retort, disprove, confute, contradict
RECALCITRANT	resisting authority or control	stubborn, defiant, unruly, headstrong, willful
RECANT	to retract a statement or opinion	disavow, disclaim, disown, renounce, repudiate
REDOLENT	exuding fragrance; evocative	ambrosial, aromatic, balmy, fragrant; reminiscent
REDUNDANCY	unnecessary repetition	duplication, superfluity, tautology, pleonasm, wordiness
REFRACTORY	resisting control or authority, stubborn	bullheaded, headstrong, intractable, mulish, obdurate, unyielding
REGIMEN	government rule; systematic plan	control, procedure, system, course
REMUNERATION	pay or reward for work, trouble, etc.	recompense, reimbursement, settlement, requital, redress
RENEGADE	traitor, person abandoning a cause	deserter, rebel, apostate, turncoat, defector
RENEGE	to go back on one's word	break, violate
REPOSE	relaxation, leisure	calmness, tranquility, rest, ease, idleness
REPRISE	repetition, especially of a piece of music	recurrence, return, resumption
REPROBATE	morally unprincipled person	sinner, knave, scoundrel, rogue, rake
REPROVE	to criticize or correct	rebuke, admonish, reprimand, chide, reproach
RESPITE	interval of relief	rest, pause, intermission, recess, suspension
RESTIVE	impatient, uneasy, restless	anxious, agitated, fretful
RHAPSODY	emotional literary or musical work	dithyramb, impromptu, paean
RHETORIC	persuasive use of language	eloquence, elocution, discourse
RIBALD	humorous in a vulgar way	lewd, coarse, indelicate, obscene, gross
RIDDLE (*v.*)	to make many holes in; permeate	perforate, honeycomb, prick, punch, pierce
RIFE	widespread, prevalent, abundant	numerous, prevailing
RUE	to regret	deplore, repent

RUMINATE	to contemplate, reflect upon	ponder, meditate, deliberate, mull, muse
RUSTIC	rural	bucolic, pastoral
SACCHARINE	excessively sweet or sentimental	cloying, treacly, syrupy, maudlin, fulsome
SAGACIOUS	shrewd	astute, perspicacious, wise, judicious, sage
SALLOW	sickly yellow in color	ashen, green, pasty, peaked, wan
SALUBRIOUS	healthful	curative, medicinal, tonic, therapeutic, bracing
SANGUINE	ruddy; cheerfully optimistic	rosy, rubicund; confident, positive, hopeful
SARDONIC	cynical, scornfully mocking	sarcastic, acerbic, caustic, satirical, snide
SATIATE	to satisfy	sate, cloy, glut, gorge, surfeit
SAUNTER	to amble, walk in a leisurely manner	stroll, ramble
SCABBARD	sheath for sword or dagger	sheath, holster, hanger
SCALE (*v.*)	to climb to the top of	ascend, mount
SCIMITAR	a type of sword, a saber with a curved blade with the edge on the convex side	claymore, falchion, rapier, saber
SCOFF	to deride, ridicule	mock, scorn, taunt, twit, flout
SCORE (*v.*)	to make a notch or scratch	furrow, scrape, groove, chase, rule
SECULAR	not specifically pertaining to religion	worldly, lay, laic, temporal
SEDITION	behavior promoting rebellion	insurrection, conspiracy, intrigue, mutiny, subversion
SEMINAL	relating to the beginning or seeds of something	original, creative, influential
SENTENTIOUS	having a moralizing tone	terse, pithy, aphoristic, pompous, moralistic
SENTIENT	aware, conscious, able to perceive	thinking, feeling, intelligent
SEQUESTER	to remove or set apart, put into seclusion	segregate, isolate, insulate, quarantine, cloister
SERAPHIC	angelic, pure, sublime	heavenly, celestial
SERENDIPITOUS	obtained by luck rather than actively sought out	lucky, providential, unplanned
SINECURE	well-paying job or office that requires little or no work	inaction, title
SINUOUS	winding; intricate, complex	supple, lithe, devious, serpentine, curvilinear

SKULK	to move in a stealthy or cautious manner, sneak	lurk, shirk, hide, evade, prowl
SLOUGH (*v.*) (pronounced "sluff")	to discard or shed	molt, cast
SLOVENLY	untidy, messy	negligent, slipshod, sloppy, unkempt
SMELT (*v.*)	to melt metal in order to refine it	purify, extract
SOBRIQUET	nickname	alias, pseudonym
SODDEN	thoroughly soaked, saturated	soggy, wet, drenched, steeped, waterlogged
SOJOURN	visit, stay	call, residency, stop, tenancy
SOLILOQUY	literary or dramatic speech by one character, not addressed to others	monologue, solo
SOPORIFIC	sleepy or tending to cause sleep	somnolent, narcotic, somniferous, drowsy
SPARTAN	austere, severe, grave, simple, bare	disciplined, restrained, frugal, courageous, laconic
SPURIOUS	lacking authenticity, counterfeit, false	fraudulent, ersatz, fake, phony, mock
STACCATO	marked by abrupt, clear-cut sounds	short, disconnected
STEADFAST	unwavering, loyal	faithful, true, constant, fast, staunch
STIGMA	mark of disgrace or inferiority	stain, blot, brand, taint
STINT (*v.*)	to be sparing or frugal	conserve, scrimp, skimp
STOIC	indifferent to or unaffected by emotions	impassive, stolid
STOLID	having or showing little emotion	impassive, stoic
STRIDENT	loud, harsh, unpleasantly noisy	grating, shrill, discordant
STYMIE	to block or thwart	stump, baffle, foil
SUAVE	smoothly gracious or polite; blandly ingratiating	urbane, diplomatic, politic
SUBJUGATE	to conquer, subdue, enslave	defeat, vanquish, enthrall, yoke
SUBLIMINAL	subconscious; imperceptible	unconscious; unperceived
SUBTERFUGE	trick or tactic used to avoid something	stratagem, ruse
SUBTERRANEAN	hidden, secret; underground	concealed, covered; buried, sunken
SULLEN	brooding, gloomy	morose, sulky, somber, glum

SULLY	to soil, stain, tarnish, taint	mar, defile, besmirch
SUPERCILIOUS	arrogant, haughty, overbearing, condescending	proud, disdainful, patronizing, contumelious
SUPPLICANT	one who asks humbly and earnestly	petitioner, appellant, applicant, suitor, suppliant
SURREPTITIOUS	characterized by secrecy	clandestine, stealthy, covert, furtive, underhanded
SYBARITE	person devoted to pleasure and luxury	voluptuary, hedonist, sensualist, libertine
SYCOPHANT	self-serving flatterer, yes-man	toady, lickspittle, fawner, bootlicker
SYLLABUS	outline of a course	summary, schedule
SYMBIOSIS	cooperation, mutual	helpfulness association, interdependence
SYNOPSIS	plot summary	outline, abstract, compendium, digest, epitome
TACIT	silently understood or implied	implicit, unspoken
TACITURN	uncommunicative, not inclined to speak much	reticent, reserved, secretive, uncommunicative, tightlipped
TACTILE	relating to the sense of touch	haptic, tangible, palpable
TAINT	to spoil or infect; to stain honor	contaminate, befoul, poison, pollute, besmirch
TALON	claw of an animal, especially a bird of prey	nail, claw
TANG	sharp flavor or odor	relish, savor, piquancy, bite
TAWDRY	gaudy, cheap, showy	flashy, garish, loud, meretricious
TEMPER (*v.*)	to restrain, moderate	qualify, allay, strengthen, muffle
TENET	belief, doctrine	principle, dogma, creed
TERSE	concise, brief, free of extra words	succinct, compact, compendious, pithy, laconic
TITAN	person of colossal stature or achievement	giant, colossus
TOADY	flatterer, hanger-on, yes-man	sycophant, bootlicker, fawner, lickspittle
TOME	book, usually large and academic	volume, codex
TORPID	lethargic, unable to move, dormant	benumbed, hibernating, apathetic, inactive, inert
TORRID	burning hot; passionate	parched, scorching, sweltering; ardent

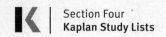
TORTUOUS	having many twists and turns; highly complex	winding, circuitous, devious; involved
TRACTABLE	obedient, yielding	governable, compliant, acquiescent, docile, malleable
TRANSITORY	short-lived, existing only briefly	transient, ephemeral, fleeting, fugitive, momentary
TRENCHANT	acute, sharp, incisive; forceful, effective	mordant, biting, cutting, caustic
TRUNCHEON	a shattered spear or lance	cudgel, bat, billy club, bludgeon, club, knobkerrie, mace, nightstick
TRYST	agreement between lovers to meet, rendezvous	assignation, date, engagement, appointment
TURGID	swollen, bloated	grandiloquent, bombastic, overwrought, orotund, distended
TURPITUDE	inherent vileness, foulness, depravity	baseness, immorality, wickedness
TYRO	beginner, novice	fledgling, neophyte, apprentice, greenhorn, tenderfoot
UBIQUITOUS	being everywhere simultaneously	omnipresent, inescapable
UMBRAGE	offense, resentment	dudgeon, pique, ire, asperity, rancor
UNCTUOUS	greasy, oily; smug and falsely earnest	fulsome, oleaginous, smarmy, phony
UNTOWARD	difficult to manage; unfavorable or unlucky	fractious, intractable, recalcitrant; hapless, unfortunate, unseemly
UPBRAID	to scold sharply	berate, tax, reproach, rebuke, chide
USURP	to seize by force	arrogate, preempt, assume, appropriate
USURY	practice of lending money at exorbitant rates	loan-sharking, interest
UXORIAL	of, relating to, or characteristic of a wife	wifely, spousal
VACILLATE	to waver, show indecision	sway, oscillate, hesitate, falter, waffle
VAUNTED	boasted about, bragged about	acclaimed, celebrated
VERDANT	green with vegetation; inexperienced	grassy, leafy, wooded; naïve, novice
VICARIOUS	surrogate; delegated imagined participation in another's experience	secondhand, proxy, substituted

VIM	energy, enthusiasm	vitality, vigor, animation, brio, esprit
VISCOUS	thick, syrupy, and sticky	adhesive, viscid, gelatinous, gummy, ropy
VORACIOUS	having a great appetite	ravenous, greedy, gluttonous, rapacious, wolfish
WAG (*n.*)	a humorous or droll person	wit, joker, humorist, jester
WAN	sickly pale	ashen, pallid, blanched, pasty, sickly
WANTON	undisciplined, unrestrained, reckless	capricious, lewd, licentious
WAX (*v.*)	to increase gradually, begin to be	enlarge, expand, swell, become, grow
WELTER	a chaotic mass or jumble	clutter, hodgepodge, mishmash
WHET	to sharpen, stimulate	hone, edge, strop, grind
WIZENED	withered, shriveled, wrinkled	wasted, atrophied, gnarled, mummified, desiccated
XENOPHOBIA	fear or hatred of foreigners or strangers	prejudice, bigotry, chauvinism
YOKE (*v.*)	to join together	pair, harness, bind, subjugate
ZENITH	highest point, summit	acme, apex, climax, crown, pinnacle
ZEPHYR	gentle breeze	breath, puff, draft

CHAPTER EIGHT

Word Root List

A: without
agnostic: one who questions the existence of God
amoral: neither moral nor immoral
anomaly: an irregularity
atheist: one who does not believe in God

AB/ABS: off, away from, apart, down
abdicate: to renounce or relinquish a throne
abduct: to take by force
abhor: to hate, detest
abstinence: forbearance from any indulgence of appetite
abstract: conceived apart from concrete realities, specific objects, or actual instances
abstruse: hard to understand; secret, hidden

AC/ACR: sharp, bitter
acerbic: sour or astringent in taste; harsh in temper
acrid: sharp or biting to the taste or smell
acrimonious: caustic, stinging, or bitter in nature
acute: sharp at the end; ending in a point
exacerbate: to increase bitterness or violence; aggravate

ACT/AG: to do, to drive, to force, to lead
agile: quick and well coordinated in movement; active, lively
agitate: to move or force into violent, irregular action
pedagogue: a teacher
synagogue: a gathering or congregation of Jews for the purpose of religious worship

AD/AL: to, toward, near
adapt: adjust or modify fittingly
adhere: to stick fast, cleave, cling
adjacent: near, close, or contiguous; adjoining
advocate: to plead in favor of

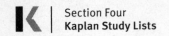

AL/ALI/ALTER: other, another

alias: an assumed name, another name
alien: one born in another country, a foreigner
allegory: figurative treatment of one subject under the guise of another
alternative: a possible choice
altruist: a person unselfishly concerned for the welfare of others

AM: love

amateur: a person who engages in an activity for pleasure rather than financial or professional gain
amenity: agreeable ways or manners
amity: friendship, peaceful harmony
amorous: inclined to love, esp. sexual love
enamored: inflamed with love, charmed, captivated
inamorata: a female lover

AMB: to go, to walk

ambient: moving freely, circulating
ambitious: desirous of achieving or obtaining power
ambulance: a wheeled vehicle equipped for carrying sick people, usually to a hospital
ambulatory: of, pertaining to, or capable of walking
perambulator: one who makes a tour of inspection on foot
preamble: an introductory statement

AMB/AMPH: both, more than one, around

ambidextrous: able to use both hands equally well
ambiguous: open to various interpretations
amphibian: any cold-blooded vertebrate, the larva of which is aquatic and the adult of which is terrestrial; a person or thing having a twofold nature

ANIM: of the life, mind, soul, spirit

animosity: a feeling of ill will or enmity
animus: hostile feeling or attitude
equanimity: mental or emotional stability, especially under tension
magnanimous: generous in forgiving an insult or injury
unanimous: in complete accord

ANNUI/ENNI: year

annals: a record of events, esp. a yearly record
anniversary: the yearly recurrence of the date of a past event
annual: of, for, or pertaining to a year; yearly
annuity: a specified income payable at stated intervals
perennial: lasting for an indefinite amount of time

ANTE: before

antebellum: before the war (especially the American Civil War)
antecedent: existing, being, or going before
antedate: precede in time
antediluvian: belonging to the period before the biblical Flood; very old or old-fashioned
anterior: placed before

ANTHRO/ANDR: man, human

androgen: any substance that promotes masculine characteristics
androgynous: being both male and female
android: robot, mechanical man
anthropocentric: regarding man as the central fact of the universe
anthropology: the science that deals with the origins of mankind
misanthrope: one who hates humans or mankind
philanderer: one who carries on flirtations

ANTI: against

antibody: a protein naturally existing in blood serum that reacts to overcome the toxic effects of an antigen
antidote: a remedy for counteracting the effects of poison, disease, etc.
antipathy: aversion
antipodal: on the opposite side of the globe
antiseptic: free from germs; particularly clean or neat

APO: away

apocalypse: prophetic revelation; disaster
apocryphal: of doubtful authorship or authenticity
apogee: the highest or most distant point
apostasy: a total desertion of one's religion, principles, party, cause, etc.
apostle: one of the 12 disciples sent forth by Jesus to preach the gospel

ARCH/ARCHI/ARCHY: chief, principal, ruler

anarchy: a state or society without government or law
archenemy: chief enemy
architect: the devisor, maker, or planner of anything
monarchy: a government in which the supreme power is lodged in a sovereign
oligarchy: a state or society ruled by a select group

AUTO: self

autocrat: an absolute ruler
automatic: self-moving or self-acting
autonomy: independence or freedom

BE: to be, to have a particular quality, to exist

belie: to misrepresent; to contradict
belittle: to regard something as less impressive than it apparently is
bemoan: to express pity for
bewilder: to confuse or puzzle completely

BEL/BELL: war

antebellum: before the war
belligerent: warlike, given to waging war
rebel: a person who resists authority, control, or tradition

BEN/BON: good

benediction: act of uttering a blessing

benefit: anything advantageous to a person or thing

benevolent: desiring to do good to others

benign: having a kindly disposition

bona fide: in good faith, without fraud

bonus: something given over and above what is due

BI: twice, double

biennial: happening every two years

bilateral: pertaining to or affecting two or both sides

bilingual: able to speak one's native language and another with equal facility

bipartisan: representing two parties

CAD/CID: to fall, to happen by chance

accident: happening by chance, unexpected

cascade: a waterfall descending over a steep surface

coincidence: a striking occurrence of two or more events at one time, apparently by chance

decadent: decaying, deteriorating

recidivist: one who repeatedly relapses, as into crime

CANT/CENT/CHANT: to sing

accent: prominence of a syllable in terms of pronunciation

chant: a song, singing

enchant: to subject to magical influence, bewitch

incantation: the chanting of words purporting to have magical power

incentive: that which incites action

recant: to withdraw or disavow a statement

CAP/CIP/CEPT: to take, to get

anticipate: to realize beforehand, foretaste, or foresee

capture: to take by force or stratagem

emancipate: to free from restraint

percipient: having perception, discerning, discriminating

precept: a commandment or direction given as a rule of conduct

susceptible: capable of receiving, admitting, undergoing, or being affected by something

CAP/CAPIT/CIPIT: head, headlong

capital: the city or town that is the official seat of government

capitulate: to surrender unconditionally or on stipulated terms

caption: a heading or title

disciple: one who is a pupil of the doctrines of another

precipice: a cliff with a vertical face

precipitate: to hasten the occurrence of, to bring about prematurely

CARD/CORD/COUR: heart

cardiac: pertaining to the heart

concord: agreement, peace, amity

concordance: agreement, concord, harmony

discord: lack of harmony between persons or things

encourage: to inspire with spirit or confidence

CARN: flesh
   carnage: the slaughter of a great number of people
   carnival: a traveling amusement show
   carnivorous: eating flesh
   incarnation: a being invested with a bodily form
   reincarnation: rebirth of a soul in a new body

CAST/CHAST: cut
   cast: to throw, hurl, or fling
   caste: a hereditary social group, limited to people of the same rank
   castigate: to punish in order to correct
   chaste: free from obscenity, decent
   chastise: to discipline, esp. by corporal punishment

CED/CEED/CESS: to go, to yield, to stop
   antecedent: existing, being, or going before
   cessation: a temporary or complete discontinuance
   concede: to acknowledge as true, just, or proper; admit
   incessant: without stop
   predecessor: one who comes before another in an office, position, etc.

CENTR: center
   centrifuge: an apparatus that rotates at high speed that separates substances of different densities
      using centrifugal force
   centrist: of or pertaining to moderate political or social ideas
   concentrate: to bring to a common center, converge, or direct toward one point
   concentric: having a common center, as in circles or spheres
   eccentric: off center, strange

CERN/CERT/CRET/CRIM/CRIT: to separate, to judge, to distinguish, to decide
   ascertain: to make sure of, to determine
   certitude: freedom from doubt
   criterion: a standard of judgment or criticism
   discreet: judicious in one's conduct of speech, esp. with regard to maintaining silence about
      something of a delicate nature
   discrete: detached from others, separate
   hypocrite: a person who pretends to have beliefs that she does not

CHRON: time
   anachronism: an obsolete or archaic form
   chronic: constant, habitual
   chronology: the sequential order in which past events occurred
   chronometer: a timepiece with a mechanism to adjust for accuracy
   synchronize: to occur at the same time or agree in time

CIRCU: around, on all sides
   circuit: the act of going or moving around
   circuitous: roundabout, indirect
   circumambulate: to walk about or around
   circumference: the outer boundary of a circular area
   circumstances: the existing conditions or state of affairs surrounding and affecting an agent

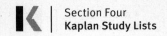

CIS: to cut

exorcise: to seek to expel an evil spirit by ceremony

incision: a cut, gash, or notch

incisive: penetrating, cutting

precise: definitely stated or defined

scissors: cutting instrument for paper

CLA/CLO/CLU: shut, close

claustrophobia: an abnormal fear of enclosed places

cloister: a courtyard bordered with covered walks, esp. in a religious institution

conclude: to bring to an end, finish, terminate

disclose: to make known, reveal, or uncover

exclusive: not admitting of something else; shutting out others

preclude: to prevent the presence, existence, or occurrence of

CLAIM/CLAM: to shout; to cry out

clamor: a loud uproar

disclaim: to deny interest in or connection with

exclaim: to cry out or speak suddenly and vehemently

proclaim: to announce or declare in an official way

reclaim: to claim or demand the return of a right or possession

CLI: to lean toward

climax: the most intense point in the development of something

decline: to cause to slope or incline downward

disinclination: aversion, distaste

proclivity: inclination, bias

recline: to lean back

CO/COL/COM/CON: with, together

coerce: to compel by force, intimidation, or authority

collaborate: to work with another, cooperate

collide: to strike one another with a forceful impact

commensurate: suitable in measure, proportionate

compatible: capable of existing together in harmony

conciliate: to placate, win over

connect: to bind or fasten together

CRE/CRESC/CRET: to grow

accretion: an increase by natural growth

accrue: to be added as a matter of periodic gain

creation: the act of producing or causing to exist

increase: to make greater in any respect

increment: something added or gained, an addition or increase

CRED: to believe; to trust

credentials: anything that provides the basis for belief

credit: trustworthiness

credo: any formula of belief

credulity: willingness to believe or trust too readily

incredible: unbelievable

CRYP: hidden
apocryphal: of doubtful authorship or authenticity
crypt: a subterranean chamber or vault
cryptography: procedures of making and using secret writing
cryptology: the science of interpreting secret writings, codes, ciphers, and the like

CUB/CUMB: to lie down
cubicle: any small space or compartment that is partitioned off
incubate: to sit upon for the purpose of hatching
incumbent: holding an indicated position
recumbent: lying down, reclining; leaning
succumb: to give away to superior force, yield

CULP: blame
culpable: deserving blame or censure
culprit: a person guilty for an offense
inculpate: to charge with fault
mea culpa: through my fault, my fault

COUR/CUR: running, a course
courier: a messenger traveling in haste who bears news
cursive: handwriting in flowing strokes with the letters joined together
cursory: hasty, superficial
excursion: a short journey or trip
incursion: a hostile entrance into a place, esp. suddenly
recur: to happen again

DE: away, off, down, completely, reversal
decipher: to make out the meaning, to interpret
defame: to attack the good name or reputation of
deferential: respectful; yielding to judgment
defile: to make foul, dirty, or unclean
delineate: to trace the outline of, sketch or trace in outline
descend: to move from a higher to a lower place

DEM: people
democracy: government by the people
demographics: vital and social statistics of populations
endemic: peculiar to a particular people or locality
epidemic: affecting at the same time a large number of people and spreading from person to person
pandemic: general, universal

DI/DIA: apart, through
diagnose: to determine the identity of something from the symptoms
dialogue: conversation between two or more persons
dichotomy: division into two parts, kinds, etc.
dilate: to make wider or larger, to cause to expand
dilatory: inclined to delay or procrastinate

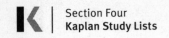
DIC/DICT/DIT: to say, to tell, to use words
dictionary: a book containing a selection of the words of a language
interdict: to forbid, prohibit
predict: to tell in advance
verdict: judgment, decree

DIGN: worth
condign: well-deserved, fitting, adequate
deign: to think fit or in accordance with one's dignity
dignitary: a person who holds a high rank or office
dignity: nobility or elevation of character; worthiness
disdain: to look upon or treat with contempt

DIS/DIF: away from, apart, reversal, not
diffuse: to pour out and spread, as in a fluid
disperse: to drive or send off in various directions
disseminate: to scatter or spread widely, promulgate
dissipate: to scatter wastefully
dissuade: to deter by advice or persuasion

DAC/DOC: to teach
didactic: intended for instruction
docile: easily managed or handled, tractable
doctor: someone licensed to practice medicine; a learned person
doctrine: a particular principle advocated, as of a government or religion
indoctrinate: to imbue a person with learning

DOG/DOX: opinion
dogma: a system of tenets, as of a church
orthodox: sound or correct in opinion or doctrine
paradox: an opinion or statement contrary to accepted opinion

DOL: suffer, pain
condolence: expression of sympathy with one who is suffering
doleful: sorrowful, mournful
dolorous: full of pain or sorrow, grievous
indolence: a state of being lazy or slothful

DON/DOT/DOW: to give
anecdote: a short narrative about an interesting event
antidote: something that prevents or counteracts ill effects
donate: to present as a gift or contribution
endow: to provide with a permanent fund
pardon: kind indulgence, forgiveness

DUB: doubt
dubiety: doubtfulness
dubious: doubtful
indubitable: unquestionable

DUC/DUCT: to lead

abduct: to carry off or lead away

conducive: contributive, helpful

conduct: personal behavior, way of acting

induce: to lead or move by influence

induct: to install in a position with formal ceremonies

produce: to bring into existence, give cause to

DUR: hard

dour: sullen, gloomy

durable: able to resist decay

duration: the length of time something exists

duress: compulsion by threat, coercion

endure: to hold out against, to sustain without yielding

DYS: faulty, abnormal

dysfunctional: poorly functioning

dyslexia: an impairment of the ability to read due to a brain defect

dyspepsia: impaired digestion

dystrophy: faulty or inadequate nutrition or development

EPI: upon

epidemic: affecting a large number of people at the same time and spreading from person to person

epidermis: the outer layer of the skin

epigram: a witty or pointed saying tersely expressed

epilogue: a concluding part added to a literary work

epithet: a word or phrase used invectively as a term of abuse

EQU: equal, even

adequate: equal to the requirement or occasion

equation: the act of making equal

equidistant: equally distant

iniquity: gross injustice, wickedness

ERR: to wander

arrant: downright, thorough, notorious

err: to go astray in thought or belief, to be mistaken

erratic: deviating from the proper or usual course in conduct

error: a deviation from accuracy or correctness

ESCE: becoming

adolescent: between childhood and adulthood

convalescent: recovering from illness

incandescent: glowing with heat, shining

obsolescent: becoming obsolete

reminiscent: reminding or suggestive of

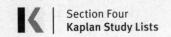
EU: good, well

eugenics: improvement of qualities of race by control of inherited characteristics

eulogy: speech or writing in praise or commendation

euphemism: pleasant-sounding term for something unpleasant

euphony: pleasantness of sound

euthanasia: killing a person painlessly, usually one who has an incurable, painful disease

E/EF/EX: out, out of, from, former, completely

efface: to rub or wipe out; to surpass, eclipse

evade: to escape from, avoid

exclude: to shut out, leave out

exonerate: to free or declare free from blame

expire: to come to an end, cease to be valid

extricate: to disentangle, release

EXTRA: outside, beyond

extract: to take out, obtain against person's will

extradite: to hand over one accused of a crime to another state where the crime was committed

extraordinary: beyond the ordinary

extrapolate: to estimate (unknown facts or values) from known data

extrasensory: derived by means other than known senses

FAB/FAM: speak

affable: friendly, courteous

defame: attack the good name of

fable: fictional tale, esp. legendary

famous: well-known, celebrated

ineffable: too great for description in words; that which must not be uttered

FAC/FIC/FIG/FAIT/FEIT/FY: to do, to make

configuration: manner of arrangement, shape

counterfeit: imitation, forgery

deficient: incomplete or insufficient

effigy: sculpture or model of person

faction: small dissenting group within larger one, esp. in politics

factory: building for manufacture of goods

prolific: producing many offspring or much output

ratify: to confirm or accept by formal consent

FER: to bring; to carry; to bear

confer: to grant, bestow

offer: to present for acceptance, refusal, or consideration

proffer: to offer

proliferate: to reproduce, produce rapidly

referendum: to vote on political question open to the entire electorate

FERV: to boil, to bubble

effervescent: with the quality of giving off bubbles of gas

fervid: ardent, intense

fervor: passion, zeal

FID: faith, trust

affidavit: written statement on oath

confide: to entrust with a secret

fidelity: faithfulness, loyalty

fiduciary: of a trust, held or given in trust

infidel: disbeliever in the supposed true religion

FIN: end

confine: to keep or restrict within certain limits, imprison

definitive: decisive, unconditional, final

final: at the end, coming last

infinite: boundless, endless

infinitesimal: infinitely or very small

FLAG/FLAM: to burn

conflagration: large, destructive fire

flagrant: blatant, scandalous

flambeau: a lighted torch

flammable: easily set on fire

FLECT/FLEX: to bend

deflect: to bend or turn aside from a purpose

flexible: able to bend without breaking

genuflect: to bend knee, esp. in worship

inflect: to change or vary pitch of

reflect: to throw back

FLU/FLUX: to flow

confluence: merging into one

effluence: flowing out of (light, electricity, etc.)

fluctuation: something that varies, rising and falling

fluid: substance, esp. gas or liquid, capable of flowing freely

mellifluous: pleasing, musical

FORE: before

foreshadow: to warn of or indicate a future event

foresight: care or provision for future

forestall: to prevent by advance action

forthright: straightforward, outspoken, decisive

FORT: chance

fortuitous: happening by luck

fortunate: lucky, auspicious

fortune: chance or luck in human affairs

FORT: strength

forte: strong point, something a person does well

fortify: to provide with fortifications, strengthen

fortissimo: very loud

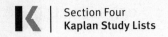

FRA/FRAC/FRAG/FRING: to break
>   fractious: irritable, peevish
>   fracture: breakage, esp. of a bone
>   fragment: a part broken off
>   infringe: to break or violate (law, etc.)
>   refractory: stubborn, unmanageable, rebellious

FUS: to pour
>   diffuse: to spread widely or thinly
>   fusillade: continuous discharge of firearms or outburst of criticism
>   infusion: infusing; liquid extract so obtained
>   profuse: lavish, extravagant, copious
>   suffuse: to spread throughout or over from within

GEN: birth, creation, race, kind
>   carcinogenic: producing cancer
>   congenital: existing or as such from birth
>   gender: classification roughly corresponding to the two sexes and sexlessness
>   generous: giving or given freely
>   genetics: study of heredity and variation among animals and plants
>   miscegenation: interbreeding of races
>   progeny: offspring, descendants

GN/GNO: know
>   agnostic: person who believes that existence of God is not provable
>   diagnose: to make an identification of disease or fault from symptoms
>   ignoramus: a person lacking knowledge, uninformed
>   ignore: to refuse to take notice of
>   incognito: with one's name or identity concealed
>   prognosis: to forecast, especially of disease
>   recognize: to identify as already known

GRAT: pleasing
>   gracious: kindly, esp. to inferiors; merciful
>   grateful: thankful
>   gratuity: money given for good service
>   ingratiate: to bring oneself into favor

GRAD/GRESS: to step
>   aggressive: given to hostile act or feeling
>   degrade: to humiliate, dishonor, reduce to lower rank
>   digress: to depart from main subject
>   egress: going out; a way out
>   progress: forward movement
>   regress: to move backward, revert to an earlier state

HER/HES: to stick
adherent: able to adhere; believer or advocate of a particular thing
adhesive: tending to remain in memory; sticky; an adhesive substance
coherent: logically consistent; having waves in phase and of one wavelength
heredity: the qualities genetically derived from one's ancestors and the transmission of those qualities
inherent: involved in the constitution or essential character of something

(H)ETERO: different
heterodox: different from acknowledged standard; holding unorthodox opinions or doctrines
heterogeneous: of other origin; not originating in the body
heterosexual: of or pertaining to sexual orientation toward members of the opposite sex; relating to different sexes

(H)OM: same
anomaly: deviation from the common rule
homeostasis: a relatively stable state of equilibrium
homogeneous: of the same or a similar kind of nature; of uniform structure of composition throughout
homonym: one of two or more words spelled and pronounced alike but different in meaning
homosexual: of, relating to, or exhibiting sexual desire toward a member of one's own sex

HYPER: over, excessive
hyperactive: excessively active
hyperbole: purposeful exaggeration for effect
hyperglycemia: an abnormally high concentration of sugar in the blood

HYPO: under, beneath, less than
hypochondriac: one affected by extreme depression of mind or spirits often centered on imaginary physical ailments
hypocritical: affecting virtues or qualities one does not have
hypodermic: relating to the parts beneath the skin
hypothesis: assumption subject to proof

IDIO: one's own
idiom: a language, dialect, or style of speaking particular to a people
idiosyncrasy: peculiarity of temperament, eccentricity
idiot: an utterly stupid person

IM/IN/EM/EN: in, into
embrace: to clasp in the arms; to include or contain
enclose: to close in on all sides
implicit: not expressly stated, implied
incarnate: given a bodily, esp. a human, form
indigenous: native; innate, natural
influx: the act of flowing in, inflow
intrinsic: belonging to a thing by its very nature

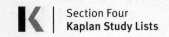

IM/IN: not, without

impartial: not partial or biased, just

inactive: not active

indigent: deficient in what is requisite

indolence: showing a disposition to avoid exertion, slothful

innocuous: not harmful or injurious

INTER: between, among

interim: a temporary or provisional arrangement; meantime

interloper: one who intrudes in the domain of others

intermittent: stopping or ceasing for a time

intersperse: to scatter here and there

interstate: connecting or jointly involving states

JECT: to throw, to throw down

abject: utterly hopeless, humiliating, or wretched

conjecture: formation of opinion on incomplete information

dejected: sad, depressed

eject: to throw out, expel

inject: to place (a quality, etc.) where needed in something

JOIN/JUNCT: to meet; to join

adjoin: to be next to and joined with

junction: the act of joining, combining

junta: clique, usually military, that takes power after a coup d'état

rejoinder: to reply, retort

subjugate: to conquer

JUR: to swear

abjure: to renounce on oath

adjure: to beg or command

perjury: willful lying while on oath

LECT/LEG: to select, to choose

collect: to gather together or assemble

eclectic: selecting ideas, etc. from various sources

elect: to choose, decide

predilection: preference, liking

select: to choose with care

LEV: lift, light, rise

alleviate: to make easier to endure, lessen

levee: embankment against river flooding

levitate: to rise in the air or cause to rise

levity: humor, frivolity, gaiety

relevant: bearing on or pertinent to information at hand

relieve: to mitigate; to free from a burden

LOC/LOG/LOQU: word, speech

colloquial: of ordinary or familiar conversation
dialogue: conversation, esp. in a literary work
elocution: art of clear and expressive speaking
eulogy: speech or writing in praise of someone
grandiloquent: pompous or inflated in language
loquacious: talkative
prologue: introduction to a poem, play, etc.

LUC/LUM/LUS: light

illuminate: to supply or brighten with light
illustrate: to make intelligible with examples or analogies
illustrious: highly distinguished
lackluster: lacking brilliance or radiance
lucid: easily understood, intelligible
luminous: bright, brilliant, glowing
translucent: permitting light to pass through

LUD/LUS: to play

allude: to refer casually or indirectly
delude: to mislead the mind or judgment of, deceive
elude: to avoid capture or escape defection by
illusion: something that deceives by producing a false impression of reality
ludicrous: ridiculous, laughable
prelude: a preliminary to an action, event, etc.

LAV/LUT/LUV: to wash

ablution: act of cleansing
antediluvian: before the biblical Flood; extremely old
deluge: a great flood of water
dilute: to make thinner or weaker by the addition of water
lavatory: a room with equipment for washing hands and face
pollute: to make foul or unclean

MAG/MAJ/MAX: big

magnanimous: generous in forgiving an insult or injury
magnate: a powerful or influential person
magnify: to increase the apparent size of
magnitude: greatness of size, extent, or dimensions
maxim: an expression of general truth or principle
maximum: the highest amount, value, or degree attained

MAL/MALE: bad, ill, evil, wrong

maladroit: clumsy, tactless
malady: a disorder or disease of the body
malapropism: humorous misuse of a word
malediction: a curse
malfeasance: misconduct or wrongdoing often committed by a public official
malfunction: failure to function properly
malicious: full of or showing malice
malign: to speak harmful untruths about, to slander

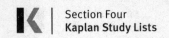

MAN: hand

emancipate: to free from bondage
mandate: an authoritative order or command
manifest: readily perceived by the eye or the understanding
manual: operated by hand
manufacture: to make by hand or machinery

MIN: small

diminish: to lessen
diminution: the act or process of diminishing
miniature: a copy or model that represents something in greatly reduced size
minute: a unit of time equal to one-sixtieth of an hour, or sixty seconds
minutiae: small or trivial details

MIN: to project, to hang over

eminent: towering above others; projecting
imminent: about to occur, impending
minatory: menacing, threatening
preeminent: superior to or notable above all others
prominent: projecting outward

MIS/MIT: to send

emissary: a messenger or agent sent to represent the interests of another
intermittent: stopping and starting at intervals
remission: a lessening of intensity or degree
remit: to send money
transmit: to send from one person, thing, or place to another

MISC: mixed

miscegenation: the interbreeding of races, esp. marriage between white and nonwhite persons
miscellaneous: made up of a variety of parts or ingredients
promiscuous: consisting of diverse and unrelated parts or individuals

MON/MONIT: to remind, to warn

admonish: to counsel against something, caution
monitor: one that admonishes, cautions, or reminds
monument: a structure, such as a building, tower, or sculpture, erected as a memorial
premonition: forewarning, presentiment
remonstrate: to say or plead in protect, objection, or reproof
summon: to call together, convene

MORPH: shape

amorphous: without definite form, lacking a specific shape
anthropomorphism: attribution of human characteristics to inanimate objects, animals, or
    natural phenomena
metamorphosis: a transformation, as by magic or sorcery

MORT: death

immortal: not subject to death
morbid: susceptible to preoccupation with unwholesome matters
moribund: dying, decaying

MUT: change

commute: to substitute, exchange, interchange
immutable: unchangeable, invariable
mutation: the process of being changed
permutation: a complete change, transformation
transmutation: the act of changing from one form into another

NAT/NAS/NAI: to be born

cognate: related by blood, having a common ancestor
naive: lacking worldliness and sophistication, artless
nascent: starting to develop
native: belonging to one by nature, inborn, innate
natural: present due to nature, not to artificial or man-made means
renaissance: rebirth, esp. referring to culture

NIC/NOC/NOX: harm

innocent: uncorrupted by evil, malice, or wrongdoing
innocuous: having no adverse effect, harmless
noxious: injurious or harmful to health or morals
obnoxious: highly disagreeable or offensive

NOM: rule, order

astronomy: the scientific study of the universe beyond the earth
autonomy: independence, self-governance
economy: the careful or thrifty use of resources, as of income, materials, or labor
gastronomy: the art or science of good eating
taxonomy: the science, laws, or principles of classification

NOM/NYM/NOUN/NOWN: name

acronym: a word formed from the initial letters of a name
anonymous: having an unknown or unacknowledged name
nomenclature: a system of names, systematic naming
nominal: existing in name only; negligible
nominate: to propose by name as a candidate
synonym: a word having a meaning similar to that of another word of the same language

NOV/NEO/NOU: new

innovate: to begin or introduce something new
neologism: a newly coined word, phrase, or expression
neophyte: a recent convert
nouveau riche: one who has lately become rich
novice: a person new to any field or activity
renovate: to restore to an earlier condition

NOUNC/NUNC: to announce

announce: to proclaim
pronounce: to articulate
renounce: to give up, especially by formal announcement

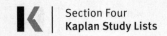
OB/OC/OF/OP: toward, to, against, over
    obese: extremely fat, corpulent
    obfuscate: to render indistinct or dim, darken
    oblique: having a slanting or sloping direction
    obsequious: overly submissive
    obstinate: stubbornly adhering to an idea, inflexible
    obstreperous: noisily defiant, unruly
    obstruct: to block or fill with obstacles
    obtuse: not sharp, pointed, or acute in any form

OMNI: all
    omnibus: an anthology of the works of one author or of writings on related subjects
    omnipotent: all-powerful
    omnipresent: everywhere at one time
    omniscient: having infinite knowledge

PAC/PEAC: peace
    appease: to bring peace to
    pacifier: something or someone that eases the anger or agitation of
    pacify: to ease the anger or agitation of
    pact: a formal agreement, as between nations

PAN: all, everyone
    pandemic: widespread, general, universal
    panegyric: formal or elaborate praise at an assembly
    panoply: a wide-ranging and impressive array or display
    panorama: an unobstructed and wide view of an extensive area
    pantheon: a public building containing tombs or memorials of the illustrious dead of a nation

PAR: equal
    apartheid: any system or caste that separates people according to race, etc.
    disparage: to belittle, speak disrespectfully about
    disparate: essentially different
    par: an equality in value or standing
    parity: equally, as in amount, status, or character

PARA: next to, beside
    parable: a short, allegorical story designed to illustrate a moral lesson or religious principle
    paragon: a model of excellence
    parallel: extending in the same direction
    paranoid: suffering from a baseless distrust of others
    parasite: an organism that lives on or within a plant or animal of another species from which it obtains nutrients
    parody: to imitate for purposes of satire

PAS/PAT/PATH: feeling, suffering, disease

compassion: a feeling of deep sympathy for someone struck by misfortune accompanied by a desire to alleviate suffering

dispassionate: devoid of personal feeling or bias

empathy: the identification with the feelings or thoughts of others

impassive: showing or feeling no emotion

pathogenic: causing disease

sociopath: a person whose behavior is antisocial and who lacks a sense of moral responsibility

sympathy: harmony or of agreement in feeling

PAU/PO/POV/PU: few, little, poor

impoverish: to deplete

paucity: smallness of quantity, scarcity, scantiness

pauper: a person without any personal means of support

poverty: the condition of being poor

puerile: childish, immature

pusillanimous: lacking courage or resolution

PED: child, education

encyclopedia: book or set of books containing articles on various topics, covering all branches of knowledge or of one particular subject

pedagogue: a teacher

pedant: one who displays learning ostentatiously

pediatrician: a doctor who primarily has children as patients

PED/POD: foot

antipodes: places diametrically opposite each other on the globe

expedite: to speed up the progress of

impede: to retard progress by means of obstacles or hindrances

pedal: a foot-operated lever or part used to control

pedestrian: a person who travels on foot

podium: a small platform for an orchestra conductor, speaker, etc.

PEN/PUN: to pay, to compensate

penal: of or pertaining to punishment, as for crimes

penalty: a punishment imposed for a violation of law or rule

penance: a punishment undergone to express regret for a sin

penitent: contrite

punitive: serving for, concerned with, or inflicting punishment

PEND/PENS: to hang, to weight, to pay

appendage: a limb or other subsidiary part that diverges from the central structure

appendix: supplementary material at the end of a text

compensate: to counterbalance, offset

depend: to rely on, to place trust in

indispensable: absolutely necessary, essential, or requisite

stipend: a periodic payment, fixed or regular pay

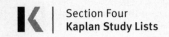

PER: completely

perforate: to make a way through or into something

perfunctory: performed merely as routine duty

perplex: to cause to be puzzled or bewildered over what is not understood

persistent: lasting or enduring tenaciously

perspicacious: shrewd, astute

pertinacious: resolute

peruse: to read with thoroughness or care

PERI: around

perimeter: the border or outer boundary of a two-dimensional figure

peripatetic: walking or traveling about, itinerant

periscope: an optical instrument for seeing objects in an obstructed field of vision

PET/PIT: to go, to seek, to strive

appetite: a desire for food or drink

centripetal: moving toward the center

compete: to strive to outdo another for acknowledgment

impetuous: characterized by sudden or rash action or emotion

petition: a formally drawn request soliciting some benefit

petulant: showing sudden irritation, esp. over some annoyance

PHIL: love

bibliophile: one who loves or collects books

philatelist: one who loves or collects postage stamps

philology: the study of literary texts to establish their authenticity and determine their meaning

philosophy: the rational investigation of the truths and principles of being, knowledge, or conduct

PLAC: to please

complacent: self-satisfied, unconcerned

complaisant: inclined or disposed to please

implacable: unable to be pleased

placebo: a substance with no pharmacological effect that acts to placate a patient who believes it to be a medicine

placid: pleasantly calm or peaceful

PLE: to fill

complete: having all parts or elements

deplete: to decrease seriously or exhaust the supply of

implement: an instrument, tool, or utensil for accomplishing work

plethora: excess, overabundance

replete: abundantly supplied

supplement: something added to supply a deficiency

PLEX/PLIC/PLY: to fold, twist, tangle, or bend

complex: composed of many interconnected parts

duplicity: deceitfulness in speech or conduct, double-dealing

implicate: to show to be involved, usually in an incriminating manner

implicit: not expressly stated, implied

replica: any close copy or reproduction

supplicate: to make humble and earnest entreaty

PON/POS/POUND: to put, to place
component: a constituent part, elemental ingredient
expose: to lay open to danger, attack, or harm
expound: to set forth in detail
juxtapose: to place close together or side by side, esp. for contract
repository: a receptacle or place where things are deposited

PORT: to carry
deportment: conduct, behavior
disport: to divert or amuse oneself
export: to transmit abroad
import: to bring in from a foreign country
importune: to urge or press with excessive persistence
portable: easily carried

POST: after
post facto: after the fact
posterior: situated at the rear
posterity: succeeding in future generations collectively
posthumous: after death

PRE: before
precarious: dependent on circumstances beyond one's control
precedent: an act that serves as an example for subsequent situations
precept: a commandment given as a rule of action or conduct
precocious: unusually advanced or mature in mental development or talent
premonition: a feeling of anticipation over a future event
presentiment: foreboding

PREHEND/PRISE: to take, to get, to seize
apprehend: to take into custody
comprise: to include or contain
enterprise: a project undertaken
reprehensible: deserving rebuke or censure
reprisals: retaliation against an enemy
surprise: to strike with an unexpected feeling of wonder or astonishment

PRO: much, for, a lot
prodigal: wastefully or recklessly extravagant
prodigious: extraordinary in size, amount, or extent
profuse: spending or giving freely
prolific: highly fruitful
propound: to set forth for consideration
proselytize: to convert or attempt to recruit
provident: having or showing foresight

PROB: to prove, to test
approbation: praise, consideration
opprobrium: the disgrace incurred by shameful conduct
probe: to search or examine thoroughly
probity: honesty, high-mindedness
problematic: questionable
reprobate: a depraved or wicked person

PUG: to fight
impugn: to challenge as false
pugilist: a fighter or boxer
pugnacious: to quarrel or fight readily
repugnant: objectionable or offensive

PUNC/PUNG/POIGN: to point, to prick
compunction: a feeling of uneasiness for doing wrong
expunge: to erase, eliminate completely
point: a sharp or tapering end
punctilious: strict or exact in the observance of formalities
puncture: the act of piercing
pungent: caustic or sharply expressive

QUE/QUIS: to seek
acquire: to come into possession of
conquest: vanquishment
exquisite: of special beauty or charm
inquisitive: given to research, eager for knowledge
perquisite: a gratuity, tip
querulous: full of complaints
query: a question, inquiry

QUI: quiet
acquiesce: to comply, give in
disquiet: lack of calm or peace
quiescence: the condition of being at rest, still, inactive
quiet: making little or no sound
tranquil: free from commotion or tumult

RID/RIS: to laugh
derision: the act of mockery
riddle: a conundrum
risible: causing laughter

ROG: to ask
abrogate: to abolish by formal means
arrogant: making claims to superior importance or rights
arrogate: to claim unwarrantably or presumptuously
derogatory: belittling, disparaging
interrogate: to ask questions of, esp. formally
surrogate: a person appointed to act for another

SAL/SIL/SAULT/SULT: to leap, to jump
> assault: a sudden or violent attack
> desultory: at random, unmethodical
> exult: to show or feel triumphant joy
> insolent: boldly rude or disrespectful
> insult: to treat with contemptuous rudeness
> resilient: able to spring back to an original form after compression
> salient: prominent or conspicuous
> somersault: to roll the body end over end, making a complete revolution

SACR/SANCT/SECR: sacred
> execrable: abominable
> sacrament: something regarded as possessing sacred character
> sacred: devoted or dedicated to a deity or religious purpose
> sacrifice: the offering of some living or inanimate thing to a deity in homage
> sacrilege: the violation of anything sacred
> sanctify: to make holy
> sanction: authoritative permission or approval

SCI: to know
> conscience: the inner sense of what is right or wrong impelling one toward right action
> conscious: aware of one's own existence
> omniscient: knowing everything
> prescient: having knowledge of things before they happen
> unconscionable: unscrupulous

SCRIBE/SCRIP: to write
> ascribe: to credit or assign, as to a cause or course
> circumscribe: to draw a line around
> conscription: draft
> describe: to tell or depict in words
> postscript: any addition or supplement
> proscribe: to condemn as harmful or odious
> scribble: to write hastily or carelessly
> script: handwriting
> transcript: a written or typed copy

SE: apart
> secede: to withdraw formally from an association
> sedition: incitement of discontent or rebellion against a government
> seduce: to lead astray
> segregate: to separate or set apart from others
> select: to choose in preference to another
> separate: to keep apart, divide
> sequester: to remove or withdraw into solitude or retirement

SEC/SEQU: to follow
> non sequitur: an inference or a conclusion that does not follow from the premise
> prosecute: to seek to enforce by legal process
> second: next after the first
> sequence: the following of one thing after another

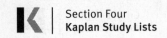
SED/SESS/SID: to sit, to be still, to plan, to plot
- assiduous: diligent, persistent, hardworking
- dissident: disagreeing, as in opinion or attitude
- insidious: intended to entrap or beguile
- preside: to exercise management or control
- residual: remaining, leftover
- subsidiary: serving to assist or supplement

SENS/SENT: to feel, to be aware
- dissent: to differ in opinion, esp. from the majority
- insensate: without feeling or sensitivity
- resent: to feel or show displeasure
- sensory: of or pertaining to the senses or sensation
- sentiment: an attitude or feeling toward something
- sentinel: a person or thing that stands watch

SOL: to loosen, to free
- absolution: forgiveness for wrongdoing
- dissolute: indifferent to moral restraints
- dissolution: the act or process of dissolving into parts or elements
- dissolve: to make a solution of, as by mixing in a liquid
- resolution: a formal expression of opinion or intention made
- soluble: capable of being dissolved or liquefied

SPEC/SPIC/SPIT: to look, to see
- circumspect: watchful and discreet, cautious
- perspicacious: having keen mental perception and understanding
- retrospective: contemplative of past situations
- specious: deceptively attractive
- spectrum: a broad range of related things that form a continuous series
- speculation: the contemplation or consideration of some subject

STA/STI: to stand, to be in place
- apostasy: renunciation of an object of one's previous loyalty
- constitute: to make up
- destitute: without means of subsistence
- obstinate: stubbornly adhering to a purpose, opinion, or course of action
- stasis: the state of equilibrium or inactivity caused by opposing equal forces
- static: of bodies or forces at rest or in equilibrium

SUA: smooth
- assuage: to make less severe, ease, relieve
- dissuade: to deter
- persuade: to encourage; to convince
- suave: smoothly agreeable or polite

SUB/SUP: below
> subliminal: existing or operating below the threshold of consciousness
> submissive: inclined or ready to submit
> subsidiary: serving to assist or supplement
> subterfuge: an artifice or expedient used to evade a rule
> subtle: thin, tenuous, or rarefied
> supposition: the act of assuming

SUPER/SUR: above
> supercilious: arrogant, haughty, condescending
> superfluous: extra, more than necessary
> superlative: the highest kind or order
> supersede: to replace in power, as by another person or thing
> surmount: to get over or across, to prevail
> surpass: to go beyond in amount, extent, or degree
> surveillance: a watch kept over someone or something

TAC/TIC: to be silent
> reticent: disposed to be silent or not to speak freely
> tacit: unspoken understanding
> taciturn: uncommunicative

TAIN/TEN/TENT/TIN: to hold
> abstention: the act of refraining voluntarily
> detain: to keep from proceeding
> pertain: to have reference or relation
> pertinacious: persistent, stubborn
> sustenance: nourishment, means of livelihood
> tenable: capable of being held, maintained, or defended
> tenacious: holding fast
> tenure: the holding or possessing of anything

TEND/TENS/TENT/TENU: to stretch; to thin
> attenuate: to weaken or reduce in force
> contentious: quarrelsome, disagreeable, belligerent
> distend: to expand by stretching
> extenuating: making less serious by offering excuses
> tendentious: having a predisposition towards a point of view
> tension: the act of stretching or straining
> tentative: of the nature of, or done as a trial, attempt

THEO: god
> apotheosis: glorification, glorified ideal
> atheist: one who does not believe in a deity or divine system
> theocracy: a form of government in which a deity is recognized as the supreme ruler
> theology: the study of divine things and the divine faith

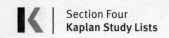
TRACT: to drag, to pull, to draw
>abstract: to draw or pull away, remove
>attract: to draw either by physical force or by an appeal to emotions or senses
>contract: a legally binding document
>detract: to take away from, esp. a positive thing
>protract: to prolong, draw out, extend
>tractable: easily managed or controlled
>tractor: a powerful vehicle used to pull farm machinery

TRANS: across
>intransigent: refusing to agree or compromise
>transaction: the act of carrying on or conduct to a conclusion or settlement
>transcendent: going beyond ordinary limits
>transgress: to violate a law, command, or moral code
>transition: a change from one way of being to another
>transparent: easily seen through, recognized, or detected

US/UT: to use
>abuse: to use wrongly or improperly
>usage: a customary way of doing something
>usurp: to seize and hold
>utilitarian: efficient, functional, useful

VEN/VENT: to come or to move toward
>adventitious: accidental
>contravene: to come into conflict with
>convene: to assemble for some public purpose
>intervene: to come between disputing factions, mediate
>venturesome: showing a disposition to undertake risks

VER: truth
>aver: to affirm, to declare to be true
>veracious: habitually truthful
>verdict: any judgment or decision
>verisimilitude: the appearance or semblance of truth
>verity: truthfulness

VERD: green
>verdant: green with vegetation; inexperienced
>verdure: fresh, rich vegetation

VERS/VERT: to turn
>aversion: dislike
>avert: to turn away from
>covert: hidden, clandestine
>diverse: of a different kind, form, character
>inadvertent: unintentional
>revert: to return to a former habit

VI: life

convivial: sociable

joie de vivre: joy of life (French expression)

viable: capable of living

vicarious: performed, exercised, received, or suffered in place of another

vivacity: the quality of being lively, animated, spirited

vivid: strikingly bright or intense

VID/VIS: to see

evident: plain or clear to the sight or understanding

vista: a view or prospect

VIL: base, mean

revile: to criticize with harsh language

vile: loathsome, unpleasant

vilify: to slander, to defame

VOC/VOK: to call

advocate: to support or urge by argument

avocation: something one does in addition to a principal occupation

equivocate: to use ambiguous or unclear expressions

invoke: to call on a deity

vocation: a particular occupation

vociferous: crying out noisily

VOL: to wish

benevolent: characterized by or expressing goodwill

malevolent: characterized by or expressing bad will

volition: free choice, free will; act of choosing

voluntary: undertaken of one's own accord or by free choice

VOR: to eat

carnivorous: meat-eating

omnivorous: eating or absorbing everything

voracious: having a great appetite

CHAPTER NINE

Specialized Vocabulary Study Lists

WORDS ABOUT WORDS

TERM	DEFINITION
acronym	A word made up of the first letters of other words it describes. Examples: *SCUBA* (self-contained underwater breathing apparatus), *UFO* (unidentified flying object).
adjective	A word that serves as a modifier of a noun to denote a quality of the thing named. Examples: *happy, strong, thin, green*.
adverb	A word serving as a modifier of a verb, an adjective, another adverb, a preposition, etc., which often but not always ends in *–ly*. Examples: *slowly, sadly, well, often*.
alliteration	Repetition of the same sound beginning several words in sequence. Example: "Veni, vidi, vici."—Julius Caesar
anagram	A word that is formed when the letters of a word or phrase are rearranged. For example, *Minnesota* is an anagram of *nominates*.
article	One of a small set of words or affixes (*a, an,* and *the*) used with nouns to limit or give definiteness to the application. English has an indefinite article (*a, an*) and a definite article (*the*).
conjunction	A word that joins together sentences, clauses, phrases, or words. There are two kinds of conjunctions: coordinating conjunctions (such as *and* and *or*) and subordinating conjunctions (such as *although* and *because*).
consonance	Recurrence or repetition of consonants, especially at the end of stressed syllables without the similar correspondence of vowels. Example: *stroke of luck*.

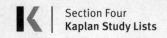
diaeresis	(¨) Two dots placed side-by-side over a vowel (like an umlaut), indicating that the vowel is considered a separate vowel, even though it would normally be considered part of a diphthong. Example: *coöperation*.
diphthong	A gliding, monosyllabic speech item that starts at or near the articulatory position for one vowel and moves to or toward the position for another (as the vowel combination that forms the last part of *toy*).
hyperbole	Exaggeration for emphasis or for rhetorical effect.
intransitive verb	A verb that does not act on an object (unlike a transitive verb). For example, *sleep* is intransitive. I *sleep*. I do not *sleep it*.
irony	Expression of something that is contrary to the intended meaning; the words say one thing but mean another.
metaphor	Implied comparison achieved through a figurative use of words; the word is used not in its literal sense but in one analogous to it. Example: "Life's but a walking shadow; a poor player, That struts and frets his hour upon the stage."—Shakespeare, *Macbeth*
noun	A word that is the name of something (as a person, animal, place, thing, quality, idea, or action).
onomatopoeia	Use of words to imitate natural sounds; accommodation of sound to sense. Examples: *hiss, whack, hum, cough, scratch*.
oxymoron	Apparent paradox achieved by the juxtaposition of words that seem to contradict one another. Examples: *jumbo shrimp, random order*.
palindrome	A word spelled the same forward as backward. Examples: *radar, kayak*.
plural	More than one, often (but not always) indicated with the letter *s* at the end of a word. Examples: *stars, dogs, boxes, geese, mice*.
paradox	An assertion seemingly opposed to common sense but that may have some truth in it.
person	A segment of discourse that pertains to the speaker (first person), to the one spoken to (second person), or the one spoken of (third person).
portmanteau	A word created by blending two words together to form a new word that is related to both of the original words. Example: *brunch = breakfast + lunch*.
possessive	A grammatical case that denotes ownership or a relation analogous to ownership. Example: *owner's manual*. Examples of possessive pronouns: *hers, his, my, mine, your, yours, our, ours, their, theirs, its, whose*.
predicate	The part of a sentence or clause that expresses what is said of the subject and that usually consists of a verb with or without objects, complements, or adverbial modifiers. The predicate excludes the subject itself.
preposition	A (usually small) word that combines with a noun, pronoun, or noun equivalent to form a prepositional phrase that modifies part of the sentence. Examples: *after, at, before, by, for, with*.

prepositional phrase	A phrase that starts with a preposition. *With a preposition* is a prepositional phrase.
pronoun	A word that is used as a substitute for a noun or noun equivalent, takes noun constructions, and refers to persons or things named or understood in the context. Examples: *I, you, he, she, it, we, they, me, him, her, us, them.*
simile	An explicit comparison between two things using *like* or *as*. Example: "Let us go then, you and I, /While the evening is spread out against the sky/ Like a patient etherized upon a table...."—T. S. Eliot, "The Love Song of J. Alfred Prufrock"
subject	The part of a sentence that indicates what acts upon the verb. It is always a noun, pronoun, or noun clause. For example, *Skiing* is the subject of the sentence "Skiing is one of my favorite activities."
superlative	The degree of grammatical comparison that denotes an extreme or unsurpassed level or extent, denoted usually by an *–est* ending. Examples: *best, worst, fastest, smartest.*
tautology	Repetition of an idea in a different word, phrase, or sentence. Example: "Cease and desist that activity."
transitive verb	A verb that can act upon an object. One might say that a transitive verb is one that is object oriented. Examples: *see, buy* (I *saw my friend* when I *bought a bagel.*).
verb	A word that expresses an action, occurrence, or mode of being. It is the grammatical center of a predicate. For example, *make* is a verb in the sentence "It is possible to make a verb out of any noun."

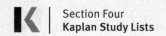
-OLOGIES

TERM	THE STUDY OF ...
alology	algae
anthropology	human beings
apiology	bees
archeology	remains of past human life and activities
axiology	values and value judgments (e.g., ethics)
bacteriology	bacteria
biology	life and living organisms
cartology	maps and mapmaking
cetology	whales
conchology	shells
cosmology	nature and origin of the universe
cryptology	codes and ciphers
cytology	the cell and its functions
deontology	ethics
enology	wines and wine making
entomology	insects
epistemology	the nature, grounds, and limits of knowledge
eschatology	the end of the world
ethology	animal behavior in the wild
etiology	causes of phenomena
etymology	the origins of words
geology	the earth and its history
gerontology	aging and problems of the aged
graphology	handwriting
hagiology	saints and revered persons
herpetology	reptiles and amphibians
hippology	horses
histology	living tissue
horology	measurement of time
hydrology	water

ichthyology	fishes
kinesiology	principles of human movement
limnology	fresh waters
mammalogy	mammals
meteorology	climate and weather
morphology	structure and forms of plants and animals
mycology	fungi
myrmecology	ants
nephology	clouds
numismatology	coins
oncology	tumors
ontology	nature of existence
ophiology	snakes
opthalmology	structure, function, and diseases of the eye
ornithology	birds
otology	ears
paleontology	fossils
pathology	diseases
pedology	children
petrology	rocks
philology	language, speech, linguistics, and literature
physiology	functions and activities of living organisms
pyrology	fire
seismology	earthquakes
speleology	caves
teleology	final causes or purpose in nature
teratology	malformations or serious deviations from the norm in organisms; monsters and monstrosities
thanatology	death and dying
virology	viruses
vulcanology	volcanos
zoology	animals

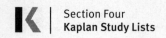

FOREIGN PHRASES

FOREIGN PHRASE	MEANING
a posteriori	based on inductive reasoning
a priori	based on deductive reasoning
ad hoc	for a specific purpose
alter ego	a second self
amicus curiae	friend of the court
beau geste	noble gesture
bête noire	someone or something particularly disliked; literally, "black beast"
bon mot	witty remark or comment; literally, "good word"
bona fide	in good faith; genuine
carpe diem	seize the day
carte blanche	unrestricted power; literally, "blank document"
casus beli	pretext for war
caveat emptor	let the buyer beware
corpus delicti	body of the crime; substantial fact necessary to prove the commission of a crime
de facto	actual
de jure	by right; technically true
deus ex machina	contrived device to resolve a situation; literally, "god from a machine"
dies irae	day of wrath; Judgment Day
dolce vita	the sweet life; a life of indulgence
ecce homo	behold the man
ex cathedra	by virtue of one's office
ex parte	from a partisan point of view
ex post facto	after the fact; retroactively
fait accompli	an accomplished fact; a done deed
faux pas	social blunder; literally, a "false step"
hoi polloi	the common people
idée fixe	obsession; literally, "fixed idea"
in camera	in private; secretly
in extremis	near death

in loco parentis	in the place of a parent
in vino veritas	in wine there is truth
ipso facto	by the fact itself; as an inevitable result
joie de vivre	joy of living; buoyant enjoyment of life
mea culpa	I am to blame
memento mori	a reminder that you must die
modus operandi	method of operating
mot juste	the appropriate word
nolo contendere	no contest
non sequitur	something that does not logically follow
nota bene	note well
persona non grata	unwelcome person
prima facie	on the face of it
pro bono	free of charge; literally, "for good"
pro forma	done as a matter of form; perfunctory
quid pro quo	an equal exchange; literally, "this for that"
quo vadis	where are you going
rara avis	rare bird; an unusual specimen
sangfroid	self-possession or equanimity, especially under strain; literally, "cold blood"
schadenfreude	enjoyment obtained from the troubles of others; literally, "harm joy"
sic transit gloria mundi	thus passes away the glory of the world
sine qua non	something indispensible; literally, "without which not"
sui generis	one of a kind
tabula rasa	a blank slate
tout le monde	all the world; everyone of importance
veni, vidi, vici	I came, I saw, I conquered
vox populi	voice of the people
weltanschauung	a comprehensive apprehension of the world; literally, "world view"
weltschmerz	sorrow over the evils of the world; literally, "world pain"

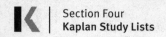
IRREGULAR PLURALS

SINGULAR	PLURAL
alga	algae
alumna	alumnae
alumnus	alumni
analysis	analyses
antenna	antennae
bacillus	bacilli
basis	bases
cactus	cacti
calf	calves
cherub	cherubim
child	children
cod	cod
corps	corps
corpus	corpora
crisis	crises
criterion	criteria
curriculum	curricula
datum	data
deer	deer
desideratum	desiderata
diagnosis	diagnoses
die	dice
elf	elves
elk	elk
erratum	errata
fauna	faunae
fish	fish
flora	florae
foot	feet
fungus	fungi

genus	genera
goose	geese
grouse	grouse
hake	hake
half	halves
hypothesis	hypotheses
knife	knives
larva	larvae
leaf	leaves
life	lives
loaf	loaves
louse	lice
magus	magi
man	men
memorandum	memoranda
metamorphosis	metamorphoses
millennium	millennia
moose	moose
mouse	mice
nebula	nebulae
neurosis	neuroses
nucleus	nuclei
oasis	oases
offspring	offspring
ox	oxen
passerby	passersby
phenomenon	phenomena
radius	radii
roe	roe
salmon	salmon
self	selves
seraph	seraphim
series	series

sheaf	sheaves
sheep	sheep
shelf	shelves
son-in-law	sons-in-law
species	species
stimulus	stimuli
stratum	strata
swine	swine
thesis	theses
thief	thieves
trout	trout
wife	wives
wildebeest	wildebeest
wolf	wolves
woman	women

CHAPTER QUIZ: SPECIALIZED VOCABULARY STUDY LISTS

Note that some of the analogies in this set feature grammar and wordplay bridges. Review chapter 3 if you find these challenging.

1. ETHOLOGY : PALEONTOLOGY :: (a. wild animals, b. ethics, c. ear, nose, and throat, d. linguistics) : FOSSILS

2. STOP : POTS :: CANOE : (a. ocean, b. rack, c. paddle, d. float)

3. SPECIES : SPECIE :: NEWS : (a. cast, b. sewn, c. new, d. capsule)

4. REGAL : DELIVER :: LAGER : (a. pizza, b. soldier, c. reviled, d. crown)

5. BREAKFAST : LUNCH :: SMOKE : (a. fire, b. cigarette, c. chimney, d. fog)

6. ALUMNA : ALUMNUS :: (a. albumin, b. alumina, c. alumnae, d. aluminum) : ALUMNI

7. CHERUB: CHERUBIM :: MOOSE : (a. angel, b. moose c. mouse, d. seraph)

8. ONOMATOPOEIA : BUZZ :: (a. palindrome, b. oxymoron, c. dipthong, d. paradox) : RACECAR

9. AMICUS CURIAE : (a. resurrection, b. friend of the court, c. seize the day, d. let the buyer beware) :: DE FACTO : ACTUAL

10. GERRYMANDER : LON NOL :: (a. politician, b. puzzle, c. portmanteau, d. pundit) : PALINDROME

11. DOG : NOUN :: AFTER : (a. preposition, b. dead pan, c. hit and miss, d. kitchen sink)

12. PRO BONO : PRO FORMA :: FREEBIE : (a. formidable, b. formality, c. genuine, d. secret)

13. EX POST FACTO : NON SEQUITUR :: MOT JUSTE : (a. sangfroid, b. ipso facto, c. weltanschauung, d. cassus belli)

14. ALOLOGY : CETOLOGY :: (a. anthropology, b. myrmecology, c. vulcanology, d. zoology) : HIPPOLOGY

15. PEDOLOGY : OOLOGY :: GERONTOLOGY : (a. ornithology, b. palaeontology, c, virology, d. ophiology)

16. MAGUS : PASSERBY :: MAGI : (a. passerbys, b. passerbies, c. passerbyes, d. passersby)

17. RONALD REAGAN : MICHAEL MOORE :: WIDE-EYED WONDER : (a. dancing stars, b. pitter patter, c. ploughshare, d. garden of luxury)

18. CYTOLOGY: CELLS :: (a. conchology, b. eschatology, c. hagiology, d. numismatology) :: COINS

19. GRAPHOLOGY : PYROLOGY :: HANDWRITING : (a. fire, b. pencil, c. underwriter, d. principles)

20. ENTOMOLOGY : ETYMOLOGY :: INSECTS : (a. elephants, b. beetles, c. bones, d. words)

21. CARTE BLANCHE : TABULA RASA :: (a. unexplored territory , b. social blunder, c. unrestricted power, d. new moon) : CLEAN SLATE

22. IN CAMERA : PERSONA NON GRATA :: (a. false, b. mysterious, c. hidden, d. exposed) : INVITED

23. GOOSE : GEESE :: GROUSE : (a. grease, b. gander, c. gale, d. grouse)

24. LIVES : LIFE :: (a. dead, b. dice, c. dyed, d. dies) : DIE

25. SAINTS : SHELLS :: HAGIOLOGY : (a. shellacology, b. nautilology, c. conchology, d. podology)

Answers

1. **(a)** Paleontology is the study of fossils and ethology is the study of animal behavior in the wild.

2. **(a)** Stop and pots are anagrams of each other, as are canoe and ocean.

3. **(c)** Species and news are words that look like plural of other words (specie and new, respectively), but aren't.

4. **(c)** Lager is regal spelled backward, and reviled is deliver spelled backward.

5. **(d)** Breakfast and lunch form the portmanteau word *brunch*, and smoke and fog form the portmanteau word *smog*.

6. **(c)** Alumnae is the plural of alumna, while alumni is the plural of alumnus.

7. **(b)** The plural of cherub is cherubim, while the plural of moose is moose.

8. **(a)** Buzz is an example of onomatopoeia, while racecar is an example of a palindrome.

9. **(b)** *Amicus curiae* means "friend of the court" and *de facto* means "actual."

10. **(c)** Lon Nol was a Cambodian politician whose name is a palindrome, and gerrymander is a portmanteau (Governor Elbridge Gerry + salamander).

11. **(a)** The word "dog" is an example of a noun, while the word "after" is an example of a preposition.

12. **(b)** Something done *pro bono* is done free of charge (literally, "for the good"), while something done *pro forma* is done as a formality, without any true meaning or substance.

13. **(a)** *Ex post facto* ("after the fact") and *non sequitur* ("something that does not logically follow") are expressions derived from Latin, while *mot juste* ("appropriate word") and *sangfroid* ("self-possession") are derived from French.

14. **(b)** This analogy references the size of the creatures—small or large—being studied: algae (alology) and ants (myrmecology) as opposed to whales (cetology) and horses (hippology).

15. **(a)** This analogy references the age of the subjects under study: pedology is the study of children, and gerontology, the study of the elderly, while oology is the study of eggs and ornithology, the study of birds.

16. **(d)** The plural of magus is magi, and the plural of passerby is passersby.

17. **(b)** Ronald Reagan and Michael Moore are alliterative names. Wide-eyed wonder and pitter patter are alliterative expressions.

18. **(d)** Cytology is the study of living cells, while numismatology is the study of coins.

19. **(a)** Graphology is the study of handwriting, while pyrology is the study of fire.

20. **(d)** Entomology is the study of insects, while etymology, a word with which is it sometimes confused, is the study of words.

21. **(c)** *Carte blanche* is an expression that means "unrestricted power," while *tabula rasa* means "clean slate."

22. **(d)** *In camera*, a Latin expression meaning "secret or in private," is opposite to "exposed"; "persona non grata," or "unwelcome person," is the opposite of "invited."

23. **(d)** The plural of goose is geese, and the plural of grouse is grouse.

24. **(b)** Lives is the plural of life, and dice is the plural of die.

25. **(c)** Hagiology is the study of saints and conchology is the study of shells.

CHAPTER TEN

Humanities Study Lists

LITERARY TERMS

TERM	DEFINITION
allegory	Written piece in which ideas or morals are represented by individual characters or things.
allusion	A reference within an artistic work to another artistic work.
antagonist	In a literary work, the character whose actions oppose those of the hero (protagonist).
ballad	A story-poem, often sung aloud.
Beat movement	A group of American poets and artists whose expressions of alienation in the 1950s became a calling card of the underground. (Ginsberg, Kerouac)
blank verse	Nonrhyming verse consisting of 10-syllable lines.
canto	A subdivision of an epic poem.
Classicism	Artistic or literary movement that is aesthetically based on the Ancient Greeks or Romans.
climax	The point in any story at which the action reaches its zenith.
couplet	Two rhyming lines of poetry in succession, most often of a similar or like meter.
denouement	The conclusion or resolution following the climax of a story.
elegy	A poem of remembrance.
Existentialism	French philosophical idea that the individual lives in an indifferent world and must take responsibility for his or her own choices. (Sartre, Camus)
fable	An allegorical story often employing animals as characters. (Aesop)

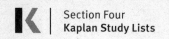

genre	A category of work within art or letters, usually of a distinctive style.
haiku	A Japanese poem containing 3 lines and 17 syllables in a structured order (5-7-5).
irony	A literary style in which a situation is shown with the intent of representing its opposite.
lost generation	A group of expatriate writers and artists in Paris in the 1920s centered around Gertrude Stein. (Hemingway, Fitzgerald)
metaphor	The comparison of two things in which one item represents another.
Modernism	High intellectual movement whose goal was the examination of pure art. (Pound, Stein, Woolf)
motif	A recurring element or theme in an artistic work.
ode	A lyric poem of rigidly structured stanzas.
parable	A story depicting a message of a moral or religious nature.
pathos	Evoking pity in a literary work.
Realism	An artistic and literary style in which society and events are depicted as they appear in real life.
Restoration	The period of intensely active literary and artistic activity in England 1660–1688 when Charles II returned to the throne. (Dryden)
Romantic movement	Predominately English movement in the 19th century whose basic belief was that passion should supercede logic and whose main opposition was Classicism. (Keats, Wordsworth, Coleridge, Byron)
satire	A literary work in which, through the use of irony, sarcasm and wit, the absurd in humanity is brought to light. (Swift's *A Modest Proposal*)
sonnet	A verse of 14 lines and written in one of several rhyme schemes. (Shakespeare, Petrarch)
stanza	One division within a poem, usually of commonly metered verse.
stream of consciousness	A literary device in which a character's thoughts emerge on the page as they occur. (Joyce, Woolf)
Transcendentalism	American movement in which insight and experience took precedence over logic and reason and that held the belief that all things coexist in nature. (Thoreau, Emerson)
Victorian Age	Nineteenth-century England, considered the height of the British industrial revolution and the apex of the British Empire. Characterized by rigid social manners and conservativism. (Dickens, Hardy)

MAJOR LITERARY FIGURES

Aeschylus (525–456 B.C.E.): Ancient Greek dramatist who specialized in tragedies, among them *Prometheus Bound*.

Aesop (c. 620–560 B.C.E.): Ancient Greek fabulist whose allegorical fables have inspired many writers.

Aligheri, Dante (1265–1321): Early Renaissance Italian writer who is called the father of modern literature. His *Divine Comedy* is one of literature's great triumphs.

Anderson, Sherwood (1876–1941): American short-story writer whose most famous collection is *Winesburg, Ohio*.

Austen, Jane (1775–1817): Nineteenth-century English author whose novels include *Sense and Sensibility*, *Pride and Prejudice*, and *Emma*.

Balzac, Honoré de (1799–1850): Early 19th-century French writer best known for his series *La Comédie Humaine*.

Beckett, Samuel (1906–1989): Irish-born French novelist and playwright whose Existentialist works include *Malloy* and *Waiting for Godot*.

Bellow, Saul (1915–2005): American novelist awarded the Nobel Prize in Literature in 1976. His works include the novels *Herzog* and *Humboldt's Gift*.

Blake, William (1757–1827): British artist, poet, and engraver who wrote *Songs of Innocence and Experience*.

Brontë, Charlotte (1816–1855): English novelist, sister to Emily, who wrote under the pen name Currer Bell. Best known for the novels *Jane Eyre* and *Shirley*.

Brontë, Emily (1818–1848): One of three literary sisters, this English novelist wrote under the pen name Ellis Bell. Her novel *Wuthering Heights* is considered one of the great Romantic novels.

Bunyan, John (1628–1688): English preacher and writer of allegorical stories, most famously *The Pilgrim's Progess*.

Byron, Lord George (1788–1824): Prominent Romantic poet known for his adventurous life and writings. Important works include *Don Juan* and *Childe Harold's Pilgrimage*.

Camus, Albert (1913–1960): French writer and Existentialist best known for his novels *The Stranger* and *The Plague*.

Carroll, Lewis (Charles Dodgson) (1832–1898): Prominent British writer, mathematician, and artist, Carroll wrote the classic children's tales *Alice In Wonderland* and *Through the Looking Glass*.

Cervantes, Miguel de (1547–1616): Spanish writer whose book *Don Quixote* is considered the first modern novel.

Chaucer, Geoffrey (c. 1340–1400): Early English poet who wrote the influential *The Canterbury Tales*.

Chekhov, Anton Pavlovich (1860–1904): Late 19th- and early 20th-century Russian playwright and short-story writer who wrote *The Seagull* and *The Cherry Orchard*.

Coleridge, Samuel Taylor (1772–1834): One of the first English Romantics, widely remembered for "The Rime of the Ancient Mariner." Together with William Wordsworth, he published *Lyrical Ballads* in 1798.

Colette, Sidonie-Gabrielle (1873–1954): Late 19th-century French female author who published the Claudine novels as well as *The Innocent Wife*.

Conrad, Joseph (1857–1924): Polish-born British writer whose most famous books are the novella *Heart of Darkness* and the novel *Under Western Eyes*.

Crane, Stephen (1871–1900): American author of the Civil War novel *Red Badge of Courage*.

Dickens, Charles (1812–1870): English writer immensely popular with his Victorian audience. A contemporary of Thomas Hardy. Some important works are *A Tale of Two Cities*, *Great Expectations,* and *A Christmas Carol*.

Dickinson, Emily (1830–1886): One of American's great 19th-century poets whose emotional poems were never published in her lifetime.

Donne, John (1572–1631): English writer, essayist, and religious scholar considered the greatest of the metaphysical poets due to his highly original poems, including "The Flea" and "Death Be Not Proud."

Dostoevsky, Fyodor (1821–1881): Prominent Russian novelist whose major works include *Crime and Punishment* and *The Idiot*.

Dreiser, Theodore (1871–1945): American writer of the naturalist school whose novels include *Sister Carrie* and *An American Tragedy*.

Eliot, George (Mary Ann Evans) (1819–1880): Victorian English female novelist who wrote the realist novels *Middlemarch* and *Adam Bede*.

Eliot, T. S. (1888–1965): American-born British Modernist poet who wrote the poems "The Waste Land" and "The Love Song of J. Alfred Prufrock."

Emerson, Ralph Waldo (1803–1882): Important American Transcendentalist writer and philosopher. The mentor of Thoreau, he wrote the essay "Nature."

Euripedes (c. 480–406 B.C.E.): Along with Sophocles and Aeschylus, a preeminent Ancient Greek dramatist.

Faulkner, William (1897–1962): Acclaimed American Southern novelist had a major influence on contemporary literature. Some major works include *The Sound and The Fury*, *Absolom! Absolom!,* and *As I Lay Dying*.

Fitzgerald, F. Scott (1896–1940): One of the 20th century's literary stars, his writing chronicled the Jazz Age. His novel *The Great Gatsby* is considered an American masterpiece.

Flaubert, Gustave (1821–1880): French writer who coined the phrase *le mot juste* (the perfect word) and had a notoriously meticulous style. His masterpiece is *Madame Bovary*.

Frost, Robert (1874–1963): Popular American poet of the 20th century who penned such notable poems as "Stopping by Woods on a Snowy Evening" and "Mending Wall."

Ginsberg, Allen (1926–1997): American Beat poet and active political figure who became the face of a generation's underground. Perhaps his most famous work is the collection *Howl*.

Goethe, Johann Wolfgang von (1749–1832): Prominent German writer, critic, and scientist who is most famous for his classic *Faust*.

Hammett, Dashiell (1894–1961): Popular American writer of noir, or detective, fiction. Many of his novels, including *Maltese Falcon* and *The Thin Man,* became successful movies.

Hardy, Thomas (1840–1928): One of the great English writers of the 19th century, his popular novels include *Far From the Madding Crowd* and *Tess of the D'Urbervilles.*

Hawthorne, Nathaniel (1804–1864): Important 19th-century American writer who wrote celebrated novels and short stories, including *The Scarlet Letter* and "The Minister's Black Veil."

Hemingway, Ernest (1899–1961): Holds a place as one of America's most influential writers due to a terse style he honed as a journalist. Best known among his works are the novels *The Sun Also Rises* and *A Farewell to Arms.*

Hesse, Hermann (1877–1962): Swiss-born German writer who wrote often about the duality of life. His novels include *Siddhartha* and *Steppenwolf.*

Homer (c. 850 B.C.E.): Ancient Greek writer sometimes called the father of literature. His epics *Iliad* and *Odyssey* are two of history's most important achievements.

Hughes, Langston (1902–1967): Twentieth-century African American poet, novelist, and playwright who helped shape the Harlem Renaissance. Famous poems include "Weary Blues," "Mother to Son," "Harlem," and "Theme for English B."

Hugo, Victor (1802–1885): Prominent Victorian French novelist who wrote *Les Misérables.*

James, Henry (1843–1916): Expatriate American writer and critic at the turn of the 19th century whose novels include *The Turn of the Screw* and *Daisy Miller.*

Johnson, Samuel (1709–1784): The leading thinker of his era, this English writer wrote the first modern dictionary in 1755.

Joyce, James (1882–1941): Irish author is one of the towering figures of modern literature due to his groundbreaking narratives, shown most spectacularly in the novels *Ulysses* and *Finnegans Wake.*

Kafka, Franz (1883–1924): German existentialist novelist who penned the classic *The Metamorphosis.*

Keats, John (1795–1821): English Romantic poet who wrote "Ode to a Nightingale" and "Ode on a Grecian Urn," among many others.

Kerouac, Jack (1922–1969): American Beat poet and novelist and voice of the counterculture who wrote *On the Road.*

Longfellow, Henry Wadsworth (1807–1882): Popular 19th-century American Romantic poet who wrote "Songs of Hiawatha."

Marlowe, Christopher (1564–1593): English playwright was Shakespeare's contemporary and is often thought to have influenced him greatly. He wrote *Tamburlaine the Great* as well as *Dr. Faustus.*

Melville, Herman (1819–1891): One of the greatest American novelists, his works include the masterpiece *Moby Dick* and the short story "Bartleby the Scrivener."

Miller, Arthur (1915–2005): Acclaimed 20th-century American playwright who wrote many Pulitzer Prize-winning plays, including *Death of a Salesman* and *The Crucible.*

Miller, Henry (1891–1980): Twentieth-century American writer who wrote several controversial works, including *Tropic of Cancer.*

Milton, John (1608–1674): Considered one of the great English-language poets. An outspoken essayist during the Reformation, his major works include *Paradise Lost* and *Paradise Regained.*

Molière, Jean-Baptiste Poquelin (1622–1673): French playwright and actor who helped define modern theater with such acclaimed plays as *Tartuffe* and *The Misanthrope.*

Morrison, Toni (1931–): Contemporary African American novelist whose fiction is widely acclaimed, she won the Nobel Prize in 1993. Her major works include *Beloved* and *Song of Solomon.*

Nabokov, Vladimir (1899–1977): Russian American writer and essayist who is probably best known for his controversial novel *Lolita* and its effete protagonist Humbert Humbert.

O'Neill, Eugene (1888–1953): Twentieth-century playwright widely thought to be America's greatest dramatist. His major works include *Desire Under the Elms, The Hairy Ape,* and *The Iceman Cometh.*

Orwell, George (Eric Blair) (1903–1950): English author who penned the satirical political novels *1984* and *Animal Farm.* Also known for his critical works and essays.

Ovid (43 B.C.E.–17 C.E.): Roman poet whose poems, including the crucial *Metamorphoses,* were a major source of inspiration for Renaissance and Baroque writers.

Petrarch (1304–1374): Renaissance Italian poet whose love poems and writings were widely translated and had great influence on 16th- and 17th-century British writers.

Plath, Sylvia (1932–1963): American poet and novelist of the confessional school whose tempestuous life was the subject of many of her poems. The author of "Daddy" and the novel *The Bell Jar* committed suicide in 1963.

Plutarch (c. 46–120): Greek essayist and biographer whose monumental tome, *The Parallel Lives,* influenced many scholars and writers, including Shakespeare.

Poe, Edgar Allan (1809–1849): One of 19th-century America's greatest writers and forefather of the modern horror genre. His works include the poem "The Raven" and the stories "The Tell-tale Heart" and "The Cask of Amontillado."

Pound, Ezra (1885–1972): American-born poet and editor (of poet T. S. Eliot and others) who typified the Modernist movement.

Proust, Marcel (1871–1922): French novelist who wrote complex novels and stories, among which is the series of books that make up *Remembrance of Things Past.*

Rushdie, Salman (1947–): British novelist most notable for the death sentence imposed on him by the Ayatollah Khomeini, who thought his novel *The Satanic Verses* to be blasphemous.

Sappho (c. 620 B.C.E.): Greek female poet of whose work little remains today except fragments of love poems.

Scott, Sir Walter (1771–1832): Scottish novelist whose historical novels were extremely popular. His most famous work is *Ivanhoe.*

Shakespeare, William (1564–1616): Considered the master of playwrights in the English language, Shakespeare has influenced much of modern literature from poetry to tragedy. Just a few of his major works include *Romeo and Juliet, Othello, Hamlet, Macbeth,* and *King Lear.*

Shaw, George Bernard (1856–1950): Irish playwright and Nobel Prize winner wrote many notable plays, including *Pygmalion* and *Saint Joan.*

Shelley, Percy Bysshe (1792–1822): English poet during the Romantic movement who was also the husband of writer Mary Shelley (*Frankenstein*). A vocal social critic, he published the great lyrical drama *Prometheus Unbound.*

Sophocles (c. 496–406 B.C.E.): Greek dramatist who, along with Aeschylus and Euripides, wrote some of the greatest Greek tragedies. His classic *Oedipus Rex* is among the greatest plays ever written.

Spenser, Edmund (1552–1599): A master of the epic poem and friend of prominent British statesmen, Spenser is best known for his elegant *The Faerie Queen.*

Stein, Gertrude (1874–1946): An American writer who lived most of her life in Paris in the 1920s, coining the term "lost generation" in reference to her fellow expatriate writers (including Hemingway and Fitzgerald).

Steinbeck, John (1902–1968): Twentieth-century American novelist whose stories often centered around the plight of the worker. He was awarded the Nobel Prize in 1962, and his novels include *The Grapes of Wrath* and *East of Eden.*

Stevenson, Robert Louis (1850–1894): English writer of the 19th century who wrote such well-known novels as *Treasure Island* and *The Strange Case of Dr. Jekyll and Mr. Hyde.*

Swift, Jonathan (1667–1745): Irish-born English writer who is widely acknowledged as one of the world's great satirists. He published the classic *Gulliver's Travels* and the widely acclaimed satire "A Modest Proposal."

Thoreau, Henry David (1817–1862): Nineteenth-century American thinker and essayist who, along with his mentor Ralph Waldo Emerson, championed the Transcendentalist movement. His book *Walden* is a classic text in Western thought.

Tolstoy, Count Leo (1828–1910): Prominent Russian novelist and philosopher who wrote some of the world's most famous novels, including *War and Peace* and *Anna Karenina.*

Twain, Mark (Samuel Clemens) (1835–1910): One of America's greatest 19th-century writers and humorists whose novels, including *Huckleberry Finn* and *Tom Sawyer,* are considered classics of American literature.

Updike, John (1932–2009): Contemporary American novelist who wrote many popular novels, including *Rabbit, Run* and *Bech at Bay.*

Virgil (Vergil) (70–19 B.C.E.): Roman poet who wrote the epic *Aeneid.*

Voltaire (1694–1778): Important 18th-century French philosopher and author whose achievements helped shape the Age of Enlightenment. Principal among his work is the masterpiece *Candide.*

Walker, Alice (1944–   ): African American novelist who wrote *The Color Purple.*

Whitman, Walt (1819–1892): One of the greatest American poets, whose seminal collection, *Leaves of Grass*, is still considered among the greatest of American poetical works.

Wilde, Oscar (1854–1900): Controversial Irish writer whose works included *The Importance of Being Earnest* and *Salomé.*

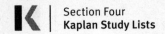

Williams, Tennessee (1914–1983): Major American playwright from the South who wrote, among others, *A Streetcar Named Desire* and *The Glass Menagerie.*

Woolf, Virginia (1882–1941): British novelist and a major influence in modern fiction, her unconventional stream-of-consciousness style has influenced many writers. Among her most well-known works are *To the Lighthouse* and *Mrs. Dalloway.*

Wordsworth, William (1770–1850): Poet of the English Romantic movement who, along with Coleridge, published the seminal *Lyrical Ballads.*

Yeats, William Butler (1865–1939): Irish playwright and poet who penned *The Winding Stair.*

Zola, Emile (1840–1902): French writer and essayist from the naturalist school whose most famous work is "J'Accuse," an article decrying the French government's role in the Dreyfus Affair.

MYTHOLOGICAL FIGURES

NAME	ROLE
Aphrodite	Greek goddess of love. Roman counterpart is **Venus**.
Apollo	Greek sun god. Roman counterpart is **Apollo**.
Ares	Greek god of war. Roman counterpart is **Mars**.
Artemis	Greek goddess of the hunt, wild animals, and chastity. Roman counterpart is **Diana**.
Athena	Greek warrior goddess. Goddess of wisdom. Roman counterpart is **Minerva**.
Calliope	Greek muse of epic poetry and eloquence.
Centaurs	Half-man, half-horse creatures of Greek myth.
Clio	Greek muse of history.
Dionysus	Greek god of wine and pleasure. Roman counterpart is **Bacchus**.
Erato	Greek muse of love poetry.
Euterpe	Greek muse of music.
Frigg (Frija)	Norse goddess of love and marriage. Wife of **Odin**. *Friday* is based on her name.
Griffin	Mythical beast that is part lion, part eagle.
Hades	Greek god of the underworld. Roman counterpart is **Pluto**.
Helen	Famed Greek beauty whose "face launched a thousand ships." Also known as "Helen of Troy." Was kidnapped by **Paris** to start the Trojan War.
Hera	Greek goddess of marriage and maternity. **Zeus**'s wife. Roman counterpart is **Juno**.
Heracles	Greek hero who personified strength. Completed the Twelve Labors of Heracles. Roman counterpart is **Hercules**.
Hermes	Greek god of travellers, commerce, and profit. Messenger of the gods. Roman counterpart is **Mercury**.
Loki	Norse god of mischief.
Melpomene	Greek muse of tragedy.
Muses	Greek goddesses of memory and poetic inspiration.
Odin	Supreme god of Norse mythology. *Wednesday* is based on his name.
Perseus	Greek hero who rode the winged horse **Pegasus**. Slew **Medusa**, the snake-headed gorgon.
Polyhymnia	Greek muse of sacred poetry, sacred music, and pantomime.
Poseidon	Greek god of the sea. Roman counterpart is **Neptune**.
Prometheus	Greek titan who lived on Olympus. Stole fire from the gods and gave it to humans.
Satyrs	Half-man, half-goat creatures associated with **Dionysus**, indulgence, and sensuality.

Sirens	Sea monsters with women's heads. Sirens' songs lured sailors and travellers to their deaths.
Terpsichore	Greek muse of lyric poetry and dance.
Thalia	Greek muse of comedy.
Theseus	Greek hero who slayed the **Minotaur of Crete** in the Labyrinth.
Thor	Norse god of thunder. *Thursday* is based on his name.
Tiw (Tyr)	Norse god of war. *Tuesday* is based on his name.
Urania	Greek muse of astronomy.
Valkyries	Norse superwomen who served the gods in Valhalla. Tremendous warriors.
Zeus	Supreme god of Greek mythology. Roman counterpart is **Jupiter.**

RELIGIOUS TERMS

TERM	DEFINITION
apostate	One who abandons his or her religious loyalty.
apostle	One of an authoritative New Testament group sent forth by Christ to preach the gospel.
Bhagavad Gita	A sacred book of Hinduism.
Brahmin	Highest of Hindu castes reserved for priests, spiritual leaders, etc.
Buddhism	Faith centered around achieving enlightenment. Based on the teachings of the Buddha, Siddhartha Gotama. Its main tenet is that life is suffering. Through meditative practice, one can escape Samsara (the Wheel of Suffering) and achieve a state of Nirvana (spiritual enlightenment).
Christianity	Monotheistic faith based on the teachings of Jesus Christ in which there are three aspects of a single divinity: God the Father, Jesus Christ, and the Holy Spirit. These three aspects comprise the Trinity. The Christian Bible is split into the Old Testament and New Testament (including the four books of the Gospel).
Confucianism	System of codes and ethics originating under Confucius. Religion centers around individuals understanding and fulfilling their roles within society.
disciple	One who accepts and assists in the spreading of doctrines of another.
Episcopalianism	Protestant faith that recognizes the Church of England.
heathen	An unconverted member of a people or nation that does not acknowledge the God of the Bible.
Hinduism	Polytheistic religion based primarily in South Asia. Known for its use of the caste system.
infidel	An unbeliever in respect to a particular religion.
Islam	Faith based on the teachings of the prophet Muhammad. Monotheistic worship of Allah centers around the holy cities of Mecca and Medina.
John Calvin	Founder of Calvinism, a strict Protestant faith centered around the concept of predestination.
Judaism	Monotheistic religion based on the Torah (Old Testament) and the Talmud texts.
Koran	The holy book of Islam.
Martin Luther	Founder of Lutheran faith. Began the Reformation with his posting of The Ninety-Five Theses on the church door in Wittenberg, Germany.
pagan	A follower of a polytheistic religion.
pagoda	A Far Eastern tower generally erected as a temple or memorial.
pariah	Outcasts or "untouchables" comprising the lowest of the Hindu castes.

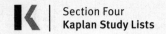

predestination   Belief that those who will achieve Salvation are a select few who are preordained prior to birth.

Presbyterianism Protestant faith that originated in Scotland.

proselytize   To attempt to convert others to a faith or religion.

Shintoism   Japanese religion based on the polytheistic worship of nature and ancestors.

Taoism   Pantheistic religion and philosophy originating in China focused on principles that allow people to live in harmony with the natural order. Founded by Lao-tzu.

HISTORICAL TERMS

TERM	DEFINITION
abolitionism	The movement to abolish slavery in the United States.
Allies	Nations that united against the Germans, Italians, and Japanese (Axis) forces during World War II. Mainly comprised of the United States, England, and France. Russia joined later.
apartheid	A former policy of South Africa in which the races were separated by law.
Axis	Nations opposed to the Allies during World War II, including Germany, Italy, and Japan.
Balfour Declaration	Great Britain's 1917 proclamation supporting the establishment of a separate homeland for Jews in Palestine.
blitzkrieg	"Lightning war" in which surprise attacks by aircraft are immediately followed by massive attacks by ground forces, as in Hitler's 1939 invasion of Poland.
bourgeoisie	According to Marx and Engels, the middle class; in prerevolutionary France, a portion of the Third Estate comprised of a middle class of artisans and merchants.
caste	One of the four hereditary classes of society in Hinduism.
Code of Hammurabi	Babylonian legal code that established governmental responsibility for criminal justice.
Cold War	Long-term period of poor relations between the United States and the Soviet Bloc from the end of World War II until the early 1990s.
colony	A territory under direct control of a stronger country.
communism	Economic system in which the workers (the proletariat) control the means of production.
Communist Manifesto	Seminal work by Karl Marx and Friedrich Engel in which the basic principles of communism are outlined.
Constitution	The U.S. Constitution, "the law of the land," was drafted in 1787 and ratified in 1789.
Cultural Revolution	Campaign carried out by the Chinese Red Guards 1966–1976 with the goal of revitalizing the Chinese Communist Party and consolidating Mao Zedong's leadership.
cuneiform	Sumerian system of writing.
Cyrillic alphabet	The alphabet of the Russian language and other Slavic languages.
czar (or tsar)	A Russian emperor.
Declaration of Independence	Written by Thomas Jefferson in 1776, this document proclaimed the American colonies' independence from Great Britain.
détente	A cooling of Cold War tensions initiated during the administrations of Nixon and Brezhnev.

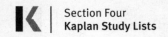
diaspora	The scattering of specific ethnic groups throughout various parts of the world.
dictator	A sole ruler with absolute power.
domino theory	An idea prevalent during the Cold War that if one nation fell to communism, neighboring nations would likewise fall.
Five-Year Plans	Economic plans to increase industrial and agricultural productivity in the Soviet Union, China, and India.
Fourteen Points	Post–World War I peace plan proposed by Woodrow Wilson; major points included the principle of self-determination and the establishment of an association of nations.
Geneva Conference	Conference held in 1954 that divided Vietnam at the 17th parallel.
glasnost	A Soviet policy introduced in 1985 by Mikhail Gorbechev emphasizing "openness" in the sharing of information and ideas.
Gulf of Tonkin Resolution	Resolution passed by the U.S. Congress in 1964 authorizing President Johnson to send troops into Vietnam.
hieroglyphics	Ancient Egyptian picture writing.
Huns	A nomadic group from central Asia who undertook a mass migration to the Roman Empire in the 400s C.E.
imperialism	The political, economic, or social domination of a strong nation over another nation or territory.
laissez-faire capitalism	Economic system in which no governmental regulation of the market is advocated.
Lend-Lease Act	A policy passed by the U.S. Congress in 1941 allowing President Roosevelt to give arms and other supplies to any nation considered vital to the security of the United States.
Magna Carta	Document drafted in 1215 that specifies English political and civil liberties. It forms the basis of English common law.
Manhattan Project	The U.S. plan to develop an atomic bomb during World War II.
Manifest Destiny	Belief first articulated in the mid-1800s that it was the destiny of the United States to continue to expand to the west and the Pacific Ocean.
Marshall Plan	Plan put forth by U.S. Secretary of State George C. Marshall describing how to rebuild Europe after the conclusion of World War II.
NATO (North Atlantic Treaty Organization)	A 1949 defense alliance initiated by the United States, Canada, and 10 Western European nations.
New Deal	Set of domestic programs set forth by FDR's administration to help the United States overcome the Great Depression.
Prussia	Old name for current-day Germany. Ruled by Frederick the Great at its height of power.

republic	Government in which citizens are ruled by elected representatives.
suffrage	The right or privilege of voting; franchise.
teetotaler	One pledged to abstinence from all intoxicating drinks.
totalitarianism	One-party political system with the goal of supporting the welfare of the state above all else.
Versailles	Palace near Paris that was the seat of power for many French kings, including Louis XIV. Also the site of the Treaty of Versailles, which marked the conclusion of World War I.
Warsaw Pact	A 1955 defense alliance organized by the Soviet Union and several Eastern European nations.
Waterloo	Site where Napoleon suffered his greatest defeat.
Yalta	Island where Churchill, Roosevelt, and Stalin met to discuss the partitioning of Europe at the conclusion of World War II.

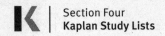

HISTORICAL TERMS: U.S. CONSTITUTION AND BILL OF RIGHTS

TERM	DEFINITION
Anti-Federalists	Name given to those figures critical of the 1787 Constitution because they objected to a stronger U.S. government, which they believed would weaken the sovereignty and prestige of the individual states. The Bill of Rights was crafted in response to their criticisms.
Anti-Federalist Papers	The name given to the loose collection of writings, dating from after the first draft of the U.S Constitution, by those opposed to the firmer union of states envisioned by that draft.
Articles of Confederation	The agreement between the original thirteen states, ratified in 1781. Due to concerns that it created an overly weak federal government, it was superseded by the U.S. Constitution in 1789.
Bill of Rights	The collective name for the United States Constitution's first ten amendments, which list specific rights and limit the power of Congress: created September 25, 1789, and ratified December 15, 1791.
Connecticut (or Great) Compromise of 1787	The name for the agreement, narrowly accepted by the Constitutional Convention, that resolved the debate between large and small states over representation in the new government. It outlined the House of Representatives (with proportional representation) and Senate (with two representatives for each state).
Delaware	The first state to ratify the U.S. Constitution, by unanimous vote, on December 7, 1787.
Federalist Papers	The collection of writings by Alexander Hamilton, John Jay, and James Madison, under the pseudonym Publius, that promoted ratification of the U.S. Constitution without a Bill of Rights. Published as a collection in 1788.
Alexander Hamilton	The first Secretary of the United States Treasury, founder of the Federalist Party, and chief author of the Federalist Papers.
Patrick Henry	Prominent revolutionary orator and Anti-Federalist.
Incorporation	The process by which portions of the Bill of Rights, originally intended only to limit federal government powers, have been applied to state governments by the U.S. Supreme Court.
John Jay	First chief justice of the United States Supreme Court, and delegate to the First and Second Continental Congresses. One of the pseudonymous authors of the Federalist Papers.
James Madison	A founding father who played a pivotal role in drafting both the U.S. Constitution and the Bill of Rights, and one of the authors of the Federalist Papers, who later became the 4th President of the United States.
Marbury v. Madison (decided 1803)	U.S. Supreme Court ruling that held that Congress cannot pass laws contrary to the Constitution, and that the role of the judicial system includes interpreting what the Constitution permits. It is the basis for the exercise of judicial review under Article III of the U.S. Constitution.

Massachusetts Compromise	The compromise that led to the inclusion of the Bill of Rights in the Constitution.
National Archives, Washington, D.C.	The agency of the United States Government responsible for preserving government and historical documents, including the copy of the Bill of Rights retained by the First Congress.
Philadelphia, Pennsylvania	Site of the Constitutional Convention, May 25–September 17, 1787, where the U.S. Constitution was drafted.
1st Amendment	Constitutional amendment establishing the freedoms of religion, speech, and the press. Ratified 1791.
2nd Amendment	Constitutional amendment establishing the right to bear arms. Ratified 1791.
4th Amendment	Constitutional amendment prohibiting unreasonable search and seizure. Ratified 1791.
5th Amendment	Constitutional amendment protecting rights of life, liberty, and property, guaranteeing due process, and protecting against double jeopardy. Ratified 1791.
8th Amendment	Constitutional amendment protecting against cruel and unusual punishment. Ratified 1791.
13th Amendment	Constitutional amendment abolishing slavery. Ratified 1865.
14th Amendment	Constitutional amendment protecting the rights of former slaves. Ratified 1868.
15th Amendment	Constitutional amendment granting African American men the right to vote. Ratified 1870.
18th Amendment	Constitutional amendment prohibiting the sale and consumption of alcohol. Ratified 1919.
19th Amendment	Constitutional amendment granting women the right to vote. Ratified 1920.
21st Amendment	Constitutional amendment repealing the 18th Amendment. Ratified 1933.

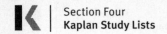
HISTORICAL FIGURES

Anthony, Susan B. (1820–1906): American leader of the suffrage movement to grant women the right to vote.

Bolívar, Simón (1783–1830): South and Central American general and liberator. Liberated Venezuela, Panama, Colombia, Ecuador, Bolivia and Peru from Spanish rule in the 19th century.

Castro, Fidel (1926–): Cuban Communist revolutionary and dictator.

Churchill, Winston (1874–1965): British Prime Minister during World War II.

Cromwell, Oliver (1599–1658): British general, member of Parliament, and revolutionary who ruled as Lord Protector without a king during the mid-1600s.

Davis, Jefferson (1808–1889): President of the Confederacy during the U.S. Civil War.

Douglass, Frederick (1817–1895): Perhaps the foremost African American abolitionist.

Gandhi, Mohandas K. (Mohatma) (1869–1948): Indian leader who achieved independence for India from the British through an organized campaign of nonviolent resistance and civil disobedience.

Garrison, William Lloyd (1805–1879): Noted American abolitionist.

Grant, Ulysses S. (1822–1885): U.S. president after being general of the Union forces during the U.S. Civil War.

Guevara, Che (1928–1967): Famous communist revolutionary in South and Central America.

Henry VIII (1491–1547): British monarch who began the Church of England in the 16th century.

Jefferson, Thomas (1743–1826): U.S. president and author of the Declaration of Independence in 1776.

Kennedy, John F. (1917–1963): U.S. president during the Cuban Missile Crisis and the beginning of the Civil Rights Movement. Assassinated by Lee Harvey Oswald.

Lee, Robert E. (1807–1870): The most successful general of the Confederate forces during the U.S. Civil War.

Lenin, Vladimir (1870–1924): Leader of the Russian Revolution of 1917. First leader of the Soviet Union. Bolshevik and Communist.

Lincoln, Abraham (1809–1865): U.S. president who governed during the U.S. Civil War. Issued the Emancipation Proclamation. Was assassinated by John Wilkes Booth.

Louis XIV (1638–1715): Known also as the "Sun King." His rule represents the height of the French monarchy at Versailles. He was an absolute monarch who claimed to rule by Divine Right.

Louis XVI (1754–1793): French monarch who ruled until the French Revolution.

Mao Tse-Tung (or Zedong) (1893–1976): Chinese revolutionary who established communism in mainland China.

Marx, Karl (1818–1883): Philosopher who first articulated the economic principles of communism.

Napoleon Bonaparte (1769–1821): Emperor who ruled France and much of Europe following the French Revolution. Nearly conquered Europe but waged an unsuccessful campaign in Russia and two years later lost a key battle at Waterloo.

Nation, Carry (1846–1911): Leader of the temperance movement (banning alcohol).

Robespierre, Maximilien (1758–1794): French revolutionary who ruled brutally during the early years of the French Revolution.

Roosevelt, Franklin Delano (1882–1945): U.S. president elected to four terms of office. President during the New Deal and the bulk of World War II.

Smith, Adam (1723–1790): British economist and author. Wrote *The Wealth of Nations* (1776), which outlines the basic ideas of free-market (laissez-faire) capitalism.

Stalin, Joseph (1879–1953): Soviet leader during World War II and the Cold War years that followed.

Stanton, Elizabeth Cady (1815–1902): American leader of the women's rights movement.

Washington, Booker T. (1856–1915): Important African American spokesperson and scholar of the late 19th and early 20th centuries.

Washington, George (1732–1799): First U.S. president and general of the American Colonies' revolutionary army.

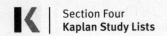

PHILOSOPHY TERMS

TERM	DEFINITION
empiricism	Belief that all knowledge is derived from experience.
existentialism	The belief that existence only acquires value and meaning through active reflection on one's own existence.
idealism	Belief that the so-called external world exists first and foremost in the perceiver's mind.
logical positivism	Belief that a concept is meaningful only if it can be empirically verified.
neoplatonism	Rebirth of Platonic thought in Europe from C.E. 250–1250. Incorporated the ideas of Aristotle, Pythagoras, and others into the teachings of Plato.
rationalism	Belief that the world can be known through reason alone.
tabula rasa	Belief put forth by John Locke that the human mind begins as a blank slate.
utilitarianism	System of ethics based on maximizing the collective good.

PHILOSOPHY FIGURES

Aquinas, St. Thomas (1225–1274): Thirteenth-century Christian philosopher. Wrote "The Five Ways," which outlined five proofs for the existence of God.

Aristotle (384–322 B.C.E.): Plato's student who criticized the theory of Forms and developed a systematized logic.

Augustine of Hippo (354–430): Fourth- and 5th-century bishop, philosopher, and neoplatonist.

Berkeley, George (1685–1753): Irish idealist philosopher who viewed mental representations and impressions as fundamental.

Descartes, René (1596–1650): Important French rationalist philosopher and mathematician. Saw mind and body as distinct (Cartesian dualism). He is also famous for the quote "I think, therefore I am."

Hegel, Georg Wilhelm Friedrich (1770–1831): German idealist philosopher known for his theory of dialectic: "The thesis combines with the antithesis to form the synthesis of the two." Also known for his teleological orientation.

Heidegger, Martin (1889–1976): German philosopher who had a major influence on existentialism.

Hobbes, Thomas (1588–1679): British materialist philosopher who viewed human existence as "nasty, brutish, and short."

Hume, David (1711–1776): Scottish empiricist philosopher. Questioned the necessity of the connection between cause and effect.

Husserl, Edmund (1859–1938): German philosopher known as the father of phenomenology.

James, William (1842–1910): American empiricist philosopher and psychologist. Known for his description of the flow of ideas as a "stream of consciousness."

Kant, Immanuel (1724–1804): German idealist philosopher best known for the "categorical imperative," which states that a moral agent acts only in ways that could become universal laws.

Kierkegaard, Søren (1813–1855): Danish existentialist philosopher.

Leibnitz, Gottfried Wilhelm von (1646–1716): German rationalist philosopher and mathematician.

Locke, John (1632–1704): English empiricist philosopher who put forth many of the basic ideas of empiricism, including *tabula rasa*. Important figure in the Age of Enlightenment.

Mill, John Stuart (1806–1873): English empiricist philosopher known for his ethical writings on Utilitarianism.

Nietzsche, Friedrich (1844–1900): German philosopher best known for his concept of the *Ubermensch* (superman).

Occam, William of (c. 1285–c. 1349): Fourteenth-century English philosopher who developed the notion of "parsimony." According to Occam's Razor, simpler explanations are preferable to more complex ones.

Pascal, Blaise (1623–1662): French philosopher, mathematician, and theologian best known for "Pascal's Bargain," which argues for belief in the existence of God.

Plato (c. 427–347 B.C.E.): Greek philosopher who studied under Socrates and developed a theory of Forms in which things in this world are mere reflections or shadows of objects of knowledge, which are universals. His writings form the basis of much of Western philosophy.

Pythagoras (c. 570–c. 495 B.C.E.): Pre-Socratic philosopher and mathematician.

Rousseau, Jean Jaqcues (1712–1778): French Romantic philosopher and philosopher of education.

Russell, Bertrand (1872–1970): British philosopher and linguist.

Ryle, Gilbert (1900–1976): British philosopher of language and logical positivist.

Sartre, Jean Paul (1905–1980): French existentialist philosopher.

Socrates (c. 470–399 B.C.E.): Greek philosopher whose oral teachings were transcribed in part by his student, Plato.

St. Anselm of Canterbury (c. 1033–1109): Christian philosopher. Developed an ontological argument for the existence of God.

Wittgenstein, Ludwig (1889–1951): Austrian philosopher who began as a logical positivist and later developed important ideas in the philosophy of language.

ART TERMS AND MOVEMENTS

TERM	DEFINITION
Abstract Expressionism	Twentieth-century American movement based on nonfigurative, dramatic expressiveness. (Pollock, Rothko)
Art Deco	Art and architecture style of the 1920s and 1930s that used abstraction, distortion, and simplification, particularly geometric shapes and highly intense colors. Examples of art deco style include the Chrysler Building.
Art Nouveau	Early 20th-century art movement that emphasized nature in art and often featured floral motifs.
Baroque	Heavily stylized movement prominent in Europe in the late 16th to early 18th centuries characterized by lavish ornamentation.
Bauhaus	Important architecture and design school in the early 20th century that emphasized many geometrical motifs. (Klee, Kandinsky)
Classicism	Art of or in the style of ancient Greek and Roman art.
Cubism	Early 20th-century artistic movement predicated on the fragmentation of reality; a direct reaction to Impressionism. (Picasso)
Dada	Absurdist movement of the early 20th century. (Duchamp)
Futurism	Early 20th-century Italian art movement that emphasized the machine as art.
Gothic	Architectural style of the 12th through 16th centuries characterized by elaborate arches and stained glass. Examples of gothic style include Notre Dame in Paris.
Impressionism	Late 19th-century French school of art that emphasized the artist's visual impressions over realism. (Monet, Renoir)
lithograph	A print technique in which plates are pressed onto a crayon drawing.
Minimalism	Art movement in late 20th century that stressed cold restraint over emotional expression.
motif	In an artistic work, a recurring theme or element.
Neoclassicism	Late 18th-century art movement that rejected the ornate rococo style and returned to a Greek and Roman model.
performance art	Contemporary theatrical art technique often intended to shock viewers.
pointillism	Artistic style characterized by use of tiny dots of paint that when seen together make up a whole image. (Seurat)

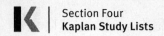
Pop Art (also Op Art)	Contemporary art movement that borrows heavily from popular culture and commercial art sources. (Warhol)
Realism	Nineteenth-century art movement in which reality of vision is emphasized over idealization or romanticization.
Renaissance	Era of renewed interest in the arts and humanities; began in Italy in the 15th century.
Rococo	Eighteenth-century art movement that was typified by playful and intricate design.
Surrealism	Movement begun in the 1920s that sought to show the world through fantastic landscapes and dream imagery. (Magritte, Dali)

WORLD MUSEUMS

MUSEUM	LOCATION
The British Museum	London, England
Frick Collection	New York City, United States
Solomon R. Guggenheim Museum	New York City, United States
Hagia Sophia	Istanbul, Turkey
Hermitage	St. Petersburg, Russia
The Louvre	Paris, France
The Met (Metropolitan Museum of Art)	New York City, United States
MOMA (Museum of Modern Art)	New York City, United States
Musee d'Orsay	Paris, France
Pergamon	Berlin, Germany
Prado	Madrid, Spain
Rijksmuseum	Amsterdam, Netherlands
The Tate Britain	London, England
The Tate Modern	London, England
Tretyakov	Moscow, Russia
Uffizi	Florence, Italy
Whitney Museum of American Art	New York City, United States

MAJOR ARTISTS

Bosch, Hieronymus (c.1450–1516): Flemish painter of the late 15th and early 16th centuries whose most famous works are *The Garden of Earthly Delights* and *Mocking of Christ*.

Botticelli, Sandro (c.1444–1510): Florentine painter whose work, such as *Fortitude*, is marked by refined figures and brilliant coloring.

Bounarroti, Michelangelo (1475–1564): Sculptor, painter, and architect whose creations typified the Renaissance in Italy. His sculptures, such as *David* and *Pieta*, are internationally recognized. His painting includes the magnificent ceiling of the Sistine Chapel.

Bruegel, Peter (c.1525–1569): Also known as "The Elder," Flemish painter renown for his fantastic landscapes and characters, including *The Fall of the Rebel Angels*.

Calder, Alexander (1898–1976): Mid-20th-century American sculptor best known for his use of mobiles and motorized pieces.

Cassatt, Mary (1844–1926): American artist who specialized in figure painting and etchings. Prominent in her work are several versions of Mother and Child.

Cézanne, Paul (1839–1906): French Post-Impressionist painter who is said to have created a bridge from Impressionism to Cubism.

Chagall, Marc (1887–1985): Russian painter whose work strongly presaged the Surrealist movement. Chagall is also well known for his stained-glass windows and illustrated books.

Dalí, Salvador (1904–1989): Spanish Surrealist painter of the 20th century. Famous for *The Persistence of Memory*.

Degas, Edgar (1834–1917): Late 19th-century French painter and sculptor known for his paintings of ballet dancers and sculptures of horses. Generally thought of as one of the great French artists. His work greatly influenced Toulouse-Lautrec and Picasso, among others.

Donatello (1386–1466): Italian sculptor who made major innovations to art in the 15th century and shaped the Renaissance.

Dürer, Albrecht (1471–1528): German artist whose woodcuts and engravings are among the greatest in history. Major works include *Four Horsemen of the Apocalypse*, a series of woodcuts, and the engraving *Melencolia I*.

Angelico, Fra (c. 1400–1455): Fifteenth-century Florentine monk and painter who supervised or created many of the frescoes in the St. Mark's convent in Florence.

Ernst, Max (1891–1976): German painter of the Dada movement who went on to help shape the Surrealist movement with his collages and paintings, including *Two Children Are Threatened by a Nightingale*.

Gainsborough, Thomas (1727–1788): English painter of portraits and landscapes whose many drawings greatly influenced 19th-century landscape artists.

Gauguin, Paul (1848–1903): French post-Impressionist painter who greatly influenced modern art. Many of his most famous pieces are of life on the islands of Tahiti and Marquesas, including his masterwork *Where do we come from? What are we? Where are we going?*

Gehry, Frank (1929–): Canadian-born modern architect whose groundbreaking designs include the Guggenheim museum in Bilbao, Spain.

Goya, Francisco (1746–1828): Spanish painter generally considered the greatest painter of his era. His portraits and graphic arts pieces can be found in collections the world over.

El Greco (c. 1541–1614): Sixteenth-century Greek painter who settled in Spain and specialized in expressive portraits of nobility and in magnificent cathedral altars.

Hopper, Edward (1882–1967): American painter and engraver well known for his stark street scenes, among the best known of which are *Early Sunday Morning* and the noir *Nighthawks.*

Javacheff, Christo (1935–) and Jeanne-Claude (1935–2009): Married Bulgarian and Moroccan artists whose large-scale Earth pieces (wraps and plastic) are among the biggest art installations ever produced.

Jefferson, Thomas (1743–1826): American political figure and architect. He designed and built Monticello as well as the University of Virginia campus.

Johns, Jasper (1930–): Twentieth-century American painter helped introduce the Pop Art movement as well as carried the torch for Abstract Expressionists. Familiar works include *Beer Cans* and his series of paintings of the American flag.

Kandinsky, Vasily (1866–1944): Russian-born Expressionist painter who helped found the Bauhaus school. Closely associated with Klee.

Klee, Paul (1879–1940): Swiss-born avant-garde Expressionist painter who helped found the Bauhaus school. Closely associated with Kandinsky.

Klimt, Gustav (1862–1918): German Art Nouveau painter best known for *The Kiss.*

Leonardo Da Vinci (1452–1519): A painter, sculptor, engineer, and inventor, Leonardo Da Vinci is a towering figure of the Italian Renaissance. *Madonna of the Rocks* and the world-famous *Mona Lisa* are among his many works.

Manet, Edouard (1832–1883): French painter who had an important influence on the later Impressionist movement. His paintings evoked outrage among critics and viewers when released in the mid-1800s.

Marc, Franz (1880–1916): Emotionally troubled German-born Expressionist painter, whose colorful paintings include *Yellow Cow, Blue Horses.*

Matisse, Henri (1869–1954): One of the great modern artists and a lasting influence on painting. French Fauve artist painted still-life subjects and is widely exhibited at major museums the world over.

Miró, Joan (1893–1983): Surrealist Spanish painter and sculptor best known for his fantastic landscapes.

Monet, Claude (1840–1926): French painter and founder of the Impressionist school. Considered one of the great landscape artists in history and a major influence on modern art. Among his works are the Water Lily paintings.

Moses, Anna Mary ("Grandma") (1860–1961): Immensely popular American artist known for her simple landscapes and views of New England life.

Munch, Edvard (1863–1944): Norwegian painter of Expressonist pieces, including *The Scream.*

O'Keeffe, Georgia (1887–1986): Twentieth-century American painter whose paintings often have a largely southwestern motif. One example is *Cow's Skull, Red, White, and Blue.*

Pei, I. M. (1917–): Postmodern Chinese-American architect who designed, in addition to many prominent skyscrapers, the entrance to the Louvre in Paris and the Rock-and-Roll Hall of Fame in Cleveland.

Picasso, Pablo (1881–1973): Spanish artist who settled in France and whose skill and vision pioneered the course of 20th-century art. He also helped found the Cubist movement. Among the most famous of his many works include *The Three Musicians* and *Guernica.*

Pissarro, Camille (1830–1903): French Impressionist known for painting broad landscapes.

Pollock, Jackson (1912–1956): American artist whose giant canvases and splatter designs characterize the Abstract Expressionist movement.

Rembrandt, Harmenszoon (1606–1669): Seventeenth-century Dutch master whose skill ranks him among the great painters of all time. Among his masterworks are *Anatomy Lesson of Dr. Tulp* and *The Shooting Company of Capt. Frans Banning Cocq.*

Renoir, Pierre (1841–1919): French painter and founder of the Impressionist movement. His paintings, including *Moulin de la Galette* and *Bather*, are widely exhibited throughout the world.

Rubens, Peter Paul (1577–1640): Flemish painter was among the most famous artists of the Baroque era and is known for his pieces *Venus and Adonis* and *The Judgment of Paris*, among many others.

Rodin, Auguste (1840–1917): Late 19th-century French sculptor of many world-famous works of art, including *The Thinker* and *The Kiss.*

Rothko, Mark (1903–1970): Russian-born American painter of the Abstract Expressionist school. A student of Max Weber.

Seurat, George (1859–1891): Late 19th-century painter was a forerunner of the Impressionist movement and created the pointillist style of painting. His masterpiece is the colossal *Un Dimanche à la Grande Jatte.*

Tiffany, Louis Comfort (1848–1933): American craftsman known for his stained-glass pieces.

Van Gogh, Vincent (1853–1890): Nineteenth-century Dutch painter is one of the most recognizable painters in history. His highly post-Impressionistic works, such as *Starry Night* and *The Sunflowers*, are among the most well-known in the world.

Warhol, Andy (1928–1987): Pop artist of the latter half of the 20th century who helped define a modern aesthetic with his movies and with such pieces as his series of Marilyn Monroe silkscreens.

Wright, Frank Lloyd (1867–1959): American considered among the greatest architects of the 20th century. His designs include Fallingwater in Pennsylvania and the Solomon R. Guggenheim Museum in New York City.

MUSICAL TERMS

TERM	DEFINITION
adagio	Slow tempo; a slow movement.
allegro	Fast tempo. Not as fast as presto.
alto	The singing range between tenor and soprano.
andante	Moderate tempo.
aria	A solo song for voice in an opera or oratorio.
baroque	Predominately 17th-century movement characterized by flourish and ornamentation.
bass	Lowest male vocal range.
buffo	An comic operatic bass vocalist.
chord	Two or more notes played simultaneously.
coda	The conclusion; the concluding portion of a musical composition.
concerto	A classical piece written for an orchestra and one or more soloists, most often in three movements.
consonance	Comfort brought about in tone or playing.
contralto	Lowest female vocal range.
crescendo	Gradually become louder; opposite of *diminuendo*.
diminuendo (also decrescendo)	Gradually become softer; opposite of *crescendo*.
dissonance	Discord brought about in tone or playing.
étude	A musical piece written to display of specific talent or technique.
forte	Loud volume.
fortissimo	Extremely loud volume.
grave	Extremely slow and moody.
jazz	Distinctly American form of music with a basis in African American folk traditions.
largo	Extremely slow tempo.
lento	Slower tempo.
libretto	The text of an opera.
madrigal	Musical piece utilizing poetry and stanzas.
mezzo forte	Moderately loud volume.
mezzo piano	Moderately soft volume.

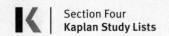

nocturne	A composition, especially for piano, of a slow and dreamy nature.
oratorio	Religious music composed for orchestra, chorus, and soloists.
pianissimo	Exceptionally soft volume.
piano	Soft volume.
polyphony(-ic)	With two or more lines of melody.
presto	Very fast tempo.
rondo	A musical piece of alternating and contrasting themes.
soprano	Highest female vocal range.
sonata	A piece written for more than one soloist and usually consisting of three or more movements.
staccato	The playing or singing of tones or chords marked by short, clear-cut sounds
symphony	A musical composition for full symphony orchestra; an orchestra with full wind and brass accompaniment.
tempo	The pace at which music is played.
tenor	Highest adult male vocal range.
timbre	The quality that allows tones to be discerned from each other.
vivace	Up-tempo and upbeat.

MAJOR MUSICIANS AND COMPOSERS

Bach, Johann Sebastian (1685–1750): Well-known German Baroque composer of *The Brandenberg Concertos* and many pieces for organ.

Beethoven, Ludwig von (1770–1827): Late 18th-, early 19th-century composer is widely considered among the greatest ever. He composed nine symphonies and scores of concertos.

Berlioz, Hector (1803–1869): French composer of innovative pieces, including *Symphonie Fantastique.*

Bernstein, Leonard (1918–1990): Contemporary American composer and conductor who wrote the musical *West Side Story.*

Brahms, Johannes (1833–1897): German composer and pianist well known for his chamber music.

Caruso, Enrico (1873–1921): Popular Italian tenor of the late 19th and early 20th centuries.

Casals, Pablo (1876–1973): Popular 20th-century Spanish cellist.

Chopin, Frederic (1810–1849): Polish music composer of the 19th century known for his piano compositions.

Coltrane, John (1926–1967): American jazz innovator and saxophonist who composed experimental and far-reaching pieces of "bop" jazz.

Copland, Aaron (1900–1990): Twentieth-century American composer who utilized folk and jazz in his compositions, which include *Rodeo* and *Appalachian Spring.*

Davis, Miles (1926–1992): American trumpet player whose free form and experimental style changed jazz music forever.

Debussy, Claude (1862–1918): French Impressionist composer of the late 19th and early 20th centuries.

Dvorak, Antonin (1841–1904): Nineteenth-century Czech composer of symphonies, including *New World Symphony.*

Gershwin, George (1898–1937): Prominent American composer of symphony and jazz music, as well as musicals. Among his most famous compositions are *Porgy and Bess, Rhapsody in Blue,* and *An American in Paris.*

Handel, George Frideric (1685–1759): German Baroque composer of oratorio and other music in the late 17th and early 18th centuries. Handel's *Messiah* is frequently performed.

Liszt, Franz (1811-1886): Nineteenth-century Hungarian composer and virtuoso pianist.

Mozart, Wolfgang Amadeus (1756–1791): Important Austrian composer of the 18th century whose operas (*The Marriage of Figaro* and *The Magic Flute)* and concertos are among the most famous in history.

Parker, Charlie (1920–1955): American saxophonist nicknamed "Bird." One of jazz's true innovators.

Prokofiev, Sergei (1891–1953): Twentieth-century composer who wrote *Peter and the Wolf.*

Puccini, Giacomo (1858–1924): Italian composer of operas, including *La Bohème* and *Madame Butterfly.*

Purcell, Henry (1659–1695): English composer of opera and church music, known for his *Dido and Aeneas.*

Ravel, Maurice (1857–1937): French composer known for nationalistic symphonies. Major work is *Bolero.*

Rodgers, Richard (1902–1979): American composer who worked first with lyricist Lorenz Hart and later with lyricist Oscar Hammerstein on some of 20th century's best-loved musicals, including *The Sound of Music* and *Oklahoma!*

Rossini, Gioacchino (1792–1868): Italian composer of operas, including *The Barber of Seville.*

Schubert, Franz (1797–1828): Nineteenth-century Austrian composer primarily of piano and vocal pieces.

Shostakovich, Dmitri (1906–1974): Russian composer of the 20th century, known for his political motivations.

Sousa, John Phillip (1854–1932): Early 20th-century American band conductor and composer of marches such as the classic *Stars and Stripes Forever.*

Strauss, Johann (1825–1899): Austrian composer known for waltzes such as *The Blue Danube.*

Strauss, Richard (1864–1949): German composer known for his tone poems, operas, and songs (*Lieder*).

Stravinsky, Igor (1882–1971): Russian-born composer is best known for his conducting and for his compositions for ballets.

Suzuki, Shin'ichi (1898–1998): Japanese music educator who promoted learning by repetition as well as by instruction.

Tchaikovsky, Pyotr (1840–1893): Prominent 19th-century Russian composer wrote the ballets *Swan Lake* and *The Nutcracker,* among others.

Verdi, Giuseppe (1813–1901): Italian composer of operas, including *Rigoletto, La Traviata,* and *Aïda.*

Vivaldi, Antonio (1678–1741): Late 17th-early 18th-century composer and violinist who wrote the well-known *The Four Seasons.*

Wagner, Richard (1813–1883): Nineteenth-century German composer whose use of *leitmotif* revolutionized opera. Among his contributions are *Tristan and Isolde* and *Der Ring des Nibelungen.*

CHAPTER QUIZ: HUMANITIES STUDY LISTS

1. SATIRE : IRONY :: FABLE : (a. allusion, b. Aesop, c. allegory, d. genre)

2. 2 : 14 :: (a. pair, b. couplet, c. doubling, d. duet) : SONNET

3. MEMORY : (a. Proust, b. Twain, c. Wilde, d. Voltaire) :: DEATH : POE

4. SAPPHO : BALZAC :: GREEK : (a. French, b. Hungarian, c. Polish, d. Czech)

5. (a. Dryden, b. Cervantes, c. Nabokov, d. Virgil) : MODERN NOVEL :: HOMER : WESTERN LITERATURE

6. GINSBERG : (a. Donne, b. Aeschylus, c. Plutarch, d. Spenser) :: HOWL : THE FAERIE QUEENE

7. THE STRANGER : EXISTENTIALIST :: TESS OF THE D'URBERVILLES : (a. Modernist, b. Restoration, c. Beat, d. Victorian)

8. PRIDE AND PREJUDICE : AUSTEN :: BELOVED : (a. Morrison, b. Bellow, c. Miller, d. Chekhov)

9. CENTAUR : HORSE :: SATYR : (a. dragon, b. lion, c. goat, d. griffin)

10. WINE : LOVE :: DIONYSUS : (a. Athena, b. Aphrodite, c. Minerva, d. Apollo)

11. BHAGAVAD GITA : KORAN :: (a. Hinduism, b. Buddhism, c. Brahmin, d. Taoism) : ISLAM

12. UNCARVED BLOCK : (a. Hinduism, b. Buddhism, c. Confucianism, d. Taoism) :: BREAD AND WINE : CHRISTIANITY

13. XVIII : XIX :: (a. dictator, b. colonialist, c. abolitionist, d. teetotaler) : SUFFRAGIST

14. (a. Fourteen Points, b. New Deal, c. Manifest Destiny, d. Gulf of Tonkin Resolution) : GREAT DEPRESSION :: MARSHALL PLAN : WORLD WAR II

15. ADAM SMITH : LAISSEZ-FAIRE :: KARL MARX : (a. communism, b. imperialism, c. socialism, d. capitalism)

16. KIERKEGAARD : MILL :: (a. idealism, b. existentialism, c. logical positivism, d. rationalism) : UTILITARIANISM

17. KANT : HEGEL :: (a. theory of Forms, b. categorical imperative, c. ubermensch, d. Cartesian dualism) : DIALECTIC

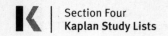
18. CHRYSLER BUILDING : NOTRE DAME :: (a. Art Deco, b. Bauhaus, c. Cubism, d. Futurism) : GOTHIC

19. BERLIN : (a. Pergamon, b. Frick Collection, c. Tretyakov, d. Hagia Sophia) :: MADRID : PRADO

20. BOSCH : (a. Four Horsemen of the Apocalypse, b. The Fall of the Rebel Angels, c. Guernica, d. The Mocking of Christ) :: DALI : THE PERSISTENCE OF MEMORY

21. KLIMT : ART NOUVEAU :: (a. Pissarro, b. Warhol, c. Rothko, d. Angelico) : ABSTRACT EXPRESSIONISM

22. KLEE : KANDINSKY :: MONET : (a. Chagall, b. Renoir, c. Goya, d. Rubens)

23. PRESTO : (a. mezzo, b. allegro, c. largo, d. vivace) :: PIANO : FORTE

24. BACH : BRAHMS :: (a. Verdi, b. Shostakovich, c. Debussy, d. Dvorak) : PUCCINI

25. (a. alto saxophone, b. drums, c. piano, d. vibraphone) : BIRD :: TRUMPET : MILES

Answers

1. **(c)** Satires use irony to communicate its message, and fables use allegory.

2. **(b)** Two lines of poetry are required to compose a couplet, and fourteen lines is the traditional length of a sonnet.

3. **(a)** Memory is one of Marcel Proust's main themes, whereas death is one of Edgar Allan Poe's main themes.

4. **(a)** Sappho wrote in Greek while Balzac wrote in French.

5. **(b)** Literary critics and historians refer to Miguel de Cervantes as the creator of the modern novel and to Homer as the founder of Western literature.

6. **(d)** Allen Ginsberg's most well-known work is *Howl*, and Edmund Spenser's best known work is *The Faerie Queene*.

7. **(d)** Albert Camus's *The Stranger* is a quintessential piece of Existentialist literature, while Thomas Hardy's *Tess of the d'Urbervilles* is a prime work of Victorian literature.

8. **(a)** *Pride and Prejudice* is one of Jane Austen's most famous novels, and *Beloved* is one of Toni Morrison's most famous novels.

9. **(c)** A centaur is half-man and half-horse just as a satyr is half-man and half-goat.

10. **(b)** Wine belongs to the domain of Dionysus, and love falls under the aegis of Aphrodite.

11. **(a)** The Bhagavad Gita is a central religious text of Hinduism, and the Koran is the central religious text of Islam.

12. **(d)** The uncarved block is an integral symbol of the untouched natural order, a principal tenet of Taoism. Bread and wine are fundamental symbols of sacrifice and forgiveness, principal tenets of Christianity.

13. **(d)** The Eighteenth Amendment to the U.S. Constitution was supported by teetotalers, while the Nineteenth Amendment was supported by suffragists.

14. **(b)** The New Deal was the U.S. government's response to the economic damage caused by the Great Depression. The Marshall Plan was the U.S. response to the carnage in Europe caused by World War II.

15. **(a)** Adam Smith advocated an economic system of *laissez-faire* capitalism, whereas Karl Marx advocated communism.

16. **(b)** Soren Kierkegaard's writings explored the philosophy of existentialism, and John Stuart Mill's writings explored the ideas of utilitarianism.

17. **(b)** One of Immanuel Kant's most important contributions to philosophy was the categorical imperative, and one of Hegel's most important contributions was concept of the dialectic, now known as the Hegelian dialectic.

18. **(a)** The Chrysler building exemplifies Art Deco architecture, and the Cathédrale Notre-Dame de Paris exemplifies Gothic architecture.

19. **(a)** Berlin is the location of the Pergamon museum, just as Madrid is the location of the Prado museum.

20. **(d)** One of Hieronymus Bosch's best known paintings is *The Mocking of Christ.* *Similarly,* one of Salvador Dalí's best known paintings is *The Persistence of Memory.*

21. **(c)** Gustav Klimt's paintings exhibit the Art Nouveau style while Mark Rothko's paintings exhibit features of Abstract Expressionism.

22. **(b)** Paul Klee and Vasily Kandinsky were contemporaries who co-founded the Bauhaus school of art. Similarly, Claude Monet and Pierre Renoir were contemporaries of each other and both founders of the Impressionist movement.

23. **(c)** In musical notation, presto and largo are opposite tempos whereas piano and forte are opposite dynamic markings.

24. **(a)** Both Johann Sebastian Bach and Ludwig van Beethoven were German composers, just as both Verdi and Puccini were Italian composers.

25. **(a)** Alto saxophone was the main instrument of Charlie Parker, who often went by the nickname "Bird." Similarly, trumpet was the main instrument of Miles Davis, who often went by simply "Miles."

CHAPTER ELEVEN

Social Sciences Study Lists

EXPLORERS AND DISCOVERERS

Aldrin Jr., Edwin ("Buzz") (1930–): Astronaut and the second man to walk on the moon.

Amundsen, Roald (1872–1928): Explorer known for leading the first successful party to the South Pole.

Armstrong, Neil Alden (1930–2012): Astronaut and first person to walk on the moon. Upon his first step on the moon, Armstrong said, "One small step for man, one giant leap for mankind."

Boone, Colonel Daniel (1734–1820): American pioneer, soldier, and explorer who founded the first U.S. settlement west of the Appalachian mountains.

Byrd, Admiral Richard Evelyn (1888–1957): Arctic and Antarctic explorer, pioneering aviator, and U.S. Naval officer. On May 9, 1926, Byrd (the navigator) and Floyd Bennett (the pilot) made what may have been the first airplane trip over the North Pole in a 15½-hour flight.

Cortés, Hernán (also spelled Cortez) (1485–1547): Spanish adventurer and conquistador (he was also a failed law student) who overthrew the Aztec empire and claimed Mexico for Spain (1519–1521).

da Gama, Vasco (1460–1524): Portuguese explorer who discovered an ocean route from Portugal to the East (India).

Dias, Bartolomeu (1457–1500): Portuguese navigator and explorer who led the first European expedition to sail around Africa's Cape of Good Hope in 1487.

Erik the Red (c. 950–1003): Viking explorer was the first European to sail to Greenland.

Erikson, Leif (c. 980–1020): Viking (Norse) explorer who was possibly the first European to sail to North America. Landed in what is now called Newfoundland (he called this *Vinland*). Ericson sailed around the year 1000.

Gagarin, Colonel Yuri (1934–1968): Soviet cosmonaut and the first human in space.

Glenn, John (1921–): Piloted the first American-manned orbital mission on February 20, 1962.

Hillary, Sir Edmund Percival (1919–2008): Mountain climber, Antarctic explorer, and beekeeper from New Zealand whose expedition was the first to reach the top of Mount Everest on May 29, 1953.

Hudson, Henry (1565–1611): English explorer and navigator who explored parts of the Arctic Ocean and northeastern North America. The Hudson River, Hudson Strait, and Hudson Bay are named for him.

La Salle, René-Robert Cavalier, Sieur de (1643–1687): French explorer who was the first European to travel the length of the Mississippi River (1682).

Lewis, Meriwether (1774–1809) and William Clark (1770–1838): American surveyors who set out in 1804 to explore and map the American West. Lewis and Clark were accompanied by a crew of men and an Indian guide and interpreter, Sacagawea, and her infant son.

Magellan, Ferdinand (1480–1521): Portuguese explorer who led the first expedition that sailed around the earth (1519–1522). Magellan also named the Pacific Ocean.

Peary, Robert Edwin (1856–1920): American explorer and naval officer who led the first expedition to the North Pole in 1909.

Pizarro, Francisco (1478–1541): Spanish conquistador "discovered" the Incan empire and conquered it brutally and quickly, stealing immense hoards of gold, silver, and other treasures.

Polo, Marco (1254–1324): Italian voyager and merchant who was one of the first Europeans to travel across Asia through China, visiting the Kublai Khan in Beijing. He left in 1271 (he was a teenager at the time) with his father (Nicolo Polo) and uncle (Maffeo Polo); they spent about 24 years traveling.

Ponce de Leon, Juan (c. 1460–1521): Spanish explorer and soldier was the first European to set foot in Florida. Ponce de Leon was searching for the legendary fountain of youth and other riches.

Prince Henry the Navigator (1394–1460): Portuguese royal prince, soldier, and patron of explorers. Henry sent many sailing expeditions down Africa's west coast but did not go on them himself.

Scott, Robert Falcon (1868–1912): British explorer who led multiple expeditions to the Antarctic.

Shepard Jr., Alan (1923–1998): Astronaut who piloted America's first manned space mission.

Vespucci, Amerigo (1454–1512): Italian explorer who was the first person to realize that the Americas were separate from the continent of Asia. America was named for him in 1507, when the German mapmaker Martin Waldseemüller printed the first map that used the name *America* for the New World.

ECONOMIC, GEOGRAPHICAL, AND GEOLOGICAL TERMS

TERM	DEFINITION
agriculture	The purposeful tending of crops and livestock in order to produce food.
aquifer	An underground reservoir of water contained within a porous, water-bearing rock layer.
arable	Literally, "cultivable." Land fit for cultivation by one farming method or another.
cartography	The art and science of making maps.
contiguous	A word of some importance to geographers that means to be in contact with, adjoining, or adjacent.
continental drift	The slow movement of continents governed by the processes associated with plate tectonics.
delta alluvial	Lowland at the mouth of a river, formed when the river deposits its alluvial load upon reaching the sea. Often triangular in shape.
desert	An arid area supporting very sparse vegetation, receiving less than 10 inches (25 cm) of precipitation per year. Usually exhibits extremes of heat and cold because the moderating influence of moisture is absent.
equator	Zero degrees latitude, equidistant from the North and South Poles. Equatorial climates are among the warmest on earth.
erosion	A combination of gradational forces that shape the earth's surface landforms. Running water, wind action, and the force of moving ice combine to wear away soil and rock. Human activities often speed erosional processes, such as through the destruction of natural vegetation, careless farming practices, and overgrazing by livestock.
fjord	Narrow, steep-sided, elongated, and inundated coastal valley deepened by glacier ice that has since melted away, leaving the sea to penetrate.
gross national product (GNP)	The total value of all goods and services produced by a country during a given year.
gulf	Body of water surrounded by land on three sides.
high seas	Areas of the oceans away from land, beyond national jurisdiction, open and free for all to use.
infrastructure	The foundations of a society: urban centers; communications; farms; factories; mines; and such facilities as schools, hospitals, postal services, and police and armed forces.
irrigation	The artificial watering of croplands.
isthmus	A comparatively narrow link between larger bodies of land (e.g., Panama).
latitude	Lines of latitude are parallels that are aligned east-west across the globe, from 0 degrees latitude at the equator to 90 degrees north and south latitude at the poles.

longitude	Angular distance (0 degrees to 180 degrees) east or west as measured from the Prime Meridian (0 degrees) that passes through the Greenwich Observatory in suburban London, England.
megalopolis	Term used to designate large, coalescing supercities that are forming in diverse parts of the world (e.g., the eastern seaboard of the United States between Washington, D.C., and Boston).
meridian	Line of longitude, aligned north-south across the globe. Together with parallels of latitude, they form the global grid system.
parallel	An east-west line of latitude that is intersected at right angles by meridians of longitude.
region	A commonly used term and a geographic concept of central importance. An area on the surface of the earth, marked by certain properties.
strait	A comparatively narrow link between larger bodies of water (e.g., Straits of Gibraltar).
tectonic plates	Bonded portions of the earth's mantle and crust. Where they meet, one slides under the other, crumpling the surface crust and producing significant volcanic and earthquake activity. The shifting of these plates plays an important role in the formation of mountains and other geological events.
Tropic of Cancer	23.5 degrees north of the equator.
Tropic of Capricorn	23.5 degrees south of the equator.

PSYCHOLOGY TERMS

TERM	DEFINITION
behaviorism	Psychological school of thought that focuses entirely on observable behaviors. Does not presume the existence of a mind independent of observable behavior.
classical (Pavlovian) conditioning	Form of conditioning first discussed by Russian scientist Ivan Pavlov in which a neutral, conditioned stimulus is paired with an unconditioned stimulus until the conditioned stimulus prompts the same response as the unconditioned stimulus.
collective unconscious	In Jungian psychology, a part of the unconscious mind, shared by a society, a people, or all humankind, that is the product of ancestral experience and contains such concepts as science, religion, and morality.
ego	In Freudian theory, the conscious component of the psyche that attempts to incorporate the urges of the id with the limitations of conscience and the superego.
id	In Freudian theory, the division of the psyche that is totally unconscious and serves as the source of instinctual impulses and demands for immediate satisfaction of primitive needs.
operant conditioning	A form of conditioning in which the operator acts independently and desirable behaviors are reinforced.
phenomenology	A method of inquiry based on inspection of one's own conscious thought processes.
superego	In Freudian theory, the division of the unconscious that is formed through the internalization of moral standards of parents and society; censors and restrains the ego.

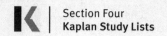
PSYCHOLOGY FIGURES

Adler, Alfred (1870–1937): American psychoanalyst who focused on birth order and feelings of inferiority and superiority as unconscious drives.

Chomsky, Noam (1928–): American philosopher and linguist. Believes in an innate "deep structure" to language.

Freud, Sigmund (1856–1939): Austrian founder of psychoanalytic thought, which presupposes the existence of an unconscious that exists independent of conscious thought.

Jung, Carl (1875–1961): Swiss psychoanalyst who departed from Freud's emphasis on the sexual nature of unconscious thought. Developed theories of personality types and the collective unconscious.

Skinner, B. F. (1904–1990): American behaviorist who believed all behavior could be understood in terms of operant conditioning.

Watson, John Broadus (1878–1958): American psychologist who first developed behaviorist thought.

CHAPTER QUIZ: SOCIAL SCIENCES STUDY LISTS

1. NEIL ARMSTRONG : (a. George Washington, b. Chuck Yeager, c. John Jay, d. King George III) :: BUZZ ALDRIN : JOHN ADAMS

2. (a. river, b. Ferdinand, c. canal, d. Cortés) : SEA :: MAGELLAN : STRAIT

3. ICELAND : ITALY :: LEIF ERIKSON : (a. Henry Hudson, b. Francisco Pizarro, c. Amerigo Vespucci, d. Leonardo da Vinci)

4. (a. Jean Paul Sartre, b. John Broadus Watson, c. Jean Piaget, d. Melanie Klein) : BEHAVIORISM :: SIGMUND FREUD : PSYCHOANALYSIS

5. ISTHMUS : PENINSULA :: FJORD : (a. sea, b. ocean, c. gulf, d. glacier)

6. SACAGAWEA : TALLCHIEF :: (a. actress, b. guide, c. US Senator, d. doctor) : DANCER

7. TROPIC OF CANCER : (a. equator, b. Aurora Australis, c. Tropic of Capricorn, d. Prime Meridian) :: NORTH : SOUTH

8. LATITUDE : LONGITUDE :: (a. Pontianak, Indonesia, b. New York City, New York, c. Bellingshausen Station, Antarctica, d. Cairo, Egypt) : GREENWICH, ENGLAND

9. SEISMOLOGY : CARTOGRAPHY :: EARTHQUAKES : (a. capitals, b. maps, c. tectonic plates, d. aquifers)

10. FRANCE : GERMANY :: VIETNAM : (a. Mauritania, b. China, c. India, d. Thailand)

11. ERIK THE RED : (a. Scotland, b. Iceland, c. Greenland, d. Newfoundland) ::
    LA SALLE : MISSISSIPPI

12. (a. infrastructure, b. megalopolis, c. neighborhood, d. capital) : CITY ::
    FEDERATION : STATE

13. GULLY : (a. river incision, b. glacial striation, c. scarp retreat, d. alluvial delta) ::
    BREAK DOWN : BUILD UP

14. GNP : (a. gross national product, b. Greater New Providence, c. generational
    nutrition parameters, d. generated nuclear power) :: IMF : INTERNATIONAL
    MONETARY FUND

15. CONTIGUOUS : (a. complex, b. pugnacious, c. separate. d. adjoining) ::
    CONGLOMERATION : AGGREGATION

16. PARALLEL : LATITUDE :: (a. strait, b. equator, c. meridian, d. region) : LONGITUDE

17. BYRD : PEARY :: AMUNDSEN : (a. Scott, b. Hillary, c. Drake, d. Franklin)

18. DANIEL BOONE : PRINCE HENRY THE NAVIGATOR :: 1734–1820 : (a. 1254–1324,
    b. 1394–1460, c. 1565–1611, d. 1856–1920)

19. PHENOMENOLOGY : CARTOGRAPHY :: THOUGHTS : (a. rivers, b. beetles, c.
    watches, d. maps)

20. CAPE OF GOOD HOPE : FLORIDA (a. Ferdinand Magellan, b. Gerardus Mercator,
    c. Vasco Da Gama, d. Bartolomeu Dias) : JUAN PONCE DE LEÓN

21. TECTONIC PLATES : EARTHQUAKES :: IMPACT EVENTS : (a. volcanoes, b. shatter
    cones, c. meteorites d. igneous rocks)

22. COLLECTIVE UNCONSCIOUS : DEEP STRUCTURE :: CARL JUNG : (a. Noam
    Chomsky, b. Grace Hopper, c. Ada Lovelace, d. Alfred Adler)

23. MARCO : NICOLO :: (a. Yuan, b. Genghis, c. Kublai, d. Ogedei) : TOLUI

24. AGRICULTURE : FOOD :: DAM : (a. hunting and gathering, b. beaver, c. concrete,
    d. irrigation)

25. LAW : INFRASTRUCTURE :: RULES : (a. society, b. courtroom, c. Congress,
    d. physical facilities)

Answers

1. **(a)** Neil Armstrong and Edwin "Buzz" Aldrin Jr. were the first and second astronauts to walk on the moon, and George Washington and John Adams were the first two presidents of the United States, respectively.

2. **(d)** The Strait of Magellan was named after the explorer Ferdinand Magellan, and the Sea of Cortez was named after the explorer Hernán Cortés.

3. **(c)** Explorer Leif Erikson was born on Iceland, and explorer Amerigo Vespucci was born in Italy. Explorers Henry Hudson and Francisco Pizarro were born in England and Spain respectively, while Italian-born Leonardo da Vinci was not an explorer.

4. **(b)** John B. Watson first developed the psychological theory of behaviorism, while Sigmund Freud founded psychoanalytic thought.

5. **(c)** An isthmus is a narrow piece of land, while a fjord is a narrow body of water. Similarly, a peninsula is a piece of land surrounded by water on three sides, while a gulf is a body of water surrounded by land on three sides.

6. **(b)** Sacagawea is famous for acting as guide for explorers Lewis and Clark, and Maria Tallchief is famous for being the first Native American to hold the rank of prima ballerina.

7. **(c)** The Tropic of Cancer is 23.5 degrees north of the equator, and the Tropic of Capricorn is 23.5 degrees south of the equator.

8. **(a)** A monument marking the equator, or 0 degrees latitude, can be found near the Indonesian city of Pontianak. Similarly, the Prime or Greenwich Meridian, or 0 degrees longitude, passes through the London district of Greenwich.

9. **(b)** Seismology is the science of earthquakes. Cartography is the science of mapmaking.

10. **(b)** France and Germany share a border, and Vietnam and China share a border.

11. **(c)** Erik the Red was the first European to sail to Greenland, while René-Robert Cavelier, Sieur de La Salle, was the first European to sail the length of the Mississippi River.

12. **(b)** A megalopolis is an amalgamation of cities, and a federation is an amalgamation of states.

13. **(d)** A gully erosion is created by running water breaking down landforms, while an alluvial delta is a river formation created by the build-up of water-borne fine-grained sediment.

14. **(a)** Gross National Product is commonly abbreviated as GNP, just as IMF stands for International Monetary Fund.

15. **(d)** Contiguous and adjoining are synonyms, and so are conglomeration and aggregation.

16. **(c)** Parallels are east-west lines of latitude; meridians are north-south lines of longitude.

17. **(a)** Byrd and Peary are both known for exploring the North Pole, while Amundsen and Scott are both known for exploring the South Pole.

18. **(b)** Daniel Boone lived in the years 1734–1820, and Prince Henry the Navigator lived in the years 1394–1460.

19. **(d)** In psychology, phenomenology is the study of one's own thought processes; cartography refers to the study of mapmaking.

20. **(d)** Bartolomeu Dias was the first European to sail around the Cape of Good Hope in southern Africa, and Juan Ponce de León was the first European to set foot in Florida.

21. **(b)** The movement of tectonic plates, segments of the earth's crust and mantle, causes earthquakes, while impact events like meteorites striking the earth's surface can create shatter cones, rare geological features that occur beneath craters.

22. **(a)** Carl Jung developed the theory of the collective unconscious, and Noam Chomsky is a linguist and philosopher associated with the notion of deep structure in language.

23. **(c)** Marco Polo and his father Nicolo Polo were among the first Europeans to travel to China, where they visited Kublai Khan and his father Tolui Khan.

24. **(d)** Agriculture is the cultivation of crops and livestock for food, while dams confine bodies of water for the purposes of irrigation.

25. **(d)** The law is a set of rules that help society function, whereas infrastructure is a set of physical structures, systems, and facilities that help society function.

CHAPTER TWELVE

Natural Sciences and Mathematics Study Lists

GENERAL SCIENCE TERMS

TERM	DEFINITION
allotrope	A substance created when an element combines with itself to become a compound. Examples include O_3 (ozone) and C_6 (diamond).
alloy	A metal that, unlike iron, gold, silver, or aluminum, is a mixture composed of metal elements. Examples include brass (copper with a bit of zinc), bronze (copper and tin with a bit of zinc), pewter (tin with a bit of lead usually), and steel (iron with nickel and titanium).
amber	Petrified sap; many early fossils have been found preserved in amber.
ambergris	A waxy substance found floating in or on the shores of tropical waters; originates in the intestines of the sperm whale.
annual	A plant that grows over only one season; examples include many common flowers such as impatiens, zinnias, and sunflowers.
apiary	A place where bees are kept.
arthropod	A huge animal phylum that includes insects, crustaceans, and arachnids (spiders).
avian	Of or relating to birds.
bryophyta (mosses)	The category of plants that includes all mosses.
Cambrian Period	Part of the Paleozoic Era, the period that began when the oldest easily identifiable fossils first appeared. (544–489 million years ago)
carnivorous	Describing an animal whose principal diet is meat based; examples include cats, birds of prey, sharks, etc.

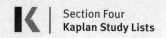

Cenozoic Era   Meaning "recent life," when mammals and flowering plants began to flourish. (65 million years ago to present)

class   A major subdivision of phyla into which organisms are classified. For instance, some of the major classes of chordata (vertebrates) are mammalia (mammals), ave (birds), reptilia (reptiles), and amphibia (amphibians).

compound   Any mixture of elements, such as H_2O (water) and NaCl (salt).

coniferous   Describing cone-bearing trees, such as pines, spruce, and yews, that don't lose their leaves in the winter and usually have needles as leaves.

Cretaceous Period   Part of the Mesozoic Era, the time during which dinosaurs peaked and then died out and mammals and flowering plants first appeared. (144–65 million years ago)

deciduous   Describing trees that lose their leaves in the winter, such as maple, oak, and sycamore.

eon   Great span of time defined by major events.

epoch   Division of geologic time less than a period and greater than an age.

era   Unit of geologic time that includes two or more periods grouped together.

eukaryote   An organism composed of one or more cells containing visibly evident nuclei and organelles. Includes all plants and animals. Compare to *prokaryote*.

eutheria   Also known as "placental." The subclass of mammals that includes most mammals, which bear young live and nourish the fetus with a placenta. This subclass includes dogs, people, bats, and even whales.

family   A subdivision of an order in the classification of living organisms. For instance, under the order of primates, humans are classified into the family of hominidae, which also includes the gorilla, chimpanzee, and orangutan (the great apes).

formicary   Another word for an ant's nest.

genus   A subdivision of a family under the classification of living organisms. For instance, under the order of primates, humans are classified into the genus *Homo*.

granivore   An animal adapted to eating grains and seeds; examples include squirrels, voles, and many bird species.

halogen   Any of the five elements fluorine (F), chlorine (Cl), bromine (Br), iodine (I), and astatine (At) that form part of group VIIA of the periodic table and exist in the free state normally as diatomic molecules.

herbivore   An animal whose principal diet is plant based; examples include deer, antelope, koala bears, rabbits, etc.

igneous rocks   Rocks that solidify from a molten or partially molten state. Examples include basalt and granite.

insectivore   An animal adapted to eating insects. Examples include anteaters, woodpeckers, etc.

Jurassic Period   Part of the Mesozoic Era, the middle period of dinosaur dominance, known as the "age of giants." (213–144 million years ago)

kingdom   The most basic classification unit of living organisms. There are five kingdoms: Plant, Animal, Fungi, Moneran (bacteria, blue-green algae, and primitive pathogens that have prokaryotic cells), and Protista (primitive, animal-like organisms distinguished by method of locomotion).

marsupial   Also known as "metatheria." A form of mammal born without a placenta and therefore nourished in its mother's pouch after birth. Its species include the kangaroo, the koala bear, and the opossum.

Mesozoic Era   Geologic era between the Paleozoic Era to the Cenozoic Era, marked by the rise and fall of the dinosaurs. (248–213 million years ago)

metamorphic rocks   Rocks that have been altered by heat, pressure, and/or the chemical action of fluids and gases. Examples include slate, quartzite, and marble.

metatheria   Also known as "marsupial." A form of mammal born without a placenta and therefore nourished in its mother's pouch after birth. Its species include the kangaroo, the koala bear, and the opossum.

mollusk   Any of a large phylum (Mollusca) of invertebrate animals (including snails, clams, octopi, and squids) with a soft, unsegmented body usually, but not always, enclosed in a shell.

Moneran   One of the basic kingdoms under which living organisms are classified. Includes all prokaryotic organisms, including bacteria, blue-green algae, and primitive pathogens.

monotreme   Also known as "protheria." A strange, primitive form of mammal that reproduces by laying eggs. Found only in Australia, the order comprises platypuses and echidnas.

noble gases   Elements found in the far right-hand side of the periodic table. They can't mix with other elements, so they are also called inert. Examples include argon (Ar), helium (He), krypton (Kr), neon (Ne), and xenon (Xe).

omnivore   An animal adapted to eating both plant and animal matter; examples include humans and other primates, bears, many turtle species, ravens, etc.

order   A subdivision of a class of living organisms. For instance, some of the orders found under the class mammalia eutheria (placental mammals) are primates, rodentia (rodents), and cetacea (whales).

perennial   A plant that has more than one growing cycle and does not need to be replanted; examples include tulips, azaleas, and maple trees.

period   Subdivision of an era marked by evolutionary changes less dramatic than those used to differentiate eras.

phylum   A primary unit of division of a kingdom. For instance, major phyla of the Animal Kingdom include Chordata (vertebrates), Arthropoda (insects, crustaceans, and arachnids), and Mollusca (including, bivalves, snails, octopi, squid, etc.)

piscivore   An animal whose principal diet is fish based; examples include seals, loons, penguins, and many fish species.

pistil   The female reproductive organ of a plant.

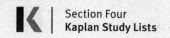

placental	See *eutheria*.
prokaryote	A cellular organism (such as a bacterium or a blue-green algae) that does not have a distinct nucleus (compare to *eukaryote*). Comprises organisms of the Moneran Kingdom only.
protheria	See *monotreme*.
Protista	One of the basic kingdoms under which living organisms are classified. Consists of primitive, animal-like organisms distinguished by method of locomotion.
sedimentary rocks	Rocks that are formed by becoming compacted and cemented over time. Examples include shale, sandstone, and limestone.
species	A subdivision of a genus and the final division of classification for living organisms. For instance, under the genus *Homo*, humans are classified as the species *Homo sapiens*.
stamen	The male reproductive organ of a plant.
tracheophyta (vascular plants)	Plants with water-carrying systems that allow them to live on land solo, unlike mosses. These include most flowering plants.
Triassic Period	Part of the Mesozoic Era, the period when dinosaurs first appeared. (248–213 million years ago)

ALL ABOUT ANIMALS

ANIMAL	BABY NAME	MALE NAME	FEMALE NAME	GROUP NAME	ADJECTIVE
bear	cub	boar	sow	sleuth/sloth	ursine
bee	larva	drone	queen/worker	swarm/hive	apian
cat	kitten	tom	queen	clutter/clowder	feline
cattle	calf	bull	cow	drove/herd	bovine
chimp/monkey	infant	male	female	cartload	simian
crocodile	crocklet	bull	cow	congregation/bask	crocodilian
crow	chick	cock	hen	murder/horde	corvine
dolphin	pup	bull	cow	pod	–
donkey	foal	jack	jenny	herd/drove	asinine
ferret	kit	hob	jill	business	ferrety
fox	kit/cub/pup	dog/todd	vixen	leash/skulk	vulpine
goat	kid	billy	nanny	trip/tribe/flock	goatish
goose	gosling	gander	goose	gaggle	–
horse	foal	stallion/colt	mare/filly	herd	equine
kangaroo	joey	buck/jack	doe/jill	mob/troop	–
lion	cub	lion	lioness	pride	leonine
pig	piglet/shoat	boar	sow	sounder	porcine
porcupine	pup	boar	sow	prickle	–
rabbit	bunny/kitten	buck	doe	nest/warren	rabbity
shark	pup	bull	female	school/shiver	sharklike
sheep	lamb	ram	ewe	flock/drove	ovine
swan	cygnet	cob	pen	bevy/wedge	swanlike

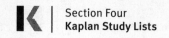
PERIODIC TABLE OF ELEMENTS

Atomic Number ——— 6
Symbol ——— C
Atomic Mass ——— 12.01

* Numbers in parentheses are the *mass numbers* of the most stable isotope of the element.

IA 1																	18
1 **H** 1.008	IIA 2															VIIA	2 **He** 4.003
3 **Li** 6.94	4 **Be** 9.012											13	14	15	16	17	
												5 **B** 10.81	6 **C** 12.01	7 **N** 14.01	8 **O** 16.00	9 **F** 19.00	10 **Ne** 20.18
11 **Na** 22.99	12 **Mg** 24.31	3	4	5	6	7	8	9	10	11	12	13 **Al** 26.98	14 **Si** 28.09	15 **P** 30.97	16 **S** 32.06	17 **Cl** 35.45	18 **Ar** 39.95
19 **K** 39.10	20 **Ca** 40.08	21 **Sc** 44.96	22 **Ti** 47.88	23 **V** 50.94	24 **Cr** 52.00	25 **Mn** 54.94	26 **Fe** 55.85	27 **Co** 58.93	28 **Ni** 58.69	29 **Cu** 63.55	30 **Zn** 65.39	31 **Ga** 69.72	32 **Ge** 72.64	33 **As** 74.92	34 **Se** 78.96	35 **Br** 79.90	36 **Kr** 83.79
37 **Rb** 85.47	38 **Sr** 87.62	39 **Y** 88.91	40 **Zr** 91.22	41 **Nb** 92.91	42 **Mo** 95.96	43 **Tc** (98)	44 **Ru** 101.1	45 **Rh** 102.9	46 **Pd** 106.4	47 **Ag** 107.9	48 **Cd** 112.4	49 **In** 114.8	50 **Sn** 118.7	51 **Sb** 121.8	52 **Te** 127.6	53 **I** 126.9	54 **Xe** 131.3
55 **Cs** 132.9	56 **Ba** 137.3	57–70	71 **Lu** 175.0	72 **Hf** 178.5	73 **Ta** 180.9	74 **W** 183.9	75 **Re** 186.2	76 **Os** 190.2	77 **Ir** 192.2	78 **Pt** 195.1	79 **Au** 197.0	80 **Hg** 200.5	81 **Tl** 204.38	82 **Pb** 207.2	83 **Bi** 209.0	84 **Po** (209)	85 **At** (210)	86 **Rn** (222)
87 **Fr** (223)	88 **Ra** (226)	89–102	103 **Lr** (262)	104 **Rf** (265)	105 **Db** (268)	106 **Sg** (271)	107 **Bh** (270)	108 **Hs** (277)	109 **Mt** (276)	110 **Ds** (281)	111 **Rg** (280)	112 **Cn** (285)	113 **Uut**	114 **Fl** (289)	115 **Uup**	116 **Lv** (293)	117 **Uus**	118 **Uuo**

57 **La** 138.9	58 **Ce** 140.1	59 **Or** 140.9	60 **Nd** 144.2	61 **Pm** (145)	62 **Sm** 150.4	63 **Eu** 152.0	64 **Gd** 157.2	65 **Tb** 158.9	66 **Dy** 162.5	67 **Ho** 164.9	68 **Er** 167.3	69 **Tm** 168.9	70 **Yb** 173.0
89 **Ac** (227)	90 **Th** 232	91 **Pa** 231	92 **U** 238	93 **Np** (237)	94 **Pu** (244)	95 **Am** (243)	96 **Cm** (247)	97 **Bk** (247)	98 **Cf** (251)	99 **Es** (252)	100 **Fm** (257)	101 **Md** (258)	102 **No** (259)

Helium, neon, argon, krypton, xenon, and radon are all **noble**, or **inert**, gases.

Fluorine, chlorine, bromine, iodine, and **astatine** are known as **halogens**—that is, they form part of group VIIA of the periodic table and exist in the free state normally as diatomic molecules.

Hydrogen, the **lightest element** in the periodic table with an atomic weight of 1.0079, is the only nonmetal in the IA group.

Nitrogen, oxygen, and **sulfur** constitute the **"other" nonmetals**. Oxygen and nitrogen both occur naturally as **gases** and make up most of the **atmosphere (nitrogen = 78%, oxygen = 21%)**. Sulfur occurs naturally as a brittle **solid**, is a constituent of proteins, and is used extensively in the chemical and paper industries.

Lithium, sodium, potassium, rubidium, cesium, and **francium** are known as **alkali metals**, a group of univalent, mostly basic metals of group IA of the periodic table.

Magnesium, calcium, strontium, barium, and **radium** constitute that **alkaline earth metals**, a group of bivalent, strongly basic metals of group IIA of the periodic table.

A large group of 29 metallic elements (examples include **chromium**, **iron**, **nickel**, **copper**, **silver**, and **gold**) are called **transition metals**, meaning they have valence electrons in two shells instead of one. Of the transition metals, only **mercury** (Hg) exists naturally as a liquid.

Boron, **carbon**, **silicon**, **germanium**, **arsenic**, **antimony**, **polonium**, and **astatine** constitute the **metalloids**, elements intermediate in properties between the typical metals and nonmetals.

Aluminum, **gallium**, **indium**, **tin**, **thallium**, **lead**, and **bismuth** are called the **"other" metals**. While these elements are ductile and malleable, they are not the same as the transition metals, because they do not exhibit variable oxidation states and their valence electrons are only present in their outer shell.

Thirty elements (examples include **uranium [U]**, which occurs naturally, and **einsteinium [ES]**, which does not) constitute the **rare earth metals**.

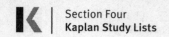
UNITS OF MEASUREMENT

UNIT	DEFINITION
ampere	A measure of electrical current.
Avogadro's number	A unit of relative quantity equal to the number of atoms or molecules per mole of a substance. The currently accepted value is 6.0221415×10^{23} per mole.
avoirdupois	Fancy name for the weight scale based on a pound containing 16 ounces.
baker's dozen	13 units (one more than an ordinary dozen).
barrel	A measure of liquid volume equal in the United States to 31.5 gallons; it's also half a hogshead and one-quarter of a butt.
Beaufort	A scale that measures wind speed; also used for measuring hurricanes.
bit	The smallest unit of information used in computer engineering, equal to one-eighth of a byte.
bolt	A large roll of cloth.
bucket	2 pecks or 16 quarts (dry measure).
bushel	2 buckets or 4 pecks (dry measure).
butt	2 hogsheads or 4 barrels—i.e., 126 gallons (liquid measure).
byte	A unit of information used in computer engineering, equal to 8 bits.
caliber	A measure of the diameter of a bullet or shell.
carat	A jeweler's measure of weight (for diamonds) or purity (for gold).
Celsius	A temperature scale, also called centigrade, that places the freezing point of water at 0° and the boiling point at 100°.
coulomb	A measure of electric charge.
cord	A quantity of logs measuring 128 cubic feet.
cubit	An ancient unit of length equal to about 18 inches.
curie	A unit of radioactivity.
decibel	A customary logarithmic measure most commonly used for measuring sound.
dram	One sixteenth of an ounce.
elite	A unit of type measurement.
Fahrenheit	A temperature scale that places the freezing point of water at 32° and the boiling point at 212°.
fathom	A measure of water depth equal to 6 feet.
flagon	A traditional unit of liquid measurement equal to a gallon.
furlong	Unit of distance equal to 220 yards or one-eighth of a mile.
gill	4 ounces (liquid measure).

grain	One seven-thousandth of a pound.
hectare	A unit of land measurement equal to 2.47 acres.
hertz	Measure of frequency.
hogshead	2 barrels or one-half of a butt—i.e., 63 gallons (liquid measure).
joule	A quantity of energy.
Kelvin	A temperature scale that sets absolute zero (the freezing point of all matter) at 0°; its degrees are equivalent to degrees Celsius + 273.
knot	A measure of speed on the sea.
league	A unit of distance, used nautically, equaling 3 miles or 4.8 kilometers.
ohm	A measure of electrical resistance.
peck	8 quarts or one-quarter of a bushel (dry measure).
pH	A scale that measures whether a substance is an acid or a base. It goes from 0 to 14: 0 is an acid, 14 is a base, and 7 is neutral.
pica	A unit of type measurement.
quintal	A unit of weight equal to 100 kilograms.
Richter	A logarithmic scale that measure tremors, earthquakes, and the like.
rod	16.5 feet or 5.5 yards.
Saffir-Simpson	A scale that measures the intensity (called a category) of an earthquake.
score	A traditional unit of quantity equal to 20.
stone	A unit of weight equal to 14 pounds or 6.4 kilograms.
troy	A weight scale in which, unlike the more common avoirdupois scale, a pound contains only 12 ounces.
volt	A unit of electrical output.
watt	A measurement of power.

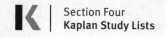

BASIC MATHEMATICAL TERMS AND CONCEPTS

TERM	DEFINITION
absolute value	The magnitude of a number, irrespective of its sign. Written as a number inside vertical lines: $\lvert 3 \rvert = 3$ and $\lvert -3 \rvert = 3$.
acute angle	An angle measuring less than 90°. A triangle with three acute angles is called an acute triangle.
angle	Two line segments coming together at a point called the vertex.
area	A measure, in square units, of the size of a region in a plane. Finding the area of a figure usually involves multiplying two dimensions, such as length and width or base and height. The area of a circle is found by multiplying π by the square of the radius.
composite number	An integer that has more factors than one and itself; i.e., a nonprime integer greater than 1. The first ten composite integers are 4, 6, 8, 9, 10, 12, 14, 15, 16, 18.
complementary angles	Two angles whose measures add up to 90°. A 30° angle and a 60° angle are complementary.
cone	A solid generated by rotating a right triangle about one of its legs; also called right circular cone.
cube	A rectangular solid whose faces are all squares.
edge	A line segment formed by the intersection of two faces of a three-dimensional shape.
dividend	A number to be divided (e.g., in $12 \div 3 = 4$, 12 is the dividend).
divisor	A number that divides into another number (e.g., in $12 \div 3 = 4$, 3 is the divisor).
ellipse	An oval shape, literally a set of points in a plane for which the sum of the distances from two points (called foci) is constant.
equilateral triangle	A triangle with three equal sides and three equal angles of 60°.
even number	An integer that is a multiple of 2. The set of even numbers includes not only 2, 4, 6, etc. but also 0, –2, –4, –6, etc.
face	A polygon formed by edges of a solid.
factor (of n)	A positive integer that divides into n with no remainder (e.g., the complete list of factors of 18 is 1, 2, 3, 6, 9, and 18).
hypotenuse	The side of a right triangle opposite the right angle. Note: The hypotenuse is always the longest side; if c is the hypotenuse and a and b are the legs of the right triangle, $c^2 = a^2 + b^2$.
imaginary number	A number that cannot be represented on the number line because it contains a factor of i, which is $\sqrt{-1}$. Thus, for example, $(3i)^2 = -9$.
integer	Any of the natural numbers (also known as "whole numbers"), the negatives of these numbers, or zero.

isosceles triangle	A triangle with two sides of equal length.
legs	The two sides of a right triangle that are not the hypotenuse (i.e., are not opposite the right angle).
multiple (of *n*)	A number that *n* will divide into with no remainder. Some of the multiples of 18 are 0, 18, 36, 54, 72, and 90.
obtuse	An obtuse angle measures more than 90° and less than 180°. An obtuse triangle is one that has one obtuse angle.
odd number	An integer that is not a multiple of 2. Any integer that is not even is odd.
parallelogram	A quadrilateral with two parallel sides.
perimeter	The sum of the lengths of the sides of a polygon. Two polygons with the same area do not necessarily have the same perimeter.
perpendicular	Intersecting at a right angle. The altitude and base of a triangle are perpendicular.
pi	An irrational number, represented by the symbol π, approximately equal to 3.14, which is equal to the ratio of the circumference of any circle to its diameter. The area of a circle equals πr^2, and the circumference equals $2\pi r$.
power	A product obtained by multiplying a quantity by itself one or more times (e.g., the fifth power of 2 or 2^5 is 32).
prime number	An integer greater than 1 that has no factors other than 1 and itself. The first ten prime numbers are 2, 3, 5, 7, 11, 13, 17, 23, 29, and 31. Notice that 2 is the only even prime number.
product	The result of multiplication (e.g., the product of 3 and 4 is 12).
pyramid	A polyhedron having for its base a polygon and for faces triangles with a common vertex.
Pythagorean theorem	The rule that states, "For any right triangle, the sum of the squares of the legs is equal to the square of the hypotenuse" (or $a^2 + b^2 = c^2$).
quadrilateral	A four-sided polygon. Squares, rectangles, parallelograms, and trapezoids are all quadrilaterals.
quotient	The result of division (e.g., in $12 \div 3 = 4$, 4 is the quotient).
radical	The symbol $\sqrt{}$, which by itself represents the square root. With a little number written in (as in $\sqrt[3]{8}$ = the cube root of 8, or 2), it represents a higher root. By convention, $\sqrt{}$ represents the positive root only.
radius	The length of a line segment connecting the center and a point on a circle. The radius is half the diameter.
real	Having a place on the number line (as opposed to imaginary numbers). For instance, π is a real number because it has a location on the number line (somewhere just to the right of 3.14).
reciprocals	A pair of numbers whose product is 1. To get the reciprocal of a fraction, switch the numerator and denominator (e.g., the reciprocal of $\frac{2}{7}$ is $\frac{7}{2}$).

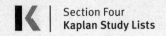

rectangle	A quadrilateral with four right angles. All rectangles are parallelograms, but not all parallelograms are rectangles.
rhombus	A quadrilateral with four equal sides.
right angle	An angle measuring exactly 90°.
root	A number that multiplied by itself a certain number of times will yield the given quantity (e.g., the square root of 4 is 2, and the cube root of 8 is 2).
scalene triangle	A triangle with sides of different lengths. A 3-4-5 triangle is a scalene triangle.
solid	A three-dimensional figure.
supplementary angles	Two angles whose measures add up to 180°.
trapezoid	A quadrilateral with two parallel sides and two nonparallel sides.
torus	A doughnut-shaped surface generated by a circle rotated about an axis in its plane that does not intersect the circle.
volume	The amount of three-dimensional space taken up by a three-dimensional object.

NUMERICAL PREFIXES

PREFIX	MEANING	EXAMPLES
bi-	2 (Latin)	binary, bifocal, bifurcate
cent-	100 (Latin)	centimeter, century, centenary
dec(a)-	10 (Latin, Greek)	decimal, decade, decennial, decahedron
di-/dy-	2 (Greek)	dichotomy, dyad, diatonic
dodec(a)-	12 (Greek)	dodecahedron, dodecathlon
duo-	2 (Latin)	duet, dual, duo
duode(c)-	12 (Latin)	duodecimal, duodecennial
ennea-	9 (Greek)	enneahedron, enneangle, ennead
hecato-	100 (Greek)	hecatogon, hecatohedron
hendec(a)-	11 (Greek)	hendecagon, hendecathlon
hepta-	7 (Greek)	heptagon, heptahedron, heptangle
hexa-	6 (Greek)	hexagon, hexameter, hexahedron
mille-/milli-	1,000 (Latin)	millennium, millimeter
mono-	1 (Greek)	monarch, monotone, monad
nov-/non-	9 (Latin)	novenniel, nonilateral, nonuple
oct-	8 (Latin, Greek)	octopus, octagon, octet
pendca-	15 (Greek)	pendecagon, pendecahedron
penta-	5 (Greek)	pentagon, pentangle, pentahedron
quadr-/quart-	4 (Latin)	quaternary, quadruple, quartet
quatuor-	14 (Greek)	quatuordecimal, quatuordenary
quinde(c)-	15 (Greek)	quindecimal, quinedanry
quinquage-	50 (Latin)	quinquagesimal, quinquagenary
quinque-/quint-	5 (Latin)	quintet, quituple, quinquennial
sep(t)-	7 (Latin)	septennial, September
sesqui-	1.5 (Greek)	sesquicentennial
sex(t)-	6 (Latin)	sextet, sextuple, sexennial
tetra-	4 (Greek)	tetrahedron, tetremeter, tetrathlon
tetra(kai)deca-	14 (Greek)	tetradecagon, tetrakaidecahedron
tri-	3 (Latin, Greek)	tricycle, triangle, trilateral
tride(c)-	13 (Greek)	tridecimal, tridenary
triskaideka-	13 (Greek)	triskaidecahedron, triskaidekaphobia
unde(c)-	11 (Latin)	undecillion, undecennial
uni-	1 (Latin)	unit, unify, unicorn

MAJOR SCIENTISTS, MATHEMATICIANS, AND INVENTORS

Ampère, André-Marie (1775–1836): French teacher and physicist whose name was given to the unit by which we measure electrical current.

Avogadro, Amedeo (1776–1856): Italian scientist after whom is named Avogadro's law, which states, "Equal volumes of different gases, pressure and temperature being equal, contain the same number of molecules." Also came up with Avogadro's number (6.02×10^{23}), which is the number of molecules in one mole of a substance.

Becquerel, Antoine Henri (1852–1908): French physicist who was one of the discoverers of radioactivity.

Bell, Alexander Graham (1847–1922): American inventor of the telephone.

Bernoulli, Daniel (1700–1782): Dutch-born scientist who derived the central formula of fluid dynamics.

Bohr, Niels Henrik David (1885–1962): Danish scientist and major contributor to quantum theory.

Carrier, Willis (1876–1950): American inventor of modern air-conditioning.

Carson, Rachel (1907–1964): Influential 20th-century American environmentalist who wrote *Silent Spring*, a book that is often credited with the launch of the global environmental movement.

Celsius, Anders (1701–1744): Swedish astronomer who devised the Celsius temperature scale, which places 100 degrees between the freezing point (0°C) and boiling point (100° C) of pure water at sea-level air pressure.

Copernicus, Nicolaus (1473–1543): Polish astronomer who founded modern astronomy and declared the sun the center of the solar system (in rejection of the geocentric theory of Ptolomy).

Cray, Seymour (1925–1996): American inventor of the Cray supercomputer.

Curie, Marie (1867–1934) & Pierre (1859–1906): Married French scientists who conducted joint research on radiation phenomena; discovered radium, polonium.

Darwin, Charles (1809–1882): British naturalist who developed a theory of evolution, called natural selection, which was highly supported by real evidence.

Dawkins, Richard (1941–   ): British popularizer of, and contributor to, the theory of evolution, famous for such works as *The Selfish Gene*.

Diesel, Rudolf (1858–1913): German inventor of the internal combustion engine.

Edison, Thomas Alva (1847–1931): American inventor of the lightbulb and the phonograph, among many other important devices.

Einstein, Albert (1879–1955): German-Jewish theoretical physicist who devised the Theory of Relativity and the Electromagnetic Theory of Light.

Euclid (c. 300–275 B.C.E.): Greek mathematician known as "the father of geometry." Wrote *The Elements*, the fundamental textbook of geometry.

Fahrenheit, Daniel Gabriel (1686–1736): German physicist who invented the alcohol thermometer in 1709 and the mercury thermometer in 1714 and, in 1724, introduced the Fahrenheit temperature scale, with a freezing point of 32°F and a boiling point of 212°F.

Faraday, Michael (1791–1867): British experimental physicist, founder of the science of electromagnetism, and inventor of the earliest form of the Bunsen burner.

Farnsworth, Philo T. (1906–1971): American inventor who conceived the basic operating principles of electronic television while still a teenager.

Fermi, Enrico (1901–1954): Italian-American scientist who performed fundamental research into radioactivity, chain reactions, and the H-bomb.

Franklin, Benjamin (1706–1790): American scientist, statesman, and inventor of bifocals and the lightning rod, among many other important devices.

Galen (c. 130–201): Ancient Greek physician who carefully dissected animals and gathered and wrote about all the medical knowledge of his time. First to give a diagnosis by taking a person's pulse.

Galileo (1564–1642): Italian astronomer, mathematician and physicist who used techniques of the scientific method to contribute significantly to physics and astronomy.

Gauss, Carl Friedrich (1777–1855): German mathematician and astronomer who made contributions to number theory.

Gould, Gordon (1920–2005): American inventor of the laser.

Gould, Stephen Jay (1941-2002): American evolutionary biologist and popularizer of evolutionary theory through such works as *Ever Since Darwin* (1977).

Halley, Edmund (1656–1742): British mathematician and astronomer for whom Halley's Comet was named.

Heisenberg, Werner (1901–1976): German physicist who was a founder of quantum mechanics and who formulated the uncertainty principle.

Hertz, Heinrich Rudolf (1857–1894): German-Jewish physicist who conducted pioneering studies on electromagnetic waves. The hertz (SI unit of frequency) is named for him.

Hippocrates (c. 460–377 B.C.E.): Ancient Greek physician, considered the father of medicine, whose ethics formed the basis of the Hippocratic Oath pledged by modern doctors.

Kepler, Johannes (1571–1630): German astronomer, mathematician, and physicist and developer of the laws of planetary motion.

Lamarck, Jean-Baptiste (1744–1829): French naturalist, whose theory of inheritance of acquired characteristics was later refuted by the work of Darwin.

Leakey, Louis (1903-1972): British archaeologist, who, in East Africa, discovered the fossilized remains of a number of "pre-men."

Lister, Joseph (1827–1912): British surgeon who pioneered antiseptic methods.

Marconi, Guglielmo Marchese (1874–1937): Italian inventor of the radio.

Maxwell, James Clerk (1831–1879): Scottish physicist who created a celebrated set of equations for the basic laws of electricity and magnetism.

McClintock, Barbara (1902–1992): American cytogeneticist who discovered moving genetic material known as transposons, or "jumping genes."

Mendel, Gregor Johann (1822–1884): Austrian monk and botanist who proved the existence of dominant and recessive characteristics in living things (Mendelian law), forming the basis of modern genetics.

Mendeleev, Dmitri (1834–1907): Russian chemist; one of two scientists who invented the modern periodic table of elements.

Morse, Samuel F. B. (1791–1872): American inventor who invented the electric telegraph and Morse code.

Newton, Sir Isaac (1642–1727): British mathematician, natural philosopher (physicist), and inventor who was primarily responsible for the mechanistic theory that accounts for the perceivable universe (Law of Universal Gravitation). Independently and simultaneously, he and **Gottfried Wilhelm von Liebnitz** discovered the branch of mathematics known as calculus. Also invented the reflecting telescope.

Nobel, Alfred (1833–1896): Swedish industrialist, engineer, and inventor of dynamite. Bequeathed his wealth to the creation of the Nobel Prize.

Pascal, Blaise (1623–1662): French mathematician and man of letters, credited with the invention of the barometer and certain mathematical formulations that heralded the invention of the differential calculus. Along with **Pierre de Fermat** (1601–1665), cocreated probability theory.

Planck, Max (1858–1947): German theoretical physicist who originated quantum theory and came up with Planck's constant, $h = 6.626 \times 10^{-34}$.

Ptolemy (c. 90–168): Ancient Greek astronomer who developed the geocentric theory of the solar system, which was later rejected by Copernicus.

Röntgen, Wilhelm Conrad (1845–1923): German scientist who discovered X-rays.

Sabin, Albert (1906–1993): Polish-American scientist who developed an oral vaccine against polio.

Salk, Jonas (1914–1995): American scientist who developed the first vaccine against polio.

Tesla, Nikola (1856–1943): Serbian-American inventor and researcher who discovered the rotating magnetic field, the basis of most alternating-current machinery. Colleague and then rival of Thomas Edison.

Volta, Alessandro, Count (1745–1827): Italian physicist who gave name to *volt*, describing a unit of electric pressure; developed the theory of current electricity; invented the electric battery.

Watson, James D. (1928–): American biophysicist who along with **Francis Crick** (1916–2004, British) discovered the structure of the DNA molecule (double helix).

Wegener, Alfred (1880–1930): German originator of the theory of continental drift, which evolved into the theory of tectonic plates.

CHAPTER QUIZ: NATURAL SCIENCES AND MATHEMATICS STUDY LISTS

1. PISTIL : FEMALE:: (a. phylum, b. moneran, c.order, d.stamen) : MALE

2. BIT : ONE :: BYTE : (a. two, b. eight, c. twelve, d. one hundred)

3. CELSIUS : (a. 0, b. 32, c. 100, d. 200) :: FAHRENHEIT : 212

4. (a. Copernicus, b. Euclid, c. Galen, D. Pascal) : DARWIN :: GEOMETRY : EVOLUTION

5. OHM : RESISTANCE :: (a. watt, b. ampere, c. hertz, d. joule) : CURRENT

6. BOAR : SOW :: COCK : (a. bull, b. hen, c. gander, d. colt)

7. ANNUAL : PERENNIAL :: (a. none, b. one, c. most, d. all): MANY

8. ERA : PERIOD :: (a. Cenozoic, b. Cambrian, c. Cretaceous, d. Jurassic) : TRIASSIC

9. (a. carnivore, b. omnivore, c. piscivore, d. herbivore) : GRANIVORE :: PLANT : GRAIN

10. KRYPTON : NOBLE GAS :: (a. chlorine, b. nitrogen, c. hydrogen, d. cesium) : HALOGEN

11. CRETACEOUS : CAMBRIAN :: MESOZOIC : (a. Cenozoic, b. Paleozoic, c. Jurassic, d. Triassic)

12. (a. moneran, b. eukaryote, c. animal, d. mollusca): PHYLUM :: FUNGI : KINGDOM

13. GOAT : BILLY :: GOOSE : (a. gosling, b. gaggle, c. kid, d. gander)

14. BEE : SWARM :: FERRET : (a. skulk, b. business, c. herd, d. clutter)

15. ALKALI : ALKALINE EARTH :: (a. lithium, b. radium, c. barium, d. hydrogen): MAGNESIUM

16. RABBIT : SHARK :: (a. lamb, b. shoat, c. joey, d. bunny) : PUP

17. SIMIAN : CHIMPANZEE :: (a. apian, b. ursine, c. bovine, d. corvine) : BEE

18. FEMALE : MALE :: (a. horse, b. foal, c. mare, d. equine) : STALLION

19. ARGON : CHLORINE :: (a. neon, b. krypton, c. xenon, d. helium) : FLOURINE

20. CUBIT : ROD :: POUND : (a. fathom, b. decibel, c. stone, d. caliber)

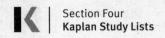

21. (a. hogshead, b. barrel, c. gallon, d. bucket) : PECK :: BUTT : BUSHEL

22. RECTANGLE : ISOSCELES TRIANGLE :: (a. square, b. cube, c. trapezoid, d. parallelogram): EQUILATERAL TRIANGLE

23. PLANCK : PHYSICIST :: NOBEL : (a. writer, b. mathematician, c. engineer, d. archaeologist)

24. MONO : (a. uni, b. solo, c. unde, d. tri) :: GREEK : LATIN

25. $10 : x :: 1000 :$ (a. $3x$, b. x^3, c. x^2, d. $2x$)

Answers

1. **(d)** The pistil is the female reproductive organ of a plant; likewise, the stamen is the male reproductive organ of a plant.

2. **(b)** A bit is the smallest unit of information used in computer engineering. A byte consists of eight bits.

3. **(c)** The boiling point of water in the Fahrenheit scale is 212 degrees, and in the Celsius scale is 100 degrees.

4. **(b)** Charles Darwin developed the theory of evolution, and Euclid wrote the fundamental textbook of geometry.

5. **(b)** Electrical resistance is measured in ohms, while electrical current is measured in amperes.

6. **(b)** Boar and sow are, respectively, the male and female names for many mammals, including bears, pigs, and porcupines. For birds, the respective male and female names are cock and hen.

7. **(b)** In botany, an annual plant has only one growing cycle, whereas a perennial has more than one and so does not need to be replanted each year.

8. **(a)** Triassic refers to a period of geological time, and Cenozoic refers to an era of geological time.

9. **(d)** A granivore is an animal adapted to eating grain, and an herbivore is an animal adapted to eating plants.

10. **(a)** Krypton is a noble gas, and chlorine is a halogen.

11. **(b)** The Cretaceous period is part of the Mesozoic Era, while the Cambrian Period is part of the Paleozoic era.

12. **(d)** In the taxonomic system of biological classification, Mollusca is a type of phylum, and Fungi is a type of kingdom.

13. **(d)** A billy is a male goat, and a gander is a male goose.

14. **(b)** A swarm is a group of bees, and a business is a group of ferrets.

15. **(a)** Magnesium is an alkaline earth metal, and lithium is an alkali metal.

16. **(d)** A pup is a baby shark, and a bunny is a baby rabbit.

17. **(a)** Simian is an adjective used to describe chimpanzees and other primates, and apian is an adjective used to describe bees.

18. **(c)** A stallion is a male horse, and mare is a female horse.

19. **(a)** Argon is the inert gas one atomic number greater than chlorine, and neon is the inert gas one atomic number greater than fluorine.

20. **(c)** The cubit and the rod are units of length, while the pound and the stone are units of weight.

21. **(b)** A barrel is a quarter of a butt; a peck is a quarter of a bushel.

22. **(a)** An equilateral triangle (all sides are the same) is a specific type of isosceles triangle (two sides are the same). Likewise, a square (all sides are the same and the angles are all 90 degrees) is a specific type of rectangle (two pairs of sides are the same and the angles are all 90 degrees)

23. **(c)** Max Planck was a theoretical physicist, and Alfred Nobel was an engineer.

24. **(a)** Mono is the Greek root for "one," and uni is the Latin root for "one."

25. **(b)** 1000 is 10 cubed, and x^3 is x cubed.

Full-Length Practice Tests

SCORING YOUR PRACTICE TESTS

The MAT will have 120 questions, but only 100 of them will count towards your score. Each time you finish a practice test in this book, you will have completed 120 questions. In order to approximate your raw score, give yourself 1 point for every correct answer, divide that number by 120, and multiply by 100. A raw score in the low 40s will produce a scaled score of about 400, which is the average scaled score on the MAT.

ANSWER SHEET FOR PRACTICE TEST 1

1. (a) (b) (c) (d)	41. (a) (b) (c) (d)	81. (a) (b) (c) (d)
2. (a) (b) (c) (d)	42. (a) (b) (c) (d)	82. (a) (b) (c) (d)
3. (a) (b) (c) (d)	43. (a) (b) (c) (d)	83. (a) (b) (c) (d)
4. (a) (b) (c) (d)	44. (a) (b) (c) (d)	84. (a) (b) (c) (d)
5. (a) (b) (c) (d)	45. (a) (b) (c) (d)	85. (a) (b) (c) (d)
6. (a) (b) (c) (d)	46. (a) (b) (c) (d)	86. (a) (b) (c) (d)
7. (a) (b) (c) (d)	47. (a) (b) (c) (d)	87. (a) (b) (c) (d)
8. (a) (b) (c) (d)	48. (a) (b) (c) (d)	88. (a) (b) (c) (d)
9. (a) (b) (c) (d)	49. (a) (b) (c) (d)	89. (a) (b) (c) (d)
10. (a) (b) (c) (d)	50. (a) (b) (c) (d)	90. (a) (b) (c) (d)
11. (a) (b) (c) (d)	51. (a) (b) (c) (d)	91. (a) (b) (c) (d)
12. (a) (b) (c) (d)	52. (a) (b) (c) (d)	92. (a) (b) (c) (d)
13. (a) (b) (c) (d)	53. (a) (b) (c) (d)	93. (a) (b) (c) (d)
14. (a) (b) (c) (d)	54. (a) (b) (c) (d)	94. (a) (b) (c) (d)
15. (a) (b) (c) (d)	55. (a) (b) (c) (d)	95. (a) (b) (c) (d)
16. (a) (b) (c) (d)	56. (a) (b) (c) (d)	96. (a) (b) (c) (d)
17. (a) (b) (c) (d)	57. (a) (b) (c) (d)	97. (a) (b) (c) (d)
18. (a) (b) (c) (d)	58. (a) (b) (c) (d)	98. (a) (b) (c) (d)
19. (a) (b) (c) (d)	59. (a) (b) (c) (d)	99. (a) (b) (c) (d)
20. (a) (b) (c) (d)	60. (a) (b) (c) (d)	100. (a) (b) (c) (d)
21. (a) (b) (c) (d)	61. (a) (b) (c) (d)	101. (a) (b) (c) (d)
22. (a) (b) (c) (d)	62. (a) (b) (c) (d)	102. (a) (b) (c) (d)
23. (a) (b) (c) (d)	63. (a) (b) (c) (d)	103. (a) (b) (c) (d)
24. (a) (b) (c) (d)	64. (a) (b) (c) (d)	104. (a) (b) (c) (d)
25. (a) (b) (c) (d)	65. (a) (b) (c) (d)	105. (a) (b) (c) (d)
26. (a) (b) (c) (d)	66. (a) (b) (c) (d)	106. (a) (b) (c) (d)
27. (a) (b) (c) (d)	67. (a) (b) (c) (d)	107. (a) (b) (c) (d)
28. (a) (b) (c) (d)	68. (a) (b) (c) (d)	108. (a) (b) (c) (d)
29. (a) (b) (c) (d)	69. (a) (b) (c) (d)	109. (a) (b) (c) (d)
30. (a) (b) (c) (d)	70. (a) (b) (c) (d)	110. (a) (b) (c) (d)
31. (a) (b) (c) (d)	71. (a) (b) (c) (d)	111. (a) (b) (c) (d)
32. (a) (b) (c) (d)	72. (a) (b) (c) (d)	112. (a) (b) (c) (d)
33. (a) (b) (c) (d)	73. (a) (b) (c) (d)	113. (a) (b) (c) (d)
34. (a) (b) (c) (d)	74. (a) (b) (c) (d)	114. (a) (b) (c) (d)
35. (a) (b) (c) (d)	75. (a) (b) (c) (d)	115. (a) (b) (c) (d)
36. (a) (b) (c) (d)	76. (a) (b) (c) (d)	116. (a) (b) (c) (d)
37. (a) (b) (c) (d)	77. (a) (b) (c) (d)	117. (a) (b) (c) (d)
38. (a) (b) (c) (d)	78. (a) (b) (c) (d)	118. (a) (b) (c) (d)
39. (a) (b) (c) (d)	79. (a) (b) (c) (d)	119. (a) (b) (c) (d)
40. (a) (b) (c) (d)	80. (a) (b) (c) (d)	120. (a) (b) (c) (d)

Practice Test 1

Time: 60 minutes
Length of Test: 120 Questions

Directions: For each of the following questions, you will find three capitalized terms and, in parentheses, four answer choices designated *a*, *b*, *c*, and *d*. Select the one answer choice that best completes the analogy with the three capitalized terms. (To record your answers, use the answer sheet that precedes this test.)

1. CITIZENSHIP : PASSPORT :: PURCHASE : (a. receipt, b. product, c. ticket, d. visa)

2. (a. Barnabas, b. Ivan, c. Akim, d. Vlad) : ATTILA :: IMPALER : HUN

3. REAM : PAPER :: CORD : (a. twine, b. outlet, c. pulp, d. wood)

4. VULPINE : FOX :: SIMIAN : (a. swan, b. ape, c. seed, d. self)

5. GRAIN : CHAFF :: METAL : (a. alloy, b. iron, c. dross, d. luster)

6. (a. shade, b. canopy, c. cot, d. blanket) : AWNING :: BED : STOREFRONT

7. (a. 4, b. 5, c. 6, d. 7) : JUPITER :: 3 : EARTH

8. SATISFY : CURIOSITY :: (a. slake, b. parch, c. whet, d. sip) : THIRST

9. BEAUFORT : TORNADO :: RICHTER : (a. scale, b. storm, c. tremor, d. radiation)

10. SWEETBREAD : ARUGULA :: ORGAN : (a. condiment, b. kidney, c. herb, d. gourd)

11. ABYSSINIA : (a. Ethiopia, b. Tehran, c. Sudan, d. Euphrates) :: PERSIA : IRAN

12. 0 : (a. 32, b. 180, c. 212, d. 273) :: CELSIUS : KELVIN

13. FISH : MERMAN :: (a. bull, b. lion, c. goat, d. horse) : CENTAUR

14. (a. excommunication, b. dethronement, c. abdication, d. regicide) : MONARCH ::
    RESIGNATION : PRESIDENT

15. STRAIT : (a. difficulty, b. peninsula, c. isthmus, d. moraine) :: WATER : LAND

16. III : L :: XV : (a. CL, b. DC, c. CCL, d. XC)

17. WALRUS : (a. whale, b. fish, c. penguin, d. octopus) :: WARTHOG : ELEPHANT

18. 1 : DROMEDARY :: 2 : (a. Bactrian, b. camel, c. quaternary, d. ovine)

19. AWL : (a. perforation, b. divination, c. measurement, d. compass) :: SEXTANT :
    NAVIGATION

20. APACHE : GERONIMO :: (a. Sequoia, b. Navaho, c. Custer, d. Lakota) : SITTING
    BULL

21. (a. road, b. port, c. furnace, d. navy) : SEA :: STEVEDORE : MARINER

22. CIRCUMFERENCE : (a. perimeter, b. vertex, c. area, d. trapezoid) :: CIRCLE :
    POLYGON

23. DRAWL : SPEAK :: LOPE : (a. throw, b. aim, c. run, d. slice)

24. DOMESTIC : (a. electric, b. flavored, c. foreign, d. up-to-date) :: AU PAIR : AU
    COURANT

25. OAK : DECIDUOUS :: (a. perennial, b. baobab, c. cactus, d. yew) : CONIFEROUS

26. SILICATE : LYE :: GLASS : (a. alkaline, b. soap, c. quartz, d. tumbler)

27. IOWA : IA :: ARKANSAS : (a. AA, b. AK, c. AR, d. AS)

28. LONDON : PARIS :: GATWICK : (a. Gautier, b. Marais, c. Halles, d. Orly)

29. BYTE : BIT :: (a. 8, b. 10, c. 16, d. 1,000) : 1

30. TACT : (a. faux pas, b. diplomat, c. boor, d. deck) :: WIT : CARD

31. OX : FLORA :: OXEN : (a. florae, b. flora, c. florum, d. floral)

32. (a. dock, b. vein, c. bribe, d. tissue) : GRAFT :: SHIP : MOOR

33. LINCOLN : JEFFERSON :: 1 : (a. 5, b. 10, c. 20, d. 25)

34. SHINGLE : ROOF :: (a. floor, b. tessera, c. mullion, d. apse) : MOSAIC

35. CORSET : GIRDLE :: PINCE-NEZ : (a. umbrella, b. briefcase, c. eyeglasses, d. hat)

36. TRIENNIAL : 3 :: DUODECENNIAL : (a. 2, b. 12, c. 20, d. 120)

37. HARPSICHORD : RECORDER :: PIANO : (a. flute, b. cassette, c. synthesizer, d. trombone)

38. LIFT : (a. drop, b. elevator, c. chorizo, d. impose) :: BANGER : SAUSAGE

39. DIRGE : (a. allegro, b. grave, c. forte, d. presto) :: LULLABY : PIANO

40. DIRNDL : (a. Hawaii, b. Turkey, c. Wales, d. Germany) :: KIMONO : JAPAN

41. CALIPER : PLUMB LINE :: WIDTH : (a. weight, b. length, c. verticality, d. flatness)

42. LONDON : TATE :: (a. St. Petersburg, b. Prague, c. Moscow, d. Warsaw) : HERMITAGE

43. (a. camel, b. buffalo, c. elephant, d. zebra) : PACHYDERM :: BEAVER : RODENT

44. (a. green, b. purple, c. yellow, d. brown) : ORANGE :: RED : BLUE

45. MESO : MIDDLE :: ENDO : (a. outside, b. within, c. above, d. distant)

46. WARDEN : CONCIERGE :: ZOO : (a. animal, b. prison, c. park, d. hotel)

47. UNGAINLY : GRACEFUL :: UNTOWARD : (a. away, b. pleasant, c. annoying, d. clumsy)

48. GRIN : (a. grain, b. flat, c. flit, d. blip) :: GROAN : FLOAT

49. RISK : (a. daredevil, b. actuary, c. investor, d. seminarian) :: WORTH : APPRAISER

50. SCABBARD : (a. spade, b. sword, c. pummel, d. sheath) :: CUDGEL : CLUB

51. BELLICOSE : (a. gullible, b. mendacious, c. contrary, d. sonorous) :: FIGHT : DECEIVE

52. ROOSEVELT : NEW DEAL :: (a. Truman, b. Kennedy, c. Johnson, d. Reagan) : GREAT SOCIETY

53. CLIO : (a. theater, b. journalism, c. advertising, d. cosmetology) :: TONY : BROADWAY

54. POLYMATH : (a. numerical, b. size, c. knowledgeable, d. small) :: LEVIATHAN : LARGE

55. FLETCHER : COBBLER :: ARROW : (a. fruit, b. bow, c. shoe, d. stone)

56. HERESY : SOLECISM :: DOGMA : (a. crowd, b. grammar, c. belief, d. unity)

57. (a. incredulous, b. mealymouthed, c. atavistic, d. impecunious) : CHURLISH :: DIRECT : REFINED

58. (a. Emerson, b. Hume, c. Locke, d. Thoreau) : CIVIL DISOBEDIENCE :: PAINE : COMMON SENSE

59. (a. Pollock, b. Calder, c. Monet, d. Warhol) : BRAQUE :: MOBILE : COLLAGE

60. PROFLIGATE : PRECIPITATE :: WASTEFUL : (a. sudden, b. solvent, c. thrifty, d. spendthrift)

61. IGNEOUS : CIRRUS :: (a. vapor, b. rock, c. combustion, d. dishonor) : CLOUD

62. REDOLENT : REFRACTORY :: FRAGRANT : (a. smelly, b. diffuse, c. unruly, d. mute)

63. (a. lung, b. kidney, c. pancreas, d. intestine) : DUODENUM :: HEART : VENA CAVA

64. MEESE : (a. Nixon, b. Carter, c. Reagan, d. Bush Sr.) :: RENO : CLINTON

65. COMPLAIN : (a. carp, b. cower, c. flush, d. fowl) :: GROUSE : QUAIL

66. (a. puce, b. chartreuse, c. ochre, d. ecru) : BEIGE :: AZURE : BLUE

67. SWEDEN : STOCKHOLM :: TURKEY : (a. Ankara, b. Istanbul, c. Izmir, d. Adana)

68. (a. arson, b. assault, c. unrest, d. bankruptcy) : MANSLAUGHTER :: CIVIL : CRIMINAL

69. (a. Doyle, b. Moriarty, c. Watson, d. Sherlock) : GRENDEL :: HOLMES : BEOWULF

70. (a. Dante, b. Marlowe, c. Milton, d. Goethe) : MOLIERE :: FAUST : TARTUFFE

71. SIDEREAL : (a. oceans, b. wind, c. stars, d. minerals) :: TERRESTRIAL : EARTH

72. RADIUS : DIAMETER :: 2 : (a. 1, b. 2, c. 4, d. 8)

73. BROCADE : FILIGREE :: FABRIC : (a. silk, b. embellishment, c. metal, d. purity)

74. EDDIE : CHRISTIAN SCIENCE :: (a. Campbell, b. Brown, c. Parham, d. Smith) : MORMONISM

75. BLANCH : WHITE :: DELIQUESCE : (a. ironic, b. black, c. sophisticated, d. fluid)

76. SYBARITE : SYCOPHANT :: (a. hedonist, b. aesthete, c. naysayer, d. sloth) : LACKY

77. GLOBE : FREE PRESS :: BOSTON : (a. Cleveland, b. Detroit, c. New York, d. San Francisco)

78. MASCARA : ROUGE :: (a. eyeliner, b. makeup, c. cameras d. maracas) : ROGUE

79. SHIP : (a. flask, b. shield, c. yawl, d. sword) :: JUNK : FALCHION

80. PAUSE : (a. obstacle, b. contemplation, c. cessation, d. onslaught) :: GLITCH : SETBACK

81. SILAS : MARNER :: ADAM : (a. Eve, b. West, c. Bede, d. Ant)

82. PHLEBOTOMIST : (a. language, b. blood, c. blemish, d. disease) :: ELECTROLOGIST : HAIR

83. FORMICARY : WARREN :: (a. rodent, b. sand, c. ant, d. mammal) : RABBIT

84. EOHIPPUS : AUSTRALOPITHECUS :: HORSE : (a. emu, b. kangaroo, c. man, d. pig)

85. TERPSICHORE : HOMILETICS :: DANCE : (a. minuet, b. preach, c. compare, d. choreograph)

86. LEWD : SAP :: (a. dwell, b. vulgar, c. wild, d. stop) : PASS

87. FEMUR : (a. humerus, b. ulna, c. tibia, d. radius) :: LEG : ARM

88. FOUNDLING : QUISLING :: ORPHAN : (a. traitor. b. teenager, c. seeker, d. coward)

89. SALAZAR : (a. Cervantes, b. Juan Carlos, c. Lopez, d. Franco) :: PORTUGAL : SPAIN

90. MATURATE : MACULATE :: RIPE : (a. spotted, b. pure, c. green, d. lucid)

91. ZLOTY : POLAND :: DINAR : (a. Jordan, b. Ukraine, c. Estonia, d. Thailand)

92. AND THE LIKE : (a. in comparison, b. that is, c. through, d. for instance) :: ETC. : VIZ.

93. PEI : GEHRY :: CHINA : (a. England, b. Canada, c. Germany, d. Holland)

94. MOON : LUNAR :: (a. day, b. earth, c. tide, d. twilight) : DIURNAL

95. CROMWELL : DISRAELI :: (a. 15th, b. 16th, c. 17th, d. 18th) : 19TH

96. YOKNAPATAWPHA : FAULKNER :: WINESBURG : (a. Cather, b. Anderson, c. Inge, d. Dreiser)

97. ABOLITION OF SLAVERY : XIII :: WOMEN'S SUFFRAGE : (a. XVIII, b. XIX, c. XX, d. XXI)

98. VOLUME : (EDGE)^3 :: SURFACE AREA : (a. 3(edge)^2, b. 4(edge)^2, c. 6(edge)^2, d. 8(edge)^2)

99. HERCULEAN : EASY :: PROCRUSTEAN : (a. original, b. industrious, c. challenging, d. accommodating)

100. (a. soil, b. monsters, c. continents, d. insects) : SPIDERS :: TERATOLOGIST : ARACHNOLOGIST

101. SEERSUCKER : STRIPES :: (a. corduroy, b. georgette, c. felt, d. damask) : RIDGES

102. (a. Greek, b. Celtic, c. Slavic, d. Austro-Asiatic) : ROMANCE :: POLISH : FRENCH

103. GARDNER : MULTIPLE INTELLIGENCES :: (a. Piaget, b. Erickson, c. Sartre, d. Rousseau) : THEORY OF COGNITIVE DEVELOPMENT

104. MANUSCRIPT : SCRIPTORIUM :: PAINTING : (a. monastery, b. guild, c. atelier, d. genre)

105. ZIMBABWE : RHODESIA :: GHANA : (a. Liberia, b. Mali, c. Gold Coast, d. Belgian Congo)

106. (a. Ni, b. H, c. Sb, d. N) : P :: O : S

107. (a. Goya, b. Manet, c. Titian, d. Bruegel) : VELÁZQUEZ :: FERDINAND VII : PHILIP IV

108. (a. England, b. Germany, c. America, d. Scotland) : JAPAN :: PRESBYTERIAN : SHINTO

109. HERTZ : FREQUENCY :: (a. pundit, b. liter, c. land, d. hectare) : LAND

110. MILES DAVIS : TRUMPET :: JOHN COLTRANE : (a. drums, b. bass, c. saxophone, d. piano)

111. BLACK-FIGURE : RED-FIGURE :: (a. Greek, b. amphora, c. Attic, d. archaic) : CLASSICAL

112. DC : EDISON :: AC : (a. Michelson, b. Morley, c. Faraday, d. Westinghouse)

113. DORIC : IONIC :: RENAISSANCE : (a. Corinthian, b. neoclassical, c. modern, d. Baroque)

114. GANDHI : (a. Germany, b. India, c. Great Britain, d. Pakistan) :: BOLIVAR : SPAIN

115. TIN : (a. Ti, b. Pb, c. Sn, d. Tl) :: SILICON : SI

116. CUNEIFORM : ORACLE BONES :: SUMERIA : (a. China, b. Babylon, c. Japan, d. Egypt)

117. ASCETIC : MISER :: (a. assiduous, b. self-denying, c. artistic, d. greedy) : STINGY

118. CAVE PAINTINGS : LASCAUX :: HOMO HABILIS : (a. Neander Valley, b. The Badlands, c. Mesopotamia, d. Olduvai Gorge)

119. VASCO DA GAMA : (a. Dias, b. Magellan, c. De La Salle, d. Pizarro) :: INDIA : AFRICA

120. VERB : (a. adverb, b. renege, c. beside, d. affinity) :: PREPOSITION : BENEATH

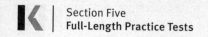

ANSWERS AND EXPLANATIONS

1. CITIZENSHIP : PASSPORT :: PURCHASE : (**a. receipt**, b. product, c. ticket, d. visa)
   (**a**) A passport is a proof of citizenship, and a receipt is a proof of purchase.

2. (a. Barnabas, b. Ivan, c. Akim, **d. Vlad**) : ATTILA :: IMPALER : HUN
   (**d**) Attila the Hun was one of history's famous bad men, as was Vlad the Impaler.

3. REAM : PAPER :: CORD : (a. twine, b. outlet, c. pulp, **d. wood**)
   (**d**) A ream is a large quantity of paper, and a cord is a large quantity of wood.

4. VULPINE : FOX :: SIMIAN : (a. swan, **b. ape**, c. seed, d. self)
   (**b**) *Vulpine* means of, relating to, or resembling a fox, and *simian* means of, relating to, or resembling an ape.

5. GRAIN : CHAFF :: METAL : (a. alloy, b. iron, **c. dross**, d. luster)
   (**c**) The unusable part of grain is called the called the chaff, and the unusable by-product in the production of metal is called the dross.

6. (a. shade, **b. canopy**, c. cot, d. blanket) : AWNING :: BED : STOREFRONT
   (**b**) A canopy is a covering that is suspended over a bed, and an awning is a covering that is suspended over a storefront.

7. (a. 4, **b. 5**, c. 6, d. 7) : JUPITER :: 3 : EARTH
   (**b**) Jupiter is the fifth planet from the sun, and earth is the third planet from the sun.

8. SATISFY : CURIOSITY :: (**a. slake**, b. parch, c. whet, d. sip) : THIRST
   (**a**) To satisfy a curiosity is to gratify it, just as to slake a thirst is to gratify it.

9. BEAUFORT : TORNADO :: RICHTER : (a. scale, b. storm, **c. tremor**, d. radiation)
   (**c**) A Beaufort scale measures the intensity of tornados, and a Richter scale measures the intensity of tremors.

10. SWEETBREAD : ARUGULA :: ORGAN : (a. condiment, b. kidney, **c. herb**, d. gourd)
    (**c**) A sweetbread is a type of organ that people consume, and arugula is a type of herb that people consume.

11. ABYSSINIA : (**a. Ethiopia**, b. Tehran, c. Sudan, d. Euphrates) :: PERSIA : IRAN
    (**a**) Abyssinia is the former name of Ethiopia, and Persia is the former name of Iran.

12. 0 : (a. 32, b. 180, c. 212, **d. 273**) :: CELSIUS : KELVIN
    (**d**) Zero degrees Celsius (the freezing point for water) is equal to 273 kelvins.

13. FISH : MERMAN :: (a. bull, b. lion, c. goat, **d. horse**) : CENTAUR
    (**d**) A merman is a mythological creature with the body of a fish, and a centaur is a mythological creature with the body of a horse.

14. (a. excommunication, b. dethronement, **c. abdication**, d. regicide) : MONARCH :: RESIGNATION : PRESIDENT
(**c**) Abdication is what you call it when a monarch voluntarily steps down from the throne, and resignation is what you call it when a president voluntarily steps down from the office.

15. STRAIT : (a. difficulty, b. peninsula, **c. isthmus**, d. moraine) :: WATER : LAND
(**c**) A strait is a narrow passageway connecting two larger bodies of water, and an isthmus is a narrow passageway connecting two larger bodies of land.

16. III : L :: XV : (a. CL, b. DC, **c. CCL**, d. XC)
(**c**) In Roman numerals, III (3) is one-fifth of XV (15), and L (50) is one-fifth of CCL (250).

17. WALRUS : (**a. whale**, b. fish, c. penguin, d. octopus) :: WARTHOG : ELEPHANT
(**a**) A walrus and a whale are both marine mammals (unlike the fish, penguin, and octopus, who lay eggs), and a warthog and an elephant are both land mammals.

18. 1 : DROMEDARY :: 2 : (**a. Bactrian**, b. camel, c. quaternary, d. ovine)
(**a**) A dromedary camel has 1 hump, and a Bactrian camel has 2 humps.

19. AWL : (**a. perforation**, b. divination, c. measurement, d. compass) :: SEXTANT : NAVIGATION
(**a**) An awl is a tool used for perforation, and a sextant is a tool used for navigation.

20. APACHE : GERONIMO :: (a. Sequoia, b. Navaho, c. Custer, **d. Lakota**) : SITTING BULL
(**d**) Geronimo was a leader of the Apaches, and Sitting Bull was a leader of the Lakota.

21. (a. road, **b. port**, c. furnace, d. navy) : SEA :: STEVEDORE : MARINER
(**b**) A mariner works at sea, and a stevedore works in a port.

22. CIRCUMFERENCE : (**a. perimeter**, b. vertex, c. area, d. trapezoid) :: CIRCLE : POLYGON
(**a**) The circumference is the external boundary of a circle, and the perimeter is the external boundary of a polygon.

23. DRAWL : SPEAK :: LOPE : (a. throw, b. aim, **c. run**, d. slice)
(**c**) To drawl is to speak in a slow, drawn-out manner, and to lope is to run in a slow, drawn-out manner.

24. DOMESTIC : (a. electric, b. flavored, c. foreign, **d. up-to-date**) :: AU PAIR : AU COURANT
(**d**) An *au pair* is a synonym for a *domestic*, and *au courant* is a synonym for *up-to-date*.

25. OAK : DECIDUOUS :: (a. perennial, b. baobab, c. cactus, **d. yew**) : CONIFEROUS
(**d**) An oak tree is a deciduous plant, and a yew is an coniferous plant.

26. SILICATE : LYE :: GLASS : (a. alkaline, **b. soap**, c. quartz, d. tumbler)
(**b**) Silicate is a basic ingredient in the making of glass, and lye is a basic ingredient in the making of soap.

27. IOWA : IA :: ARKANSAS : (a. AA, b. AK, **c. AR**, d. AS)
(**c**) The postal abbreviation for Iowa is IA, and the postal abbreviation for Arkansas is AR.

28. LONDON : PARIS :: GATWICK : (a. Gautier, b. Marais, c. Halles, **d. Orly**)
(**d**) Gatwick is one of London's major airports, and Orly is one of Paris's major airports.

29. BYTE : BIT :: (**a. 8**, b. 10, c. 16, d. 1,000) : 1
(**a**) There are 8 bits in every byte.

30. TACT : (a. faux pas, **b. diplomat**, c. boor, d. deck) :: WIT : CARD
(**b**) A diplomat is a person who has tact, and a card is slang for a person who has wit.

31. OX : FLORA :: OXEN : (**a. florae**, b. flora, c. florum, d. floral)
(**a**) The plural form of *ox* is *oxen*, and the plural form of *flora* is *florae*.

32. (a. dock, b. vein, c. bribe, **d. tissue**) : GRAFT :: SHIP : MOOR
(**d**) To graft is to attach tissue (to an organism), and to moor is to attach a ship (to a dock, etc.).

33. LINCOLN : JEFFERSON :: 1 : (**a. 5**, b. 10, c. 20, d. 25)
(**a**) Abraham Lincoln's likeness appears on a penny (1 cent), and Thomas Jefferson's likeness appears on a nickel (5 cents).

34. SHINGLE : ROOF :: (a. floor, **b. tessera**, c. mullion, d. apse) : MOSAIC
(**b**) A shingle is a constituent piece of a roof, and a tessera is a constituent piece of a mosaic.

35. CORSET : GIRDLE :: PINCE-NEZ : (a. umbrella, b. briefcase, **c. eyeglasses**, d. hat)
(**c**) A corset is a girdle from the Victorian era, and a pince-nez is a pair of eyeglasses from the Victorian era.

36. TRIENNIAL : 3 :: DUODECENNIAL : (a. 2, **b. 12**, c. 20, d. 120)
(**b**) A triennial event happens after 3 years, and a duodecennial event happens after 12 years.

37. HARPSICHORD : RECORDER :: PIANO : (**a. flute**, b. cassette, c. synthesizer, d. trombone)
(**a**) The harpsichord was a precursor to the piano, and the recorder was a precursor to the flute.

38. LIFT : (a. drop, **b. elevator**, c. chorizo, d. impose) :: BANGER : SAUSAGE
(b) *Lift* in British English means *elevator* in American English, and *banger* in British English means *sausage* in American English.

39. DIRGE : (a. allegro, **b. grave**, c. forte, d. presto) :: LULLABY : PIANO
(b) A dirge should be played grave (slowly and solemnly), and a lullaby should be played piano (softly).

40. DIRNDL : (a. Hawaii, b. Turkey, c. Wales, **d. Germany**) :: KIMONO : JAPAN
(d) A dirndl is a traditional woman's garment from Germany, and a kimono is a traditional woman's garment from Japan.

41. CALIPER : PLUMB LINE :: WIDTH : (a. weight, b. length, **c. verticality**, d. flatness)
(c) A caliper is used to measure width, and a plumb line is used to measure verticality.

42. LONDON : TATE :: (**a. St. Petersburg**, b. Prague, c. Moscow, d. Warsaw) : HERMITAGE
(a) The Tate museums are located in London, and the Hermitage Museum is located in St. Petersburg.

43. (a. camel, b. buffalo, **c. elephant**, d. zebra) : PACHYDERM :: BEAVER : RODENT
(c) An elephant is a pachyderm, and a beaver is a rodent.

44. (**a. green**, b. purple, c. yellow, d. brown) : ORANGE :: RED : BLUE
(a) Green and red are complementary colors, and orange and blue are complementary colors.

45. MESO : MIDDLE :: ENDO : (a. outside, **b. within**, c. above, d. distant)
(b) The prefix *meso–* means middle, and the prefix *endo–* means within.

46. WARDEN : CONCIERGE :: ZOO : (a. animal, b. prison, c. park, **d. hotel**)
(d) A caretaker at a zoo is called a warden, and a caretaker at a hotel is called a concierge.

47. UNGAINLY : GRACEFUL :: UNTOWARD : (a. away, **b. pleasant**, c. annoying, d. clumsy)
(b) Someone or something ungainly is not graceful, and someone or something untoward is not pleasant.

48. GRIN : (a. grain, b. flat, **c. flit**, d. blip) :: GROAN : FLOAT
(c) *Grin* becomes *groan* if you replace the *i* with *oa*, and *flit* becomes *float* if you replace the *i* with *oa*.

49. RISK : (a. daredevil, **b. actuary**, c. investor, d. seminarian) :: WORTH : APPRAISER
(b) An actuary assesses the risk of something, and an appraiser assesses the worth of something.

50. SCABBARD : (a. spade, b. sword, c. pummel, **d. sheath**) :: CUDGEL : CLUB
(**d**) A scabbard is a type of sheath, and a cudgel is a type of a club.

51. BELLICOSE : (a. gullible, **b. mendacious**, c. contrary, d. sonorous) :: FIGHT : DECEIVE
(**b**) Someone who's bellicose tends to fight, and someone who's mendacious tends to deceive.

52. ROOSEVELT : NEW DEAL :: (a. Truman, b. Kennedy, **c. Johnson**, d. Reagan) : GREAT SOCIETY
(**c**) Franklin Roosevelt called his domestic program the New Deal, and Lyndon Johnson called his domestic program the Great Society.

53. CLIO : (a. theater, b. journalism, **c. advertising**, d. cosmetology) :: TONY : BROADWAY
(**c**) The Clio award is given to people in the advertising industry, and the Tony award is given to people in theater.

54. POLYMATH : (a. numerical, b. size, **c. knowledgeable**, d. small) :: LEVIATHAN : LARGE
(**c**) A polymath, by definition, is knowledgeable, and a leviathan, by definition, is large.

55. FLETCHER : COBBLER :: ARROW : (a. fruit, b. bow, **c. shoe**, d. stone)
(**c**) A fletcher makes arrows, and a cobbler makes shoes.

56. HERESY : SOLECISM :: DOGMA : (a. crowd, **b. grammar**, c. belief, d. unity)
(**b**) A heresy is a violation of, or deviation from, dogma, and a solecism is a violation of, or deviation from, grammar.

57. (a. incredulous, **b. mealymouthed**, c. atavistic, d. impecunious) : CHURLISH :: DIRECT : REFINED
(**b**) Someone who's mealymouthed is not direct, and someone who's churlish is not refined.

58. (a. Emerson, b. Hume, c. Locke, **d. Thoreau**) : CIVIL DISOBEDIENCE :: PAINE : COMMON SENSE
(**d**) Henry David Thoreau wrote *Civil Disobedience*, and Thomas Paine wrote *Common Sense*.

59. (a. Pollock, **b. Calder**, c. Monet, d. Warhol) : BRAQUE :: MOBILE : COLLAGE
(**b**) The artist Alexander Calder is famous for his mobiles, and the artist Georges Braque is famous for his collages.

60. PROFLIGATE : PRECIPITATE :: WASTEFUL : (**a. sudden**, b. solvent, c. thrifty, d. spendthrift)
(**a**) *Profligate* is a synonym for *wasteful*, and *precipitate* is a synonym for *sudden*.

61. IGNEOUS : CIRRUS :: (a. vapor, **b. rock**, c. combustion, d. dishonor) : CLOUD
(**b**) Igneous is a type of rock, and cirrus is a type of cloud.

62. REDOLENT : REFRACTORY :: FRAGRANT : (a. smelly, b. diffuse, **c. unruly**, d. mute)
(**c**) *Redolent* is a synonym for *fragrant*, and *refractory* is a synonym for *unruly*.

63. (a. lung, b. kidney, c. pancreas, **d. intestine**) : DUODENUM :: HEART : VENA CAVA
(**d**) The duodenum is a part of the intestine, and the vena cava is a part of the heart.

64. MEESE : (a. Nixon, b. Carter, **c. Reagan**, d. Bush Sr.) :: RENO : CLINTON
(**c**) Edwin Meese was the U.S. attorney general during the Reagan administration, and Janet Reno was the U.S. attorney general during the Clinton administration.

65. COMPLAIN : (a. carp, **b. cower**, c. flush, d. fowl) :: GROUSE : QUAIL
(**b**) To complain is to grouse, and to cower is to quail.

66. (a. puce, b. chartreuse, c. ochre, **d. ecru**) : BEIGE :: AZURE : BLUE
(**d**) Ecru is a shade of beige, and azure is a shade of blue.

67. SWEDEN : STOCKHOLM :: TURKEY : (**a. Ankara**, b. Istanbul, c. Izmir, d. Adana)
(**a**) The capital of Sweden is Stockholm, and the capital of Turkey is Ankara.

68. (a. arson, b. assault, c. unrest, **d. bankruptcy**) : MANSLAUGHTER :: CIVIL : CRIMINAL
(**d**) Bankruptcy is covered under civil law, and manslaughter is covered under criminal law.

69. (a. Doyle, **b. Moriarty**, c. Watson, d. Sherlock) : GRENDEL :: HOLMES : BEOWULF
(**b**) Professor Moriarty was the archenemy of Sherlock Holmes, and Grendel was the archenemy of Beowulf.

70. (a. Dante, b. Marlowe, c. Milton, **d. Goethe**) : MOLIÈRE :: FAUST : TARTUFFE
(**d**) Johann Goethe created the character of Faust, and Jean-Baptiste Molière created the character of Tartuffe.

71. SIDEREAL : (a. oceans, b. wind, **c. stars**, d. minerals) :: TERRESTRIAL : EARTH
(**c**) *Sidereal* means of or relating to stars, and *terrestrial* means of or relating to the earth.

72. RADIUS : DIAMETER :: 2 : (a. 1, b. 2, **c. 4**, d. 8)
(**c**) If the radius of a circle is 2, the diameter is 4 (i.e., the diameter is two times the radius).

73. BROCADE : FILIGREE :: FABRIC : (a. silk, b. embellishment, **c. metal**, d. purity)
(**c**) A brocade is a raised pattern on fabric, and a filigree is a raised pattern on metal.

74. EDDIE : CHRISTIAN SCIENCE :: (a. Campbell, b. Brown, c. Parham, **d. Smith**) : MORMONISM
(**d**) Mary Baker Eddie was the spiritual founder of Christian Science, and Joseph Smith was the spiritual founder of Mormonism.

75. BLANCH : WHITE :: DELIQUESCE : (a. ironic, b. black, c. sophisticated, **d. fluid**)
(**d**) To blanch is to become white, and to deliquesce is to become fluid.

76. SYBARITE : SYCOPHANT :: (**a. hedonist**, b. aesthete, c. naysayer, d. sloth) : LACKY
(**a**) *Sybarite* is a synonym for *hedonist*, and *sycophant* is a synonym for *lacky*.

77. GLOBE : FREE PRESS :: BOSTON : (a. Cleveland, **b. Detroit**, c. New York, d. San Francisco)
(**b**) Boston has a daily newspaper called the *Globe*, and Detroit has a daily newspaper called the *Free Press*.

78. MASCARA : ROUGE :: (a. eyeliner, b. makeup, c. cameras, **d. maracas**) : ROGUE
(**d**) An anagram for *mascara* is *maracas*, and an anagram for *rouge* is *rogue*.

79. SHIP : (a. flask, b. shield, c. yawl, **d. sword**) :: JUNK : FALCHION
(**d**) A junk is a type of ship, and a falchion is a type of sword.

80. PAUSE : (a. obstacle, b. contemplation, **c. cessation**, d. onslaught) :: GLITCH : SETBACK
(**c**) A pause is a temporary cessation, and a glitch is a temporary setback.

81. SILAS : MARNER :: ADAM : (a. Eve, b. West, **c. Bede**, d. Ant)
(**c**) George Eliot wrote *Silas Marner*, and she also wrote *Adam Bede*.

82. PHLEBOTOMIST : (a. language, **b. blood**, c. blemish, d. disease) :: ELECTROLOGIST : HAIR
(**b**) A phlebotomist is someone who removes (withdraws) blood, and an electrologist is someone who removes hair.

83. FORMICARY : WARREN :: (a. rodent, b. sand, **c. ant**, d. mammal) : RABBIT
(**c**) A formicary is a nest for ants, and a warren is a nest for rabbits.

84. EOHIPPUS : AUSTRALOPITHECUS :: HORSE : (a. emu, b. kangaroo, **c. man**, d. pig)
(**c**) Eohippus was an ancient ancestor of the modern horse, and Australopithecus was an ancient ancestor of modern man.

85. TERPSICHORE : HOMILETICS :: DANCE : (a. minuet, **b. preach**, c. compare, d. choreograph)
(**b**) Terpsichore is the art of dancing, and homiletics is the art of preaching.

86. LEWD : SAP :: (**a. dwell**, b. vulgar, c. wild, d. stop) : PASS
    (a) If you write *lewd* backwards and repeat the last letter, you get *dwell*, and if you write *sap* backwards and repeat the last letter, you get *pass*.

87. FEMUR : (**a. humerus**, b. ulna, c. tibia, d. radius) :: LEG : ARM
    (a) The femur is the upper leg (thigh) bone, and the humerus is the upper arm bone.

88. FOUNDLING : QUISLING :: ORPHAN : (**a. traitor**, b. teenager, c. seeker, d. coward)
    (a) A foundling is an orphan, and a quisling is a traitor.

89. SALAZAR : (a. Cervantes, b. Juan Carlos, c. Lopez, **d. Franco**) :: PORTUGAL : SPAIN
    (d) Antonio Salazar was a 20th-century dictator of Portugal, and Francisco Franco was a 20th-century dictator of Spain.

90. MATURATE : MACULATE :: RIPE : (**a. spotted**, b. pure, c. green, d. lucid)
    (a) *Maturate* means to become ripe, and *maculate* means to become spotted.

91. ZLOTY : POLAND :: DINAR : (**a. Jordan**, b. Ukraine, c. Estonia, d. Thailand)
    (a) The zloty is the unit of currency in Poland, and the dinar is the unit of currency in Jordan.

92. AND THE LIKE : (a. in comparison, **b. that is**, c. through, d. for instance) :: ETC. : VIZ.
    (b) The abbreviation *etc.* (*et cetera*) means *and the like*, and the abbreviation *viz.* (*videlicet*) means *that is* (*to say*).

93. PEI : GEHRY :: CHINA : (a. England, **b. Canada**, c. Germany, d. Holland)
    (b) The famed architect I. M. Pei was born in China, and the famed architect Frank Gehry was born in Canada.

94. MOON : LUNAR :: (**a. day**, b. earth, c. tide, d. twilight) : DIURNAL
    (a) *Lunar* means of or relating to the moon, and *diurnal* means of or relating to the day.

95. CROMWELL : DISRAELI :: (a. 15th, b. 16th, **c. 17th**, d. 18th) : 19TH
    (c) Oliver Cromwell was active in English politics in the 17th century, and Benjamin Disraeli was active in English politics in the 19th century.

96. YOKNAPATAWPHA : FAULKNER :: WINESBURG : (a. Cather, **b. Anderson**, c. Inge, d. Dreiser)
    (b) William Faulkner wrote about a fictional place called Yoknapatawpha County, Mississippi, and Sherwood Anderson wrote about a fictional town called Winesburg, Ohio.

97. ABOLITION OF SLAVERY : XIII :: WOMEN'S SUFFRAGE: (a. XVIII, **b. XIX**, c. XX, d. XXI)
(b) Amendment XIII of the U.S. Constitution guaranteed the abolition of slavery, and Amendment XIX of the U.S. Constitution guaranteed women's suffrage.

98. VOLUME : (EDGE)^3 :: SURFACE AREA : (a. 3(edge)^2, b. 4(edge)^2, **c. 6(edge)^2**, d. 8(edge)^2)
(c) The volume of a cube is (edge)^3, and the surface area of a cube is 6(edge)^2.

99. HERCULEAN : EASY :: PROCRUSTEAN : (a. original, b. industrious, c. challenging, **d. accommodating**)
(d) Something described as herculean is not easy, and something described as procrustean is not accommodating.

100. (a. soil, **b. monsters**, c. continents, d. insects) : SPIDERS :: TERATOLOGIST : ARACHNOLOGIST
(b) An arachnologist studies spiders, and a teratologist studies monsters.

101. SEERSUCKER : STRIPES :: (**a. corduroy**, b. georgette, c. felt, d. damask) : RIDGES
(a) Stripes are the distinguishing feature of the seersucker fabric, and ridges are the distinguishing feature of corduroy fabric.

102. (a. Greek, b. Celtic, **c. Slavic**, d. Austro-Asiatic) : ROMANCE :: POLISH : FRENCH
(c) An example of a Slavic language is Polish, and an example of a Romance language is French.

103. GARDNER : MULTIPLE INTELLIGENCES :: (**a. Piaget**, b. Erickson, c. Sartre, d. Rousseau) : THEORY OF COGNITIVE DEVELOPMENT
(a) Howard Gardner wrote the theory of multiple intelligences in children, and Jean Piaget wrote the theory of cognitive development in children.

104. MANUSCRIPT : SCRIPTORIUM :: PAINTING : (a. monastery, b. guild, **c. atelier**, d. genre)
(c) Medieval manuscripts were created in monastic scriptoriums, while paintings are made in artists' ateliers.

105. ZIMBABWE : RHODESIA :: GHANA : (a. Liberia, b. Mali, **c. Gold Coast**, d. Belgian Congo)
(c) Today, the Gold Coast is known as Ghana, and the colony known as Rhodesia is now known as the independent state of Zimbabwe.

106. (a. Ni, b. H, c. Sb, **d. N**) : P :: O : S
(d) Oxygen (O) is one period higher than Sulfur (S) in Group 16, and Nitrogen (N) is one period higher than Phosphorus (P) in Group 15.

107. (**a. Goya**, b. Manet, c. Titian, d. Bruegel) : VELÁZQUEZ :: FERDINAND VII : PHILIP IV
(**a**) Francisco Goya served as court painter to Ferdinand VII, and Diego Velázquez served as court painter to Philip IV.

108. (a. England, b. Germany, c. America, **d. Scotland**) : JAPAN :: PRESBYTERIAN : SHINTO
(**d**) The Presbyterian faith is native to Scotland, and Shintoism is native to Japan.

109. HERTZ : FREQUENCY :: (a. pundit, b. liter, c. land, **d. hectare**) : LAND
(**d**) Hertz is a unit to measure frequency, and hectare is a unit to measure land.

110. MILES DAVIS : TRUMPET :: JOHN COLTRANE : (a. drums, b. bass, **c. saxophone**, d. piano)
(**c**) Miles Davis was a jazz trumpeter who died in 1991, and John Coltrane was a jazz saxophonist who died in 1967.

111. BLACK-FIGURE : RED-FIGURE :: (a. Greek, b. amphora, c. Attic, **d. archaic**) : CLASSICAL
(**d**) Black-figure was the preferred technique of vase painting in the Greek archaic period, and red-figure vase painting took over in popularity in the classical period.

112. DC : EDISON :: AC : (a. Michelson, b. Morley, c. Faraday, **d. Westinghouse**)
(**d**) Thomas Edison championed the DC current, and George Westinghouse championed the AC current.

113. DORIC : IONIC :: RENAISSANCE : (a. Corinthian, b. neoclassical, c. modern, **d. Baroque**)
(**d**) The ionic order of classical architecture was a more stylized and lyrical successor to the doric order, and the Baroque was a more stylized and decorative aesthetic following the Renaissance period.

114. GANDHI : (a. Germany, b. India, **c. Great Britain**, d. Pakistan) :: BOLIVAR : SPAIN
(**c**) Mohandas K. (Mahatma) Gandhi liberated India from British control, and Simon de Bolivar liberated Bolivia from the Spanish.

115. TIN : (a. Ti, b. Pb, **c. Sn**, d. Tl) :: SILICON : SI
(**c**) Si is the symbol for silicon, and Sn is the symbol for tin.

116. CUNEIFORM : ORACLE BONES :: SUMERIA : (**a. China,** b. Babylon, c. Japan, d. Egypt)
(**a**) Oracle bones are a form of ancient Chinese writing, while cuneiform is ancient Sumerian writing.

117. ASCETIC : MISER :: (a. assiduous, **b. self-denying**, c. artistic, d. greedy) : STINGY
(**b**) An ascetic is self-denying, and a miser is stingy.

118. CAVE PAINTINGS : LASCAUX :: HOMO HABILIS : (a. Neander Valley, b. The Badlands, c. Mesopotamia, **d. Olduvai Gorge**)
(**d**) Prehistoric cave paintings were discovered in Lascaux, France, and the skeleton of *Homo habilis* was discovered at Olduvai Gorge, Tanzania.

119. VASCO DA GAMA : (**a. Dias**, b. Magellan, c. De La Salle, d. Pizarro) :: INDIA : AFRICA
(**a**) Vasco da Gama was the explorer who discovered a water route to India, and Bartolomeu Dias was the explorer who discovered the water route around Africa.

120. VERB : (a. adverb, **b. renege**, c. beside, d. affinity) :: PREPOSITION : BENEATH
(**b**) An example of a verb is *renege* (to go back on one's word), and an example of a preposition is *beneath*.

ANSWER SHEET FOR PRACTICE TEST 2

1. (a) (b) (c) (d)   41. (a) (b) (c) (d)   81. (a) (b) (c) (d)
2. (a) (b) (c) (d)   42. (a) (b) (c) (d)   82. (a) (b) (c) (d)
3. (a) (b) (c) (d)   43. (a) (b) (c) (d)   83. (a) (b) (c) (d)
4. (a) (b) (c) (d)   44. (a) (b) (c) (d)   84. (a) (b) (c) (d)
5. (a) (b) (c) (d)   45. (a) (b) (c) (d)   85. (a) (b) (c) (d)
6. (a) (b) (c) (d)   46. (a) (b) (c) (d)   86. (a) (b) (c) (d)
7. (a) (b) (c) (d)   47. (a) (b) (c) (d)   87. (a) (b) (c) (d)
8. (a) (b) (c) (d)   48. (a) (b) (c) (d)   88. (a) (b) (c) (d)
9. (a) (b) (c) (d)   49. (a) (b) (c) (d)   89. (a) (b) (c) (d)
10. (a) (b) (c) (d)   50. (a) (b) (c) (d)   90. (a) (b) (c) (d)
11. (a) (b) (c) (d)   51. (a) (b) (c) (d)   91. (a) (b) (c) (d)
12. (a) (b) (c) (d)   52. (a) (b) (c) (d)   92. (a) (b) (c) (d)
13. (a) (b) (c) (d)   53. (a) (b) (c) (d)   93. (a) (b) (c) (d)
14. (a) (b) (c) (d)   54. (a) (b) (c) (d)   94. (a) (b) (c) (d)
15. (a) (b) (c) (d)   55. (a) (b) (c) (d)   95. (a) (b) (c) (d)
16. (a) (b) (c) (d)   56. (a) (b) (c) (d)   96. (a) (b) (c) (d)
17. (a) (b) (c) (d)   57. (a) (b) (c) (d)   97. (a) (b) (c) (d)
18. (a) (b) (c) (d)   58. (a) (b) (c) (d)   98. (a) (b) (c) (d)
19. (a) (b) (c) (d)   59. (a) (b) (c) (d)   99. (a) (b) (c) (d)
20. (a) (b) (c) (d)   60. (a) (b) (c) (d)   100. (a) (b) (c) (d)
21. (a) (b) (c) (d)   61. (a) (b) (c) (d)   101. (a) (b) (c) (d)
22. (a) (b) (c) (d)   62. (a) (b) (c) (d)   102. (a) (b) (c) (d)
23. (a) (b) (c) (d)   63. (a) (b) (c) (d)   103. (a) (b) (c) (d)
24. (a) (b) (c) (d)   64. (a) (b) (c) (d)   104. (a) (b) (c) (d)
25. (a) (b) (c) (d)   65. (a) (b) (c) (d)   105. (a) (b) (c) (d)
26. (a) (b) (c) (d)   66. (a) (b) (c) (d)   106. (a) (b) (c) (d)
27. (a) (b) (c) (d)   67. (a) (b) (c) (d)   107. (a) (b) (c) (d)
28. (a) (b) (c) (d)   68. (a) (b) (c) (d)   108. (a) (b) (c) (d)
29. (a) (b) (c) (d)   69. (a) (b) (c) (d)   109. (a) (b) (c) (d)
30. (a) (b) (c) (d)   70. (a) (b) (c) (d)   110. (a) (b) (c) (d)
31. (a) (b) (c) (d)   71. (a) (b) (c) (d)   111. (a) (b) (c) (d)
32. (a) (b) (c) (d)   72. (a) (b) (c) (d)   112. (a) (b) (c) (d)
33. (a) (b) (c) (d)   73. (a) (b) (c) (d)   113. (a) (b) (c) (d)
34. (a) (b) (c) (d)   74. (a) (b) (c) (d)   114. (a) (b) (c) (d)
35. (a) (b) (c) (d)   75. (a) (b) (c) (d)   115. (a) (b) (c) (d)
36. (a) (b) (c) (d)   76. (a) (b) (c) (d)   116. (a) (b) (c) (d)
37. (a) (b) (c) (d)   77. (a) (b) (c) (d)   117. (a) (b) (c) (d)
38. (a) (b) (c) (d)   78. (a) (b) (c) (d)   118. (a) (b) (c) (d)
39. (a) (b) (c) (d)   79. (a) (b) (c) (d)   119. (a) (b) (c) (d)
40. (a) (b) (c) (d)   80. (a) (b) (c) (d)   120. (a) (b) (c) (d)

Practice Test 2

Time: 60 minutes
Length of Test: 120 Questions

Directions: For each of the following questions, you will find three capitalized terms and, in parentheses, four answer choices designated *a*, *b*, *c*, and *d*. Select the one answer choice that best completes the analogy with the three capitalized terms. (To record your answers, use the answer sheet that precedes this test.)

1. GUN : HOLSTER :: ARROW : (a. archer, b. bow, c. quiver, d. target)

2. COMET : SHIP :: (a. Halley, b. meteor, c. tail, d. rocket) : WAKE

3. MOON : WANE :: (a. eclipse, b. tide, c. crater, d. sun) : EBB

4. LINCOLN MEMORIAL : MONTICELLO :: 1 : (a. 2, b. 5, c. 10, d. 25)

5. HAT : HEAD :: COZY : (a. chest, b. lap, c. fireplace, d. teapot)

6. LEAF : (a. bean, b. bark, c. clove, d. root) :: MINT : CINNAMON

7. BEAUTY : PROOF :: EYE OF THE BEHOLDER : (a. pudding, b. puzzle, c. product, d. taking)

8. SATURN : MOON :: SATURDAY : (a. Uranus, b. Thursday, c. astronomy, d. Monday)

9. BAKER'S DOZEN : SCORE :: 13 : (a. 20, b. gross, c. donuts, d. 26)

10. (a. whisper, b. garble, c. chortle, d. yell) : TALK :: GUFFAW : LAUGH

11. YOU : ME :: SECOND : (a. first, b. second, c. third, d. fourth)

12. (a. circumference, b. area, c. sector, d. arc) : VOLUME :: CIRCLE : SPHERE

13. (a. North America, b. Europe, c. Africa, d. Australia) : ASIA :: MATTERHORN : EVEREST

14. EMU : (a. reptilian, b. mammalian, c. insectival, d. avian) :: NEWT : AMPHIBIAN

15. (a. electron, b. ganglia, c. nucleus, d. neutron) : PIT :: ATOM : CHERRY

16. HOMBURG : MACKINTOSH :: (a. boot, b. hat, c. slicker, d. umbrella) : RAINCOAT

17. (a. plaster, b. linen, c. linoleum, d. rayon) : DRYWALL :: FLAX : GYPSUM

18. 1912 : (a. 1910, b. 1915, c. 1920, d. 1925) :: TITANIC : LUSITANIA

19. RUBBER : MATCH :: (a. racquetball, b. squash, c. cribbage, d. bridge) : TENNIS

20. (a. Rhine, b. Rhone, c. Danube, d. Oder) : VIENNA :: SEINE : PARIS

21. LAPIDARY : TOPIARY :: (a. ice, b. leather, c. stone, d. wood) : plant

22. TRAIN : (a. caboose, b. engineer, c. locomotive, d. porter) :: SHELL : COXSWAIN

23. COULD : SHOULD :: (a. capacity, b. desire, c. necessity, d. expediency) : PROPRIETY

24. SANE : SON :: GAIN : (a. loss, b. gone, c. gun, d. cone)

25. (a. geneticist, b. linguist, c. historian, d. pharmocologist) : ECONOMIST :: HGP : GNP

26. OH : BUCKEYE :: CT : (a. buckwheat, b. chestnut, c. maple, d. nutmeg)

27. INTERREGNUM : INTERMISSION :: (a. development, b. government, c. propriety, d. conversation) : ENTERTAINMENT

28. ROCK : EROSION :: IRON : (a. conduction, b. oxidation, c. metallurgy, d. smelting)

29. CEL : CELL :: CARTOON : (a. carton, b. organism, c. protoplasm, d. animation)

30. (a. agora, b. academy, c. monastery, d. saturnalia) : SPA :: ASCETIC : SALUBRIOUS

31. ADMIRE : LIONIZE :: (a. belittle, b. betray, c. dislike, d. vituperate) : ABHOR

32. CLEOPATRA : (a. asp, b. hemlock, c. knife, d. illness) :: MARIE ANTOINETTE : GUILLOTINE

33. COWBOY : GAUCHO :: UNITED STATES : (a. Brazil, b. Argentina, c. Portugal, d. Spain)

34. FREUD : PSYCHOANALYSIS :: (a. Rogers, b. Skinner, c. Chomsky, d. Maslow) : BEHAVIORISM

35. BLUE BLOOD : (a. red herring, b. red light, c. red letter, d. red tape) :: ARISTOCRACY : BUREAUCRACY

36. WOMAN : WOMEN :: STIMULUS : (a. stimulus, b. stimula, c. stimuluses, d. stimuli)

37. MERCURY : SILVER :: (a. Ac, b. Hg, c. Me, d. Nr) : AG

38. (a. kid, b. lamb, c. pup, d. foal) : CUB :: OVINE : URSINE

39. (a. Apollo, b. Ares, c. Poseidon, d. Saturn) : NEPTUNE :: ZEUS : JUPITER

40. TETRA : SESQUI :: 4 : (a. 1.5, b. 2.5, c. 6, d. 7)

41. PITHY : EPIGRAMMATIC :: (a. lugubrious, b. prolix, c. trenchant, d. discursive) : MORDANT

42. AC : DC :: (a. Franklin, b. Marconi, c. Tesla, d. Bell) : Edison

43. 2 : (a. 0, b. 7, c. 12, d. 16) :: ACIDIC : ALKALINE

44. (a. dulcimer, b. lute, c. timpani, d. virginal) : KEYBOARD :: PINBOX : CAMERA

45. (a. snake, b. fish, c. pig, d. tree) : STONE :: CIRCE : MEDUSA

46. SCENT : CENTER :: COUGH : (a. hub, b. coffer, c. cougar, d. lozenge)

47. (a. gammon, b. venison, c. buck, d. veal) : DOE :: BEEF : COW

48. BRAID : UPBRAID :: (a. plait, b. buckle, c. chastise, d. recant) : REBUKE

49. HUNTER GATHERER : AGRARIAN :: (a. stone, b. arrow, c. urn, d. steel) : BRONZE

50. (a. basalt, b. sandstone, c. slate, d. marble) : SEDIMENTARY :: GRANITE : IGNEOUS

51. SPELEOLOGY : (a. caves, b. games, c. lexicons, d. rocks) :: ZOOLOGY : ANIMALS

52. ROMAN : ENGLISH :: (a. Alexandrian, b. Cyrillic, c. Slavic, d. Greek) : RUSSIAN

53. WORRY : (a. fear, b. panic, c. vex, d. assuage) :: ANNOY : EXCRUCIATE

54. GREEK : NORSE :: ZEUS : (a. Asgard, b. Njord, c. Odin, d. Thor)

55. INFER : CONCLUDE :: IMPLY : (a. intimate, b. initiate, c. state, d. terminate)

56. (a. buffoon, b. constable, c. dupe, d. scaramouch) : CHARLATAN :: PREY : PREDATOR

57. SOPERIFIC : ANALGESIC :: (a. hunger, b. thirst, c. wakefulness, d. lethargy) : PAIN

58. SEMPER : CARPE :: FIDELIS : (a. absurdem, b. diem, c. factotum, d. lector)

59. (a. preface, b. encomium, c. peroration, d. homily) : SPEECH :: CODA : SONATA

60. (a. ale, b. kvass, c. gin, d. sake) : CLARET :: RICE : GRAPE

61. SERENDIPITOUS : SURREPTITIOUS :: (a. planned, b. slow, c. desirable, d. understood) : OPEN

62. TROY : 12 :: (a. SI, b. metric, c. avoirdupois, d. Winchester) : 16

63. CONGRESS : (a. bills, b. senators, c. Capitol Hill, d. representatives) :: PARLIAMENT : COMMONS

64. C : MM :: (a. VI, b. IX, c. XI, d. XIV) : CLXXX

65. FICKLE : (a. unsteady, b. corpulent, c. gloomy, d. incisive) :: MERCURIAL : SATURNINE

66. SECT : SECTOR :: DENOMINATION : (a. circumference, b. division, c. remuneration, d. excision)

67. (a. Mercury, b. Venus, c. Sun, d. Earth) : NEPTUNE :: ALPHA : OMEGA

68. (a. Cali, b. Caracas, c. Quito, d. Bogotá) : BUDAPEST :: COLOMBIA : HUNGARY

69. LOW : BRAY :: (a. idiotic, b. bovine, c. subterranean, d. canine) : ASININE

70. BATTLE : CREEK :: GRAND : (a. Canyon, b. Dame, c. Rapids, d. Teton)

71. (a. Baum, b. Dodgson, c. Feiffer, d. Potter) : CARROLL :: OZ : WONDERLAND

72. WELT : WELTER :: LUMP : (a. pummel, b. jumble, c. prole, d. lumber)

73. OSS : (a. CIA, b. FBI, c. IRS, d. SSI) :: LEAGUE OF NATIONS : UNITED NATIONS

74. MEASURED : ORGIASTIC :: (a. Apollonian, b. Bacchanalian, c. Melpomenian, d. Panglossian) : DIONYSIAN

75. PRIDE : SENSE :: PREJUDICE : (a. nonsense, b. sensibility, c. tolerance, d. logic)

76. NAPOLEON : WATERLOO :: LEE : (a. Antietam, b. Appomattox, c. Gettysburg, d. Sumter)

77. AMERICAN GOTHIC : (a. Hart, b. Poe, c. Whistler, d. Wood) :: NIGHTHAWKS : HOPPER

78. FETED : FETID :: ENTERTAINED : (a. considered, b. piquant, c. noisome, d. cacophonous)

79. (a. Manhattan, b. Wall Street, c. Midtown, d. Second City) : NEW YORK :: THE CITY : LONDON

80. INVISIBLE MAN : (a. Baldwin, b. Bradbury, c. Ellison, d. Himes) :: THE THIN MAN : HAMMETT

81. KNEECAP : PATELLA :: (a. collarbone, b. hip bone, c. elbow, d. tibia) : CLAVICLE

82. HENRY DAVID THOREAU : TRANSCENDENTALISM :: (a. Camus, b. Pound, c. Jameson, d. Crane) : EXISTENTIALISM

83. WOLF : DRUM :: (a. flower, b. assassin, c. end, d. start) : MURDER

84. (a. room, b. closet, c. suitcase, d. building) : VESTIBULE :: CONSTITUTION : PREAMBLE

85. QUART : PINT :: (a. butt, b. hogshead, c. kellion, d. drum) : BARREL

86. SINE : (a. cosecant, b. cosine, c. secant, d. tangent) :: TANGENT : COTANGENT

87. RUFF : COLLAR :: PERUKE : (a. hat, b. coat, c. pipe, d. wig)

88. HOMERIC : SWIFTIAN :: EPIC : (a. classical, b. epistolary, c. satirical, d. naturalistic)

89. (a. plebian, b. tyro, c. fop, d. tycoon) : NOVICE :: MAVEN : EXPERT

90. PANEGYRIC : CRITICAL :: POLEMIC : (a. succinct, b. impartial, c. verbose, d. direct)

91. PROUST : SARTRE :: STUPOR : (a. artist, b. teaser, c. arrest, d. roused)

92. SEMIOTICS : SIGNS :: SEMANTICS : (a. location, b. language, c. laws, d. meanings)

93. RADAR : SMOG :: ACRONYM : (a. anagram, b. portmanteau, c. epigram, d. synecdoche)

94. $1^{10} : 10^0 :: 2^1 :$ (a. 2^0, b. 1^2, c. $\frac{1}{2}^{-1}$, d. 10^0)

95. MERETRICIOUS : MERITORIOUS :: (a. commendable, b. gaudy, c. lamentable, d. formidable) : LAUDABLE

96. OBEISANCE : PROSTRATION :: (a. defiance, b. deference, c. insolence, d. indifference) : SUBMISSION

97. BECQUEREL : (a. fluid dynamics, b. quantum mechanics, c. electromagnetism, d. radiation) :: McCLINTOCK : TRANSPOSONS

98. FLUVIAL : UXORIAL :: RIVER : (a. wealth, b. uncle, c. oil, d. wife)

99. CUBIT : QUINTAL :: LENGTH : (a. energy, b. weight, c. volume, d. pressure)

100. CHINK : CHINE :: (a. cleft, b. sling, c. nexus, d. spunk) : SPINE

101. CHUKKER : POLO :: (a. heat, b. period, c. half, d. inning) : BASEBALL

102. BOUGH : THOROUGH :: (a. know, b. tough, c. cow, d. brought) : BURRO

103. COMMODORE PERRY : MARCO POLO :: (a. America, b. Japan, c. India, d. Mexico) : CHINA

104. LINEAR : (a. sculptural, b. painterly, c. Impressionist, d. circular) :: INGRES : DELACROIX

105. $\dfrac{14}{7} : \dfrac{1}{2} :: \dfrac{25}{15} :$ (a. 2, b. $\dfrac{5}{3}$, c. $\dfrac{3}{5}$, d. $\dfrac{1}{2}$)

106. TRAJAN : (a. temple, b. villa, c. basilica, d. column) :: CONSTANTINE : ARCH

107. DNA : THYMINE :: RNA : (a. cytosine, b. uracil, c. adenine, d. guanine)

108. SANTIAGO DE COMPOSTELA : ROMANESQUE :: NOTRE DAME : (a. ancient, b. Gothic, c. Baroque, d. Rococo)

109. HYDROLOGY : (a. hydrogen, b. horses, c. water, d. electricity) :: PYROLOGY : FIRE

110. ODIN : ZEUS :: (a. Frigg, b. Loki, c. Baldr, d. Tyr) : APHRODITE

111. PINETOP PERKINS : PIANO :: B. B. KING : (a. fiddle, b. harmonica, c. banjo, d. guitar)

112. PAGODA : (a. Shintoism, b. Taoism, c. Buddhism, d. Confucianism) :: MOSQUE : ISLAM

113. GOLDEN GATE BRIDGE : SAN FRANCISCO :: LAKE PONTCHARTRAIN CAUSEWAY : (a. Salt Lake City, b. Seattle, c. Key West, d. New Orleans)

114. FAMILY : GENUS :: (a. Hominidae, b. Primate, c. Chordata, d. Sapien) : HOMO

115. (a. communism, b. imperialism, c. nationalism, d. industrialism) : EUROPEAN
COLONIZATION :: CONTAINMENT : MONROE DOCTRINE

116. METACARPAL : METATARSAL :: ULNA : (a. scapula, b. fibula, c. femur, d. phlanges)

117. (a. calumny, b. silence, c. lampoon, d. cacophony) : NOISE :: CARICATURE :
PORTRAIT

118. $\sqrt{117} : \sqrt{13} :: 72 :$ (a. 24, b. $\sqrt{66}$, c. 48, d. 12)

119. (a. Rodin, b. Goya, c. Van Gogh, d. Blake) : CLAUDEL :: DEGAS : VALADON

120. THROW : (a. reflexive, b. indicative, c. transitive, d. subjunctive) :: COMPLAIN :
INTRANSITIVE

ANSWERS AND EXPLANATIONS

1. GUN : HOLSTER :: ARROW : (a. archer, b. bow, **c. quiver**, d. target)
   (c) A gun is carried in a holster, just as an arrow is carried in a quiver.

2. COMET : SHIP :: (a. Halley, b. meteor, **c. tail**, d. rocket) : WAKE
   (c) A comet is followed by its tail, and a ship is followed by its wake.

3. MOON : WANE :: (a. eclipse, **b. tide**, c. crater, d. sun) : EBB
   (b) The receding moon wanes, just as the receding tide ebbs.

4. LINCOLN MEMORIAL : MONTICELLO : 1 : (a. 2, **b. 5**, c. 10, d. 25)
   (b) The Lincoln Memorial appears on the back of the penny, or 1-cent piece, and Monticello appears on the back of the nickel, or 5-cent piece.

5. HAT : HEAD :: COZY : (a. chest, b. lap, c. fireplace, **d. teapot**)
   (d) A hat keeps a head warm, and a cozy keeps a teapot warm.

6. LEAF : (a. bean, **b. bark**, c. clove, d. root) :: MINT : CINNAMON
   (b) Mint is a kind of leaf, and cinnamon is a kind of bark.

7. BEAUTY : PROOF :: EYE OF THE BEHOLDER : (**a. pudding**, b. puzzle, c. product, d. taking)
   (a) One adage says, "Beauty is in the eye of the beholder," just as another adage says, "The proof is in the pudding."

8. SATURN : MOON :: SATURDAY : (a. Uranus, b. Thursday, c. astronomy, **d. Monday**)
   (d) Saturn is the origin of the word *Saturday,* and the moon is the origin of the word *Monday.*

9. BAKER'S DOZEN : SCORE :: 13 : (**a. 20**, b. gross, c. donuts, d. 26)
   (a) A baker's dozen is 13 items, and a score is 20 items.

10. (a. whisper, b. garble, c. chortle, **d. yell**) : TALK :: GUFFAW : LAUGH
    (d) To yell is to talk loudly, just as to guffaw is to laugh loudly.

11. YOU : ME :: SECOND : (**a. first**, b. second, c. third, d. fourth)
    (a) *You* is a second-person pronoun, and *me* is a first-person pronoun.

12. (a. circumference, **b. area**, c. sector, d. arc) : VOLUME :: CIRCLE : SPHERE
    (b) Area is the space in a circle, just as volume is the space in a sphere.

13. (a. North America, **b. Europe**, c. Africa, d. Australia) : ASIA :: MATTERHORN : EVEREST
    (b) The Matterhorn is located in Europe, and Everest is located in Asia.

14. EMU : (a. reptilian, b. mammalian, c. insectival, **d. avian**) :: NEWT : AMPHIBIAN
(**d**) An emu is a member of the Avian class (birds), just as a newt is a member of the Amphibian class.

15. (a. electron, b. ganglia, **c. nucleus**, d. neutron) : PIT :: ATOM : CHERRY
(**c**) A nucleus is at the center of an atom, and a pit is at the center of a cherry.

16. HOMBURG : MACKINTOSH :: (a. boot, **b. hat**, c. slicker, d. umbrella) : RAINCOAT
(**b**) The homburg is a type of hat, and the mackintosh is a type of raincoat.

17. (a. plaster, **b. linen**, c. linoleum, d. rayon) : DRYWALL :: FLAX : GYPSUM
(**b**) Linen is made of flax, and drywall is made of gypsum.

18. 1912 : (a. 1910, **b. 1915**, c. 1920, d. 1925) :: TITANIC : LUSITANIA
(**b**) The *Titanic* sank in 1912, just as the *Lusitania* sank in 1915.

19. RUBBER : MATCH :: (a. racquetball, b. squash, c. cribbage, **d. bridge**) : TENNIS
(**d**) A rubber is a completed game of bridge, and a match is a completed game of tennis.

20. (a. Rhine, b. Rhone, **c. Danube**, d. Oder) : VIENNA :: SEINE : PARIS
(**c**) The Danube river flows through Vienna, just as the River Seine flows through Paris.

21. LAPIDARY : TOPIARY :: (a. ice, b. leather, **c. stone**, d. wood) : plant
(**c**) Lapidary refers to working with stone, and topiary refers to working with plants.

22. TRAIN : (a. caboose, **b. engineer**, c. locomotive, d. porter) :: SHELL : COXSWAIN
(**b**) An engineer oversees operation of a train, just as a coxswain oversees operation of a shell, or small crew boat.

23. COULD : SHOULD :: (**a. capacity**, b. desire, c. necessity, d. expediency) : PROPRIETY
(**a**) The term *could* implies a capacity to act, while the term *should* implies a propriety to act. For example, "I *could* go to the market" means that I have the capacity and the ability to go to the market, while "I *should* go the market" means that it would be appropriate for me to go to the market.

24. SANE : SON :: GAIN : (a. loss, b. gone, **c. gun**, d. cone)
(**c**) *Sane* rhymes with *gain*, just as *son* rhymes with *gun*.

25. (**a. geneticist**, b. linguist, c. historian, d. pharmocologist) : ECONOMIST :: HGP : GNP
(**a**) A geneticist works with the HGP, or Human Genome Project, and an economist works with the GNP, or gross national product.

26. OH : BUCKEYE :: CT : (a. buckwheat, b. chestnut, c. maple, **d. nutmeg**)
    (**d**) OH, or Ohio, is known as the Buckeye State, and CT, Connecticut, was at one time known as the Nutmeg State. (It is now known as the Constitution State.)

27. INTERREGNUM : INTERMISSION :: (a. development, **b. government**, c. propriety, d. conversation) : ENTERTAINMENT
    (**b**) An interregnum is a temporary suspension in government, and an intermission is a temporary suspension of entertainment.

28. ROCK : EROSION :: IRON : (a. conduction, **b. oxidation**, c. metallurgy, d. smelting)
    (**b**) Erosion is a gradual destruction of rock, just as oxidation is a gradual destruction of iron.

29. CEL : CELL :: CARTOON : (a. carton, **b. organism**, c. protoplasm, d. animation)
    (**b**) A cel (short for celluloid) is the smallest unit in a cartoon, and a cell is the smallest unit in an organism.

30. (a. agora, b. academy, **c. monastery**, d. saturnalia) : SPA :: ASCETIC : SALUBRIOUS
    (**c**) A monastery is an ascetic environment, and a spa is a salubrious environment.

31. ADMIRE : LIONIZE :: (a. belittle, b. betray, **c. dislike**, d. vituperate) : ABHOR
    (**c**) To lionize is to greatly admire, just as to abhor is to greatly dislike.

32. CLEOPATRA : (**a. asp**, b. hemlock, c. knife, d. illness) :: MARIE ANTOINETTE : GUILLOTINE
    (**a**) Cleopatra was killed by an asp, and Marie Antoinette was killed by a guillotine.

33. COWBOY : GAUCHO :: UNITED STATES : (a. Brazil, **b. Argentina**, c. Portugal, d. Spain)
    (**b**) The cowboy is a horseman native to the United States, and the gaucho is a horseman native to Argentina.

34. FREUD : PSYCHOANALYSIS :: (a. Rogers, **b. Skinner**, c. Chomsky, d. Maslow) : BEHAVIORISM
    (**b**) Sigmund Freud is the founder of psychoanalysis, and B.F. Skinner is the founder of behaviorism.

35. BLUE BLOOD : (a. red herring, b. red light, c. red letter, **d. red tape**) :: ARISTOCRACY : BUREAUCRACY
    (**d**) *Blue blood* is another term for the aristocracy, just as *red tape* is another term for bureaucracy.

36. WOMAN : WOMEN :: STIMULUS : (a. stimulus, b. stimula, c. stimuluses, **d. stimuli**)
    (**d**) The plural of woman is women, just as the plural of stimulus is stimuli.

37. MERCURY : SILVER :: (a. Ac, **b. Hg**, c. Me, d. Nr) : AG
    (**b**) The periodic symbol for mercury is Hg, and the periodic symbol for silver is Ag.

38. (a. kid, **b. lamb**, c. pup, d. foal) : CUB :: OVINE : URSINE
    (**b**) A lamb is a young member of the ovine family, and a cub is a young member of the ursine family.

39. (a. Apollo, b. Ares, **c. Poseidon**, d. Saturn) : NEPTUNE :: ZEUS : JUPITER
    (**c**) The god of the sea in Roman mythology is Neptune and in Greek mythology is Poseidon, and the supreme god in Roman mythology is Jupiter and in Greek mythology is Zeus.

40. TETRA : SESQUI :: 4 : (**a. 1.5**, b. 2.5, c. 6, d. 7)
    (**a**) *Tetra–* is a prefix meaning 4, just as *sesqui–* is a prefix meaning 1.5.

41. PITHY : EPIGRAMMATIC :: (a. lugubrious, b. prolix, **c. trenchant**, d. discursive) : MORDANT
    (**c**) *Pithy* and *epigrammatic* both mean concise, and *trenchant* and *mordant* both mean caustic.

42. AC : DC :: (a. Franklin, b. Marconi, **c. Tesla**, d. Bell) : Edison
    (**c**) Nikola Tesla discovered alternating current, or AC, and Thomas Edison discovered direct current, or DC.

43. 2 : (a. 0, b. 7, **c. 12**, d. 16) :: ACIDIC : ALKALINE
    (**c**) A pH number of 2 denotes an acidic substance, and a pH number of 12 denotes an alkaline substance.

44. (a. dulcimer, b. lute, c. timpani, **d. virginal**) : KEYBOARD :: PINBOX : CAMERA
    (**d**) A virginal is an antique version of a keyboard, and a pinbox is an antique version of a camera.

45. (a. snake, b. fish, **c. pig**, d. tree) : STONE :: CIRCE : MEDUSA
    (**c**) In Greek mythology, Circe turned men into pigs, and Medusa turned men into stone.

46. SCENT : CENTER :: COUGH : (a. hub, **b. coffer**, c. cougar, d. lozenge)
    (**b**) The word *center* begins with the sound "scent," just as the word *coffer* begins with the sound "cough."

47. (a. gammon, **b. venison**, c. buck, d. veal) : DOE :: BEEF : COW
    (**b**) Venison is the meat of a doe, or female deer, and beef is the meat of a cow.

48. BRAID : UPBRAID :: (**a. plait**, b. buckle, c. chastise, d. recant) : REBUKE
    (**a**) *Plait* means to braid, and *upbraid* means to rebuke.

49. HUNTER GATHERER : AGRARIAN :: (**a. stone**, b. arrow, c. urn, d. steel) : BRONZE
(**a**) A hunter-gatherer society dominated the Stone Age, and an agrarian society dominated the Bronze Age.

50. (a. basalt, **b. sandstone**, c. slate, d. marble) : SEDIMENTARY :: GRANITE : IGNEOUS
(**b**) Sandstone is a sedimentary type of rock, just as granite is an igneous type of rock.

51. SPELEOLOGY : (**a. caves**, b. games, c. lexicons, d. rocks) :: ZOOLOGY : ANIMALS
(**a**) Speleology is the study of caves, and zoology is the study of animals.

52. ROMAN : ENGLISH :: (a. Alexandrian, **b. Cyrillic**, c. Slavic, d. Greek) : RUSSIAN
(**b**) English writing is based on the Roman alphabet, just as Russian writing is based on the Cyrillic alphabet.

53. WORRY : (a. fear, **b. panic**, c. vex, d. assuage) :: ANNOY : EXCRUCIATE
(**b**) To panic is to worry extremely, and to excruciate is to annoy extremely.

54. GREEK : NORSE :: ZEUS : (a. Asgard, b. Njord, **c. Odin**, d. Thor)
(**c**) Zeus was king of the Greek gods, and Odin was king of the Norse gods.

55. INFER : CONCLUDE :: IMPLY : (**a. intimate**, b. initiate, c. state, d. terminate)
(**a**) Infer means to conclude a meaning, and imply means to intimate a meaning.

56. (a. buffoon, b. constable, **c. dupe**, d. scaramouch) : CHARLATAN :: PREY : PREDATOR
(**c**) A charlatan dupes, just as a predator preys—or alternately, a charlatan goes after a dupe, and a predator goes after prey.

57. SOPERIFIC : ANALGESIC :: (a. hunger, b. thirst, **c. wakefulness**, d. lethargy) : PAIN
(**c**) A soporific alleviates wakefulness, and an analgesic alleviates pain.

58. SEMPER : CARPE :: FIDELIS : (a. absurdem, **b. diem**, c. factotum, d. lector)
(**b**) *Semper fidelis* is a Latin adage meaning "always faithful," and *carpe diem* is a Latin adage meaning "seize the day".

59. (a. preface, c. encomium, **c. peroration**, d. homily) : SPEECH :: CODA : SONATA
(**c**) A peroration is a recapitulation at the end of a speech, just as a coda is a recapitulation at the end of a sonata.

60. (a. ale, b. kvass, c. gin, **d. sake**) : CLARET :: RICE : GRAPE
(**d**) Sake is a wine made from rice, just as a claret is a wine made from grapes.

61. SERENDIPITOUS : SURREPTITIOUS :: (**a. planned**, b. slow, c. desirable, d. understood) : OPEN
(**a**) Something serendipitous, or discovered by luck or chance, is not planned, and something surreptitious, or hidden, is not open.

62. TROY : 12 :: (a. SI, b. metric, c. avoirdupois, d. Winchester) : 16
    (**c**) A troy pound has 12 ounces, and an avoirdupois pound has 16 ounces.

63. CONGRESS : (a. bills, b. senators, c. Capitol Hill, **d. representatives**) ::
    PARLIAMENT : COMMONS
    (**d**) The lower house of America's Congress is the House of Representatives, just as the
    lower house of Britain's Parliament is the House of Commons.

64. C : MM :: (a. VI, **b. IX**, c. XI, d. XIV) : CLXXX
    (**b**) Two thousand, Roman numeral MM, is 20 times 100, Roman numeral C, just as
    180, Roman numeral CLXXX, is 20 times 9, Roman numeral IX.

65. FICKLE : (a. unsteady, b. corpulent, **c. gloomy**, d. incisive) :: MERCURIAL : SATURNINE
    (**c**) A fickle person is mercurial, and a gloomy person is saturnine.

66. SECT : SECTOR :: DENOMINATION : (a. circumference, **b. division**,
    c. remuneration, d. excision)
    (**b**) *Sect* and *denomination* both refer to a religious group, and *sector* and *division* both
    refer to a subset.

67. (**a. Mercury**, b. Venus, c. Sun, d. Earth) : NEPTUNE :: ALPHA : OMEGA
    (**a**) Mercury is the first planet in the solar system and Neptune the last, while *alpha* is
    Greek for first and *omega* Greek for last.

68. (a. Cali, b. Caracas, c. Quito **d. Bogotá**) : BUDAPEST :: COLOMBIA : HUNGARY
    (**d**) Bogotá is the capital of Colombia, just as Budapest is the capital of Hungary.

69. LOW : BRAY :: (a. idiotic, **b. bovine**, c. subterranean, d. canine) : ASININE
    (**b**) A low is the noise of a bovine animal, or cow, and a bray is the noise of an asinine
    animal, or donkey.

70. BATTLE : CREEK :: GRAND : (a. Canyon, b. Dame, **c. Rapids**, d. Teton)
    (**c**) Battle Creek is a city in Michigan, as is Grand Rapids.

71. (**a. Baum**, b. Dodgson, c. Feiffer, d. Potter) : CARROLL :: OZ : WONDERLAND
    (**a**) Frank Baum created the fictional world of *The Wizard of Oz*, and Lewis Carroll
    created the fictional world of *Alice in Wonderland*.

72. WELT : WELTER :: LUMP : (a. pummel, **b. jumble**, c. prole, d. lumber)
    (**b**) A welt is a lump on the body, and a welter is a jumble.

73. OSS : (**a. CIA**, b. FBI, c. IRS, d. SSI) :: LEAGUE OF NATIONS : UNITED NATIONS
    (**a**) The OSS was the precursor to the CIA, just as the League of Nations was the
    precursor to the United Nations.

74. MEASURED : ORGIASTIC :: (**a. Apollonian**, b. Bacchanalian, c. Melpomenian, d. Panglossian) : DIONYSIAN
(**a**) *Measured* and *Apollonian* both mean characterized by restraint, and *orgiastic* and *Dionysian* both mean characterized by excess.

75. PRIDE : SENSE :: PREJUDICE : (a. nonsense, **b. sensibility**, c. tolerance, d. logic)
(**b**) *Pride and Prejudice* is a novel by Jane Austen, as is *Sense and Sensibility*.

76. NAPOLEON : WATERLOO :: LEE : (a. Antietam, **b. Appomattox**, c. Gettysburg, d. Sumter)
(**b**) Napoleon Bonaparte suffered his final defeat at Waterloo, just as Robert E. Lee suffered his final defeat at Appomattox.

77. AMERICAN GOTHIC : (a. Hart, b. Poe, c. Whistler, **d. Wood**) :: NIGHTHAWKS : HOPPER
(**d**) *American Gothic* is a painting by artist Grant Wood, and *Nighthawks* is a painting by artist Edward Hopper.

78. FETED : FETID :: ENTERTAINED : (a. considered, b. piquant, **c. noisome**, d. cacophonous)
(**c**) *Feted* is a state of being entertained, and *fetid* is a state of noisome, or offensive, odor.

79. (a. Manhattan, **b. Wall Street**, c. Midtown, d. Second City) : NEW YORK :: THE CITY : LONDON
(**b**) Wall Street is the financial district of New York City, and The City is the financial district of London.

80. INVISIBLE MAN : (a. Baldwin, b. Bradbury, **c. Ellison**, d. Himes) :: THE THIN MAN : HAMMETT
(**c**) *Invisible Man* is a novel by author Ralph Ellison, and *The Thin Man* is a novel by author Dashell Hammett.

81. KNEECAP : PATELLA :: (**a. collarbone**, b. hip bone, c. elbow, d. tibia) : CLAVICLE
(**a**) *Patella* is another name for the kneecap, just as *clavicle* is another name for the collarbone.

82. HENRY DAVID THOREAU : TRANSCENDENTALISM :: (**a. Camus**, b. Pound, c. Jameson, d. Crane) : EXISTENTIALISM
(**a**) Henry David Thoreau was a founder of the philosophical movement of transcendentalism, just as Albert Camus was a founder of the philosophical movement of existentialism.

83. WOLF : DRUM :: (**a. flower**, b. assassin, c. end, d. start) : MURDER
(**a**) Remove the letters *–er* and reverse the remaining letters in *flower* to get the word *wolf*, just as you remove the letters *–er* and reverse the remaining letters in *murder* to get the word *drum*.

84. (a. room, b. closet, c. suitcase, **d. building**) : VESTIBULE :: CONSTITUTION : PREAMBLE
(**d**) The first part of a building is a vestibule, and the first part of a constitution is a preamble.

85. QUART : PINT :: (a. butt, **b. hogshead**, c. kellion, d. drum) : BARREL
(**b**) A quart equals two pints, just as a hogshead equals two barrels.

86. SINE : (**a. cosecant**, b. cosine, c. secant, d. tangent) :: TANGENT : COTANGENT
(**a**) A cosecant is the reciprocal of the sine, and the cotangent is the reciprocal of the tangent.

87. RUFF : COLLAR :: PERUKE : (a. hat, b. coat, c. pipe, **d. wig**)
(**d**) A ruff is an antique type of collar, just as a peruke is an antique type of wig.

88. HOMERIC : SWIFTIAN :: EPIC : (a. classical, b. epistolary, **c. satirical**, d. naturalistic)
(**c**) *Homeric*, from the Greek author Homer, refers to a piece with an epic tone, and *Swiftian*, from writer Jonathan Swift, refers to a piece with a satirical tone.

89. (a. plebian, **b. tyro**, c. fop, d. tycoon) : NOVICE :: MAVEN : EXPERT
(**b**) A tyro is a novice, or beginner, just as a maven is an expert.

90. PANEGYRIC : CRITICAL :: POLEMIC : (a. succinct, **b. impartial**, c. verbose, d. direct)
(**b**) Being critical is the opposite of being panegryic, or praising, and being impartial is the opposite of being polemic, or argumentative.

91. PROUST : SARTRE :: STUPOR : (a. artist, b. teaser, **c. arrest**, d. roused)
(**c**) Rearrange the letters of *Proust* to get *stupor*, and rearrange the letters of *Sartre* to get *arrest*.

92. SEMIOTICS : SIGNS :: SEMANTICS : (a. location, b. language, c. laws, **d. meanings**)
(**d**) Semiotics is the study of signs, and semantics is the study of meanings.

93. RADAR : SMOG :: ACRONYM : (a. anagram, **b. portmanteau**, c. epigram, d. synecdoche)
(**b**) RADAR is an acronym for <u>RA</u>dio <u>D</u>etection <u>A</u>nd <u>R</u>anging, and smog is a portmanteau from <u>SM</u>oke and f<u>OG</u>.

94. $1^{10} : 10^0 :: 2^1 :$ (a. 2^0, b. 1^2, **c.** $\frac{1}{2}^{-1}$, d. 10^0)
(**c**) One to the tenth power equals 10 to the zero power, just as 2 to the first power equals $\frac{1}{2}$ to the negative first power.

95. MERETRICIOUS : MERITORIOUS :: (a. commendable, **b. gaudy**, c. lamentable, d. formidable) : LAUDABLE
(b) *Meretricious* means gaudy, and *meritorious* means laudable.

96. OBEISANCE : PROSTRATION :: (a. defiance, **b. deference**, c. insolence, d. indifference) : SUBMISSION
(b) An obeisance expresses deference, while a prostration expresses submission.

97. BECQUEREL : (a. fluid dynamics, b. quantum mechanics, c. electromagnetism, **d. radiation**) :: McCLINTOCK : TRANSPOSONS
(d) Antoine Henri Becquerel was the scientist credited with first discovering natural radiation, and Barbara McClintock was the geneticist credited with first discovering transposons (jumping genes).

98. FLUVIAL : UXORIAL :: RIVER : (a. wealth, b. uncle, c. oil, **d. wife**)
(d) *Fluvial* means relating to a river, just as *uxorial* means relating to a wife.

99. CUBIT : QUINTAL :: LENGTH : (a. energy, **b. weight**, c. volume, d. pressure)
(b) A cubit is a measure of length, and a quintal is a measure of weight.

100. CHINK : CHINE :: (**a. cleft**, b. sling, c. nexus, d. spunk) : SPINE
(a) A chink is another term for a cleft, or missing piece, while chine is another term for the spine.

101. CHUKKER : POLO :: (a. heat, b. period, c. half, **d. inning**) : BASEBALL
(d) Chukkers are the playing periods in polo, and innings are the playing periods in baseball.

102. BOUGH : THOROUGH :: (a. know, b. tough, **c. cow**, d. brought) : BURRO
(c) *Bough* rhymes with *cow*, just as *thorough* rhymes with *burro*.

103. COMMODORE PERRY : MARCO POLO :: (a. America, **b. Japan**, c. India, d. Mexico) : CHINA
(b) Commodore Perry opened Japanese ports to Western trade, and Marco Polo facilitated trade between China and the West.

104. LINEAR : (a. sculptural, **b. painterly**, c. Impressionist, d. circular) :: INGRES : DELACROIX
(b) The so-called linear style of Jean-Auguste-Dominique Ingres emphasized draftsmanship and line, while his contemporary Eugène Delacroix exhibited a painterly style with more expressive brushstrokes.

105. $\frac{14}{7} : \frac{1}{2} :: \frac{25}{15} :$ (a. 2, b. $\frac{5}{3}$, **c. $\frac{3}{5}$**, d. $\frac{1}{2}$)
(c) $\frac{1}{2}$ is the reciprocal of $\frac{14}{7}$, and $\frac{3}{5}$ is the reciprocal of $\frac{25}{15}$.

106. TRAJAN : (a. temple, b. villa, c. basilica, **d. column**) :: CONSTANTINE : ARCH
(**d**) Trajan's Column and the Arch of Constantine both commemorate the triumph of the Roman emperors for whom they are named.

107. DNA : THYMINE :: RNA : (a. cytosine, **b. uracil**, c. adenine, d. guanine)
(**b**) Thymine is an acid used only by DNA, and uracil is an acid used only by RNA.

108. SANTIAGO DE COMPOSTELA : ROMANESQUE :: NOTRE DAME : (a. ancient, **b. Gothic**, c. Baroque, d. Rococo)
(**b**) Santiago de Compostela is a Spanish Romanesque cathedral, and Notre Dame is a French Gothic cathedral.

109. HYDROLOGY : (a. hydrogen, b. horses, **c. water**, d. electricity) :: PYROLOGY : FIRE
(**c**) *Hydrology* is the study of water, while *pyrology* is the study of fire.

110. ODIN : ZEUS :: (**a. Frigg**, b. Loki, c. Baldr, d. Tyr) : APHRODITE
(**a**) Odin is the supreme being in Norse mythology, as Zeus is in Greek mythology; Frigg is the goddess of love in Norse mythology, as Aphrodite is in Greek mythology.

111. PINETOP PERKINS : PIANO :: B. B. KING : (a. fiddle, b. harmonica, c. banjo, **d. guitar**)
(**d**) Pinetop Perkins was a Grammy Award-winning pianist, and B. B. King was a Grammy Award-winning blues guitarist.

112. PAGODA : (a. Shintoism, b. Taoism, **c. Buddhism**, d. Confucianism) :: MOSQUE : ISLAM
(**c**) Pagodas are sacred Buddhist temples found in the East, and Mosques are sacred spaces in Islam.

113. GOLDEN GATE BRIDGE : SAN FRANCISCO :: LAKE PONTCHARTRAIN CAUSEWAY : (a. Salt Lake City, b. Seattle, c. Key West, **d. New Orleans**)
(**d**) The Golden Gate Bridge connects travelers to San Francisco, and the Lake Pontchartrain Causeway connects travelers to New Orleans.

114. FAMILY : GENUS :: (**a. Hominidae**, b. Primate, c. Chordata, d. Sapien) : HOMO
(**a**) *Homo* is a genus, and *Hominidae* is a family.

115. (**a. communism**, b. imperialism, c. nationalism, d. industrialism) : EUROPEAN COLONIZATION :: CONTAINMENT : MONROE DOCTRINE
(**a**) Containment was a policy that focused on stopping the spread of communism. The Monroe Doctrine was a policy that focused on stopping the spread of European influence and colonization in the Western Hemisphere.

116. METACARPAL : METATARSAL :: ULNA : (a. scapula, **b. fibula**, c. femur, d. phlanges)
(**b**) The ulna is connected to metacarpals, and the fibula is connected to metatarsals.

117. (a. calumny, b. silence, c. lampoon, **d. cacophony**) : NOISE :: CARICATURE : PORTRAIT
    (**d**) A cacophony is a type of noise, and a caricature is a type of portrait.

118. $\sqrt{117} : \sqrt{13} :: 72 : $ (a. 24, b. $\sqrt{66}$, c. 48, d. 12)
    (**a**) $\sqrt{117}$ is 3 times $\sqrt{13}$, and 72 is 3 times 24.

119. (**a. Rodin**, b. Goya, c. Van Gogh, d. Blake) : CLAUDEL :: DEGAS : VALADON
    (**a**) The sculptor Camille Claudel was a muse, model, and student of Auguste Rodin, and the artist Suzanne Valadon shared a parallel relationship with Edgar Degas.

120. THROW : (a. reflexive, b. indicative, **c. transitive**, d. subjunctive) :: COMPLAIN : INTRANSITIVE
    (**c**) *Throw* is a transitive verb, while *complain* is an intransitive verb.

ANSWER SHEET FOR PRACTICE TEST 3

1. (a) (b) (c) (d)
2. (a) (b) (c) (d)
3. (a) (b) (c) (d)
4. (a) (b) (c) (d)
5. (a) (b) (c) (d)
6. (a) (b) (c) (d)
7. (a) (b) (c) (d)
8. (a) (b) (c) (d)
9. (a) (b) (c) (d)
10. (a) (b) (c) (d)
11. (a) (b) (c) (d)
12. (a) (b) (c) (d)
13. (a) (b) (c) (d)
14. (a) (b) (c) (d)
15. (a) (b) (c) (d)
16. (a) (b) (c) (d)
17. (a) (b) (c) (d)
18. (a) (b) (c) (d)
19. (a) (b) (c) (d)
20. (a) (b) (c) (d)
21. (a) (b) (c) (d)
22. (a) (b) (c) (d)
23. (a) (b) (c) (d)
24. (a) (b) (c) (d)
25. (a) (b) (c) (d)
26. (a) (b) (c) (d)
27. (a) (b) (c) (d)
28. (a) (b) (c) (d)
29. (a) (b) (c) (d)
30. (a) (b) (c) (d)
31. (a) (b) (c) (d)
32. (a) (b) (c) (d)
33. (a) (b) (c) (d)
34. (a) (b) (c) (d)
35. (a) (b) (c) (d)
36. (a) (b) (c) (d)
37. (a) (b) (c) (d)
38. (a) (b) (c) (d)
39. (a) (b) (c) (d)
40. (a) (b) (c) (d)

41. (a) (b) (c) (d)
42. (a) (b) (c) (d)
43. (a) (b) (c) (d)
44. (a) (b) (c) (d)
45. (a) (b) (c) (d)
46. (a) (b) (c) (d)
47. (a) (b) (c) (d)
48. (a) (b) (c) (d)
49. (a) (b) (c) (d)
50. (a) (b) (c) (d)
51. (a) (b) (c) (d)
52. (a) (b) (c) (d)
53. (a) (b) (c) (d)
54. (a) (b) (c) (d)
55. (a) (b) (c) (d)
56. (a) (b) (c) (d)
57. (a) (b) (c) (d)
58. (a) (b) (c) (d)
59. (a) (b) (c) (d)
60. (a) (b) (c) (d)
61. (a) (b) (c) (d)
62. (a) (b) (c) (d)
63. (a) (b) (c) (d)
64. (a) (b) (c) (d)
65. (a) (b) (c) (d)
66. (a) (b) (c) (d)
67. (a) (b) (c) (d)
68. (a) (b) (c) (d)
69. (a) (b) (c) (d)
70. (a) (b) (c) (d)
71. (a) (b) (c) (d)
72. (a) (b) (c) (d)
73. (a) (b) (c) (d)
74. (a) (b) (c) (d)
75. (a) (b) (c) (d)
76. (a) (b) (c) (d)
77. (a) (b) (c) (d)
78. (a) (b) (c) (d)
79. (a) (b) (c) (d)
80. (a) (b) (c) (d)

81. (a) (b) (c) (d)
82. (a) (b) (c) (d)
83. (a) (b) (c) (d)
84. (a) (b) (c) (d)
85. (a) (b) (c) (d)
86. (a) (b) (c) (d)
87. (a) (b) (c) (d)
88. (a) (b) (c) (d)
89. (a) (b) (c) (d)
90. (a) (b) (c) (d)
91. (a) (b) (c) (d)
92. (a) (b) (c) (d)
93. (a) (b) (c) (d)
94. (a) (b) (c) (d)
95. (a) (b) (c) (d)
96. (a) (b) (c) (d)
97. (a) (b) (c) (d)
98. (a) (b) (c) (d)
99. (a) (b) (c) (d)
100. (a) (b) (c) (d)
101. (a) (b) (c) (d)
102. (a) (b) (c) (d)
103. (a) (b) (c) (d)
104. (a) (b) (c) (d)
105. (a) (b) (c) (d)
106. (a) (b) (c) (d)
107. (a) (b) (c) (d)
108. (a) (b) (c) (d)
109. (a) (b) (c) (d)
110. (a) (b) (c) (d)
111. (a) (b) (c) (d)
112. (a) (b) (c) (d)
113. (a) (b) (c) (d)
114. (a) (b) (c) (d)
115. (a) (b) (c) (d)
116. (a) (b) (c) (d)
117. (a) (b) (c) (d)
118. (a) (b) (c) (d)
119. (a) (b) (c) (d)
120. (a) (b) (c) (d)

Practice Test 3

Time: 60 minutes
Length of Test: 120 Questions

Directions: For each of the following questions, you will find three capitalized terms and, in parentheses, four answer choices designated *a*, *b*, *c*, and *d*. Select the one answer choice that best completes the analogy with the three capitalized terms. (To record your answers, use the answer sheet that precedes this test.)

1. TAVERNS : SERVANT :: HOTELS : (a. custodian, b. pub, c. waiter, d. hostel)

2. SUSPECT : BOOK :: (a. investigator, b. convict, c. evidence, d. witness) : INTERVIEW

3. HINDENBERG : (a. *Lusitania*, b. *Titanic*, c. zeppelin, d. Kitty Hawk) :: FIRE : ICEBERG

4. ROPE : SPLICE :: (a. braid , b. knot, c. captain, d. metal) : SOLDER

5. POEM : LOPE :: MOPE : (a. strut, b. pole, c. lift, d. diverge)

6. APPOMATTOX : (a. Yorktown, b. Boston, c. Richmond, d. New York) :: CIVIL WAR : REVOLUTIONARY WAR

7. STRAND : EPISODE :: (a. cable, b. castaway, c. epistle, d. yarn) : EPIC

8. 3 : 2 :: CUBE : (a. square, b. sphere, c. axis, d. 8)

9. (a. underground, b. secret, c. dead, d. original) : NECROPOLIS :: LARGE : MEGAPOLIS

10. (a. 120°, b. 360°, c.180°, d. 45°) : 90° :: SUPPLEMENTARY : COMPLEMENTARY

11. STONE : PICTURE :: SETTING : (a. engraving, b. lithograph, c. canvas, d. frame)

12. BRAZEN : (a. bold, b. raze, c. zen, d. colorful) :: CHIDED : HIDE

13. APOTHECARY : CHANDLER :: MEDICINE : (a. shoes, b. candles, c. bells, d. rope)

14. SHIFTING : DOGMATIC :: WHIMSICAL : (a. softened, b. careless, c. determined, d. accurate)

15. OSTRICH : FLY :: ELEPHANT : (a. bird, b. walk, c. jump, d. masticate)

16. EXCULPATE : (a. ingratiate, b. incriminate, c. terraform, d. attack) :: FLOUNDER : SUCCEED

17. 3 : 2 :: 27 : (a. 4, b. 6, c. 8, d. 28)

18. PLANT : SEED :: FUNGUS : (a. root, b. parasite, c. spore, d. flower)

19. 4.4 : (a. 1, b. 2, c. 4, d. 8) :: POUNDS : KILOS

20. (a. pound, b. tilde, c. pipe, d. asterisk) : CARET :: * : ^

21. FILM : (a. aperture, b. shutter, c. retina, d. cornea) :: CAMERA : EYE

22. TRUMP : UPSTAGE :: (a. play, b. trick, c. scale, d. virtuoso) : PERFORMANCE

23. SNAFU : DETARTRATED :: ACRONYM : (a. onomatopoeia, b. homophone, c. palindrome, d. spoonerism)

24. RIGHT ANGLE : (a. line, b. vertical, c. complementary, d. congruent) :: 90 : 180

25. ULTRA– : (a. intro–, b. inter–, c. hyper–, d. infra–) :: OVER : UNDER

26. SHARPEN : HONE :: WIPE : (a. dust, b. burnish, c. cleanse, d. neaten)

27. RAIN : (a. wind, b. thunder, c. humidity, d. water) :: LIGHTNING : ELECTRICITY

28. CART : WAGON :: (a. 1, b. 2, c. 4, d. 6) : 4

29. GAGARIN : MAGELLAN :: ORBIT : (a. Everest, b. circumnavigation, c. red tide, d. Northwest Passage)

30. (a. 2nd, b. 5th, c. 11th, d. 13th) : 18TH :: SLAVERY : ALCOHOL

31. SWIFT : KIPLING :: (a. Gunga Din, b. Alice, c. Quartermain, d. Gulliver) : MOWGLI

32. FOLLICLE : (a. hair, b. vesicle, c. cuticle, d. fluid) :: OVUM : NAIL

33. VIDI : I SAW :: (a. veni, b. viri, c. vici, d. verdi) : I CONQUERED

34. PLANE : WASH :: (a. streamlined, b. smooth, c. lightweight, d. buoyant) : CLEAN

35. NELSON : (a. Magellan, b. Napoleon, c. Drake, d. Wellington) :: TRAFALGAR : WATERLOO

36. GRAVITY : NEWTON :: QUANTUM MECHANICS : (a. Heisenberg, b. Einstein, c. Morse, d. Farnsworth)

37. RICE : (a. Pakistani, b. Yanomamo, c. !Kung, d. Swede) :: TARO : FIJIAN

38. DIAMETER : (a. radius, b. dissection, c. diagonal, d. hypotenuse) :: CIRCLE : SQUARE

39. RAT : (a. primate, b. evolution, c. pea, d. flora) :: SKINNER : MENDEL

40. HEPATITIS : LIVER :: ENCEPHALITIS : (a. skull, b. pharynx, c. brain, d. endometrium)

41. MOLIÈRE : TARTUFFE :: (a. Scott, b. Marlowe, c. Stevenson, d. Colette) : TREASURE ISLAND

42. VOLATILE : (a. flammable, b. hydrogenated, c. noble, d. acidic) :: REACTIVE : INERT

43. (a. assemblage, b. solo, c. faction, d. bellow) : ENSEMBLE :: ARIA : CHORUS

44. PLANE : EUCLIDIAN :: (a. sphere, b. point, c. line, d. triangle) : NON-EUCLIDIAN

45. FORUM : (a. formum, b. foruma, c. fora, d. forons) :: PHENOMENON : PHENOMENA

46. ZEPPELIN : AIR :: (a. trireme, b. propeller, c. oxygen, d. wagon) : WATER

47. BALEEN : (a. carnivorous, b. aquatic, c. toothed, d. cetacean) :: BLUE WHALE : KILLER WHALE

48. (a. odious, b. infested, c. sagacious, d. obligatory) : DEVOID :: RIFE : BEREFT

49. (a. Buddha, b. Pythagoras, c. Euclid, d. Krishna) : SIDDHARTHA :: $2\pi r$: CIRCUMFERENCE

50. SHALE : SEDIMENTARY :: BASALT : (a. igneous, b. latent, c. metamorphic, d. conglomerate)

51. BACTERIA : (a. praxae, b. praxes, c. praxi, d. praxum) :: BACTERIUM : PRAXIS

52. MINIMALIST : SPARTAN :: MANNERIST : (a. ostentatious, b. dour, c. saturnine, d. titan)

53. YETI : TIBET :: (a. chimera, b. bigfoot, c. chupacabra, d. habanero) : MEXICO

54. (a. myself, b. you, c. whom, d. anyone) : INDEFINITE :: IT : DEFINITE

55. MARSUPIAL : (a. monotreme, b. prokariotic, c. placental, d. metatheria) :: KOALA : DOG

56. SPANISH-AMERICAN WAR : WORLD WAR I :: (a. Battleship *Maine*, b. San Juan Hill, c. Wounded Knee, d. Bay of Pigs) : ARCHDUKE FERDINAND

57. CENOZOIC : AGE OF MAMMALS :: (a. Tertiary, b. Formicary, c. Cambrian, d. Cretaceous) : AGE OF DINOSAURS

58. CANDLE : LUMINOSITY :: (a. trumpet, b. amplifier, c. wave, d. decibel) : SOUND

59. ADAM SMITH : (a. *Democracy in America*, b. *Civil Disobedience*, c. *Wealth of Nations*, d. *Nature*) :: MARX : DAS KAPITAL

60. LOS ALAMOS : OPPENHEIMER :: MENLO PARK : (a. Ford, b. Bell, c. Edison, d. Franklin)

61. SOUTHERN : NORTHERN :: (a. polaris, b. capricornus, c. equitorus, d. australis) : BOREALIS

62. (a. fennel, b. rutabaga, c. beet, d. rhubarb) : TURNIP :: DAIKON : RADISH

63. QUADRILLE : (a. circle, b. triangle, c. square, d. spiral) :: CONGA : LINE

64. (a. tride, b. cent, c. penta, d. duo) : LATIN :: HECATO : GREEK

65. BÉARNAISE : HOLLANDAISE :: (a. Flemish, b. French, c. Portuguese, d. Swedish) : DUTCH

66. BRASS : (a. iron, b. silver, c. zinc, d. chrome) :: BRONZE : TIN

67. CARAT : GEMSTONE :: (a. pace, b. stone, c. hand, d. caliber) : HORSE

68. (a. Locke, b. More, c. Boswell, d. Swift) : UTOPIA :: ORWELL : DYSTOPIA

69. CHURLISH : EFFRONTERY :: HURL : (a. immature, b. goading, c. front, d. vague)

70. LAMP : LIGHTHOUSE :: (a. clock, b. bell, c. steeple, d. watchman) : CAMPANILE

71. (a. Daniel, b. Joseph, c. Ezekiel, d. Habukuk) : WHEEL :: JACOB : LADDER

72. BRANDO : STREETCAR NAMED DESIRE :: (a. Gable, b. Stewart, c. Bogart, d. Grant) : MALTESE FALCON

73. MALORY : KING ARTHUR :: LANGLAND (a. Wife of Bath, b. Beowulf, c. Polonius, d. Piers Ploughman)

74. FETTER : BRACE :: TRAMMELED : (a. fried, b. transported, c. supported, d. surrounded)

75. BENTHAM : UTILITARIANISM :: (a. Hobbes, b. Steinem, c. Cixous, d. Daly) : LIBERAL FEMINISM

76. ZEPHYROS : (a. Euros, b. Notos, c. Boreas, d. Anemoi) :: WEST : SOUTH

77. AHAB : PEQUOD :: (a. Nemo, b. Marlow, c. Ishmael, d. Hornblower) : NAUTILUS

78. VESICLE : (a. contain, b. contract, c. leak, d. monitor) :: DUCT : PASS

79. FLAUBERT : DOSTOYEVSKY :: BOVARY : (a. Bezukov, b. Tolstoy, c. Karamazov, d. Rostov)

80. (a. 062, b. 348, c. 1111, d. XXI) : BINARY :: 0F : HEXADECIMAL

81. BRANCUSI : BERNINI :: MODERN : (a. romantic, b. neoclassical, c. postmodern, d. baroque)

82. SPARTAN : BYZANTINE :: AUSTERE : (a. Olympian, b. golden, c. convoluted, d. orthodox)

83. EMERALD : SAPPHIRE :: MAY : (a. January, b. September, c. March, d. December)

84. GURKHA : NEPAL :: (a. Hessian, b. Basque, c. Huguenot, d. Thracian) : GERMANY

85. CHEESE : RENNET :: (a. yogurt, b. butter, c. jelly, d. toast) : PECTIN

86. (a. Sikes, b. Magwich, c. Raffles, d. Choakumchild) : OLIVER TWIST :: ANTAGONIST : PROTAGONIST

87. WIND : BLOW :: SPRING : (a. nature, b. coil, c. season, d. horn)

88. RELIGIOUS : HIERATIC :: SECULAR : (a. commercial, b. demotic, c. dorian, d. seraphic)

89. JAPAN : (a. shakuhachi, b. kabuki, c. nori, d. ikebana) :: EUROPE : FLUTE

90. (a. apparition, b. revenant, c. lunatic, d. doppleganger) : RETURN :: LYCANTHROPE : TRANSFORM

91. EMPEROR : KING :: (a. empire, b. penguin, c. crown, d. python) : COBRA

92. LONGITUDE : (a. tropical, b. equatorial, c. great circle, d. meridian) :: LATITUDE : PARALLEL

93. DIOGENES : (a. epicurean, b. cynic, c. sophist, d. Pythagorean) :: EPICTETUS : STOIC

94. (a. aroma, b. ardor, c. apathy, d. apprehension) : ODIUM :: AVARICE : MUNIFICENCE

95. THITHER : THERE :: WHEREFORE : (a. what, b. where, c. why, d. how)

96. PAPER : WOOD PULP :: VELLUM : (a. plant, b. rag, c. parchment, d. skin)

97. BADGERS : CETE :: APES : (a. pack, b. shrewdness, c. pride, d. lair)

98. ABSTRACT : REPRESENTATIVE :: (a. Michaelangelo, b. Rothko, c. Constable, d. van Eyck) : REMBRANDT

99. RICHARDSON : HARDY :: CLARISSA : (a. Juliet, b. Lolita, c. Tess, d. Nancy)

100. (a. cortisol, b. serotonin, c. dopamine, d. melatonin) : SLEEP :: ADRENALINE : FLIGHT

101. NAAN : (a. Thailand, b. Ethiopia, c. India, d. Greece) :: FOCACCIA : ITALY

102. (a. etymologist, b. navigator, c. paragon, d. titan) : ARCHITECT :: MAPS : BLUEPRINTS

103. NAPOLEON : WATERLOO :: GODWINSON : (a. Yprès, b. Agincourt, c. Marne, d. Hastings)

104. OBOE : WOODWIND :: VIBRAPHONE: (a. string, b. brass, c. percussion, d. reed)

105. (a. Ni, b. Cu, c. Na, d. Mg) : CHLOROPHYLL :: FE : HEMOGLOBIN

106. MINNEAPOLIS : ST. PAUL :: DETROIT : (a. Toledo, b. Ann Arbor, c. Windsor, d. Indianapolis)

107. (a. *sfumato*, b. *disegno*, c. *chiaroscuro*, d. *sprezzatura*) : FLORENCE :: COLORITO : VENICE

108. LORDS : SERFS :: BOURGEOISIE : (a. middle class, b. nobility, c. proletariat, d. clergy)

109. PROLIX : GARRULOUS :: (a. wifely, b. clever, c. unctuous, d. wanton) : UXORIAL

110. XC : LIV :: CM : (a. DXL, b. CCM, c. DL, d. XC)

111. MOUZINHO DE ALBURQUERQUE : (a. Mozambique, b. Madagascar, c. Morocco, d. Malaysia) :: AMERIGO VESPUCCI : UNITED STATES OF AMERICA

112. WATER : ICE :: CARBON DIOXIDE : (a. bauxite, b. limestone, c. dry ice, d. steam)

113. STEICHEN : CARRACCI :: (a. Moholy-Nagy, b. Poussin, c. Stieglitz, d. Eggleston) : CARAVAGGIO

114. WASHINGTON : (a. Mohammed, b. Ataturk, c. Lawrence, d. Faisal) :: AMERICA : TURKEY

115. MARINETTI : FUTURISM :: BALL : (a. Dada, b. Surrealism, c. Abstraction, d. Vorticism)

116. PETROLOGY : ROCK :: (a. pomology, b. speliology, c. seismology, d. phytology) : EARTHQUAKES

117. TORNADO : BREEZE :: RAVINE : (a. ditch, b. hurricane, c. raven, d. quagmire)

118. LAISSEZ-FAIRE : GOVERNMENTAL DEFICIT SPENDING :: SMITH : (a. Marx, b. Fleming, c. Greenspan, d. Keynes)

119. NORTHERN RENAISSANCE : HARLEM RENAISSANCE :: JAN VAN EYCK : (a. Carrie Mae Weems, b. Grandma Moses, c. Jacob Lawrence, d. Wilfredo Lam)

120. STRATUM : THESIS :: (a. stratums, b. stratus, c. strata, d. stratas) : THESES

ANSWERS AND EXPLANATIONS

1. TAVERNS : SERVANT :: HOTELS : (a. custodian, b. pub, c. waiter, **d. hostel**)
    (**d**) *Taverns* is an anagram of *servant*; *hotels* is an anagram of *hostel*.

2. SUSPECT : BOOK :: (a. investigator, b. convict, c. evidence, **d. witness**) : INTERVIEW
    (**d**) *Book* is a verb here rather than a noun as might be expected. A suspect is someone who is booked (as in an investigation). A witness is someone who is interviewed.

3. HINDENBERG : (a. *Lusitania*, **b. Titanic**, c. zeppelin, d. Kitty Hawk) :: FIRE : ICEBERG
    (**b**) The *Hindenberg* airship was disasterously destroyed by fire; the *Titanic* was destroyed by an iceberg.

4. ROPE : SPLICE :: (a. braid , b. knot, c. captain, **d. metal**) : SOLDER
    (**d**) Two pieces of rope are joined by a splice; two pieces of metal are joined by a solder.

5. POEM : LOPE :: MOPE : (a. strut, **b. pole**, c. lift, d. diverge)
    (**b**) *Poem* is an anagram of *mope*; *lope* is an anagram of *pole*.

6. APPOMATTOX : (**a. Yorktown**, b. Boston, c. Richmond, d. New York) :: CIVIL WAR : REVOLUTIONARY WAR
    (**a**) Appomattox is the site of the surrender that ended the Civil War; Yorktown is the site of the surrender that ended the Revolutionary War.

7. STRAND : EPISODE :: (**a. cable**, b. castaway, c. epistle, d. yarn) : EPIC
    (**a**) A bundle of strands makes up a cable; a bundle of episodes makes up an epic.

8. 3 : 2 :: CUBE : (**a. square**, b. sphere, c. axis, d. 8)
    (**a**) A number raised to the power of 3 is cubed; a number raised to the power of 2 is squared.

9. (a. underground, b. secret, **c. dead**, d. original) : NECROPOLIS :: LARGE : MEGAPOLIS
    (**c**) The prefix *necro–* means dead, so a necropolis is a city of the dead (as in a large graveyard). The prefix *mega–* means very large, so a megapolis is a very large city.

10. (a. 120°, b. 360°, **c.180°**, d. 45°) : 90° :: SUPPLEMENTARY : COMPLEMENTARY
    (**c**) Supplementary angles sum to 180°, just as complementary angles sum to 90°.

11. STONE : PICTURE :: SETTING : (a. engraving, b. lithograph, c. canvas, **d. frame**)
    (**d**) A stone is displayed in a setting; a picture is displayed in a frame.

12. BRAZEN : (a. bold, **b. raze**, c. zen, d. colorful) :: CHIDED : HIDE
    (**b**) *Raze* is the word *brazen* with the first and last letters truncated. *Hide* is the word *chided* with the first and last letters truncated.

13. APOTHECARY : CHANDLER :: MEDICINE : (a. shoes, **b. candles**, c. bells, d. rope)
(**b**) An apothecary makes and sells medicine; a chandler makes and sells candles.

14. SHIFTING : DOGMATIC :: WHIMSICAL : (a. softened, b. careless, **c. determined**, d. accurate)
(**c**) One who is shifting in opinions is said to be whimsical; one who is dogmatic in opinions is said to be determined.

15. OSTRICH : FLY :: ELEPHANT : (a. trunk, b. walk, **c. jump**, d. masticate)
(**c**) An ostrich is unable to fly; an elephant is unable to jump. Even if you didn't know this science fact, you should be able to eliminate one or two wrong answers—elephants can definitely walk and masticate (chew).

16. EXCULPATE : (a. ingratiate, **b. incriminate**, c. terraform, d. attack) :: FLOUNDER : SUCCEED
(**b**) To flounder is the opposite of to succeed; to exculpate is the opposite of to incriminate.

17. 3 : 2 :: 27 : (a. 4, b. 6, **c. 8**, d. 28)
(**c**) The number 3 cubed equals 27, and 2 cubed equals 8.

18. PLANT : SEED :: FUNGUS : (a. root, b. parasite, **c. spore**, d. flower)
(**c**) Plants reproduce by means of seeds; fungi reproduce by means of spores.

19. 4.4 : (a. 1, **b. 2**, c. 4, d. 8) :: POUNDS : KILOS
(**b**) One kilogram is equal to 2.2 pounds, so 4.4 pounds equals 2 kilos.

20. (a. pound, b. tilde, c. pipe, **d. asterisk**) : CARET :: * : ^
(**d**) The symbol ^ is called a caret; the symbol * is called an asterisk.

21. FILM : (a. aperture, b. shutter, **c. retina**, d. cornea) :: CAMERA : EYE
(**c**) A camera projects an image onto film; an eye projects an image onto a retina.

22. TRUMP : UPSTAGE :: (a. play, **b. trick**, c. scale, d. virtuoso) : PERFORMANCE
(**b**) To upstage is to outdo someone else's performance. To trump is to outdo someone in a trick (a round of play in a card game such as bridge).

23. SNAFU : DETARTRATED :: ACRONYM : (a. onomatopoeia, b. homophone, **c. palindrome**, d. spoonerism)
(**c**) *Snafu* is a World War II acronym ("<u>S</u>ituation <u>N</u>ormal, <u>A</u>ll <u>F</u>ouled <u>U</u>p").
Detartrated—the condition of having been made less tart—is a palindrome.

24. RIGHT ANGLE : (**a. line**, b. vertical, c. complementary, d. congruent) :: 90 : 180
(**a**) A right angle measures 90 degrees. A line measures 180 degrees.

25. ULTRA– : (a. intro–, b. inter–, c. hyper–, **d. infra–**) :: OVER : UNDER
    (d) The prefix *ultra–* means over; the prefix *infra–* means under.

26. SHARPEN : HONE :: WIPE : (a. dust, **b. burnish**, c. cleanse, d. neaten)
    (b) To hone is an extreme form of to sharpen; to burnish is an extreme form of to wipe.

27. RAIN : (a. wind, b. thunder, c. humidity, **d. water**) :: LIGHTNING : ELECTRICITY
    (d) Rain is the atmospheric manifestation of water; lightning is the atmospheric manifestation of electricity.

28. CART : WAGON :: (a. 1, **b. 2**, c. 4, d. 6) : 4
    (b) A cart has 2 wheels, just as a wagon has 4 wheels.

29. GAGARIN : MAGELLAN :: ORBIT : (a. Everest, **b. circumnavigation**, c. red tide, d. Northwest Passage)
    (b) Yuri Gagarin was the first human to orbit the earth; Ferdinand Magellan was the first human to circumnavigate the earth.

30. (a. 2nd, b. 5th, c. 11th, **d. 13th**) : 18TH :: SLAVERY : ALCOHOL
    (d) The 13th amendment outlawed slavery, just as the 18th amendment outlawed alcohol.

31. SWIFT : KIPLING :: (a. Gunga Din, b. Alice, c. Quartermain, **d. Gulliver**) : MOWGLI
    (d) Jonathan Swift wrote about a hero named Gulliver (*Gulliver's Travels*). Rudyard Kipling wrote about a hero named Mowgli (*The Jungle Book*).

32. FOLLICLE : (a. hair, b. vesicle, **c. cuticle**, d. fluid) :: OVUM : NAIL
    (c) A follicle is a structure that generates an ovum (female reproductive cell), just as a cuticle is a structure that generates a fingernail or toenail. Don't be fooled by choice (a)—while it's true that another type of follicle generates a hair, that leaves no logical connection between ovum and nail. The connection here is between the first and third words, not the first and second.

33. VIDI : I SAW :: (a. veni, b. viri, **c. vici**, d. verdi) : I CONQUERED
    (c) *Vidi* is Latin for "I saw." *Vici* is Latin for "I conquered." Both these words are taken from Julius Caesar's famous pronouncement after defeating Pharnaces at Zela in the Roman Civil Wars ("*Veni, vidi, vici,*" or "I came, I saw, I conquered.").

34. PLANE : WASH :: (a. streamlined, **b. smooth**, c. lightweight, d. buoyant) : CLEAN
    (b) To plane is to make something smooth; to wash is to make something clean. Don't be fooled by the temptation to see *plane* as a noun in this question.

35. NELSON : (a. Magellan, b. Napoleon, c. Drake, **d. Wellington**) :: TRAFALGAR : WATERLOO
(**d**) Horatio Nelson was the victorious commander at the Battle of Trafalgar. Wellington was the victorious commander at the Battle of Waterloo. Napoleon was at Waterloo, but he was defeated, not victorious.

36. GRAVITY : NEWTON :: QUANTUM MECHANICS : (**a. Heisenberg**, b. Einstein, c. Morse, d. Farnsworth)
(**a**) Sir Isaac Newton first described the principles of gravity. Werner Heisenberg first described the principles of quantum mechanics.

37. RICE : (**a. Pakistani**, b. Yanomamo, c. !Kung, d. Swede) :: TARO : FIJIAN
(**a**) Rice is a staple food of the Pakistani people, just as taro (a starchy root plant) is a staple food of the Fijian people. (Yanomamo are an aboriginal people of South America, and !Kung are the bushmen of West Africa, neither of whom consume rice as a staple food.)

38. DIAMETER : (a. radius, b. dissection, **c. diagonal**, d. hypotenuse) :: CIRCLE : SQUARE
(**c**) The longest line that can be drawn inside a circle is a diameter; the longest line that can be drawn inside a square is a diagonal.

39. RAT : (a. primate, b. evolution, **c. pea**, d. flora) :: SKINNER : MENDEL
(**c**) B. F. Skinner used rats as test subjects in his study of psychology, and Gregor Mendel used pea plants as test subjects in his study of genetics. Evolution is not the correct answer, because not only is evolution an area of study rather than a type of test subject, but Mendel studied genetics (the effects of genes on heredity) rather than evolution (the historical development of a biological group).

40. HEPATITIS : LIVER :: ENCEPHALITIS : (a. skull, b. pharynx, **c. brain**, d. endometrium)
(**c**) Hepatitis is an inflammation of the liver; encephalitis is an inflammation of the brain. Word roots can give you clues about the meaning of *encephalitis*: *en–* (inside), *cephal–* (head), *–itis* (inflammation).

41. MOLIÈRE : TARTUFFE :: (a. Scott, b. Marlowe, **c. Stevenson**, d. Colette) : TREASURE ISLAND
(**c**) Jean-Baptiste Molière wrote *Tartuffe*; Robert Louis Stevenson wrote *Treasure Island*.

42. VOLATILE : (a. flammable, b. hydrogenated, **c. noble**, d. acidic) :: REACTIVE : INERT
(**c**) A volatile gas is highly reactive. A noble gas is inert.

43. (a. assemblage, **b. solo**, c. faction, d. bellow) : ENSEMBLE :: ARIA : CHORUS
(**b**) A solo artist sings an aria, just as an ensemble sings a chorus.

44. PLANE : EUCLIDIAN :: (**a. sphere**, b. point, c. line, d. triangle) : NON-EUCLIDIAN
    (**a**) Geometry on a planar surface is Euclidian; geometry on a spherical surface is non-Euclidian.

45. FORUM : (a. formum, b. foruma, **c. fora**, d. forons) :: PHENOMENON : PHENOMENA
    (**c**) The plural form of *forum* is *fora* (although *forums* is also permissible in English); the plural form of *phenomenon* is *phenomena*.

46. ZEPPELIN : AIR :: (**a. trireme**, b. propeller, c. oxygen, d. wagon) : WATER
    (**a**) A zeppelin is a type of ship that travels through the air; a trireme is a type of ship that travels over water.

47. BALEEN : (a. carnivorous, b. aquatic, **c. toothed**, d. cetacean) :: BLUE WHALE : KILLER WHALE
    (**c**) A blue whale is a variety of baleen whale (having a mouth full of baleen for filtering krill rather than teeth); a killer whale is a variety of toothed whale.

48. (a. odious, **b. infested**, c. sagacious, d. obligatory) : DEVOID :: RIFE : BEREFT
    (**b**) Something that is infested is said to be rife. Something that is devoid is said to be bereft.

49. (**a. Buddha**, b. Pythagoras, c. Euclid, d. Krishna) : SIDDHARTHA :: $2\pi r$: CIRCUMFERENCE
    (**a**) Buddha and Siddhartha are the same person; $2\pi r$ and a circumference are the same quantity.

50. SHALE : SEDIMENTARY :: BASALT : (**a. igneous**, b. latent, c. metamorphic, d. conglomerate)
    (**a**) Shale is a type of sedimentary rock; basalt is a type of igneous rock.

51. BACTERIA : (a. praxae, **b. praxes**, c. praxi, d. praxum) :: BACTERIUM : PRAXIS
    (**b**) The plural of *bacterium* is *bacteria*; the plural of *praxis* (action) is *praxes*.

52. MINIMALIST : SPARTAN :: MANNERIST : (**a. ostentatious**, b. dour, c. saturnine, d. titan)
    (**a**) Something done in a minimalist style could be described as spartan; something done in a mannerist style could be described as ostentatious.

53. YETI : TIBET :: (a. chimera, b. bigfoot, **c. chupacabra**, d. habanero) : MEXICO
    (**c**) The yeti is a legendary creature inhabiting Tibet; the chupacabra is a legendary creature inhabiting Mexico.

54. (a. myself, b. you, c. whom, **d. anyone**) : INDEFINITE :: IT : DEFINITE
    (**d**) *Anyone* is an indefinite pronoun, and *it* is a definite pronoun.

55. MARSUPIAL : (a. monotreme, b. prokariotic, **c. placental**, d. metatheria) :: KOALA : DOG
    (**c**) A koala is a marsupial mammal; a dog is a placental mammal.

56. SPANISH-AMERICAN WAR : WORLD WAR I :: (**a. Battleship *Maine***, b. San Juan Hill, c. Wounded Knee, d. Bay of Pigs) : ARCHDUKE FERDINAND
    (**a**) The assassination of Archduke Ferdinand sparked World War I; the destruction of the Battleship *Maine* sparked the Spanish-American war.

57. CENOZOIC : AGE OF MAMMALS :: (a. Tertiary, b. Formicary, c. Cambrian, **d. Cretaceous**) : AGE OF DINOSAURS
    (**d**) The Cenozoic Era is marked by the dominance of mammals; the Cretaceous Period was marked by the dominance of dinosaurs.

58. CANDLE : LUMINOSITY :: (a. trumpet, b. amplifier, c. wave, **d. decibel**) : SOUND
    (**d**) A candle is a unit used to measure luminosity; a decibel is a unit used to measure sound. Be alert for possible secondary meanings of common words if the logic of an analogy doesn't at first make sense.

59. ADAM SMITH : (a. *Democracy in America*, b. *Civil Disobedience*, **c. *Wealth of Nations***, d. *Nature*) :: MARX : DAS KAPITAL
    (**c**) Adam Smith wrote the *Wealth of Nations*; Karl Marx wrote *Das Kapital*.

60. LOS ALAMOS : OPPENHEIMER :: MENLO PARK : (a. Ford, b. Bell, **c. Edison**, d. Franklin)
    (**c**) Robert Oppenheimer is well known for his work at Los Alamos (on the Manhattan Project). Thomas Edison is well known for his work at Menlo Park.

61. SOUTHERN : NORTHERN :: (a. polaris, b. capricornus, c. equitorus, **d. australis**) : BOREALIS
    (**d**) The *aurora borealis* (northern lights) occurs in the northern hemisphere. The *aurora australis* (southern lights) occurs in the southern hemisphere.

62. (a. fennel, **b. rutabaga**, c. beet, d. rhubarb) : TURNIP :: DAIKON : RADISH
    (**b**) The daikon is a large member of the radish family. The rutabaga is a large member of the turnip family.

63. QUADRILLE : (a. circle, b. triangle, **c. square**, d. spiral) :: CONGA : LINE
    (**c**) A conga is a dance performed in a line. A quadrille is a dance performed in a square. If you had never heard of a quadrille, the prefix *quad–* (four/square) might have clued you into the meaning of the word.

64. (a. tride, **b. cent**, c. penta, d. duo) : LATIN :: HECATO : GREEK
    (**b**) *Hecato–* is the Greek prefix for 100. *Cent–* is the Latin prefix for 100.

65. BÉARNAISE : HOLLANDAISE :: (a. Flemish, **b. French**, c. Portuguese, d. Swedish) :
DUTCH
(b) Hollandaise is a Dutch sauce (originating in the region of Holland). Béarnaise is a
French sauce (originating in the region of Béarn).

66. BRASS : (a. iron, b. silver, **c. zinc**, d. chrome) :: BRONZE : TIN
(c) Bronze is an alloy of copper and tin. Brass is an alloy of copper and zinc.

67. CARAT : GEMSTONE :: (a. pace, b. stone, **c. hand**, d. caliber) : HORSE
(c) A carat is a unit for measuring the size of a gemstone. A hand is a unit for
measuring the size of a horse.

68. (a. Locke, **b. More**, c. Boswell, d. Swift) : UTOPIA :: ORWELL : DYSTOPIA
(b) George Orwell wrote about a famous dystopia (in *1984*). Thomas More wrote
about a famous utopia (he coined the word in a work titled *Utopia*).

69. CHURLISH : EFFRONTERY :: HURL : (a. immature, b. goading, **c. front**, d. vague)
(c) The word *hurl* is contained inside the word *churlish*. The word *front* is contained
inside the word *effrontery*.

70. LAMP : LIGHTHOUSE :: (a. clock, **b. bell**, c. steeple, d. watchman) : CAMPANILE
(b) A lighthouse is a tower with a lamp in it. A campanile is a tower with a bell in it.

71. (a. Daniel, b. Joseph, **c. Ezekiel**, d. Habukuk) : WHEEL :: JACOB : LADDER
(c) The prophet Ezekiel had a vision of a wheel. The prophet Jacob had a vision of a
ladder.

72. BRANDO : STREETCAR NAMED DESIRE :: (a. Gable, b. Stewart, **c. Bogart**,
d. Grant) : MALTESE FALCON
(c) Marlon Brando played a famous role in the film version of *A Streetcar Named
Desire*. Humphrey Bogart played a famous role in the film version of *The Maltese
Falcon*.

73. MALORY : KING ARTHUR :: LANGLAND (a. Wife of Bath, b. Beowulf, c. Polonius,
d. Piers Ploughman)
(d) King Arthur is the protagonist of Thomas Malory's famous work *Le Morte
d'Arthur*. Piers Ploughman is the protagonist of William Langland's famous work *The
Vision and Creed of Piers Ploughman*. Even if you didn't know Langland's work, you
might have been able to eliminate more-famous wrong answers: the Wife of Bath
appears in Chaucer, Polonius appears in Shakespeare, and the author of *Beowulf* is
unknown.

74. FETTER : BRACE :: TRAMMELED : (a. fried, b. transported, **c. supported**,
d. surrounded)
(c) A fetter (chain) functions to make something trammeled (restricted). A brace
functions to make something supported.

75. BENTHAM : UTILITARIANISM :: (a. Hobbes, **b. Steinem**, c. Cixous, d. Daly) :
LIBERAL FEMINISM
(b) Jeremy Bentham was a proponent of utilitarianism (the greatest good for the
greatest number). Gloria Steinem is a proponent of liberal feminism (political reform
in the civil rights mode). Mary Daly was a separatist feminist, and Hélène Cixous is a
"French" feminist.

76. ZEPHYROS : (a. Euros, **b. Notos**, c. Boreas, d. Anemoi) :: WEST : SOUTH
(b) In Greek mythology, Zephyros is the god of the gentle west wind, and Notos the
god of the blustery south wind. Other Greek *Anemoi* (wind gods) are Boreas the
north wind and Euros the east wind.

77. AHAB : PEQUOD :: (**a. Nemo**, b. Marlow, c. Ishmael, d. Hornblower) : NAUTILUS
(a) Ahab is the captain of the *Pequod* in Herman Melville's *Moby Dick*. Nemo is the
captain of the *Nautilus* in Jules Verne's *20,000 Leagues Under the Sea*.

78. VESICLE : (**a. contain**, b. contract, c. leak, d. monitor) :: DUCT : PASS
(a) A vesicle functions to contain substances in the body. A duct functions to pass
substances in the body.

79. FLAUBERT : DOSTOYEVSKY :: BOVARY : (a. Bezukov, b. Tolstoy, **c. Karamazov**,
d. Rostov)
(c) Gustave Flaubert wrote about the Bovary family. Fyodor Dostoyevsky wrote about
the Karamazov family. Two other answer choices, Bezukov and Rostov, are two of the
families in Tolstoy's *War and Peace*.

80. (a. 062, b. 348, **c. 1111**, d. XXI) : BINARY :: 0F : HEXADECIMAL
(c) The number 1111 in binary numbers is equal to the decimal value 15. The
number 0F in hexadecimal numbers is equal to the decimal value 15.

81. BRANCUSI : BERNINI :: MODERN : (a. romantic, b. neoclassical, c. postmodern,
d. baroque)
(d) Constantin Brancusi was a sculptor of the Modern period. Gian Lorenzo Bernini
was a sculptor of the Baroque period.

82. SPARTAN : BYZANTINE :: AUSTERE : (a. Olympian, b. golden, **c. convoluted**,
d. orthodox)
(c) *Spartan* means austere. *Byzantine* means convoluted.

83. EMERALD : SAPPHIRE :: MAY : (a. January, **b. September**, c. March, d. December)
(b) Emerald is the birthstone associated with the month of May. Sapphire is the
birthstone associated with the month of September.

84. GURKHA : NEPAL :: (**a. Hessian**, b. Basque, c. Huguenot, d. Thracian) : GERMANY
(a) A Gurkha is a soldier from Nepal enlisted in the British army. A Hessian is a
soldier from Germany enlisted in the British army.

85. CHEESE : RENNET :: (a. yogurt, b. butter, **c. jelly**, d. toast) : PECTIN
   (c) Rennet is a coagulant used in the manufacture of cheese. Pectin is a coagulant used in the manufacture of jelly.

86. (**a. Sikes**, b. Magwich, c. Raffles, d. Choakumchild) : OLIVER TWIST :: ANTAGONIST : PROTAGONIST
   (a) Oliver Twist is the protagonist of Dickens's *Oliver Twist*. Bill Sikes is the antagonist of that novel. Raffles and Magwich are characters from Dickens's *Great Expectations*, and Choakumchild is from *Hard Times*.

87. WIND : BLOW :: SPRING : (a. nature, b. coil, c. season, **d. horn**)
   (d) To wind (long *i*) is something you do to a spring, as in winding a clock. To blow is something you do to a horn. Don't be thrown by the proximity of the word *blow* to make you think of *wind* with a short *i* (as in "the wind blows").

88. RELIGIOUS : HIERATIC :: SECULAR : (a. commercial, **b. demotic**, c. dorian, d. seraphic)
   (b) *Hieratic* means relating to the priesthood and, thus, religious. *Demotic* means relating to the populace and, thus, secular. In ancient Egypt, the complex form of writing used by the priesthood was called hieratic script, whereas the simpler form of writing used for secular purposes was called demotic script.

89. JAPAN : (**a. shakuhachi**, b. kabuki, c. nori, d. ikebana) :: EUROPE : FLUTE
   (a) The instrument referred to as a flute in Europe is called a shakuhachi in Japan. Kabuki is a style of theater, nori is a type of edible seaweed sheet, and ikebana is the art of arranging flowers.

90. (a. apparition, **b. revenant**, c. lunatic, d. doppleganger) : RETURN :: LYCANTHROPE : TRANSFORM
   (b) A lycanthrope is a legendary creature that transforms to and from human form (for example, a werewolf). A revenant is a legendary creature that returns from the dead (for example, a zombie, ghost, or vampire).

91. EMPEROR : KING :: (a. empire, **b. penguin**, c. crown, d. python) : COBRA
   (b) The emperor penguin is a species of penguin. The king cobra is a species of cobra.

92. LONGITUDE : (a. tropical, b. equatorial, c. great circle, **d. meridian**) :: LATITUDE : PARALLEL
   (d) A latitude line is also called a parallel. A longitude line is also called a meridian.

93. DIOGENES : (a. epicurean, **b. cynic**, c. sophist, d. Pythagorean) :: EPICTETUS : STOIC
   (b) Epictetus was a famous Classical Greek Stoic. Diogenes was a famous Classical Greek Cynic.

94. (a. aroma, **b. ardor**, c. apathy, d. apprehension) : ODIUM :: AVARICE : MUNIFICENCE
(b) Avarice (greed) is the opposite of munificence (generosity). Ardor (love) is the opposite of odium (hatred).

95. THITHER : THERE :: WHEREFORE : (a. what, b. where, **c. why**, d. how)
(c) *Thither* is the Elizabethan English form of *there*. *Wherefore* is the Elizabethan English form of *why*. (Juliet's famous monologue in Shakespeare actually asks "Why are you Romeo?" not "Where are you, Romeo?" as many people think. The speech is part of her "What's in a name?" line of argument for why Romeo's being named Montague should not matter.)

96. PAPER : WOOD PULP :: VELLUM : (a. plant, b. rag, c. parchment, **d. skin**)
(d) Paper is processed wood pulp used as a writing surface. Vellum is processed animal skin used as a writing surface.

97. BADGERS : CETE :: APES : (a. pack, **b. shrewdness**, c. pride, d. lair)
(b) A group of badgers is called a cete. A group of apes is called a shrewdness.

98. ABSTRACT : REPRESENTATIVE :: (a. Michaelangelo, **b. Rothko**, c. Constable, d. van Eyck) : REMBRANDT
(b) Harmenszoon Rembrandt painted in a representative style. Mark Rothko painted in an abstract style.

99. RICHARDSON : HARDY :: CLARISSA : (a. Juliet, b. Lolita, **c. Tess**, d. Nancy)
(c) The tragic heroine of Samuel Richardson's famous work was Clarissa. The tragic heroine of Thomas Hardy's famous work was Tess of the D'Ubervilles.

100. (a. cortisol, b. seretonin, c. dopamine, **d. melatonin**) : SLEEP :: ADRENALINE : FLIGHT
(d) Adrenaline is a hormone associated with flight-or-fight responses. Melatonin is a hormone associated with sleep.

101. NAAN : (a. Thailand, b. Ethiopia, **c. India**, d. Greece) :: FOCACCIA : ITALY
(c) Naan is a type of Indian bread, and focaccia is a type of Italian bread.

102. (a. etymologist, **b. navigator**, c. paragon, d. titan) : ARCHITECT :: MAPS : BLUEPRINTS
(b) A navigator works with maps, just as an architect works with blueprints.

103. NAPOLEON : WATERLOO :: GODWINSON : (a. Yprès, b. Agincourt, c. Marne, **d. Hastings**)
(d) Napoleon Bonaparte was the losing commander at the Battle of Waterloo, and Harold Godwinson was the losing commander at the Battle of Hastings.

104. OBOE : WOODWIND :: VIBRAPHONE: (a. string, b. brass, **c. percussion**, d. reed)
(**c**) An oboe is a member of the woodwind family, just as the vibraphone is a member of the percussion family.

105. (a. Ni, b. Cu, c. Na, **d. Mg**) : CHLOROPHYLL :: FE : HEMOGLOBIN
(**d**) Iron (Fe) is at the center of the porphyrin of hemoglobin, and magnesium (Mg) is at the center of the chlorophyll.

106. MINNEAPOLIS : ST. PAUL :: DETROIT : (a. Toledo, b. Ann Arbor, **c. Windsor**, d. Indianapolis)
(**c**) Windsor, Ontario, is a twin city of Detroit, Michigan; likewise, Minneapolis is a twin city of St. Paul, Minnesota.

107. (a. *sfumato*, **b. *disegno***, c. *chiaroscuro*, d. *sprezzatura*) : FLORENCE :: COLORITO : VENICE
(**b**) Florentine Renaissance painting is known for prioritizing *disegno*, or drawing, while Venetian Renaissance painting is renown for its attention to *colorito*, or color.

108. LORDS : SERFS :: BOURGEOISIE : (a. middle class, b. nobility, **c. proletariat**, d. clergy)
(**c**) Marxists compare the position of the proletariat to that of medieval serfs and the bourgeoisie to medieval lords.

109. PROLIX : GARRULOUS :: (**a. wifely**, b. clever, c. unctuous, d. wanton) : UXORIAL
(**a**) *Prolix* means garrulous, and *wifely* means uxorial.

110. XC : LIV :: CM : (**a. DXL**, b. CCM, c. DL, d. XC)
(**a**) XC (90) is one-tenth of CM (900), and LIV (54) is one-tenth of DXL (540).

111. MOUZINHO DE ALBURQUERQUE : (**a. Mozambique**, b. Madagascar, c. Morocco, d. Malaysia) :: AMERIGO VESPUCCI : UNITED STATES OF AMERICA
(**a**) Mozambique was named after Mouzinho de Alburquerque, and the United States of America was named after Amerigo Vespucci.

112. WATER : ICE :: CARBON DIOXIDE : (a. bauxite, b. limestone, **c. dry ice**, d. steam)
(**c**) Ice is the solid form of water, and dry ice is the solid form of carbon dioxide.

113. STEICHEN : CARRACCI :: (a. Moholy-Nagy, b. Poussin, **c. Stieglitz**, d. Eggleston) : CARAVAGGIO
(**c**) Edward Steichen and Alfred Stieglitz were both American photographers working contemporaneously. Annibale Carracci and Michelangelo Caravaggio were both Italian painters who were contemporaries.

114. WASHINGTON : (a. Mohammed, **b. Ataturk**, c. Lawrence, d. Faisal) :: AMERICA : TURKEY
   (b) George Washington is considered the "father of America," and Kemal Ataturk is considered the "father of modern Turkey."

115. MARINETTI : FUTURISM :: BALL : (**a. Dada**, b. Surrealism, c. abstraction, d. Vorticism)
   (a) F. T. Marinetti was the literary figurehead and manifesto writer for the Futurism movement, while Hugo Ball did much the same for the Dada movement.

116. PETROLOGY : ROCK :: (a. pomology, b. speliology, **c. seismology**, d. phytology): EARTHQUAKES
   (c) Seismology is the study of earthquakes, just as petrology is the study of rocks.

117. TORNADO : BREEZE :: RAVINE : (**a. ditch**, b. hurricane, c. raven, d. quagmire)
   (a) A tornado is an extreme form of a breeze, and a ravine is an extreme form of a ditch.

118. LAISSEZ-FAIRE : GOVERNMENTAL DEFICIT SPENDING :: SMITH :
   (a. Marx, b. Fleming, c. Greenspan, **d. Keynes**)
   (d) Adam Smith was the economist who developed the theory of laissez-faire economics. John Maynard Keynes was the economist who developed the theory of beneficial governmental deficit spending.

119. NORTHERN RENAISSANCE : HARLEM RENAISSANCE :: JAN VAN EYCK :
   (a. Carrie Mae Weems, b. Grandma Moses, **c. Jacob Lawrence**, d. Wilfredo Lam)
   (c) Jan van Eyck was a key figure of the Northern Renaissance in 15th-century Europe, and Jacob Lawrence was a preeminent painter of the Harlem Renaissance in 20th-century America.

120. STRATUM : THESIS :: (a. stratums, b. stratus, **c. strata**, d. stratas) : THESES
   (c) The irregular plural of *stratum* is *strata,* just as the irregular plural of *thesis* is *theses.*

ANSWER SHEET FOR PRACTICE TEST 4

1. (a) (b) (c) (d)
2. (a) (b) (c) (d)
3. (a) (b) (c) (d)
4. (a) (b) (c) (d)
5. (a) (b) (c) (d)
6. (a) (b) (c) (d)
7. (a) (b) (c) (d)
8. (a) (b) (c) (d)
9. (a) (b) (c) (d)
10. (a) (b) (c) (d)
11. (a) (b) (c) (d)
12. (a) (b) (c) (d)
13. (a) (b) (c) (d)
14. (a) (b) (c) (d)
15. (a) (b) (c) (d)
16. (a) (b) (c) (d)
17. (a) (b) (c) (d)
18. (a) (b) (c) (d)
19. (a) (b) (c) (d)
20. (a) (b) (c) (d)
21. (a) (b) (c) (d)
22. (a) (b) (c) (d)
23. (a) (b) (c) (d)
24. (a) (b) (c) (d)
25. (a) (b) (c) (d)
26. (a) (b) (c) (d)
27. (a) (b) (c) (d)
28. (a) (b) (c) (d)
29. (a) (b) (c) (d)
30. (a) (b) (c) (d)
31. (a) (b) (c) (d)
32. (a) (b) (c) (d)
33. (a) (b) (c) (d)
34. (a) (b) (c) (d)
35. (a) (b) (c) (d)
36. (a) (b) (c) (d)
37. (a) (b) (c) (d)
38. (a) (b) (c) (d)
39. (a) (b) (c) (d)
40. (a) (b) (c) (d)

41. (a) (b) (c) (d)
42. (a) (b) (c) (d)
43. (a) (b) (c) (d)
44. (a) (b) (c) (d)
45. (a) (b) (c) (d)
46. (a) (b) (c) (d)
47. (a) (b) (c) (d)
48. (a) (b) (c) (d)
49. (a) (b) (c) (d)
50. (a) (b) (c) (d)
51. (a) (b) (c) (d)
52. (a) (b) (c) (d)
53. (a) (b) (c) (d)
54. (a) (b) (c) (d)
55. (a) (b) (c) (d)
56. (a) (b) (c) (d)
57. (a) (b) (c) (d)
58. (a) (b) (c) (d)
59. (a) (b) (c) (d)
60. (a) (b) (c) (d)
61. (a) (b) (c) (d)
62. (a) (b) (c) (d)
63. (a) (b) (c) (d)
64. (a) (b) (c) (d)
65. (a) (b) (c) (d)
66. (a) (b) (c) (d)
67. (a) (b) (c) (d)
68. (a) (b) (c) (d)
69. (a) (b) (c) (d)
70. (a) (b) (c) (d)
71. (a) (b) (c) (d)
72. (a) (b) (c) (d)
73. (a) (b) (c) (d)
74. (a) (b) (c) (d)
75. (a) (b) (c) (d)
76. (a) (b) (c) (d)
77. (a) (b) (c) (d)
78. (a) (b) (c) (d)
79. (a) (b) (c) (d)
80. (a) (b) (c) (d)

81. (a) (b) (c) (d)
82. (a) (b) (c) (d)
83. (a) (b) (c) (d)
84. (a) (b) (c) (d)
85. (a) (b) (c) (d)
86. (a) (b) (c) (d)
87. (a) (b) (c) (d)
88. (a) (b) (c) (d)
89. (a) (b) (c) (d)
90. (a) (b) (c) (d)
91. (a) (b) (c) (d)
92. (a) (b) (c) (d)
93. (a) (b) (c) (d)
94. (a) (b) (c) (d)
95. (a) (b) (c) (d)
96. (a) (b) (c) (d)
97. (a) (b) (c) (d)
98. (a) (b) (c) (d)
99. (a) (b) (c) (d)
100. (a) (b) (c) (d)
101. (a) (b) (c) (d)
102. (a) (b) (c) (d)
103. (a) (b) (c) (d)
104. (a) (b) (c) (d)
105. (a) (b) (c) (d)
106. (a) (b) (c) (d)
107. (a) (b) (c) (d)
108. (a) (b) (c) (d)
109. (a) (b) (c) (d)
110. (a) (b) (c) (d)
111. (a) (b) (c) (d)
112. (a) (b) (c) (d)
113. (a) (b) (c) (d)
114. (a) (b) (c) (d)
115. (a) (b) (c) (d)
116. (a) (b) (c) (d)
117. (a) (b) (c) (d)
118. (a) (b) (c) (d)
119. (a) (b) (c) (d)
120. (a) (b) (c) (d)

Practice Test 4

Time: 60 minutes
Length of Test: 120 Questions

Directions: For each of the following questions, you will find three capitalized terms and, in parentheses, four answer choices designated *a*, *b*, *c*, and *d*. Select the one answer choice that best completes the analogy with the three capitalized terms. (To record your answers, use the answer sheet that precedes this test.)

1. 60-60-60 : (a. 30-60-90, b. 50-60-70, c. 90-45-45, d. 45-60-75) :: EQUILATERAL : ISOSCELES

2. (a. battery, b. electricity, c. resistor, d. radio) : VOLTA :: LIGHTNING ROD : FRANKLIN

3. CROWN : CORONATION :: (a. diploma, b. gown, c. ceremony, d. scepter) : GRADUATION

4. BOIL : (a. dumpling, b. meal, c. steam, d. cracker) :: FRY : FRITTER

5. RECLUSE : WIDOW :: BROWN : (a. solitary, b. wan, c. black, d. lone)

6. ANGST : FEAR :: ENNUI : (a. contempt, b. boredom, c. animosity, d. confusion)

7. BORDER : ORDER :: (a. pass, b. refuse, c. abut, d. mandate) : DEMAND

8. –OR : –IZE :: NOUN : (a. adjective, b. verb, c. preposition, d. adverb)

9. ABBREVIATION : POSSESSION :: PERIOD : (a. comma, b. apostrophe, c. dash, d. colon)

10. VACCINATE : HABITUATE :: IMMUNITY : (a. receptivity, b. understanding, c. tolerance, d. addiction)

11. (a. brain, b. eyes, c. stomach, d. blood) : NERVES :: DYSPEPSIA : NEURALGIA

12. EPOCH : TIME :: LIGHT YEAR : (a. duration, b. luminosity, c. distance, d. gravity)

13. PLURAL : (a. curriculi, b. curriculae, c. curricules, d. curricula) :: SINGULAR : CURRICULUM

14. RAISIN : GRAPE :: PRUNE : (a. plum, b. date, c. apricot, d. tree)

15. RABBIT : (a. hare, b. kennel, c. warren, d. carrot) :: BEAVER : DAM

16. FALL : SPRING :: AUTUMNAL : (a. equinox, b. vernal, c. solstice, d. aquifer)

17. (a. assuage, b. meat, c. bratwurst, d. breakfast) : SAUSAGE :: GRIN : RING

18. PLUMB : VERTICAL :: (a. level, b. square, c. divider, d. rule) : HORIZONTAL

19. DREGS : WINE :: (a. alloy, b. slag, c. mint, d. coin) : METAL

20. FIB : FOIBLE :: (a. flaw, b. lie, c. equivocate, d. foil) : FAULT

21. APHORISM : PITHY :: (a. platitude, b. oratory, c. recitation, d. clever) : BANAL

22. DICTION : (a. articulation, b. charm, c. dance, d. dexterity) :: SPEECH : MOVEMENT

23. (a. pierce, b. bend, c. disperse, d. ablate) : BOUNCE :: REFRACTION : REFLECTION

24. (a. tirade, b. morale, c. kudos, d. pathos) : PRAISE :: POLEMIC : CONTROVERSY

25. PUGILIST : BOXER :: (a. theater, b. play, c. thespian, d. director) : ACTOR

26. SEVEN SCORE : (a. 70, b. 84, c. 140, d. 700) :: SIX DOZEN : 72

27. HUNGRY : (a. meal, b. peck, c. drink, d. spit) :: THIRSTY : SIP

28. ARCHIPELAGO : (a. islands, b. ocean, c. peak, d. atoll) :: RANGE : MOUNTAINS

29. FORTE : VOLUME :: (a. allegro, b. piano, c. pitch, d. soprano) : TEMPO

30. (a. –osis, b. –ism, c. –eme, d. –osa) : ABNORMAL :: –ITIS : INFLAMMATION

31. (a. cupidity, b. lethargic, c. somnambulistic, d. celeritous) : GREED :: DEFERENCE : RESPECT

32. (a. dictator, b. talented, c. few d. wealthy) : PRIESTHOOD :: MERITOCRACY : THEOCRACY

33. ALE : MALT :: MEAD : (a. honey, b. grapes, c. hops, d. cloves)

34. ROD : BUSHEL :: (a. weight, b. mass, c. purity, d. distance) : VOLUME

35. IMPUGN : DISPARAGE :: (a. laud, b. deny, c. calculate, d. illicit) : PRAISE

36. PROBABILITY : PERCENT :: (a. 0.05, b. 0.5, c. 5, d. 50) : 50

37. DOLPHIN : BLOWHOLE :: GRASSHOPPER : (a. lung, b. spiracle, c. antenna, d. tympanum

38. TILT : (a. drift, b. wind, c. direction, d. navigation) :: GYROSCOPE : ANCHOR

39. (a. isocahedron, b. octahedron, c. cube, d. dodecahedron) : TETRAHEDRON :: 12 : 4

40. SRI LANKA : BURKINA FASO :: CEYLON : (a. Congo, b. Upper Volta, c. Mali, d. Benin)

41. MONDAY : (a. dynamo, b. lunar, c. Beltane, d. weekly) :: MARCH : CHARM

42. (a. underwriting, b. guarantee, c. receipt, d. repair) : INSURANCE :: PURCHASE : ACCIDENT

43. NICKELODEON : AUTOMAT :: MUSIC : (a. food, b. pictures, c. novelties, d. laundry)

44. FLENSE : (a. carve, b. stretch, c. grind, d. congeal) :: EXFOLIATE : CRUMBLE

45. ARCH : KEYSTONE :: WHEEL : (a. axle, b. spoke, c. rim, d. linchpin)

46. (a. outside, b. into, c. between, d. around) : WITHIN :: INTER– : INTRA–

47. BOWDLERIZE : EDIT :: (a. plagiarize, b. proofread, c. cite, d. reference) : PARAPHRASE

48. BEMUSED : IRATE :: NONPLUSSED : (a. confused, b. angry, c. sympathetic, d. cheerful)

49. (a. membrane, b. transporter, c. cell, d. eater) : –PHAGE :: BODY : –SOME

50. WATER : AIR :: (a. regulator, b. submersible, c. hydrophone, d. radar) : MICROPHONE

51. EAR : (a. drum, b. canal, c. tympanum, d. skin) :: BIRD : REPTILE

52. ADAGIO : (a. loudly, b. slowly, c. quickly, d. carefully) :: PIANO : SOFTLY

53. CRANIUM : (a. psychology, b. mesmerism, c. psychometrics, d. phrenology) :: HANDWRITING : GRAPHOLOGY

54. ANTEDILUVIAN : ANTEBELLUM :: (a. trial, b. flood, c. dilution, d. battle) : WAR

55. DYNAMITE : NITROGLYCERIN :: (a. mortar, b. plaster, c. clay, d. brick) : CEMENT

56. EXAMPLE : PARADIGM :: JUDGMENT : (a. judge, b. sentence, c. precedent, d. law)

57. SERENDIPITOUS : LOUD :: PLANNED : (a. dissonant, b. scented, c. quiet, d. melodious)

58. ANEMOMETER : WINDSOCK :: (a. temperature, b. speed, c. humidity, d. altitude) : DIRECTION

59. ASSIDUOUS : (a. work, b. rope, c. lackadaisical, d. diligent) :: TAUT : SLACK

60. LINCOLN : (a. Monroe, b. Reagan, c. Kennedy, d. Wilson) :: FORD'S THEATER : DEALY PLAZA

61. (a. interregnum, b. usurper, c. play, d. opus) : INTERMISSION :: REIGNS : ACTS

62. JOYCE : BYRON :: MODERN : (a. neoclassical, b. transcendental, c. sublime, d. romantic)

63. SLIDE RULE : (a. probability, b. permutations, c. logarithms, d. square roots) :: ABACUS : ARITHMETIC

64. CONSONANCE : ALLITERATION :: (a. middle, b. end, c. rhyme, d. rhythm) : BEGINNING

65. PARIAH : ANATHEMA :: (a. canard, b. outcast, c. axiom, d. pundit) : FALSEHOOD

66. TURGID : GRANDILOQUENT :: (a. torpid, b. succinct, c. turbid, d. tacit) : MUDDLED

67. LIGATURE : ARMATURE :: (a. bind, b. speak, c. access, d. reach) : SUPPORT

68. NAPOLEON : ALEXANDER :: (a. Elba, b. Waterloo, c. Sicily, d. Corsica) : MACEDONIA

69. CIRCE : (a. *Aeneid*, b. *Odyssey*, c. *Orestia*, d. eg *Metamorphoses*) :: AGAMEMNON : ILIAD

70. (a. censorious, b. new, c. formal, d. specialized) : NEOLOGISM :: INFORMAL : COLLOQUIALISM

71. DU BOIS : PAN-AFRICANISM :: (a. Carver, b. Truth, c. Washington, d. Douglass) : ATLANTA COMPROMISE

72. HAIKU : 17 :: (a. iamb, b. sonnet, c. couplet, d. syllable) : 2

73. c : (a. E, b. K, c. l, d. g) :: 299,792,458 m/s : 9.8 m/s^2

74. (a. sail, b. wind, c. keel, d. tiller) : TACK :: RESISTANCE : COERCE

75. MULTIPLE OF 6 : 168 :: MULTIPLE OF 3 : (a. 10, b. 165, c. 295, d. 2005)

76. STRING : PIANO :: (a. drone, b. bladder, c. chanter, d. reed) : BAGPIPE

77. FRACTURE : (a. callus, b. seam, c. compound, d. bend) :: LACERATION : SCAR

78. BOMBARDIER : PILOT :: (a. bird, b. flower, c. beetle, d. lizard) : FISH

79. HIDE : HOME :: CONCEAL : (a. return, b. thrash, c. shelter, d. abide)

80. FRESCO : (a. canvas, b. paneling, c. triptych, d. plaster) :: BATIK : FABRIC

81. PRIME : 19 :: PERFECT : (a. 0, b. 1, c. 6, d. 22)

82. ASH : PALM :: WEDNESDAY : (a. Sunday, b. Monday, c. Tuesday, d. Friday)

83. BABBAGE : TESLA :: (a. difference engine, b. steam engine, c. telegraph, d. semaphore) : TRANSFORMER

84. EPIGONE : (a. outside, b. protective, c. inferiority, d. humility) :: PARAGON : EXCELLENCE

85. JUPITER : EAGLE :: JUNO : (a. owl, b. peacock, c. swan, d. dove)

86. POLYMER : LATEX :: HYDROCARBON : (a. butane, b. graphite, c. lead, d. water)

87. 3.14 : CIRCLE :: 0.618 : (a. triangle, b. spiral, c. parallelogram, d. hexagon)

88. GEORGE VI : (a. Peel, b. Gladstone, c. Palmerston, d. Churchill) :: VICTORIA I : DISRAELI

89. ATTICA : GREECE :: THRACE : (a. Thebes, b. Turkey, c. Italy, d. Britain)

90. VERDIGRIS : PATINA :: (a. liberty, b. justice, c. equality, d. fraternity) : FREEDOM

91. NAUSEOUS : NAUSEATED :: (a. fearful, b. frightening, c. uncertain, d. unwell) : AFRAID

92. SCHADENFREUDE : (a. apprehensive, b. confused, c. irritable, d. cheerful) :: SYMPATHY : JOVIAL

93. SCRUPLE : (a. peck, b. hogshead, c. dram, d. ounce) :: TRIANGLE : ANGLE

94. (a. coulomb, b. fathom, c. bolt, d. hectare) : HERTZ :: ELECTRIC CHARGE : FREQUENCY

95. MAWKISH : SENTIMENTAL :: CLOYING : (a. sweet, b. harmonious, c. cool, d. sad)

96. QUETZALCOATL : CHOCOLATE :: ZEUS : (a. blood, b. gold, c. ambrosia, d. corn)

97. EXEGESIS : (a. forensics, b. stasis, c. research, d. ballistics) :: TEXT : CRIME SCENE

98. (a. ontology, b. graphology, c. limnology, d. numismatology) : COINS :: CETOLOGY : WHALES

99. ACIDITY : pH :: WINDINESS : (a. Richter, b. Geiger, c. Beaufort, d. speed)

100. NICHOLAS : LENIN :: BATISTA : (a. Guevara, b. Stalin, c. Castro, d. DuChamp)

101. (a. Shiba Inu, b. Lhasa Apso, c. Akita, d. Basenji) : TIBET :: KOMONDOR : HUNGARY

102. WREATHES : ORGANIST :: (a. whether, b. sweater, c. threshold, d. weathers) : ROASTING

103. GRANT : (a. Wilson, b. Hoover, c. Coolidge, d. Roosevelt) :: CIVIL RIGHTS : SUFFRAGE

104. FUTURISM : NEOCLASSICISM :: (a. harmony, b. Cubism, c. perspective, d. speed) : BALANCE

105. APHRODITE : VENUS :: DIANA : (a. Artemis, b. Helen, c. Hera, d. Paris)

106. JULIUS II : (a. Pius XII, b. Max Ernst, c. Peggy Guggenheim, d. Museum of Modern Art) :: MICHELANGELO : POLLOCK

107. GENEVA : LAKE GENEVA :: CHICAGO : (a. Lake Erie, b. Lake Superior, c. Lake Michigan, d. Lake Huron)

108. QUARTZ : GRANITE :: (a. obsidian, b. calcite, c. bakelite, d. fluorite) : LIMESTONE

109. (a. pasty, b. leaden, c. convoluted, d. succinct) : PITHY :: ASHEN : RUDDY

110. RAVENNA : (a. mosaics, b. sculpture, c. jewels, d. catacombs) :: POMPEII : FRESCOES

111. (a. flute, b. piano, c. sousaphone, d. bassoon): STRING :: TROMBONE : BRASS

112. (a. Hinduism, b. Islam, c. Coptic, d. Christianity) : JUDAISM :: POLY : MONO

113. MAO ZEDONG : (a. Cultural Revolution, b. Great Leap Forward, c. Five Modernizations, d. Final Solution) :: STALIN : FIVE YEAR PLAN

114. (a. ambulatory, b. altar, c. Westwerk, d. buttress) : FAÇADE :: GROIN VAULTING : ROOF

115. BINARY : DECIMAL :: 10001 : (a. 101, b. 65, c. 12, d. 17)

116. AGINCOURT : MARNE :: (a. Germany, b. Russia, c. England, d. Spain) : FRANCE

117. DAUNT : DREAM :: TUNA : (a. dared, b. ready, c. read, d. mare)

118. ELECTRONS : (a. hadrons, b. fermions, c. neutrinos, d. mesons) :: PROTONS : BOSONS

119. MITOSIS : EUKARYOTE :: MEIOSIS : (a. gamete, b. fungoid, c. somatic, d. lymph)

120. RACECAR : (a. anagram, b. kerplunk, c. auger, d. deterred) :: PALINDROME : ONOMATOPOEIA

ANSWERS AND EXPLANATIONS

1. 60-60-60 : (a. 30-60-90, b. 50-60-70, **c. 90-45-45**, d. 45-60-75) :: EQUILATERAL : ISOSCELES
   (c) An equilateral triangle has sides all of the same length, meaning that the interior angles of the triangle are also identical at 60 degrees each. An isosceles triangle has two sides of equal length, which therefore creates two interior angles of 45 degrees and one angle of 90 degrees.

2. (**a. battery**, b. electricity, c. resistor, d. radio) : VOLTA :: LIGHTNING ROD : FRANKLIN
   (a) Alessandro Volta invented the battery, and Benjamin Franklin invented the lightning rod.

3. CROWN : CORONATION :: (**a. diploma**, b. gown, c. ceremony, d. scepter) : GRADUATION
   (a) Just as it is customary to present a crown to someone at a coronation, it is customary to present a diploma to someone who is graduating.

4. BOIL : (**a. dumpling**, b. meal, c. steam, d. cracker) :: FRY : FRITTER
   (a) In cooking, to make a fritter, you must fry the ingredients, just as to make a dumpling, you must boil the ingredients.

5. RECLUSE : WIDOW :: BROWN : (a. solitary, b. wan, **c. black**, d. lone)
   (c) A brown recluse is a type of poisonous spider, and a black widow is also a type of poisonous spider.

6. ANGST : FEAR :: ENNUI : (a. contempt, **b. boredom**, c. animosity, d. confusion)
   (b) *Angst* is a synonym for *fear*, just as *ennui* is a synonym for *boredom*.

7. BORDER : ORDER :: (a. pass, b. refuse, **c. abut**, d. mandate) : DEMAND
   (c) *Border* means the same as *abut*, and *order* means the same as *demand*.

8. –OR : –IZE :: NOUN : (a. adjective, **b. verb**, c. preposition, d. adverb)
   (b) The suffix *–or* is used to signify the noun form of a word, just as the suffix *–ize* is used to signify the verb form of a word.

9. ABBREVIATION : POSSESSION :: PERIOD : (a. comma, **b. apostrophe**, c. dash, d. colon)
   (b) A period is used to identify an abbreviation, and an apostrophe is used to identify possession.

10. VACCINATE : HABITUATE :: IMMUNITY : (a. receptivity, b. understanding, **c. tolerance**, d. addiction)
    (c) To provide immunity against infection, one must vaccinate. To provide tolerance, one must habituate, or expose through frequent repetition.

11. (a. brain, b. eyes, **c. stomach**, d. blood) : NERVES :: DYSPEPSIA : NEURALGIA
    (c) Dyspepsia is intense pain or discomfort of the stomach, just as neuralgia is intense pain of the nerves.

12. EPOCH : TIME :: LIGHT YEAR : (a. duration, b. luminosity, **c. distance**, d. gravity)
    (c) An epoch is a measurement of time, and a light year is a measurement of distance.

13. PLURAL : (a. curriculi, b. curriculae, c. curricules, **d. curricula**) :: SINGULAR : CURRICULUM
    (d) The plural of *curriculum* is *curricula*.

14. RAISIN : GRAPE :: PRUNE : (**a. plum**, b. date, c. apricot, d. tree)
    (a) Just as a raisin is a dried-out grape, a prune is a dried-out plum.

15. RABBIT : (a. hare, b. kennel, **c. warren**, d. carrot) :: BEAVER : DAM
    (c) A rabbit constructs a warren for shelter, and a beaver constructs a dam for shelter.

16. FALL : SPRING :: AUTUMNAL : (a. equinox, **b. vernal**, c. solstice, d. aquifer)
    (b) Autumnal means relating to the fall season, and vernal means relating to the spring season.

17. (**a. assuage**, b. meat, c. bratwurst, d. breakfast) : SAUSAGE :: GRIN : RING
    (a) The word *assuage* is an anagram for *sausage*, and the word *grin* is an anagram for *ring*.

18. PLUMB : VERTICAL :: (**a. level**, b. square, c. divider, d. rule) : HORIZONTAL
    (a) A plumb is a tool used to measure a vertical, and a level is a tool used to measure a horizontal.

19. DREGS : WINE :: (a. alloy, **b. slag**, c. mint, d. coin) : METAL
    (b) Dregs are what remain following the making of wine, just as slag is what remains following the production of metal.

20. FIB : FOIBLE :: (a. flaw, **b. lie**, c. equivocate, d. foil) : FAULT
    (b) *Fib* is a synonym for *lie*, and *foible* is a synonym for *fault*.

21. APHORISM : PITHY :: (**a. platitude**, b. oratory, c. recitation, d. clever) : BANAL
    (a) An aphorism, or statement of principle, is characterized by being pithy, while a platitude, or idle compliment, is characterized by being banal.

22. DICTION : (a. articulation, b. charm, c. dance, **d. dexterity**) :: SPEECH : MOVEMENT
    (d) The use of clear diction is a measure of one's skill in speech, just as dexterity is the measure of one's skill in movement.

23. (a. pierce, **b. bend**, c. disperse, d. ablate) : BOUNCE :: REFRACTION : REFLECTION
    (**b**) Refraction is the bending of light, and reflection is the bouncing of light.

24. (a. tirade, b. morale **c. kudos**, d. pathos) : PRAISE :: POLEMIC : CONTROVERSY
    (**c**) Kudos are exclamations of praise or compliments, while a polemic is a controversial speech or argument.

25. PUGILIST : BOXER :: (a. theater, b. play, **c. thespian**, d. director) : ACTOR
    (**c**) *Pugilist* is another name for a boxer, just as *thespian* is another name for an actor.

26. SEVEN SCORE : (a. 70, b. 84, **c. 140**, d. 700) :: SIX DOZEN : 72
    (**c**) A dozen is a group of 12 things, so six dozen equals 72. A score is a group of 20 things, so seven score would equal 140.

27. HUNGRY : (a. meal, **b. peck**, c. drink, d. spit) :: THIRSTY : SIP
    (**b**) A mildly hungry person might peck at his food, just as a mildly thirsty person might sip his drink.

28. ARCHIPELAGO : (**a. islands**, b. ocean, c. peak, d. atoll) :: RANGE : MOUNTAINS
    (**a**) An archipelago is a series of islands in a row, and a range is a series of mountains in a row.

29. FORTE : VOLUME :: (**a. allegro**, b. piano, c. pitch, d. soprano) : TEMPO
    (**a**) *Forte* is an Italian term used in music to indicate a lot of volume, or to play loudly, and *allegro* is an Italian term used in music to indicate a fast tempo, or to play with a lot of speed.

30. (**a. –osis**, b. –ism, c. –eme, d. –osa) : ABNORMAL :: –ITIS : INFLAMMATION
    (**a**) In medical terms, the suffix *–osis* signifies an abnormality (e.g., psychosis), just as the suffix *–itis* signifies an inflammation (e.g., appendicitis).

31. (**a. cupidity**, b. lethargic, c. somnambulistic, d. celeritous) : GREED :: DEFERENCE : RESPECT
    (**a**) Cupidity is a sign of greed, and deference is a sign of respect.

32. (a. dictator, **b. talented**, c. few, d. wealthy) : PRIESTHOOD :: MERITOCRACY : THEOCRACY
    (**b**) A meritocracy is a government based on leadership by the talented, just as a theocracy is a government based on leadership by the priesthood.

33. ALE : MALT :: MEAD : (**a. honey**, b. grapes, c. hops, d. cloves)
    (**a**) Ale is a beverage made from malt, and mead is a beverage made from honey.

34. ROD : BUSHEL :: (a. weight, b. mass, c. purity, **d. distance**) : VOLUME
    (**d**) A rod is a measure of distance, just as a bushel is a measure of volume.

35. IMPUGN : DISPARAGE :: (**a. laud**, b. deny, c. calculate, d. illicit) : PRAISE
(**a**) To impugn someone means to disparage the person, and to laud someone means to praise the person.

36. PROBABILITY : PERCENT :: (a. 0.05, **b. 0.5**, c. 5, d. 50) : 50
(**b**) Probability is generally expressed as a number between 0 and 1. Thus, a 50 percent probability is expressed as 0.5.

37. DOLPHIN : BLOWHOLE :: GRASSHOPPER : (a. lung, **b. spiracle**, c. antenna, d. tympanum
(**b**) A dolphin breathes via its blowhole, just as a grasshopper breathes via its spiracle.

38. TILT : (**a. drift**, b. wind, c. direction, d. navigation) :: GYROSCOPE : ANCHOR
(**a**) A gyroscope is a device used to offset the effects of tilt, and an anchor is a device used to offset the effects of drift.

39. (a. isocahedron, b. octahedron, c. cube, **d. dodecahedron**) : TETRAHEDRON :: 12 : 4
(**d**) A dodecahedron is a shape having 12 faces, just as a tetrahedron is a shape having 4 faces.

40. SRI LANKA : BURKINA FASO :: CEYLON : (a. Congo, **b. Upper Volta**, c. Mali, d. Benin)
(**b**) The former name for the country of Sri Lanka was Ceylon, and the former name of the country of Burkina Faso was Upper Volta.

41. MONDAY : (**a. dynamo**, b. lunar, c. Beltane, d. weekly) :: MARCH : CHARM
(**a**) The word *Monday* is an anagram for the word *dynamo*, just as the word *March* is an anagram for the word *charm*.

42. (a. underwriting, **b. guarantee**, c. receipt, d. repair) : INSURANCE :: PURCHASE : ACCIDENT
(**b**) A guarantee is a way for consumers to protect themselves against a faulty purchase, and insurance is a way for someone to protect against an accident.

43. NICKELODEON : AUTOMAT :: MUSIC : (**a. food**, b. pictures, c. novelties, d. laundry)
(**a**) Just as a nickelodeon is an automated device for purchasing music, an automat is an automated device for purchasing food.

44. FLENSE : (a. carve, b. stretch, **c. grind**, d. congeal) :: EXFOLIATE : CRUMBLE
(**c**) To flense is an extreme form of stripping away the skin, or exfoliating. Similarly, to grind is an extreme form of making into smaller chunks, or crumbling.

45. ARCH : KEYSTONE :: WHEEL : (a. axle, b. spoke, c. rim, **d. linchpin**)
    (**d**) In the same way that a keystone holds together all pieces of an arch, a linchpin holds together all parts of a wheel. While an axle, spoke, and rim are all part of a wheel construction, none of these holds together all the pieces in the same way that a keystone holds together an arch.

46. (a. outside, b. into, **c. between**, d. around) : WITHIN :: INTER– : INTRA–
    (**c**) The prefix *intra–* means within any one thing, and the prefix *inter–* means between any two or more things.

47. BOWDLERIZE : EDIT :: (**a. plagiarize**, b. proofread, c. cite, d. reference) : PARAPHRASE
    (**a**) To bowdlerize is an extreme and negative form of editing or omitting, while to plagiarize is an extreme and negative form of paraphrasing. To cite would be to state a reference directly, which is not extreme or negative.

48. BEMUSED : IRATE :: NONPLUSSED : (a. confused, **b. angry**, c. sympathetic, d. cheerful)
    (**b**) *Bemused* is a synonym for *nonplussed*, just as *irate* is a synonym for *angry*.

49. (a. membrane, b. transporter, c. cell, **d. eater**) : –PHAGE :: BODY : –SOME
    (**d**) The suffix *–phage* refers to the eating or destruction of cells, and the suffix *–some* refers to anything relating to a body (e.g., chromasome).

50. WATER : AIR :: (a. regulator, b. submersible, **c. hydrophone**, d. radar) : MICROPHONE
    (**c**) A hydrophone is a device used to pick up soundwaves underwater, while a microphone is a device used to pick up soundwaves through the air.

51. EAR : (a. drum, b. canal, **c. tympanum**, d. skin) :: BIRD : REPTILE
    (**c**) Birds are able to hear via a set of ears, while reptiles are able to hear via a set of tympana.

52. ADAGIO : (a. loudly, **b. slowly**, c. quickly, d. carefully) :: PIANO : SOFTLY
    (**b**) *Adagio* is the musical term for playing slowly, just as *piano* is the musical term for playing softly.

53. CRANIUM : (a. psychology, b. mesmerism, c. psychometrics, **d. phrenology**) :: HANDWRITING : GRAPHOLOGY
    (**d**) Phrenology is the study of the shape and size of the cranium or skull, while graphology is the study of the shape and size of handwriting.

54. ANTEDILUVIAN : ANTEBELLUM :: (a. trial, **b. flood**, c. dilution, d. battle) : WAR
    (**b**) The term *antediluvian* means before the flood, and the term *antebellum* means before the war.

55. DYNAMITE : NITROGLYCERIN :: (**a. mortar**, b. plaster, c. clay, d. brick) : CEMENT
(**a**) The active ingredient in dynamite is nitroglycerin, just as the active ingredient in mortar is cement.

56. EXAMPLE : PARADIGM :: JUDGMENT : (a. judge, **b. sentence**, c. precedent, d. law)
(**b**) A paradigm is another way of saying an example or model, and a sentence is another way of saying a judgment. Note that while the answer choice *judge* is related to the original word in question, it is not in the right form of the word to satisfy the analogy best.

57. SERENDIPITOUS : LOUD :: PLANNED : (a. dissonant, b. scented, **c. quiet**, d. melodious)
(**c**) Something that is serendipitous happens without notice and without warning, the very opposite of something planned. Similarly, *loud* is the very opposite of *quiet*.

58. ANEMOMETER : WINDSOCK :: (a. temperature, **b. speed**, c. humidity, d. altitude) : DIRECTION
(**b**) The device called an anemometer is used to measure the force, or speed, of wind. A windsock is used to measure the direction of wind.

59. ASSIDUOUS : (a. work, b. rope, **c. lackadaisical**, d. diligent) :: TAUT : SLACK
(**c**) The clear opposite of *assiduous*, or driven and consistent, is *lackadaisical*. Similarly, the clear opposite of *taut* is *slack*.

60. LINCOLN : (a. Monroe, b. Reagan, **c. Kennedy**, d. Wilson) :: FORD'S THEATER : DEALY PLAZA
(**c**) President Abraham Lincoln was shot and killed in Ford's Theatre in Washington, D.C. President John F. Kennedy was shot and killed in Dealy Plaza in Dallas, Texas.

61. (**a. interregnum**, b. usurper, c. play, d. opus) : INTERMISSION :: REIGNS : ACTS
(**a**) An interregnum is the period of time between the end of the reign of one sovereign and the beginning of the reign of the next. An intermission is the period of time between acts of a play or an opera.

62. JOYCE : BYRON :: MODERN : (a. neoclassical, b. transcendental, c. sublime, **d. romantic**)
(**d**) Irish author James Joyce is widely acknowledged as one of the masters of the modern era, while Lord Byron is widely acknowledged as one of the masters of the Romantic age.

63. SLIDE RULE : (a. probability, b. permutations, **c. logarithms**, d. square roots) :: ABACUS : ARITHMETIC
(**c**) A slide rule is designed to allow the user to calculate logarithms simply, just as an abacus is designed to simplify the calculation of arithmetic. Probability and square roots are not a part of the slide rule's design.

64. CONSONANCE : ALLITERATION :: (a. middle, **b. end**, c. rhyme, d. rhythm) : BEGINNING
(**b**) The poetic device of consonance focuses on the repetition of consonant sounds at the end of a word or phrase. Alliteration is a poetic device that focuses on the repetition of consonant sounds at the beginning of words or syllables.

65. PARIAH : ANATHEMA :: (**a. canard**, b. outcast, c. axiom, d. pundit) : FALSEHOOD
(**a**) A pariah is someone shunned by society, and the word is a synonym for *anathema*. Likewise, *canard* is synonymous with *falsehood*.

66. TURGID : GRANDILOQUENT :: (a. torpid, b. succinct, **c. turbid**, d. tacit) : MUDDLED
(**c**) The words *turgid* and *grandiloquent* are synonymous, both meaning ornate or overly complex. Likewise, *turbid* is a synonym for *muddled*.

67. LIGATURE : ARMATURE :: (**a. bind**, b. speak, c. access, d. reach) : SUPPORT
(**a**) The function of a ligature is to bind, while the function of an armature is to support.

68. NAPOLEON : ALEXANDER :: (a. Elba, b. Waterloo, c. Sicily, **d. Corsica**) : MACEDONIA
(**d**) The French Emperor Napoleon Bonaparte was originally from the island of Corsica. Emperor Alexander the Great was originally from Macedonia. Elba and Waterloo are both locales that factor into Napoleon's life, but neither fits the birthplace analogy.

69. CIRCE : (a. *Aeneid*, **b. *Odyssey***, c. *Orestia*, d. *Metamorphoses*) :: AGAMEMNON : ILLIAD
(**b**) Circe is a character in Homer's *Odyssey*. Agamemnon is a character in Homer's *Iliad*.

70. (a. censorious, **b. new**, c. formal, d. specialized) : NEOLOGISM :: INFORMAL : COLLOQUIALISM
(**b**) A neologism is a new word or expression, just as a colloquialism is an expression or word that is considered informal.

71. DU BOIS : PAN-AFRICANISM :: (a. Carver, b. Truth, **c. Washington**, d. Douglass) : ATLANTA COMPROMISE
(**c**) W. E. B. DuBois pioneered the pan-African movement, designed to unite the African Diaspora. In 1895, Booker T. Washington delivered his famous Atlanta Compromise speech.

72. HAIKU : 17 :: (**a. iamb**, b. sonnet, c. couplet, d. syllable) : 2
(**a**) A haiku is a type of poem that uses 17 syllables. An iamb is a building block of a poem that utilizes only two syllables—one stressed, one unstressed.

73. c : (a. E, b. K, c. l, **d. g**) :: 299,792,458 m/s : 9.8 m/s^2
    (**d**) The symbol c stands for the speed of light, which in mathematical terms is 299,792,458 m/s. The symbol g stands for gravity, whose mathematical equivalent is 9.8 m/s^2.

74. (a. sail, **b. wind**, c. keel, d. tiller) : TACK :: RESISTANCE : COERCE
    (**b**) In sailing, to tack is a maneuver used to overcome the wind. Similarly, to coerce is to overcome resistance.

75. MULTIPLE OF 6 : 168 :: MULTIPLE OF 3 : (a. 10, **b. 165**, c. 295, d. 2005)
    (**b**) The number 168 is divisible by 6. The number 165 is the only answer choice given that is a multiple of 3. The easiest way to figure this out quickly is to add up the digits individually. If the number you get from adding the digits is divisible by 3, then you know the larger number is also a multiple of 3.

76. STRING : PIANO :: (a. drone, b. bladder, c. chanter, **d. reed**) : BAGPIPE
    (**d**) A string is the part of the inner workings of a piano that makes the sound, just as a reed is the part of the inner workings of a bagpipe that delivers its sound.

77. FRACTURE : (**a. callus**, b. seam, c. compound, d. bend) :: LACERATION : SCAR
    (**a**) A bone fracture heals into a callus (an enlarged mass of bone). Similarly, a laceration or cut heals into a scar.

78. BOMBARDIER : PILOT :: (a. bird, b. flower, **c. beetle**, d. lizard) : FISH
    (**c**) A pilot fish is a type of fish. A bombardier beetle is a type of beetle.

79. HIDE : HOME :: CONCEAL : (**a. return**, b. thrash, c. shelter, d. abide)
    (**a**) To hide is the same as to conceal a person or thing. Also synonyms are the given word, *home*, whose verb form means to return. That all the given words are verbs should have helped you to solve the analogy.

80. FRESCO : (a. canvas, b. paneling, c. triptych, **d. plaster**) :: BATIK : FABRIC
    (**d**) A batik is made by applying color to fabric. A fresco is made by applying color to moist plaster.

81. PRIME : 19 :: PERFECT : (a. 0, b. 1, **c. 6**, d. 22)
    (**c**) Since 19 is a known prime number, then you are clearly looking for a known perfect number. Only a few are known. A perfect number is a whole integer greater than zero such that when you add up all of its factors other than the number itself, you get that number. Thus, of the choices before you, only the number 6 ($1 + 2 + 3 = 6$) is perfect.

82. ASH : PALM :: WEDNESDAY : (**a. Sunday**, b. Monday, c. Tuesday, d. Friday)
    (**a**) Both Ash Wednesday and Palm Sunday are Catholic holy days.

83. BABBAGE : TESLA :: (**a. difference engine**, b. steam engine, c. telegraph, d. semaphore) : TRANSFORMER
(**a**) Charles Babbage, a British mathematician, invented in 1822 the first predecessor of the modern computer, called a *difference engine*. Nicola Tesla, meanwhile, was the originator of the electrical transformer. All the other answer choices are prominent inventions, just not ones invented by Babbage.

84. EPIGONE : (a. outside, b. protective, **c. inferiority**, d. humility) :: PARAGON : EXCELLENCE
(**c**) A paragon is something noted for its excellence (e.g., a shining example). An epigone is something known for its inferiority (e.g., a cheap imitator).

85. JUPITER : EAGLE :: JUNO : (a. owl, **b. peacock**, c. swan, d. dove)
(**b**) The Roman gods were often associated with specific animals. Traditionally, the Roman god Jupiter was associated with the eagle. Similarly, the Roman goddess Juno was associated with the peacock.

86. POLYMER : LATEX :: HYDROCARBON : (**a. butane**, b. graphite, c. lead, d. water)
(**a**) The product called latex, which goes into many goods, is at its basic level a polymer. Butane, a fuel, is at its basic level a hydrocarbon. Graphite is carbon, not a hydrocarbon.

87. 3.14 : CIRCLE :: 0.618 : (a. triangle, **b. spiral**, c. parallelogram, d. hexagon)
(**b**) The mathematical number pi, numerically approximated as 3.14, is most often associated with finding the area of a circle, while 0.618 is numerically associated with the golden-ratio spiral.

88. GEORGE VI : (a. Peel, b. Gladstone, c. Palmerston, **d. Churchill**) :: VICTORIA I : DISRAELI
(**d**) Winston Churchill, the great British prime minister, served under King George VI. Benjamin Disraeli, the Tory prime minister and author, served with distinction as prime minister under Queen Victoria I.

89. ATTICA : GREECE :: THRACE : (a. Thebes, **b. Turkey**, c. Italy, d. Britain)
(**b**) The scattered tribes that lived in Attica eventually would found the nation-state of Greece, just as the area once known as Thrace would eventually become modern-day Turkey.

90. VERDIGRIS : PATINA :: (**a. liberty**, b. justice, c. equality, d. fraternity) : FREEDOM
(**a**) The terms *verdigris* and *patina* are synonyms, both meaning the crust or film that can cover artifacts with age. The only true synonym for *freedom* among the answer choices given is *liberty*.

91. NAUSEOUS : NAUSEATED :: (a. fearful, **b. frightening**, c. uncertain, d. unwell) : AFRAID
    (**b**) A semantics question. *Nauseous* means causing nausea, while *nauseated* means feeling nausea. Thus, *frightening* means causing fear, while *afraid* means feeling fear.

92. SCHADENFREUDE : (a. apprehensive, b. confused, **c. irritable**, d. cheerful) :: SYMPATHY : JOVIAL
    (**c**) The term *schadenfraude* means to take pleasure in the pain of others, a clear opposite of having sympathy. Looking at the other half of the analogy, only *irritable* is the clear opposite of *jovial*, meaning happy.

93. SCRUPLE : (a. peck, b. hogshead, **c. dram**, d. ounce) :: TRIANGLE : ANGLE
    (**c**) A triangle contains three angles within it. A scruple, which is a measure of weight, contains three drams.

94. (**a. coulomb**, b. fathom, c. bolt, d. hectare) : HERTZ :: ELECTRIC CHARGE : FREQUENCY
    (**a**) A coulomb is a measure of electric charge, just as a hertz is a measure of frequency.

95. MAWKISH : SENTIMENTAL :: CLOYING : (**a. sweet**, b. harmonious, c. cool, d. sad)
    (**a**) *Mawkish* is an adjective to describe something overly sentimental. *Cloying* is an adjective to describe something overly sweet.

96. QUETZALCOATL : CHOCOLATE :: ZEUS : (a. blood, b. gold, **c. ambrosia**, d. corn)
    (**c**) Quetzalcoatl, like the other Mayan gods, ate chocolate as a treat. Zeus and the other Greek gods ate ambrosia as a treat.

97. EXEGESIS : (**a. forensics**, b. stasis, c. research, d. ballistics) :: TEXT : CRIME SCENE
    (**a**) Exegesis is the examination and critical analysis of a text. Forensics, similarly, is the evaluation and analysis of a crime scene.

98. (a. ontology, b. graphology, c. limnology, **d. numismatology**) : COINS :: CETOLOGY : WHALES
    (**d**) Numismatology is the study of money and coins, just as cetology is the study of whales and whale behavior.

99. ACIDITY : pH :: WINDINESS : (a. Richter, b. Geiger, **c. Beaufort**, d. speed)
    (**c**) The pH scale is used to judge acidity in liquids. The Beaufort scale is used to judge wind speed.

100. NICHOLAS : LENIN :: BATISTA : (a. Guevara, b. Stalin, **c. Castro**, d. DuChamp)
    (**c**) Czar Nicholas was the ruler overthrown by Vladimir Lenin in 1917. Fulgencio Batista was the ruler overthrown by Fidel Castro in 1959.

101. (a. Shiba Inu, **b. Lhasa Apso**, c. Akita, d. Basenji) : TIBET :: KOMONDOR : HUNGARY
(b) The Lhasa Apso breed of dog originated in Tibet, and the Komondor breed of dog originated in Hungary.

102. WREATHES : ORGANIST :: (a. whether, b. sweater, c. threshold, **d. weathers**) : ROASTING
(d) *Wreathes* is a transposition of *weathers*, and *organist* is a transposition of *roasting*.

103. GRANT : (**a. Wilson**, b. Hoover, c. Coolidge, d. Roosevelt) :: CIVIL RIGHTS : SUFFRAGE
(a) Ulysses S. Grant was president of the United States when the 15th Amendment (civil rights) was ratified, and Woodrow Wilson was president when the 19th Amendment (women's suffrage) was ratified.

104. FUTURISM : NEOCLASSICISM :: (a. harmony, b. Cubism, c. perspective, **d. speed**) : BALANCE
(d) The Italian Futurist movement emphasized speed and mechanization, while neoclassical art prioritizes balance and symmetry.

105. APHRODITE : VENUS :: DIANA : (**a. Artemis**, b. Helen, c. Hera, d. Paris)
(a) In classical mythology, Venus is the Roman name of Greek goddess Aphrodite, and Artemis is the Roman name of Diana.

106. JULIUS II : (a. Pius XII, b. Max Ernst, **c. Peggy Guggenheim**, d. Museum of Modern Art) :: MICHELANGELO : POLLOCK
(c) Pope Julius II commissioned Michelangelo to paint the Sistine Chapel, and art patron Peggy Guggenheim commissioned Jackson Pollock to paint a large mural for her New York apartment.

107. GENEVA : LAKE GENEVA :: CHICAGO : (a. Lake Erie, b. Lake Superior, **c. Lake Michigan**, d. Lake Huron)
(c) Geneva, Switzerland, borders Lake Geneva; Chicago, Illinois, borders Lake Michigan.

108. QUARTZ : GRANITE :: (a. obsidian, **b. calcite**, c. bakelite, d. fluorite) : LIMESTONE
(b) Quartz is the principal mineral in granite, and calcite is the principal mineral in limestone.

109. (a. pasty, b. leaden, **c. convoluted**, d. succinct) : PITHY :: ASHEN : RUDDY
(c) *Convoluted* is the opposite of *pithy*, just as *ashen* is the opposite of *ruddy*.

110. RAVENNA : (**a. mosaics**, b. sculpture, c. jewels, d. catacombs) :: POMPEII : FRESCOES
(a) The churches of Ravenna are known for their elaborate mosaics, and the ruins of Pompeii are known for their colorful wall frescoes.

111. (a. flute, **b. piano**, c. sousaphone, d. bassoon) : STRING :: TROMBONE: BRASS
(**b**) The piano is a member of the string family, and the trombone is a member of the brass family.

112. (**a. Hinduism,** b. Islam, c. Coptic, d. Christianity) : JUDAISM :: POLY : MONO
(**a**) Hinduism is a polytheistic religion, and Judaism is monotheistic.

113. MAO ZEDONG : (a. Cultural Revolution, **b. Great Leap Forward**, c. Five Modernizations, d. Final Solution) :: STALIN : FIVE YEAR PLAN
(**b**) Mao's grand plan for industrializing China was the Great Leap Forward, and Josef Stalin's plan for industrializing Russia was the Five Year Plan.

114. (a. ambulatory, b. altar, **c. Westwerk**, d. buttress) : FAÇADE :: GROIN VAULTING : ROOF
(**c**) Westwerk is a particular characteristic of certain medieval cathedral façades. Groin vaulting is a feature of certain medieval cathedral roofs.

115. BINARY : DECIMAL :: 10001 : (a. 101, b. 65, c. 12, **d. 17**)
(**d**) The number 10001 in binary is the same as 17 in decimal notation.

116. AGINCOURT : MARNE :: (a. Germany, b. Russia, **c. England**, d. Spain) : FRANCE
(**c**) England won the Battle of Agincourt, and France led the Allies to victory in the First and Second Battle of the Marne.

117. DAUNT : DREAM :: TUNA : (a. dared, b. ready, c. read, **d. mare**)
(**d**) Drop the *d* from *daunt* and mix up the letters to get *tuna*. Likewise, drop the *d* from *dream* and mix up the letters to get *mare*.

118. ELECTRONS : (a. hadrons, **b. fermions**, c. neutrinos, d. mesons) :: PROTONS : BOSONS
(**b**) Protons are bosons, and electrons are fermions.

119. MITOSIS : EUKARYOTE :: MEIOSIS : (**a. gamete**, b. fungoid, c. somatic, d. lymph)
(**a**) Mitosis occurs during the formation of eukaryotes, and meiosis occurs during the formation of gametes.

120. RACECAR : (a. anagram, **b. kerplunk**, c. auger, d. deterred) :: PALINDROME : ONOMATOPOEIA
(**b**) *Racecar* is an example of a palindrome, and *kerplunk* is an example of onomatopoeia.

ANSWER SHEET FOR PRACTICE TEST 5

1. (a) (b) (c) (d)	41. (a) (b) (c) (d)	81. (a) (b) (c) (d)
2. (a) (b) (c) (d)	42. (a) (b) (c) (d)	82. (a) (b) (c) (d)
3. (a) (b) (c) (d)	43. (a) (b) (c) (d)	83. (a) (b) (c) (d)
4. (a) (b) (c) (d)	44. (a) (b) (c) (d)	84. (a) (b) (c) (d)
5. (a) (b) (c) (d)	45. (a) (b) (c) (d)	85. (a) (b) (c) (d)
6. (a) (b) (c) (d)	46. (a) (b) (c) (d)	86. (a) (b) (c) (d)
7. (a) (b) (c) (d)	47. (a) (b) (c) (d)	87. (a) (b) (c) (d)
8. (a) (b) (c) (d)	48. (a) (b) (c) (d)	88. (a) (b) (c) (d)
9. (a) (b) (c) (d)	49. (a) (b) (c) (d)	89. (a) (b) (c) (d)
10. (a) (b) (c) (d)	50. (a) (b) (c) (d)	90. (a) (b) (c) (d)
11. (a) (b) (c) (d)	51. (a) (b) (c) (d)	91. (a) (b) (c) (d)
12. (a) (b) (c) (d)	52. (a) (b) (c) (d)	92. (a) (b) (c) (d)
13. (a) (b) (c) (d)	53. (a) (b) (c) (d)	93. (a) (b) (c) (d)
14. (a) (b) (c) (d)	54. (a) (b) (c) (d)	94. (a) (b) (c) (d)
15. (a) (b) (c) (d)	55. (a) (b) (c) (d)	95. (a) (b) (c) (d)
16. (a) (b) (c) (d)	56. (a) (b) (c) (d)	96. (a) (b) (c) (d)
17. (a) (b) (c) (d)	57. (a) (b) (c) (d)	97. (a) (b) (c) (d)
18. (a) (b) (c) (d)	58. (a) (b) (c) (d)	98. (a) (b) (c) (d)
19. (a) (b) (c) (d)	59. (a) (b) (c) (d)	99. (a) (b) (c) (d)
20. (a) (b) (c) (d)	60. (a) (b) (c) (d)	100. (a) (b) (c) (d)
21. (a) (b) (c) (d)	61. (a) (b) (c) (d)	101. (a) (b) (c) (d)
22. (a) (b) (c) (d)	62. (a) (b) (c) (d)	102. (a) (b) (c) (d)
23. (a) (b) (c) (d)	63. (a) (b) (c) (d)	103. (a) (b) (c) (d)
24. (a) (b) (c) (d)	64. (a) (b) (c) (d)	104. (a) (b) (c) (d)
25. (a) (b) (c) (d)	65. (a) (b) (c) (d)	105. (a) (b) (c) (d)
26. (a) (b) (c) (d)	66. (a) (b) (c) (d)	106. (a) (b) (c) (d)
27. (a) (b) (c) (d)	67. (a) (b) (c) (d)	107. (a) (b) (c) (d)
28. (a) (b) (c) (d)	68. (a) (b) (c) (d)	108. (a) (b) (c) (d)
29. (a) (b) (c) (d)	69. (a) (b) (c) (d)	109. (a) (b) (c) (d)
30. (a) (b) (c) (d)	70. (a) (b) (c) (d)	110. (a) (b) (c) (d)
31. (a) (b) (c) (d)	71. (a) (b) (c) (d)	111. (a) (b) (c) (d)
32. (a) (b) (c) (d)	72. (a) (b) (c) (d)	112. (a) (b) (c) (d)
33. (a) (b) (c) (d)	73. (a) (b) (c) (d)	113. (a) (b) (c) (d)
34. (a) (b) (c) (d)	74. (a) (b) (c) (d)	114. (a) (b) (c) (d)
35. (a) (b) (c) (d)	75. (a) (b) (c) (d)	115. (a) (b) (c) (d)
36. (a) (b) (c) (d)	76. (a) (b) (c) (d)	116. (a) (b) (c) (d)
37. (a) (b) (c) (d)	77. (a) (b) (c) (d)	117. (a) (b) (c) (d)
38. (a) (b) (c) (d)	78. (a) (b) (c) (d)	118. (a) (b) (c) (d)
39. (a) (b) (c) (d)	79. (a) (b) (c) (d)	119. (a) (b) (c) (d)
40. (a) (b) (c) (d)	80. (a) (b) (c) (d)	120. (a) (b) (c) (d)

Practice Test 5

Directions: For each of the following questions, you will find three capitalized terms and, in parentheses, four answer choices designated *a*, *b*, *c*, and *d*. Select the one answer choice that best completes the analogy with the three capitalized terms. (To record your answers, use the answer sheet that precedes this test.)

1. PHILATELIST : (a. baseball cards, b. stamps, c. balls, d. rings) :: NUMISMATIST : COINS

2. RELIQUARY : RELIC :: HANGAR : (a. suit, b. aircraft, c. vault, d. church)

3. IMPUGN : CASTIGATE :: (a. laud, b. deny, c. calculate, d. illicit) : PRAISE

4. (a. metaphor, b. canto, c. meter, d. rhyme) : POEM :: CHAPTER : NOVEL

5. ANTARCTIC : (a. penguin, b. snowshoe rabbit, c. lemming, d. ptarmigan) :: ARCTIC : POLAR BEAR

6. (a. sleeve, b. punch, c. chomp, d. sip) : CUFF :: BITE : NIP

7. TANGO : DANCE :: MANGO : (a. trance, b. fruit, c. samba, d. rhythm)

8. (a. 6, b. 7, c. 9, d. 10) : SEPT– :: 8 : OCT–

9. (a. parallax, b. parasol, c. solipsism, d. penumbra) : SUN :: UMBRELLA : RAIN

10. NASA : ACRONYM :: DEED : (a. tmesis, b. palindrome, c. metonymy, d. alliteration)

11. (a. branch, b. delta, c. falls, d. ford) : RIVER :: CROSSWALK : STREET

12. MARTIN LUTHER : LUTHERAN :: MUHAMMAD : (a. Jewish, b. Christian, c. Buddhist, d. Muslim)

13. KOWTOW : DEFERENCE :: STRUT : (a. humility, b. swagger, c. genuflect, d. walk)

14. FORAGE : SEARCH :: (a. hunt, b. hide, c. flummox, d. clarify) : CONFUSE

15. SACROSANCT : SACRED :: PROFANE : (a. holy, b. irreverent, c. altar, d. prophet)

16. (a. dunce, b. oaf, c. wag, d. poet) : WITTY :: CURMUDGEON : ILL-TEMPERED

17. fewer : (a. imaginary, b. total, c. less, d. sum) :: COUNTABLE : UNCOUNTABLE

18. (a. ancient, b. retrospective, c. circumspective, d. retroactive) : PROSPECTIVE :: PAST : FUTURE

19. SYLLABUS : COURSE :: (a. menu, b. leg, c. itinerary, d. lesson) : TRIP

20. AMORPHOUS : SHAPE :: (a. bland, b. zesty, c. savory, d. bulbous) : FLAVOR

21. FISH : (a. swim, b. school, c. aquarium, d. pride) :: GEESE : FLOCK

22. (a. delight, b. deluge, c. drizzle, d. drift) : RAIN :: BLIZZARD : SNOW

23. MORTIFY : (a. murder, b. embalm, c. embarrass, d. exculpate) :: DENOUNCE : CRITICIZE

24. (a. actuary, b. dangerous, c. jeweler, d. statistician) : RISK :: APPRAISER : VALUE

25. MERCURY : NEPTUNE :: ALPHA : (a. beta, b. centauri, c. gamma, d. omega)

26. WASHINGTON : 1 :: (a. Jefferson, b. Kennedy, c. Hamilton, d. Lincoln) : 10

27. DEARTH : (a. dross, b. forfeit, c. surfeit, d. paucity) :: SCARCITY : ABUNDANCE

28. POSEUR : GENUINE :: (a. neophyte, b. veteran, c. gimmick, d. mendicant) : EXPERIENCED

29. TRANSITORY : ETERNAL :: (a. nanoseconds, b. radial, c. permanent, d. lengthy) : EONS

30. OZONE : OXYGEN :: (a. hydrogen peroxide, b. alcohol, c. iodine, d. carbon dioxide) : WATER

31. SLANDER : (a. insult, b. libel, c. praise, d. false) :: SPOKEN : WRITTEN

32. PLASTIC : (a. inexpensive, b. gauche, c. changeable, d. fabricated) :: WOODEN : UNRESPONSIVE

33. CENTRIPETAL : IN :: (a. force, b. spin, c. centrifugal, d. opposite) : OUT

34. BANE : BOON :: (a. inauspicious, b. haphazard, c. ad hoc, d. fortunate) : LUCKY

35. ONTOLOGY : (a. epistemology, b. philology, c. deontology, d. cosmology) :: EXISTENCE : ETHICS

36. ANTIQUARIAN : BOOKS :: LEPIDOPTERIST : (a. stamps, b. butterflies, c. coins, d. currency)

37. PLUTOCRACY : (a. strong, b. distant, c. wealthy, d. election) :: OLIGARCHY : FEW

38. STANNUM : TIN :: PLUMBUM : (a. lead, b. aluminum, c. iron, d. mercury)

39. BOOR : MANNERS :: (a. maladroit, b. diplomat, c. confidant, d. dancer) : GRACE

40. (a. treatment, b. snake oil, c. panacea, d. inoculation) : MEDICINE :: QUACK : DOCTOR

41. AFFERENT : (a. effective, b. affected, c. efferent, d. effluvia) :: TOWARDS : AWAY

42. THALIA : (a. Fate, b. Muse, c. mortal, d. witch) :: HERA : GODDESS

43. DEERE : (a. banking, b. sports, c. farming, d. television) :: KENNEDY : POLITICS

44. GROSS : (a. price, b. score, c. expense, d. revenue) :: NET : PROFIT

45. STARBOARD : PORT :: WINDWARD : (a. stern, b. sail, c. alee, d. aft)

46. APOTHEOSIS : DIVINE :: (a. classification, b. deification, c. reification, d. magnification) : REAL

47. APLOMB : POISE :: PANACHE : (a. reserve, b. calm, c. lethargy, d. flair)

48. WELDER : METAL :: JOINER : (a. clubs, b. barrels, c. wood, d. fabric)

49. (a. discoverer, b. spelunker, c. debunker, d. explorer) : CAVES :: ASTRONAUT : SPACE

50. VAINGLORIOUS : HUMILITY :: IMPROMPTU : (a. planning, b. pride, c. emphasis, d. poise)

51. FORTNIGHT : (a. 2, b. 4, c. 14, d. 29) :: LEAP YEAR : 366

52. WAN : (a. ebb, b. ashen, c. ruddy, d. sere) :: DESICCATE : DRY

53. PERQUISITE : (a. dock, b. bonus, c. requirement, d. rate) :: STIPEND : SALARY

54. PULMONARY : LUNG :: (a. cardiac, b. renal, c. ventral, d. bladder) : KIDNEY

55. BEREFT : LACKING :: BESMIRCHED : (a. cleansed, b. speckled, c. sullied, d. abundant)

56. (a. stereotype, b. prototype, c. phenotype, d. xenophobe) : EXEMPLAR :: ORIGINAL : IDEAL

57. PORTLY : LEAN :: (a. corpulent, b. svelte, c. adroit, d. upright) : EMACIATED

58. COQUETTE : FLIRTATION :: MISER : (a. generosity, b. parsimony, c. money, d. value)

59. LAGGARD : (a. thin, b. lazy, c. prompt, d. vain) :: SOT : TEMPERATE

60. GUERNICA : PICASSO :: STARRY NIGHT : (a. Rodin, b. Van Gogh, c. Matisse, d. Da Vinci)

61. SATURNINE : SULLEN :: BLITHE : (a. morose, b. astronomical, c. cheery, d. thin)

62. SYCOPHANT : (a. insults, b. poetry, c. flattery, d. criticisms) :: ORATOR : RHETORIC

63. DIAPHANOUS : (a. opaque, b. translucent, c. glowing, d. oblique) :: MELLIFLUOUS : EUPHONIOUS

64. SYMPATHETIC : (a. autonomic, b. parasympathetic, c. central, d. nervous) :: AROUSAL : RELAXATION

65. (a. moot, b. axiomatic, c. heretical, d. divine) : INCONTROVERTIBLE :: DEBATABLE : PROVEN

66. FRANK : CANDOR :: (a. absent, b. snide, c. inopportune, d. wild) : MALICE

67. PRONE : FRONTAL :: SUPINE : (a. medial, b. dorsal, c. global, d. manual)

68. ENERVATED : (a. languid, b. vigorous, c. spry, d. tacit) :: ENERGIZED : SPIRITED

69. PROLIX : CURT :: (a. speech, b. abbreviated, c. language, d. protracted) : BRIEF

70. PHENOMENOLOGY : CONSCIOUSNESS :: PSYCHOANALYSIS : (a. unconscious, b. illness, c. sleep, d. thought)

71. PHYLUM : (a. order, b. species, c. type, d. kingdom) :: NICKEL : DOLLAR

72. APATHETIC : ZEALOUS :: PRAGMATIC : (a. concomitant, b. realistic, c. romantic, d. pluralistic)

73. SYBARITE : (a. prudish, b. hedonistic, c. fanciful, d. dour) :: ASCETIC : ABSTEMIOUS

74. CHANCE : RANDOM :: SYNCHRONIZED : (a. coterminous, b. vocational, c. undulating, d. desultory)

75. CEREBRUM : CEREBELLUM :: THOUGHT : (a. idea, b. breath, c. consciousness, d. balance)

76. ENGLAND : (a. St. George, b. St. Martin, c. St. Patrick, d. St. Thomas) :: FRANCE : ST. JOAN

77. PI : (a. integral, b. real, c. rational, d. transcendental) :: *i* : IMAGINARY

78. PHLEGMATIC : (a. snotty, b. sick, c. sluggish, d. elated) :: SANGUINE : CHEERFUL

79. METASTASIS : SPREAD :: REMISSION : (a. beginning, b. abatement, c. intensification, d. transmission)

80. (a. critique, b. imprimatur, c. admission, d. conquest) : APPROVAL :: CENSURE : CRITICISM

81. GEORGIAN : AUSTEN :: (a. Romantic, b. Classical, c. Modernist, d. Restoration) : DRYDEN

82. PHYLOGENY : (a. plants, b. words, c. evolution, d. effects) :: ETIOLOGY : CAUSES

83. ARISTOTLE : PLATO :: KEPLER : (a. Gilbert, b. Bruno, c. Brahe, d. Crick)

84. (a. monkey, b. prosimian, c. *Homo sapiens*, d. chimpanzee) : SIMIAN :: LEMUR : APE

85. HEURISTIC : ALGORITHM :: EXPEDITIOUS : (a. quick, b. computerized, c. exhaustive, d. probabilistic)

86. LANGUAGE : WITTGENSTEIN :: (a. polio, b. psyche, c. phenomenology, d. genetics) : JUNG

87. FOMENT : INCITE :: MITIGATE : (a. incense, b. alleviate, c. worry, d. riot)

88. MOT JUSTE : APT :: SOLECISM : (a. inappropriate, b. witty, c. prudish, d. candid)

89. FOLIO : ONE FOLD :: OCTAVO : (a. two folds, b. four folds, c. eight folds, d. sixteen folds)

90. MODICUM : (a. modica, b. modicus, c. modicae, d. modices) :: INDEX : INDICES

91. LINDBERGH : ATLANTIC :: (a. Glenn, b. Armstrong, c. Wright, d. Smith) : PACIFIC

92. VET : MANUSCRIPT :: (a. collect, b. experience, c. preserve, d. dissect) : SPECIMEN

93. IDEALISM : BERKELEY :: RATIONALISM : (a. Liebnitz, b. Kant, c. Descartes, d. Occam)

94. PECCADILLO : FELONY :: TIFF : (a. misdemeanor, b. spat, c. exoneration, d. melee)

95. SUSURRUS : (a. melody, b. cumulonimbus, c. din, d. terminus) :: WHISPER : CACOPHONY

96. BUMBLEBEE BAT : (a. reptile, b. mammal, c. nocturnal, d. flight) :: HUMMINGBIRD : BIRD

97. VAN ALEN : CHRYSLER BUILDING :: (a. Wright, b. Graham, c. Gehry, d. Bauhaus) : SEARS TOWER

98. SOUSA : PUCCINI :: MARCH : (a. opera, b. violin, c. jazz, d. fugue)

99. CASTELLAN : CASTLE :: (a. landlord, b. butler, c. peasant, d. groundskeeper) : MANSION

100. BUSHEL : PECK :: PINT : (a. gallon, b. grain, c. gill, d. dram)

101. (a. abacus, b. furlong, c. league, d. sextant) : NAVIGATION :: RULER: MEASUREMENT

102. PURLOIN : FULMINATE :: FILCH : (a. explode, b. exude, c. repose, d. rant)

103. RHODESIA : BURMA :: (a. Zambia, b. South Africa, c. Kenya, d. Zimbabwe) : MYANMAR

104. BERNINI : BAROQUE :: WATTEAU : (a. Renaissance, b. Rococo, c. academic, d. classical)

105. HE : NOBLE GAS :: (a. U, b. Cs, c. In, d. Fe) : ACTINIDE

106. CAMUS : THE STRANGER :: SARTRE : (a. *Hunger*, b. *Nausea*, c. *Steppenwolf*, d. *The Plague*)

107. (a. Persia, b. Iraq, c. Macedonia, d. Greece) : PERSEPOLIS :: BYZANTINE EMPIRE : CONSTANTINOPLE

108. (a. Titan 7, b. Soyuz, c. Atlas 10, d. Gemini) : MERCURY :: SATURN V : APOLLO

109. (a. he, b. yourself, c. that, d. mine) : SOMEONE :: DEFINITE : INDEFINITE

110. 8TH AVENUE : LONGITUDE: (a. Broadway, b. Avenue of the Americas, c. 42nd Street, d. Grand Concourse) : LATITUDE

111. RUBENS : REMBRANDT :: (a. Flemish, b. French, c. Swiss, d. German) : DUTCH

112. KILAMAJARO : EVEREST :: (a. Kenya, b. Tanzania, c. Ethiopia, d. Somalia) : NEPAL

113. (a. Edison, b. Kodak, c. Nadar, d. Daguerre) : PHOTOGRAPHY :: LUMIÈRE : MOTION PICTURES

114. HECTOR : ACHILLES :: (a. Troy, b. Odysseus, c. Agamemnon, d. Paris) : MENELAUS

115. TIGRIS : (a. Iran, b. Iraq, c. Saudi Arabia, d. Jordan) :: ARNO : ITALY

116. MADAME BUTTERFLY : PUCCINI :: DON GIOVANNI : (a. Vivaldi, b. Rossini, c. Mozart, d. Verdi)

117. PHILISTINE : APPRECIATION :: BOOR : (a. depreciation, b. tact, c. accusations, d. perception)

118. PLANTS : CHLOROPLASTS :: ANIMALS : (a. Golgi apparatus, b. mitochondria, c. vacuoles, d. vesicles)

119. FRANK O'HARA : MOMA :: (a. E. E. Cummings, b. Kenneth Koch, c. Alan Dugan, d. Walt Whitman) : BROOKLYN DAILY EAGLE

120. STRESSED : (a. desserts, b. anxious, c. dilution, d. extreme) :: EDIT : TIDE

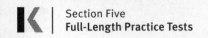
ANSWERS AND EXPLANATIONS

1. PHILATELIST : (a. baseball cards, **b. stamps**, c. balls, d. rings) :: NUMISMATIST : COINS
   (**b**) A philatelist is a collector of stamps, and a numismatist is a collector of coins.

2. RELIQUARY : RELIC :: HANGAR : (a. suit, **b. aircraft**, c. vault, d. church)
   (**b**) A reliquary is a place where relics and artifacts are kept, and a hangar is a place where aircraft are kept.

3. IMPUGN : CASTIGATE :: (**a. laud**, b. deny, c. calculate, d. illicit) : PRAISE
   (**a**) To impugn someone is to castigate or scold her. Similarly, to laud someone is to praise her.

4. (a. metaphor, **b. canto**, c. meter, d. rhyme) : POEM :: CHAPTER : NOVEL
   (**b**) A canto is a component part of a larger poem, just as a chapter is a component part of a larger novel.

5. ANTARCTIC : (**a. penguin**, b. snowshoe rabbit, c. lemming, d. ptarmigan) :: ARCTIC : POLAR BEAR
   (**a**) A penguin can be found in Antarctic regions in the same way that a polar bear can be found in Arctic regions. Among the answer choices given, only penguins live in the Antarctic.

6. (a. sleeve, **b. punch**, c. chomp, d. sip) : CUFF :: BITE : NIP
   (**b**) *Punch* and *cuff* are synonyms; similarly, *bite* and *nip* are synonyms. Note that *cuff* is used as a verb here as opposed to its more common usage as the cuff of a sleeve.

7. TANGO : DANCE :: MANGO : (a. kiwi, **b. fruit**, c. samba, d. rhythm)
   (**b**) A tango is a type of dance, and a mango is a type of fruit.

8. (a. 6, **b. 7**, c. 9, d. 10) : SEPT– :: 8 : OCT–
   (**b**) The number 7 is associated with the *sept–* prefix, and the number 8 is associated with the *oct–* prefix. Note that September was the seventh month of the ancient Roman calendar and October was the eighth.

9. (a. parallax, **b. parasol**, c. solipsism, d. penumbra) : SUN :: UMBRELLA : RAIN
   (**b**) A parasol shields a person from the sun, just as an umbrella shields a person from the rain.

10. NASA : ACRONYM :: DEED : (a. tmesis, **b. palindrome**, c. metonymy, d. alliteration)
    (**b**) *NASA* is an example of an acronym, and *deed* is an example of a palindrome.

11. (a. branch, b. delta, c. falls, **d. ford**) : RIVER :: CROSSWALK : STREET
    (**d**) A ford is a place where one can easily cross a river. A crosswalk is a place where one can easily cross a street.

12. MARTIN LUTHER : LUTHERAN :: MUHAMMAD : (a. Jewish, b. Christian, c. Buddhist, **d. Muslim**)
    (**d**) Martin Luther's teachings formed the foundation of the Lutheran faith. By the same token, Muhammad's teachings formed the foundation of the Muslim faith.

13. KOWTOW : DEFERENCE :: STRUT : (a. humility, **b. swagger**, c. genuflect, d. walk)
    (**b**) To kowtow is to show deference or obeisance, and to strut is to show swagger or arrogance.

14. FORAGE : SEARCH :: (a. hunt, b. hide, **c. flummox**, d. clarify) : CONFUSE
    (**c**) To forage is a way to search. To flummox is a way to confuse.

15. SACROSANCT : SACRED :: PROFANE : (a. holy, **b. irreverent**, c. altar, d. prophet)
    (**b**) Something sacrosanct is sacred, and something profane is irreverent.

16. (a. dunce, b. oaf, **c. wag**, d. poet) : WITTY :: CURMUDGEON : ILL-TEMPERED
    (**c**) A wag is, by definition, a witty person, just as a curmudgeon is, by definition, an ill-tempered person. A poet might also be witty, but wit is not an absolute requirement in a poet.

17. fewer : (a. imaginary, b. total, **c. less**, d. sum) :: COUNTABLE : UNCOUNTABLE
    (**c**) The word *fewer* is used with a countable number of objects, while the word *less* is used with an uncountable quantity. For example: "I had *fewer* bottles of Coors Light, so I ended up drinking *less* beer."

18. (a. ancient, **b. retrospective**, c. circumspective, d. retroactive) : PROSPECTIVE :: PAST : FUTURE
    (**b**) Something retrospective involves looking at the past. Something prospective involves looking towards the future.

19. SYLLABUS : COURSE :: (a. menu, b. leg, **c. itinerary**, d. lesson) : TRIP
    (**c**) A syllabus is an outline or schedule for a course, and an itinerary is an outline or schedule for a trip.

20. AMORPHOUS : SHAPE :: (**a. bland**, b. zesty, c. savory, d. bulbous) : FLAVOR
    (**a**) Something amorphous lacks shape, and something bland lacks flavor.

21. FISH : (a. swim, **b. school**, c. aquarium, d. pride) :: GEESE : FLOCK
    (**b**) A collective or group of fish is called a school, and a collective or group of geese is called a flock.

22. (a. delight, **b. deluge**, c. drizzle, d. drift) : RAIN :: BLIZZARD : SNOW
    (**b**) A deluge has a tremendous output of rain, and a blizzard has a tremendous output of snow.

23. MORTIFY : (a. murder, b. embalm, **c. embarrass**, d. exculpate) :: DENOUNCE : CRITICIZE
(c) To mortify is to embarrass to an extreme degree. To denounce is to criticize to an extreme degree.

24. (**a. actuary**, b. dangerous, c. jeweler, d. statistician) : RISK :: APPRAISER : VALUE
(a) An actuary assesses risk, while an appraiser assesses value.

25. MERCURY : NEPTUNE :: ALPHA : (a. beta, b. centauri, c. gamma, **d. omega**)
(d) Mercury is the first planet, closest to the sun, and Neptune is the farthest planet from the sun. Alpha is the first letter of the Greek alphabet, and omega is the last letter in the Greek alphabet.

26. WASHINGTON : 1 :: (a. Jefferson, b. Kennedy, **c. Hamilton**, d. Lincoln) : 10
(c) Washington is on the one dollar bill. Hamilton is on the ten dollar bill.

27. DEARTH : (a. dross, b. forfeit, **c. surfeit**, d. paucity) :: SCARCITY : ABUNDANCE
(c) A dearth is characterized by a scarcity of a commodity. A surfeit is characterized by an abundance of a commodity.

28. POSEUR : GENUINE :: (**a. neophyte**, b. veteran, c. gimmick, d. mendicant) : EXPERIENCED
(a) By definition, a poseur is never genuine, and a neophyte is never experienced.

29. TRANSITORY : ETERNAL :: (**a. nanoseconds**, b. radial, c. permanent, d. lengthy) : EONS
(a) Something transitory lasts only a brief period of time, like nanoseconds. Something eternal lasts for a long period of time, like eons.

30. OZONE : OXYGEN :: (**a. hydrogen peroxide**, b. alcohol, c. iodine, d. carbon dioxide) : WATER
(a) Ozone is an oxygen molecule with an extra oxygen atom. Hydrogen peroxide is a water molecule with an extra oxygen atom.

31. SLANDER : (a. insult, **b. libel**, c. praise, d. false) :: SPOKEN : WRITTEN
(b) Slander is false language spoken with the intent to harm someone's reputation. Libel is false language written with the intent to harm someone's reputation.

32. PLASTIC : (a. inexpensive, b. gauche, **c. changeable**, d. fabricated) :: WOODEN : UNRESPONSIVE
(c) Something plastic is malleable and changeable. Something wooden is stiff and unresponsive.

33. CENTRIPETAL : IN :: (a. force, b. spin, **c. centrifugal**, d. opposite) : OUT
    (c) Centripetal force points inward when something spins. Centrifugal force is the complementary force that points outward when something spins.

34. BANE : BOON :: (**a. inauspicious**, b. haphazard, c. ad hoc, d. fortunate) : LUCKY
    (a) A bane is always inauspicious. A boon is always lucky.

35. ONTOLOGY : (a. epistemology, b. philology, **c. deontology**, d. cosmology) :: EXISTENCE : ETHICS
    (c) Ontology is the study of being or existence. Deontology is the study of ethics.

36. ANTIQUARIAN : BOOKS :: LEPIDOPTERIST : (a. stamps, **b. butterflies**, c. coins, d. currency)
    (b) An antiquarian is a collector of old or rare books, and a lepidopterist is a collector of butterflies.

37. PLUTOCRACY : (a. strong, b. distant, **c. wealthy**, d. election) :: OLIGARCHY : FEW
    (c) A plutocracy is a government ruled by the wealthy. An oligarchy is a government ruled by the few.

38. STANNUM : TIN :: PLUMBUM : (**a. lead**, b. aluminum, c. iron, d. mercury)
    (a) *Stannum* is another name for the metal tin. *Plumbum* is another name for the metal lead.

39. BOOR : MANNERS :: (**a. maladroit**, b. diplomat, c. confidant, d. dancer) : GRACE
    (a) By definition, a boor lacks manners, and a maladroit lacks grace.

40. (a. treatment, **b. snake oil**, c. panacea, d. inoculation) : MEDICINE :: QUACK : DOCTOR
    (b) Snake oil is a fake or dubious medicine. A quack is a fake or dubious doctor.

41. AFFERENT : (a. effective, b. affected, **c. efferent**, d. effluvia) :: TOWARDS : AWAY
    (c) Afferent pathways move towards the central nervous system. Efferent pathways move away from the central nervous system.

42. THALIA : (a. Fate, **b. Muse**, c. mortal, d. witch) :: HERA : GODDESS
    (b) Thalia is a Greek Muse. Hera is a Greek goddess.

43. DEERE : (a. banking, b. sports, **c. farming**, d. television) :: KENNEDY : POLITICS
    (c) The Deere family is an important family in farming. The Kennedy family is an important family in politics.

44. GROSS : (a. price, b. score, c. expense, **d. revenue**) :: NET : PROFIT
    (**d**) The gross amount is all that one takes in. The net is the amount that one takes away over expenses. Similarly, the revenue is the amount of money one takes in, and the profit is the amount of money one takes away over expenses.

45. STARBOARD : PORT :: WINDWARD : (a. stern, b. sail, **c. alee**, d. aft)
    (**c**) Starboard, or right, and port, or left, are opposite nautical directions. By the same token, windward and alee are opposite nautical directions: windward is toward the wind, and alee is away from the wind.

46. APOTHEOSIS : DIVINE :: (a. classification, b. deification, **c. reification**, d. magnification) : REAL
    (**c**) The process of apotheosis makes something divine. The process of reification makes something real.

47. APLOMB : POISE :: PANACHE : (a. reserve, b. calm, c. lethargy, **d. flair**)
    (**d**) Someone with aplomb demonstrates poise. Someone with panache demonstrates flair.

48. WELDER : METAL :: JOINER : (a. clubs, b. barrels, **c. wood**, d. fabric)
    (**c**) Welders assemble pieces of metal. Joiners assemble pieces of wood.

49. (a. discoverer, **b. spelunker**, c. debunker, d. explorer) : CAVES :: ASTRONAUT : SPACE
    (**b**) A spelunker explores caves, just as an astronaut explores space.

50. VAINGLORIOUS : HUMILITY :: IMPROMPTU : (**a. planning**, b. pride, c. emphasis, d. poise)
    (**a**) Something vainglorious lacks humility. Something impromptu lacks planning.

51. FORTNIGHT : (a. 2, b. 4, **c. 14**, d. 29) :: LEAP YEAR : 366
    (**c**) A fortnight is two weeks or 14 days. A leap year is 366 days.

52. WAN : (a. ebb, **b. ashen**, c. ruddy, d. sere) :: DESICCATE : DRY
    (**b**) To wan is to become ashen or pale. To dessicate is to become dry.

53. PERQUISITE : (a. dock, **b. bonus**, c. requirement, d. rate) :: STIPEND : SALARY
    (**b**) A perquisite is a bonus associated with one's employment. A stipend is a salary associated with one's employment.

54. PULMONARY : LUNG :: (a. cardiac, **b. renal**, c. ventral, d. bladder) : KIDNEY
    (**b**) The word *pulmonary* refers to things related to the lungs. The word *renal* refers to things related to the kidneys.

55. BEREFT : LACKING :: BESMIRCHED : (a. cleansed, b. speckled, **c. sullied**,
d. abundant)
(**c**) Something or someone bereft of something is lacking that thing. Someone
besmirched is dirtied or sullied in some way.

56. (a. stereotype, **b. prototype**, c. phenotype, d. xenophobe) : EXEMPLAR :: ORIGINAL :
IDEAL
(**b**) A prototype is an original model of something. An exemplar is an ideal model of
something.

57. PORTLY : LEAN :: (**a. corpulent**, b. svelte, c. adroit, d. upright) : EMACIATED
(**a**) Someone who is corpulent is extremely portly or fat. Someone emaciated is
extremely skinny or lean.

58. COQUETTE : FLIRTATION :: MISER : (a. generosity, **b. parsimony**, c. money,
d. value)
(**b**) A coquette's behavior is characterized by flirtation. A miser's behavior is
characterized by parsimony or selfishness.

59. LAGGARD : (a. thin, b. lazy, **c. prompt**, d. vain) :: SOT : TEMPERATE
(**c**) By definition, a laggard is not prompt, and a sot is not temperate.

60. GUERNICA : PICASSO :: STARRY NIGHT : (a. Rodin, **b. Van Gogh**, c. Matisse,
d. Da Vinci)
(**b**) *Guernica* is a famous painting by Pablo Picasso. *Starry Night* is a famous painting
by Vincent Van Gogh.

61. SATURNINE : SULLEN :: BLITHE : (a. morose, b. astronomical, **c. cheery**, d. thin)
(**c**) Someone who is saturnine has a sullen disposition. Someone who is blithe has a
cheery disposition.

62. SYCOPHANT : (a. insults, b. poetry, **c. flattery**, d. criticisms) :: ORATOR :
RHETORIC
(**c**) A sycophant uses flattery when speaking, much as an orator uses rhetoric when
speaking.

63. DIAPHANOUS : (a. opaque, **b. translucent**, c. glowing, d. oblique) ::
MELLIFLUOUS : EUPHONIOUS
(**b**) *Diaphanous* is synonymous with *translucent*. *Mellifluous* is synonymous with
euphonious.

64. SYMPATHETIC : (a. autonomic, **b. parasympathetic**, c. central, d. nervous) ::
AROUSAL : RELAXATION
(**b**) The sympathetic nervous system is associated with arousal, and the
parasympathetic nervous system is associated with relaxation.

65. (**a. moot**, b. axiomatic, c. heretical, d. divine) : INCONTROVERTIBLE ::
DEBATABLE : PROVEN
(a) Something that is moot is debatable. Something that is incontrovertible has been proven.

66. FRANK : CANDOR :: (a. absent, **b. snide**, c. inopportune, d. wild) : MALICE
(b) Frank speech is characterized by candor. Snide speech is characterized by malice.

67. PRONE : FRONTAL :: SUPINE : (a. medial, **b. dorsal**, c. global, d. manual)
(b) When prone, your frontal region faces the ground (i.e., lying facedown). When supine, your dorsal region faces the ground (i.e., lying on your back).

68. ENERVATED : (**a. languid**, b. vigorous, c. spry, d. tacit) :: ENERGIZED : SPIRITED
(a) When something is enervated or weakened, it becomes languid. When something is energized, it becomes spirited.

69. PROLIX : CURT :: (a. speech, b. abbreviated, c. language, **d. protracted**) : BRIEF
(d) Something that is prolix is tediously prolonged or protracted. Something that is curt is rudely abrupt or brief.

70. PHENOMENOLOGY : CONSCIOUSNESS :: PSYCHOANALYSIS : (**a. unconscious**, b. illness, c. sleep, d. thought)
(a) Phenomenology is the study of consciousness. Psychoanalysis is the study of the unconcsious.

71. PHYLUM : (a. order, b. species, c. type, **d. kingdom**) :: NICKEL : DOLLAR
(d) A nickel is a smaller level of organization of U.S. currency than a dollar. A phylum is a smaller level of organization of an organism than a kingdom. (From the broadest level to the most specific: kingdom—phylum—class—order—family—genus—species. A handy mnemonic device to remember these: "King Philip's Class Ordered the Family-sized Gino's Special.")

72. APATHETIC : ZEALOUS :: PRAGMATIC : (a. concomitant, b. realistic, **c. romantic**, d. pluralistic)
(c) Someone who is apathetic is not zealous. Someone who is pragmatic is not romantic or fanciful.

73. SYBARITE : (a. prudish, **b. hedonistic**, c. fanciful, d. dour) :: ASCETIC : ABSTEMIOUS
(b) A sybarite is always hedonistic or fond of indulging. An ascetic is always abstemious or temperate.

74. CHANCE : RANDOM :: SYNCHRONIZED : (**a. coterminous**, b. vocational, c. undulating, d. desultory)
(**a**) Something that occurs by chance occurs at a random time. Something that is synchronized occurs at a coterminous time.

75. CEREBRUM : CEREBELLUM :: THOUGHT : (a. idea, b. breath, c. consciousness, **d. balance**)
(**d**) Conscious thought is controlled by the part of the brain called the cerebrum. Balance is controlled by the part of the brain called the cerebellum.

76. ENGLAND : (**a. St. George**, b. St. Martin, c. St. Patrick, d. St. Thomas) :: FRANCE : ST. JOAN
(**a**) St. George is the patron saint of England. St. Joan is the patron saint of France.

77. PI : (a. integral, b. real, c. rational, **d. transcendental**) :: i : IMAGINARY
(**d**) Pi is a transcendental number, and i is an imaginary number.

78. PHLEGMATIC : (a. snotty, b. sick, **c. sluggish**, d. elated) :: SANGUINE : CHEERFUL
(**c**) Something that is phlegmatic is sluggish. Something that is sanguine is cheerful.

79. METASTASIS : SPREAD :: REMISSION : (a. beginning, **b. abatement**, c. intensification, d. transmission)
(**b**) Metastasis is the spread of an illness such as cancer. Remission is the abatement of the spread of an illness such as cancer.

80. (a. critique, **b. imprimatur**, c. admission, d. conquest) : APPROVAL :: CENSURE : CRITICISM
(**b**) Imprimatur is official approval, and censure is official criticism.

81. GEORGIAN : AUSTEN :: (a. Romantic, b. Classical, c. Modernist, **d. Restoration**) : DRYDEN
(**d**) Jane Austen is a writer from the Georgian period. John Dryden is a writer from the Restoration period.

82. PHYLOGENY : (a. plants, b. words, **c. evolution**, d. effects) :: ETIOLOGY : CAUSES
(**c**) *Phylogeny* refers to the evolution of a species. *Etiology* refers to the causes of something.

83. ARISTOTLE : PLATO :: KEPLER : (a. Gilbert, b. Bruno, **c. Brahe**, d. Crick)
(**c**) Aristotle was taught by Plato. Johannes Kepler was taught by Tycho Brahe.

84. (a. monkey, **b. prosimian**, c. *Homo sapiens*, d. chimpanzee) : SIMIAN :: LEMUR : APE
(b) A lemur is a type of prosimian, and an ape is a type of simian. Even if you know nothing about prosimians, you could still find the correct answer by a process of elimination: A lemur is not a monkey, not a chimp, and not a *Homo sapiens* (human).

85. HEURISTIC : ALGORITHM :: EXPEDITIOUS : (a. quick, b. computerized, **c. exhaustive**, d. probabilistic)
(c) A heuristic is a quick rule of thumb that is an expeditious way of reaching a solution. An algorithm is a rigorous and exhaustive way of reaching a solution.

86. LANGUAGE : WITTGENSTEIN :: (a. polio, **b. psyche**, c. phenomenology, d. genetics) : JUNG
(b) Ludwig Wittgenstein studied language in depth, and Carl Jung studied the psyche in depth.

87. FOMENT : INCITE :: MITIGATE : (a. incense, **b. alleviate**, c. worry, d. riot)
(b) To foment is to incite or exacerbate. To mitigate is to alleviate or lessen.

88. MOT JUSTE : APT :: SOLECISM : (**a. inappropriate**, b. witty, c. prudish, d. candid)
(a) A mot juste (from the French) is always apt or appropriate. A solecism is always inappropriate.

89. FOLIO : ONE FOLD :: OCTAVO : (**a. two folds**, b. four folds, c. eight folds, d. sixteen folds)
(a) A folio is made with one fold, and an octavo is made with two folds.

90. MODICUM : (**a. modica**, b. modicus, c. modicae, d. modices) :: INDEX : INDICES
(a) One of the plural forms of *modicum* is *modica*. The plural form of *index* is *indices* or *indexes*.

91. LINDBERGH : ATLANTIC :: (a. Glenn, b. Armstrong, c. Wright, **d. Smith**) : PACIFIC
(d) Charles Lindbergh was the first person to fly across the Atlantic. Kingsford Smith was the first to fly across the Pacific.

92. VET : MANUSCRIPT :: (a. collect, b. experience, c. preserve, **d. dissect**) : SPECIMEN
(d) To vet a manuscript is to analyze it and break it down. To dissect a specimen is to analyze it and break it down.

93. IDEALISM : BERKELEY :: RATIONALISM : (a. Liebnitz, b. Kant, **c. Descartes**, d. Occam)
(c) George Berkeley was a proponent of idealism, the belief that ideas were the basis of reality. René Descartes was a proponent of rationalism, the belief that use of reason alone can find the basis of reality.

94. PECCADILLO : FELONY :: TIFF : (a. misdemeanor, b. spat, c. exoneration, **d. melee**)
(**d**) A peccadillo is a small sin, while a felony is an extreme offense. Similarly, a tiff is a small disagreement, while a melee is large, confused battle.

95. SUSURRUS : (a. melody, b. cumulonimbus, **c. din**, d. terminus) :: WHISPER : CACOPHONY
(**c**) A susurrus is a type of sound similar to a whisper, and a din is a type of sound similar to a cacophony.

96. BUMBLEBEE BAT : (a. reptile, **b. mammal**, c. nocturnal, d. flight) :: HUMMINGBIRD : BIRD
(**b**) The bumblebee bat is the world's smallest mammal, and the hummingbird is the world's smallest bird.

97. VAN ALEN : CHRYSLER BUILDING :: (a. Wright, **b. Graham**, c. Gehry, d. Bauhaus) : SEARS TOWER
(**b**) William Van Alen was the architect who designed the Chrysler building, and Bruce Graham was the architect who designed the Sears Tower.

98. SOUSA : PUCCINI :: MARCH : (**a. opera**, b. violin, c. jazz, d. fugue)
(**a**) John Phillip Sousa is a well-known composer of marches, and Giacomo Puccini is a well-known composer of operas.

99. CASTELLAN : CASTLE :: (a. landlord, **b. butler**, c. peasant, d. groundskeeper) : MANSION
(**b**) A castellan is the keeper or governor of a castle, and a butler is the keeper of a mansion.

100. BUSHEL : PECK :: PINT : (a. gallon, b. grain, **c. gill**, d. dram)
(**c**) There are four pecks in a bushel, and there are four gills in a pint.

101. (a. abacus, b. furlong, c. league, **d. sextant**) : NAVIGATION :: RULER: MEASUREMENT
(**d**) A sextant is a tool used in navigation, and a ruler is a tool used for measurement.

102. PURLOIN : FULMINATE :: FILCH : (a. explode, b. exude, c. repose, **d. rant**)
(**d**) *Purloin* means filch, and *fulminate* means rant.

103. RHODESIA : BURMA :: (a. Zambia, b. South Africa, c. Kenya, **d. Zimbabwe**) : MYANMAR
(**d**) Rhodesia is the former name of Zimbabwe, and Burma is the former name of Myanmar.

104. BERNINI : BAROQUE :: WATTEAU : (a. Renaissance, **b. Rococo**, c. academic, d. classical)
    (**b**) The sculptor Gian Lorenzo Bernini is placed in the Baroque period, and the painter Jean-Antoine Watteau is placed in the Rococo period.

105. HE : NOBLE GAS :: (**a. U**, b. Cs, c. In, d. Fe) : ACTINIDE
    (**a**) Helium (He) is a noble gas, and uranium (U) is an actinide.

106. CAMUS : THE STRANGER :: SARTRE : (a. *Hunger*, **b. *Nausea***, c. *Steppenwolf*, d. *The Plague*)
    (**b**) Albert Camus authored *The Stranger*, and Jean Paul Sartre authored *Nausea*.

107. (**a. Persia**, b. Iraq, c. Macedonia, d. Greece) : PERSEPOLIS :: BYZANTINE EMPIRE : CONSTANTINOPLE
    (**a**) The capital of ancient Persia was Persepolis, and the capital of the Byzantine Empire was Constantinople.

108. (a. Titan 7, b. Soyuz, **c. Atlas 10**, d. Gemini) : MERCURY :: SATURN V : APOLLO
    (**c**) The Saturn V rocket was used in the Apollo space missions, and the Atlas 10 rocket was used in the Mercury space missions.

109. (**a. he**, b. yourself, c. that, d. mine) : SOMEONE :: DEFINITE : INDEFINITE
    (**a**) *He* is a definite pronoun, and *someone* is an indefinite pronoun.

110. 8TH AVENUE : LONGITUDE : (a. Broadway, b. Avenue of the Americas, **c. 42nd Street**, d. Grand Concourse) : LATITUDE
    (**c**) New York City's 8th Avenue runs longitudinally while 42nd Street runs latitudinally across Manhattan Island.

111. RUBENS : REMBRANDT :: (**a. Flemish**, b. French, c. Swiss, d. German) : DUTCH
    (**a**) Peter Paul Rubens was a painter from the Catholic territory of Flanders, while Harmenszoon Rembrandt hailed from the Protestant Netherlands.

112. KILIMANJARO : EVEREST :: (a. Kenya, **b. Tanzania**, c. Ethiopia, d. Somalia) : NEPAL
    (**b**) Mount Kilimanjaro is located in Tanzania, and Mount Everest is located in Nepal.

113. (a. Edison, b. Kodak, c. Nadar, **d. Daguerre**) : PHOTOGRAPHY :: LUMIÈRE : MOTION PICTURES
    (**d**) Louis Daguerre was a key figure in the invention of photography, and the Lumière brothers were comparably important to the development of motion pictures.

114. HECTOR : ACHILLES :: (a. Troy, b. Odysseus, c. Agamemnon, **d. Paris**) : MENELAUS
    (**d**) During the Trojan War, Hector's archenemy was Achilles, and Paris's was King Menelaus.

115. TIGRIS : (a. Iran, **b. Iraq**, c. Saudi Arabia, d. Jordan) :: ARNO : ITALY
     (b) The Tigris River runs through Baghdad, Iraq, just as the Arno River runs through Florence, Italy.

116. MADAME BUTTERFLY : PUCCINI :: DON GIOVANNI : (a. Vivaldi, b. Rossini, **c. Mozart**, d. Verdi)
     (c) Giacomo Puccini composed the opera *Madame Butterfly*, and Wolfgang Amadeus Mozart composed the opera *Don Giovanni*.

117. PHILISTINE : APPRECIATION :: BOOR : (a. depreciation, **b. tact**, c. accusations, d. perception)
     (b) A philistine lacks appreciation, and a boor lacks tact.

118. PLANTS : CHLOROPLASTS :: ANIMALS : (a. Golgi apparatus, **b. mitochondria**, c. vacuoles, d. vesicles)
     (b) Chloroplasts produce cellular energy in plants, and mitochondria produce cellular energy in animals.

119. FRANK O'HARA : MOMA :: (a. E. E. Cummings, b. Kenneth Koch, c. Alan Dugan, **d. Walt Whitman**) : BROOKLYN DAILY EAGLE
     (d) The American poet Frank O'Hara worked at MOMA before his poetry career took off, and one of many of Walt Whitman's jobs before fully dedicating himself to poetry was editing for the *Brooklyn Daily Eagle*.

120. STRESSED : (**a. desserts**, b. anxious, c. dilution, d. extreme) :: EDIT : TIDE
     (a) *Stressed* spelled backward is *desserts*, and *edit* spelled backward is *tide*.

ANSWER SHEET FOR PRACTICE TEST 6

1. ⓐ ⓑ ⓒ ⓓ
2. ⓐ ⓑ ⓒ ⓓ
3. ⓐ ⓑ ⓒ ⓓ
4. ⓐ ⓑ ⓒ ⓓ
5. ⓐ ⓑ ⓒ ⓓ
6. ⓐ ⓑ ⓒ ⓓ
7. ⓐ ⓑ ⓒ ⓓ
8. ⓐ ⓑ ⓒ ⓓ
9. ⓐ ⓑ ⓒ ⓓ
10. ⓐ ⓑ ⓒ ⓓ
11. ⓐ ⓑ ⓒ ⓓ
12. ⓐ ⓑ ⓒ ⓓ
13. ⓐ ⓑ ⓒ ⓓ
14. ⓐ ⓑ ⓒ ⓓ
15. ⓐ ⓑ ⓒ ⓓ
16. ⓐ ⓑ ⓒ ⓓ
17. ⓐ ⓑ ⓒ ⓓ
18. ⓐ ⓑ ⓒ ⓓ
19. ⓐ ⓑ ⓒ ⓓ
20. ⓐ ⓑ ⓒ ⓓ
21. ⓐ ⓑ ⓒ ⓓ
22. ⓐ ⓑ ⓒ ⓓ
23. ⓐ ⓑ ⓒ ⓓ
24. ⓐ ⓑ ⓒ ⓓ
25. ⓐ ⓑ ⓒ ⓓ
26. ⓐ ⓑ ⓒ ⓓ
27. ⓐ ⓑ ⓒ ⓓ
28. ⓐ ⓑ ⓒ ⓓ
29. ⓐ ⓑ ⓒ ⓓ
30. ⓐ ⓑ ⓒ ⓓ
31. ⓐ ⓑ ⓒ ⓓ
32. ⓐ ⓑ ⓒ ⓓ
33. ⓐ ⓑ ⓒ ⓓ
34. ⓐ ⓑ ⓒ ⓓ
35. ⓐ ⓑ ⓒ ⓓ
36. ⓐ ⓑ ⓒ ⓓ
37. ⓐ ⓑ ⓒ ⓓ
38. ⓐ ⓑ ⓒ ⓓ
39. ⓐ ⓑ ⓒ ⓓ
40. ⓐ ⓑ ⓒ ⓓ

41. ⓐ ⓑ ⓒ ⓓ
42. ⓐ ⓑ ⓒ ⓓ
43. ⓐ ⓑ ⓒ ⓓ
44. ⓐ ⓑ ⓒ ⓓ
45. ⓐ ⓑ ⓒ ⓓ
46. ⓐ ⓑ ⓒ ⓓ
47. ⓐ ⓑ ⓒ ⓓ
48. ⓐ ⓑ ⓒ ⓓ
49. ⓐ ⓑ ⓒ ⓓ
50. ⓐ ⓑ ⓒ ⓓ
51. ⓐ ⓑ ⓒ ⓓ
52. ⓐ ⓑ ⓒ ⓓ
53. ⓐ ⓑ ⓒ ⓓ
54. ⓐ ⓑ ⓒ ⓓ
55. ⓐ ⓑ ⓒ ⓓ
56. ⓐ ⓑ ⓒ ⓓ
57. ⓐ ⓑ ⓒ ⓓ
58. ⓐ ⓑ ⓒ ⓓ
59. ⓐ ⓑ ⓒ ⓓ
60. ⓐ ⓑ ⓒ ⓓ
61. ⓐ ⓑ ⓒ ⓓ
62. ⓐ ⓑ ⓒ ⓓ
63. ⓐ ⓑ ⓒ ⓓ
64. ⓐ ⓑ ⓒ ⓓ
65. ⓐ ⓑ ⓒ ⓓ
66. ⓐ ⓑ ⓒ ⓓ
67. ⓐ ⓑ ⓒ ⓓ
68. ⓐ ⓑ ⓒ ⓓ
69. ⓐ ⓑ ⓒ ⓓ
70. ⓐ ⓑ ⓒ ⓓ
71. ⓐ ⓑ ⓒ ⓓ
72. ⓐ ⓑ ⓒ ⓓ
73. ⓐ ⓑ ⓒ ⓓ
74. ⓐ ⓑ ⓒ ⓓ
75. ⓐ ⓑ ⓒ ⓓ
76. ⓐ ⓑ ⓒ ⓓ
77. ⓐ ⓑ ⓒ ⓓ
78. ⓐ ⓑ ⓒ ⓓ
79. ⓐ ⓑ ⓒ ⓓ
80. ⓐ ⓑ ⓒ ⓓ

81. ⓐ ⓑ ⓒ ⓓ
82. ⓐ ⓑ ⓒ ⓓ
83. ⓐ ⓑ ⓒ ⓓ
84. ⓐ ⓑ ⓒ ⓓ
85. ⓐ ⓑ ⓒ ⓓ
86. ⓐ ⓑ ⓒ ⓓ
87. ⓐ ⓑ ⓒ ⓓ
88. ⓐ ⓑ ⓒ ⓓ
89. ⓐ ⓑ ⓒ ⓓ
90. ⓐ ⓑ ⓒ ⓓ
91. ⓐ ⓑ ⓒ ⓓ
92. ⓐ ⓑ ⓒ ⓓ
93. ⓐ ⓑ ⓒ ⓓ
94. ⓐ ⓑ ⓒ ⓓ
95. ⓐ ⓑ ⓒ ⓓ
96. ⓐ ⓑ ⓒ ⓓ
97. ⓐ ⓑ ⓒ ⓓ
98. ⓐ ⓑ ⓒ ⓓ
99. ⓐ ⓑ ⓒ ⓓ
100. ⓐ ⓑ ⓒ ⓓ
101. ⓐ ⓑ ⓒ ⓓ
102. ⓐ ⓑ ⓒ ⓓ
103. ⓐ ⓑ ⓒ ⓓ
104. ⓐ ⓑ ⓒ ⓓ
105. ⓐ ⓑ ⓒ ⓓ
106. ⓐ ⓑ ⓒ ⓓ
107. ⓐ ⓑ ⓒ ⓓ
108. ⓐ ⓑ ⓒ ⓓ
109. ⓐ ⓑ ⓒ ⓓ
110. ⓐ ⓑ ⓒ ⓓ
111. ⓐ ⓑ ⓒ ⓓ
112. ⓐ ⓑ ⓒ ⓓ
113. ⓐ ⓑ ⓒ ⓓ
114. ⓐ ⓑ ⓒ ⓓ
115. ⓐ ⓑ ⓒ ⓓ
116. ⓐ ⓑ ⓒ ⓓ
117. ⓐ ⓑ ⓒ ⓓ
118. ⓐ ⓑ ⓒ ⓓ
119. ⓐ ⓑ ⓒ ⓓ
120. ⓐ ⓑ ⓒ ⓓ

Practice Test 6

Time: 60 minutes
Length of Test: 120 Questions

Directions: For each of the following questions, you will find three capitalized terms and, in parentheses, four answer choices designated *a*, *b*, *c*, and *d*. Select the one answer choice that best completes the analogy with the three capitalized terms. (To record your answers, use the answer sheet that precedes this test.)

1. COSMOPOLITAN : RUSTIC :: CITY : (a. magazine, b. farm, c. tractor, d. urbane)

2. (a. viola, b. drum, c. tuba, d. olive) : VIOLIN :: BLOW : BOW

3. DISQUIETUDE : (a. serenity, b. discord, c. cacophony, d. baffle) :: ANXIETY : PEACE

4. (a. bicuspid, b. fang, c. scale, d. reptile) : SNAKE :: MOLAR : HUMAN

5. QUICKSILVER : MERCURY :: BRIMSTONE : (a. sulfur, b. lodestone, c. quicklime, d. magnesium)

6. –4 : 16 :: 0.5 : (a. 0.25, b. 2, c. 2.5, d. 4)

7. (a. besmirched, b. wet, c. immediate, d. sere) : SODDEN :: DRY : ARID

8. PARISIAN : PARIS :: NEAPOLITAN : (a. Norway, b. Nepal, c. Naples, d. Nippon)

9. E.G. : I.E. :: (a. context, b. meaning, c. abbreviation, d. example) : THAT IS

10. CUR : (a. breed, b. dog, c. wicked, d. rude) :: CHURL : PERSON

11. COMPRESSED : TABLET :: (a. hued, b. dissolved, c. magnetized, d. polarized) : TINCTURE

12. SPRINT : (a. height, b. speed, c. persistence, d. depth) :: DISCUS : DISTANCE

13. SHUT : SLAM :: (a. close, b. nudge, c. tackle, d. nod) : SHOVE

14. (a. picture, b. lamp, c. window, d. sconce) : WALL :: CHANDELIER : CEILING

15. 0 : 32 :: (a. 32, b. 98.6, c. 100, d. 273) : 212

16. MANDIBLE : JAW :: (a. probity, b. proboscis, c. mandrill, d. scent) : NOSE

17. TICK : (a. dog, b. clock, c. mark, d. tock) :: HONK : HORN

18. ORBIT : ELECTRON :: (a. neutron, b. nucleus, c. shell, d. isotope) : PROTON

19. (a. knoll, b. fen, c. desert, d. perigee) : LOW :: PLATEAU : HIGH

20. BON VIVANT : BONHOMIE :: TASTEFUL : (a. genial, b. misanthropic, c. capricious, d. blunt)

21. LOCK : CANAL :: (a. key, b. cylinder, c. chamber, d. open) : HEART

22. (a. sly, b. deft, c. abrupt, d. stout) : ADROIT :: APT : FIT

23. RIPOSTE : WIT :: (a. oratory, b. thesis, c. rebuttal, d. lectern) : DEBATER

24. EXTOL : TRIUMPH :: (a. celebrate, b. decry, c. laud, d. overcome) : DEBACLE

25. SEVERED : (a. reversed, b. retold, c. deserve, d. lopped) :: TROUNCE : RECOUNT

26. SIREN : (a. rocks, b. music, c. mermaid, d. lure) :: GORGON : PETRIFY

27. (a. extant, b. deft, c. virile, d. adroit) : DEFUNCT :: ALIVE : DEAD

28. NEST : FLEDGLING :: CRÈCHE : (a. child, b. seedling, c. tadpole, d. calf)

29. VELDT : (a. grassy, b. mountainous, c. thin, d. flat) :: ATOLL : RINGED

30. RHOMBUS : (a. 1, b. 4, c. 9, d. many) :: TRIANGLE : 3

31. TRUCK : GEAR :: HORSE : (a. bridle, b. saddle, c. hoof, d. pace)

32. MERCURIAL : QUIXOTIC :: MERCURY : (a. Quixote, b. Quito, c. quizzical, d. quasi)

33. CROW : BANTAM :: (a. moon, b. sit, c. high, d. bay) : HOUND

34. ACADEMY : (a. edifying, b. humid, c. restrictive, d. vituperative) :: PRISON : PUNITIVE

35. (a. clam, b. sea anemone, c. earthworm, d. vole) : RADIAL SYMMETRY :: GIRAFFE : BILATERAL SYMMETRY

36. EPISODIC : POLYGLOT :: EVENTS : (a. memories, b. images, c. places, d. languages)

37. HOI POLLOI : INTELLIGENTSIA :: (a. ill-mannered, b. ordinary, c. conglomerated, d. homogenous) : ELITE

38. (a. film, b. daguerreotype, c. calculator, d. camera) : PHOTOGRAPH :: ABACUS : COMPUTER

39. AMNESIAC : MEMORY :: (a. deaf, b. mute, c. forget, d. silence) : VOICE

40. TEMPLARS : SHRINE :: (a. temple, b. cavalry, c. crusade, d. tramples) : SHINER

41. (a. depression, b. transgression, c. regression, d. concession) : MATURITY :: DELUSION : REALITY

42. IMPOSTOR : IDENTITY :: MALINGERER : (a. finances, b. illness, c. competence, d. belief)

43. SLOGAN : ENCAPSULATE :: (a. footnote, b. introduction, c. abstract, d. conclusion) : SUPPLEMENT

44. HEMATO : (a. blood, b. iron, c. tomato, d. liver) :: OSTEO : BONES

45. CRADLE : GRAVE :: SOUP : (a. croutons, b. nuts, c. entrée, d. dust)

46. OBLIQUE : DIRECT :: (a. acute, b. curt, c. tactful, d. muscle) : INDISCREET

47. (a. hulk, b. punt, c. drake, d. bird) : BOAT :: PIKE : SPEAR

48. ACTIVE : TILLED :: LATENT : (a. ploughed, b. overdue, c. fallow, d. sterile)

49. RENT : (a. mend, b. lease, c. tear, d. tie) :: LACERATE : STITCH

50. AGONIST : STRUGGLE :: (a. combatant, b. skirmish, c. protagonist, d. assault) : BATTLE

51. MUTATION : (a. evolutionary, b. intentional, c. fortuitous, d. novel) :: ATAVISM : RECURRING

52. FICTIVE : GENUINE :: (a. word, b. tacit, c. verbal, d. overt) : SPOKEN

53. INTOLERANCE : BIGOT :: (a. supplication, b. assistance, c. discouragement, d. restoration) : MENDICANT

54. (a. polydactyl, b. multicephalic, c. polyandrous, d. multifarious) : TOES :: MULTILINGUAL : LANGUAGES

55. LEGERDEMAIN : COUP DE MAIN :: (a. informed, b. lawful, c. deceitful, d. legendary) : SUDDEN

56. (a. here, b. in front of, c. after, d. until) : BEFORE :: HENCEFORTH : HITHERTO

57. UNCTUOUS : OILY :: (a. dodgy, b. sere, c. ethereal, d. fastidious) : DRY

58. CLASSIFICATION : TAXONOMY :: (a. ignorance, b. persuasion, c. speech, d. deception) : RHETORIC

59. AVUNCULAR : (a. friend, b. cousin, c. uncle, d. spouse) :: FRATERNAL : BROTHER

60. (a. braid, b. billiards, c. cards, d. line) : CUE :: PINBALL : PADDLE

61. WHENEVER : ADVERB :: ALTHOUGH : (a. preposition, b. adverb, c. determiner, d. conjunction)

62. CHTHONIC : CELESTIAL :: UNDERWORLD : (a. afterlife, b. heavens, c. inferno, d. astronomy)

63. RELAY : SWITCH :: (a. resistor, b. cathode, c. circuit, d. capacitor) : ACCUMULATE

64. FARSIGHTED : (a. hyperopic, b. prescient, c. penetrating, d. conjunctivitis) :: NEARSIGHTED : MYOPIC

65. HOMAGE : DIATRIBE :: (a. righteous, b. gentle, c. critical, d. praiseworthy) : LAUDATORY

66. (a. folivore, b. granivore, c. fructivore, d. cannibal) : INSECTIVORE :: GIBBON : HEDGEHOG

67. MANTRA : CEREMONY :: (a. refrain, b. melody, c. incantation, d. theme) : SONG

68. (a. Pasteur, b. Fleming, c. Shockley, d. Wright) : PENICILLIN :: CAROTHERS : NYLON

69. QUASIMODO : (a. Dumas, b. Leroux, c. Tolstoy, d. Hugo) :: LEAR : SHAKESPEARE

70. GANGLION : (a. capillaries, b. muscles, c. ducts, d. nerves) :: SHEAF : STALKS

71. RECRUIT : VETERAN :: APPRENTICE : (a. journeyman, b. neophyte, c. proselyte, d. retiree)

72. KRISHNA : (a. Manichaeanism , b. Hellenism, c. Hinduism, d. Islam) :: ZARATHUSTRA : ZOROASTRIANISM

73. (a. prone, b. maladroit, c. sinistral, d. ventral) : LEFT :: DEXTRAL : RIGHT

74. PERDITION : SALVATION :: (a. sinner, b. condemn, c. soul, d. crime) : EXONERATE

75. UNION : EMPLOYEES :: (a. cartel, b. management, c. stewards, d. company) : CORPORATIONS

76. AUGER : BORING :: (a. lathe, b. prediction, c. grain, d. drill) : MILLING

77. HEMI– : DEMI– :: (a. alter–, b. semi–, c. pseudo–, d. sub–) : QUASI–

78. APOSTATE : BELIEF :: (a. hypocrite, b. defector, c. fanatic, d. refugee) : NATIONALITY

79. WILLIAM THE CONQUEROR : ENGLISH CHANNEL :: JULIUS CAESAR : (a. Nile, b. Rubicon, c. Thames, d. Loire)

80. DETENTE : RAPPROCHEMENT :: (a. sovereignty, b. independence, c. antipathy, d. mendacity) : ENMITY

81. GEORGE ELIOT : MARY ANN EVANS :: MARK TWAIN : (a. William Dean Howells, b. Henry James, c. Samuel Clemens, d. Willa Cather)

82. SINE QUA NON : (a. actual, b. self-evident, c. indispensable, d. unsurpassable) :: QUID PRO QUO : RECIPROCAL

83. VOLUNTARY CONTRACTIONS : DANCING :: INVOLUNTARY CONTRACTIONS : (a. grasping, b. paralysis, c. hunger, d. peristalsis)

84. PLANET : CORE :: (a. star, b. solar system, c. black hole, d. supernova) : SINGULARITY

85. DAMOCLES : SWORD :: SISYPHUS : (a. eagle, b. rock, c. bed, d. serpent)

86. METAL : ALLOY :: WOOD : (a. charcoal, b. carving, c. paper, d. laminate)

87. GRASSHOPPER : ARTHROPOD :: STARFISH : (a. pachyderm, b. echinoderm, c. nematode, d. chordate)

88. SOLVENT : (a. solution, b. conglomeration, c. precipitate, d. titration) :: WHEY : CURDS

89. ROMEO : JULIET :: PYRAMUS : (a. Euridice, b. Electra, c. Thisbe, d. Galatea)

90. (a. prodromal, b. subdural, c. sub rosa, d. predictable) : BEFORE :: INTERSTITIAL : BETWEEN

91. INAUGURATE : OFFICE :: (a. ordain, b. canonize, c. confirm, d. postulate) : SAINTHOOD

92. SEMIQUAVER : WHOLE NOTE :: (a. 2, b. 4, c. 8, d. 16) : 1

93. (a. Ariadne, b. Nile, c. Bifrost, d. Lethe) : ASGARD :: HADES : STYX

94. CHANGELING : BABY :: (a. kiwi, b. egg, c. dodo, d. cuckoo) : EGG

95. FENRIR : WOLF :: OUROBOROS : (a. raven, b. turtle, c. boar, d. snake)

96. (a. ritual, b. shibboleth, c. uniform, d. diploma) : INITIATE :: BADGE : OFFICER

97. RUBIDIUM : (a. rare earth, b. halogen, c. alkali, d. other) :: CHROMIUM : TRANSITION

98. BROBDINAGIAN : LARGE :: STENTORIAN : (a. small, b. loud, c. gradual, d. sudden)

99. IDIOGRAPHIC : (a. nominal, b. idiosyncratic, c. peripatetic, d. nomothetic) :: DIFFERENCES : NORMS

100. ANGLO-SAXON : FUTHARK :: (a. Cretan, b. Egyptian, c. Aramaic, d. Phoenician) : LINEAR A

101. BRAQUE : JOHNS :: PICASSO : (a. Rothko, b. Rauschenberg, c. Gris, d. Gleizes)

102. REPUBLIC : ROME :: DEMOCRACY : (a. Thrace, b. Attica, c. Sparta, d. Athens)

103. LIMNOLOGY : (a. forests, b. mountains, c. lakes, d. limericks) :: OCEANOGRAPHY : OCEANS

104. HUNGARY : BÉLA BARTÓK :: (a. Poland, b. Russia, c. Czechoslovakia, d. Austria) : DMITRI SHOSTAKOVICH

105. RICE : RISOTTO :: (a. couscous, b. quinoa, c. barley, d. bulgur) : TANGINE

106. WAVE : TSUNAMI :: BREEZE : (a. typhoon, b. hurricane, c. gale, d. tornado)

107. ARCHAEOLOGY : CULTURE :: HERPETOLOGY : (a. disease, b. stone, c. blood, d. reptiles)

108. ERNEST LAWRENCE : ALBERT EINSTEIN :: CYCLOTRON : (a. calculus, b. black holes, c. photoelectric effect, d. gamma rays)

109. TELEVISION : RADIO :: PHILO : (a. Guglielmo, b. Enrico, c. Niels, d. Erin)

110. EXTRA : TRANS :: BEYOND : (a. across, b. under, c. drag, d. avert)

111. (a. saltarello, b. courante, c. mambo, d. samba) : DUPLE METER :: SARABANDE : TRIPLE METER

112. WINNIPESAUKEE : (a. New York, b. Massachusetts, c. Ohio, d. New Hampshire) :: KISSIMMEE : FLORIDA

113. BHAGAVAD GITA : (a. Islam, b. Hinduism, Confucianism, d. Taoism) :: TORAH : JUDAISM

114. NILE RIVER : MEDITERRANEAN SEA :: YELLOW RIVER : (a. Yellow Sea, b. East China Sea, c. North Sea, d. Sea of Japan)

115. LEE : SHERMAN :: (a. Gettysburg, b. Fredericksburg, c. Vicksburg, d. Petersburg) : SIEGE OF ATLANTA

116. (a. Pavlov, b. Adler, c. Hegel, d. Erickson) : SKINNER :: CLASSICAL CONDITIONING : OPERANT CONDITIONING

117. DONATELLO : RAPHAEL :: (a. drawing, b. sculpture, c. architecture, d. engraving) : PAINTING

118. SONAR : ACRONYM :: KAYAK : (a. oxymoron, b. palindrome, c. portmanteau, d. alliteration)

119. TRISKAIDEKA– : (a. 3, b. 13, c. 30, d. 300) :: HENDECA– : 11

120. (a. Cassatt, b. Caillebotte, c. Van Gogh, d. Gauguin) : TAHITI :: CÉZANNE : MONT SAINTE-VICTOIRE

ANSWERS AND EXPLANATIONS

1. COSMOPOLITAN : RUSTIC :: CITY : (a. magazine, **b. farm**, c. tractor, d. urbane)
   (b) *Cosmopolitan* describes things related to a city environment. *Rustic* describes things related to a farm environment.

2. (a. viola, b. drum, **c. tuba**, d. olive) : VIOLIN :: BLOW : BOW
   (c) A tuba is played by blowing. A violin is played by bowing. The similar letters in several words suggest word transformation or anagrams, but this analogy is based on meaning, not wordplay.

3. DISQUIETUDE : (**a. serenity**, b. discord, c. cacophony, d. baffle) :: ANXIETY : PEACE
   (a) A feeling of disquietude is characterized by anxiety. A feeling of serenity is characterized by peace.

4. (a. bicuspid, **b. fang**, c. scale, d. reptile) : SNAKE :: MOLAR : HUMAN
   (b) A molar is a type of tooth that a human has. A fang is a type of tooth that a snake has.

5. QUICKSILVER : MERCURY :: BRIMSTONE : (**a. sulfur**, b. lodestone, c. quicklime, d. magnesium)
   (a) *Quicksilver* is another name for mercury, and *brimstone* is another name for sulfur.

6. −4 : 16 :: 0.5 : (**a. 0.25**, b. 2, c. 2.5, d. 4)
   (a) The number −4 squared is equal to 16; 0.5 squared is equal to 0.25.

7. (a. besmirched, **b. wet**, c. immediate, d. sere) : SODDEN :: DRY : ARID
   (b) *Arid* means extremely dry. *Sodden* means extremely wet.

8. PARISIAN : PARIS :: NEAPOLITAN : (a. Norway, b. Nepal, **c. Naples**, d. Nippon)
   (c) A person from Paris is called a Parisian. A person from Naples (called *Napoli* in Italian) is called a Neapolitan.

9. E.G. : I.E. :: (a. context, b. meaning, c. abbreviation, **d. for example**) : THAT IS
   (d) *E.g.* is the abbreviation for the Latin *exempli gratia*, meaning "for example". *I.e.* is the abbreviation for the Latin *id est*, meaning "that is".

10. CUR : (a. breed, **b. dog**, c. wicked, d. rude) :: CHURL : PERSON
    (b) A churl is a rude or ill-bred person. A cur is a rude or ill-bred dog.

11. COMPRESSED : TABLET :: (a. hued, **b. dissolved**, c. magnetized, d. polarized) : TINCTURE
    (b) A substance, such as a medicine, compressed into a form that can be administered is called a tablet. A substance dissolved into a form that can be administered is called a tincture.

12. SPRINT : (a. height, **b. speed**, c. persistence, d. depth) :: DISCUS : DISTANCE
    (b) The object of a discus throw is to achieve the best possible distance. The object of a sprint is to achieve the best possible speed.

13. SHUT : SLAM :: (a. close, **b. nudge**, c. tackle, d. nod) : SHOVE
    (b) To slam is to shut forcefully. To shove is to nudge forcefully.

14. (a. picture, b. lamp, c. window, **d. sconce**) : WALL :: CHANDELIER : CEILING
    (d) A light fixture that hangs from a ceiling is called a chandelier. A light fixture that hangs on a wall is called a sconce. Pictures also hang from walls, but they are not light fixtures. Lamps are light fixtures, but they do not hang from a wall. Windows can provide light, but they are not light fixtures, nor do they hang from walls.

15. 0 : 32 :: (a. 32, b. 98.6, **c. 100**, d. 273) : 212
    (c) The temperature of liquid water in degrees Fahrenheit ranges from 32 to 212 degrees. The temperature of liquid water in degrees Celsius ranges from 0 to 100 degrees.

16. MANDIBLE : JAW :: (a. probity, **b. proboscis**, c. mandrill, d. scent) : NOSE
    (b) *Mandible* is a synonym for jaw. *Proboscis* is a synonym for nose.

17. TICK : (a. dog, **b. clock**, c. mark, d. tock) :: HONK : HORN
    (b) The sound a horn makes is called a honk. The sound a clock makes is called a tick.

18. ORBIT : ELECTRON :: (a. neutron, **b. nucleus**, c. shell, d. isotope) : PROTON
    (b) An electron typically resides in an orbit of an atom. A proton typically resides in the nucleus of an atom.

19. (a. knoll, **b. fen**, c. desert, d. perigee) : LOW :: PLATEAU : HIGH
    (b) A plateau is a type of high place. A fen is a type of low place.

20. BON VIVANT : BONHOMIE :: TASTEFUL : (**a. genial**, b. misanthropic, c. capricious, d. blunt)
    (a) A bon vivant is a tasteful person. A bonhomie is a genial (friendly) person. Both words in the first pair incorporate the Latin root *bon–* (good), so that might have clued you in to the meanings of these words if you didn't know them.

21. LOCK : CANAL :: (a. key, b. cylinder, **c. chamber**, d. open) : HEART
    (c) A lock is an enclosure in a canal, closed by gates, that is alternately filled with and drained of water. A chamber is an enclosure in the heart, closed by valves, that is alternately filled with and drained of blood.

22. (a. sly, **b. deft**, c. abrupt, d. stout) : ADROIT :: APT : FIT
    (b) *Apt* is synonymous with *fit* or *capable*. *Deft* is synonymous with *adroit* or *skillful*.

23. RIPOSTE : WIT :: (a. oratory, b. thesis, **c. rebuttal**, d. lectern) : DEBATER
(**c**) The characteristic verbal retort of a wit is called a riposte. The characteristic verbal retort of a debater is called a rebuttal.

24. EXTOL : TRIUMPH :: (a. celebrate, **b. decry**, c. laud, d. overcome) : DEBACLE
(**b**) A triumph is likely to be extolled or praised, just as a debacle is likely to be decried or condemned.

25. SEVERED : (a. reversed, b. retold, **c. deserve**, d. lopped) :: TROUNCE : RECOUNT
(**c**) *Trounce* is an anagram of *recount*. *Severed* is an anagram of *deserve*.

26. SIREN : (a. rocks, b. music, c. mermaid, **d. lure**) :: GORGON : PETRIFY
(**d**) In Greek mythology, the characteristic action of a gorgon is to petrify men with her gaze. Likewise, the characteristic action of a siren in Greek mythology is to lure sailors to their death.

27. (**a. extant**, b. deft, c. virile, d. adroit) : DEFUNCT :: ALIVE : DEAD
(**a**) *Alive* is the opposite of *dead*; *extant* is the opposite of *defunct*.

28. NEST : FLEDGLING :: CRÈCHE : (**a. child**, b. seedling, c. tadpole, d. calf)
(**a**) The place where a fledgling is cared for is called a nest. The place where a child is cared for is called a crèche.

29. VELDT : (**a. grassy**, b. mountainous, c. thin, d. flat) :: ATOLL : RINGED
(**a**) A veldt is characteristically grassy. An atoll (ring-shaped chain of islands) is characteristically ringed.

30. RHOMBUS : (a. 1, **b. 4**, c. 9, d. many) :: TRIANGLE : 3
(**b**) A triangle has 3 sides; a rhombus has 4 sides.

31. TRUCK : GEAR :: HORSE : (a. bridle, b. saddle, c. hoof, **d. pace**)
(**d**) The different rates of travel for a truck are called gears. The different rates of travel for a horse are called paces (e.g., walk, trot, gallop).

32. MERCURIAL : QUIXOTIC :: MERCURY : (**a. Quixote**, b. Quito, c. quizzical, d. quasi)
(**a**) The word *mercurial* (changeable) is derived from the name of the mythical character Mercury. The word *quixotic* (changeable) is derived from the name of the fictional character Don Quixote.

33. CROW : BANTAM :: (a. moon, b. sit, c. high, **d. bay**) : HOUND
(**d**) The characteristic sound that a bantam (small rooster) makes is called a crow. The characteristic sound that a hound makes is called a bay.

34. ACADEMY : (**a. edifying**, b. humid, c. restrictive, d. vituperative) :: PRISON : PUNITIVE
(**a**) A prison is an institution designed to be punitive. An academy is an institution designed to be edifying or enlightening.

35. (a. clam, **b. sea anemone**, c. earthworm, d. vole) : RADIAL SYMMETRY :: GIRAFFE : BILATERAL SYMMETRY
    (b) A giraffe exhibits the characteristic of bilateral symmetry. A sea urchin exhibits the characteristic of radial symmetry.

36. EPISODIC : POLYGLOT :: EVENTS : (a. memories, b. images, c. places, **d. languages**)
    (d) Something that is episodic includes multiple events. Something that is polyglot includes multiple languages.

37. HOI POLLOI : INTELLIGENTSIA :: (a. ill-mannered, **b. ordinary**, c. conglomerated, d. homogenous) : ELITE
    (b) The intelligentsia are characteristically elite. The hoi polloi (common populace) are characteristically ordinary. Note that the idea of "general populace" does not necessarily include connotations of being either ill-mannered or homogenous.

38. (a. film, **b. daguerreotype**, c. calculator, d. camera) : PHOTOGRAPH :: ABACUS : COMPUTER
    (b) The abacus is the technological precursor of the computer. The daguerreotype is the technological precursor of the photograph.

39. AMNESIAC : MEMORY :: (a. deaf, **b. mute**, c. forget, d. silence) : VOICE
    (b) An amnesiac lacks memory. A mute lacks voice.

40. TEMPLARS : SHRINE :: (a. temple, b. cavalry, c. crusade, **d. tramples**) : SHINER
    (d) *Shrine* is an anagram of *shiner*. *Templars* is an anagram of *tramples*.

41. (a. depression, b. transgression, **c. regression**, d. concession) : MATURITY :: DELUSION : REALITY
    (c) Delusion is a loss or rejection of reality. Regression is a loss or rejection of maturity.

42. IMPOSTOR : IDENTITY :: MALINGERER : (a. finances, **b. illness**, c. competence, d. belief)
    (b) An impostor fakes an identity, just as a malingerer fakes an illness.

43. SLOGAN : ENCAPSULATE :: (**a. footnote**, b. introduction, c. abstract, d. conclusion) : SUPPLEMENT
    (a) A slogan is intended to encapsulate a set of ideas. A footnote is intended to supplement a set of ideas.

44. HEMATO : (**a. blood**, b. iron, c. tomato, d. liver) :: OSTEO : BONES
    (a) *Osteo-* is the Greek root used in words that refer to bones (e.g., *osteoporosis*). *Hemato-* is the Greek root used in words that refer to blood (e.g., *hematology*).

45. CRADLE : GRAVE :: SOUP : (a. croutons, **b. nuts**, c. entrée, d. dust)
   (b) "Cradle to grave" is an expression that means "beginning to end." "Soup to nuts" is an equivalent expression, referring to the first (soup) and last (nuts) courses of a formal dinner.

46. OBLIQUE : DIRECT :: (a. acute, b. curt, **c. tactful**, d. muscle) : INDISCREET
   (c) *Oblique* is the opposite of *direct*. *Tactful* is the opposite of *indiscreet*.

47. (a. hulk, **b. punt**, c. drake, d. bird) : BOAT :: PIKE : SPEAR
   (b) A pike is a type of spear, and a punt is a type of boat. Note that a hulk (a) is a type of ship, not a type of boat.

48. ACTIVE : TILLED :: LATENT : (a. ploughed, b. overdue, **c. fallow**, d. sterile)
   (c) A tilled field is active. A fallow field is latent. *Latent* implies the ability to become active, so that eliminates *sterile* as a possibility. *Ploughed* doesn't imply that anything has been planted or not planted.

49. RENT : (**a. mend**, b. lease, c. tear, d. tie) :: LACERATE : STITCH
   (a) Something lacerated is repaired by stitching. Something rent (torn) is repaired by mending.

50. AGONIST : STRUGGLE :: (**a. combatant**, b. skirmish, c. protagonist, d. assault) : BATTLE
   (a) An agonist is a participant in a struggle. A combatant is a participant in a battle.

51. MUTATION : (a. evolutionary, b. intentional, c. fortuitous, **d. novel**) :: ATAVISM : RECURRING
   (d) A recurring genetic arrangement is called an atavism. A novel genetic arrangement is called a mutation. A mutation is not necessarily either evolutionary (a) or fortuitous (c)—mutations can also be regressive or maladaptive.

52. FICTIVE : GENUINE :: (a. word, **b. tacit**, c. verbal, d. overt) : SPOKEN
   (b) *Fictive* means not genuine. *Tacit* means not spoken.

53. INTOLERANCE : BIGOT :: (**a. supplication**, b. assistance, c. discouragement, d. restoration) : MENDICANT
   (a) The characteristic action of a bigot is intolerance. The characteristic action of a mendicant (beggar) is supplication.

54. (**a. polydactyl**, b. multicephalic, c. polyandrous, d. multifarious) : TOES :: MULTILINGUAL : LANGUAGES
   (a) *Multilingual* means having many languages. *Polydactyl* means having many toes.

55. LEGERDEMAIN : COUP DE MAIN :: (a. informed, b. lawful, **c. deceitful**, d. legendary) : SUDDEN
(**c**) A coup de main is a sudden action. Legerdemain is a deceitful action. Notice that both these common English terms derive from French phrases involving motions of the hand (*main*). *Coup de main* literally means "stroke of hand", while *leger de main* literally means "light of hand".

56. (a. here, b. in front of, **c. after**, d. until) : BEFORE :: HENCEFORTH : HITHERTO
(**c**) *Hitherto* means before. *Henceforth* means after.

57. UNCTUOUS : OILY :: (a. dodgy, **b. sere**, c. ethereal, d. fastidious) : DRY
(**b**) *Unctuous* is a synonym for oily. *Sere* is a synonym for dry.

58. CLASSIFICATION : TAXONOMY :: (a. ignorance, **b. persuasion**, c. speech, d. deception) : RHETORIC
(**b**) Taxonomy is the science of classification. Rhetoric is the science of persuasion.

59. AVUNCULAR : (a. friend, b. cousin, **c. uncle**, d. spouse) :: FRATERNAL : BROTHER
(**c**) *Fraternal* means of or pertaining to a brother. *Avuncular* means of or pertaining to an uncle.

60. (a. braid, **b. billiards**, c. cards, d. line) : CUE :: PINBALL : PADDLE
(**b**) In pinball, the ball is struck with a paddle. In billiards, the ball is struck with a cue.

61. WHENEVER : ADVERB :: ALTHOUGH : (a. preposition, b. adverb, c. determiner, **d. conjunction**)
(**d**) The word *whenever* is an adverb. The word *although* is a conjunction.

62. CHTHONIC : CELESTIAL :: UNDERWORLD : (a. afterlife, **b. heavens**, c. inferno, d. astronomy)
(**b**) *Chthonic* means of or pertaining to the underworld. *Celestial* means of or pertaining to the heavens.

63. RELAY : SWITCH :: (a. resistor, b. cathode, c. circuit, **d. capacitor**) : ACCUMULATE
(**d**) The function of a relay is to switch electrical current. The function of a capacitor is to accumulate electrical current. Going through the other answer choices, a circuit carries current, a cathode emits current, and a resistor changes the form of a current.

64. FARSIGHTED : (**a. hyperopic**, b. prescient, c. penetrating, d. conjunctivitis) :: NEARSIGHTED : MYOPIC
(**a**) *Myopic* means nearsighted. *Hyperopic* means farsighted. While *prescient* and *penetrating* can also be metaphoric synonyms for *farsighted*, they don't match the mechanical and scientific bridge between *myopic* and *nearsighted*.

65. HOMAGE : DIATRIBE :: (a. righteous, b. gentle, **c. critical**, d. praiseworthy) : LAUDATORY
(c) An homage (praising speech) is not critical; a diatribe (critical speech) is not laudatory.

66. (a. folivore, b. granivore, **c. fructivore**, d. cannibal) : INSECTIVORE :: GIBBON : HEDGEHOG
(c) A hedgehog is an insectivore (eats primarily insects). A gibbon is a fructivore (eats primarily fruit).

67. MANTRA : CEREMONY :: (**a. refrain**, b. melody, c. incantation, d. theme) : SONG
(a) A mantra is a recurring verbal formula in a ceremony. A refrain is a recurring verbal formula in a song.

68. (a. Pasteur, **b. Fleming**, c. Shockley, d. Wright) : PENICILLIN :: CAROTHERS : NYLON
(b) Wallace Hume Carothers invented nylon. Alexander Fleming discovered penicillin. Pasteur contributed to germ theory, vaccination, and sterilization techniques.

69. QUASIMODO : (a. Dumas, b. Leroux, c. Tolstoy, **d. Hugo**) :: LEAR : SHAKESPEARE
(d) Lear is the flawed protagonist of *King Lear* by William Shakespeare. Quasimodo is the flawed protagonist of *The Hunchback of Notre Dame* by Victor Hugo.

70. GANGLION : (a. capillaries, b. muscles, c. ducts, **d. nerves**) :: SHEAF : STALKS
(d) A sheaf is a bundle of stalks. A ganglion is a bundle of nerves.

71. RECRUIT : VETERAN :: APPRENTICE : (**a. journeyman**, b. neophyte, c. proselyte, d. retiree)
(a) A recruit is a new member of a group (usually the military), and a veteran is an experienced member of a group. An apprentice is a new practitioner of a trade, and a journeyman is an experienced practitioner of a trade.

72. KRISHNA : (a. Manichaeanism, b. Hellenism, **c. Hinduism**, d. Islam) :: ZARATHUSTRA : ZOROASTRIANISM
(c) Krishna is a prophetic figure in Hinduism. Zarathustra is a prophetic figure in Zorastrianism (a religion of ancient Persia).

73. (a. prone, b. maladroit, **c. sinistral**, d. ventral) : LEFT :: DEXTRAL : RIGHT
(c) *Dextral* means of or pertaining to the right side of something. *Sinistral* means of or pertaining to the left side of something. The terms come from the Latin words for right (*dexter*) and left (*sinister*).

74. PERDITION : SALVATION :: (a. sinner, **b. condemn**, c. soul, d. crime) : EXONERATE
(b) *Perdition* means the condition of being condemned. *Salvation* means the condition of having been exonerated.

75. UNION : EMPLOYEES :: (**a. cartel**, b. management, c. stewards, d. company) :
CORPORATIONS
(**a**) A union is a group of employees united to protect their interests. A cartel is a
group of corporations united to protect their interests.

76. AUGER : BORING :: (**a. lathe**, b. prediction, c. grain, d. drill) : MILLING
(**a**) An auger is a device used for boring (making holes in) wood. A lathe is a device
for milling (reshaping) wood. Beware of potential confusion about the parts of speech
in this analogy.

77. HEMI– : DEMI– :: (a. alter–, **b. semi–**, c. pseudo–, d. sub–) : QUASI–
(**b**) *Demi–* and *quasi–* both mean "to some extent." *Hemi–* and *semi–* both mean
"half." *Psuedo–* means "false," not "half."

78. APOSTATE : BELIEF :: (a. hypocrite, **b. defector**, c. fanatic, d. refugee) :
NATIONALITY
(**b**) An apostate rejects a formerly held belief system. A defector rejects a formerly
held nationality.

79. WILLIAM THE CONQUEROR : ENGLISH CHANNEL :: JULIUS CAESAR : (a. Nile,
b. Rubicon, c. Thames, d. Loire)
(**b**) William the Conqueror started a war by crossing the English Channel (the
conquest of England). Julius Caesar started a war by crossing the Rubicon (the Roman
Civil War).

80. DETENTE : RAPPROCHEMENT :: (a. sovereignty, b. independence, **c. antipathy**,
d. mendacity) : ENMITY
(**c**) *Rapprochement* describes two or more states without enmity. *Détente* describes
states without antipathy.

81. GEORGE ELIOT : MARY ANN EVANS :: MARK TWAIN : (a. William Dean Howells,
b. Henry James, **c. Samuel Clemens**, d. Willa Cather)
(**c**) Mary Ann Evans wrote under the pen name George Eliot. Samuel Clemens wrote
under the pen name Mark Twain.

82. SINE QUA NON : (a. actual, b. self-evident, **c. indispensable**, d. unsurpassable) ::
QUID PRO QUO : RECIPROCAL
(**c**) *Quid pro quo* (something for something) means "reciprocal." *Sine qua non*
(without which nothing) means "indispensable."

83. VOLUNTARY CONTRACTIONS : DANCING :: INVOLUNTARY
CONTRACTIONS : (a. grasping, b. paralysis, c. hunger, **d. peristalsis**)
(**d**) Dancing is an activity that requires voluntary muscle contractions. Peristalsis (the
characteristic motion of smooth muscle in the digestive tract) requires involuntary
muscle contractions.

84. PLANET : CORE :: (a. star, b. solar system, **c. black hole**, d. supernova) : SINGULARITY
    (c) The center of a planet is called a core. The center of a black hole is called a singularity.

85. DAMOCLES : SWORD :: SISYPHUS : (a. eagle, **b. rock**, c. bed, d. serpent)
    (b) In Greek mythology, the punishment of Damocles involved a sword that dangled over his head suspended by a single human hair. The punishment of Sisyphus involved pushing a massive rock up a steep hill only to have it roll down again before he reached the top.

86. METAL : ALLOY :: WOOD : (a. charcoal, b. carving, c. paper, **d. laminate**)
    (d) An alloy is a blend of different types of metals. A laminate is a blend of different types of wood.

87. GRASSHOPPER : ARTHROPOD :: STARFISH : (a. pachyderm, **b. echinoderm**, c. nematode, d. chordate)
    (b) The grasshopper belongs to the phylum arthropod (literally, "jointed foot"). A starfish belongs to the phylum echinoderm (literally, "spiny skin").

88. SOLVENT : (a. solution, b. conglomeration, **c. precipitate**, d. titration) :: WHEY : CURDS
    (c) In chemistry, a precipitate is a solid substance that separates out of a solvent. In cheese making, curds are the solid clumps that separate out from the liquid whey.

89. ROMEO : JULIET :: PYRAMUS : (a. Euridice, b. Electra, **c. Thisbe**, d. Galatea)
    (c) The Shakespearian characters Romeo and Juliet are loosely based on the Greek story of Pyramus and Thisbe.

90. (**a. prodromal**, b. subdural, c. sub rosa d. predictable) : BEFORE :: INTERSTITIAL : BETWEEN
    (a) *Interstitial* means between. *Prodromal* means before.

91. INAUGURATE : OFFICE :: (a. ordain, **b. canonize**, c. confirm, d. postulate) : SAINTHOOD
    (b) To inaugurate is to install someone into an office. To canonize is to install someone into sainthood.

92. SEMIQUAVER : WHOLE NOTE :: (a. 2, b. 4, c. 8, **d. 16**) : 1
    (d) The duration of one whole note is the equivalent of 16 semiquavers (sixteenth notes) or 8 eighth notes or 4 quarter notes.

93. (a. Ariadne, b. Nile, **c. Bifrost**, d. Lethe) : ASGARD :: HADES : STYX
    (c) Styx is the river that souls cross to enter Hades in Greek myth. Bifrost is the bridge that souls cross to enter Asgard in Norse myth.

94. CHANGELING : BABY :: (a. kiwi, b. egg, c. dodo, **d. cuckoo**) : EGG
(**d**) A changeling is a fairy child maliciously left in the place of a human baby to be raised by the parents as their own child. Cuckoo birds leave their eggs in the nests of other birds to be raised by the adopted parents as their own fledglings.

95. FENRIR : WOLF :: OUROBOROS : (a. raven, b. turtle, c. boar, **d. snake**)
(**d**) Fenrir is a legendary wolf in Norse mythology. The ouroboros (literally, "world serpent") is a legendary snake that encircles the world and holds its tail in its mouth.

96. (a. ritual, **b. shibboleth**, c. uniform, d. diploma) : INITIATE :: BADGE : OFFICER
(**b**) A shibboleth is a password that demonstrates a person is an initiate in a particular group, just as a badge is an outward sign that a person is an officer of a particular group.

97. RUBIDIUM : (a. rare earth, b. halogen, **c. alkali**, d. other) :: CHROMIUM : TRANSITION
(**c**) Chromium is a transition metal; rubidium is an alkali metal.

98. BROBDINAGIAN : LARGE :: STENTORIAN : (a. small, **b. loud**, c. gradual, d. sudden)
(**b**) *Brobdinagian* means very large (from the name of the land of giants in Jonathan Swift's *Gulliver's Travels*). *Stentorian* means very loud (from the name of a very loud herald in the *Iliad*).

99. IDIOGRAPHIC : (**a. nominal**, b. idiosyncratic, c. peripatetic, d. nomothetic) :: DIFFERENCES : NORMS
(**a**) *Idiographic* means having to do with differences. *Nominal* means having to do with norms.

100. ANGLO-SAXON : FUTHARK :: (**a. Cretan**, b. Egyptian, c. Aramaic, d. Phoenician) : LINEAR A
(**a**) The Anglo-Saxon runic alphabet is called Futhark. The Cretan language (spoken on the island of Crete) was written in the undeciphered alphabet called Linear A.

101. BRAQUE : JOHNS :: PICASSO : (a. Rothko, **b. Rauschenberg**, c. Gris, d. Gleizes)
(**b**) Georges Braque and Pablo Picasso were close collaborators who cofounded Cubism. Jasper Johns and Robert Rauschenberg were closely related contemporaries in mid-20th-century New York.

102. REPUBLIC : ROME :: DEMOCRACY : (a. Thrace. b. Attica, c. Sparta, **d. Athens**)
(**d**) The republican form of government was founded in ancient Rome, and the democratic form of government was founded in ancient Athens.

103. LIMNOLOGY : (a. forests, b. mountains, **c. lakes**, d. limericks) :: OCEANOGRAPHY :
OCEANS
(**c**) Limnology is the scientific study of lakes and other bodies of freshwater, just as
oceanography is the study of (saltwater) oceans.

104. HUNGARY : BÉLA BARTÓK :: (a. Poland, **b. Russia**, c. Czechoslovakia, d. Austria) :
DMITRI SHOSTAKOVICH
(**b**) Béla Bartók was a Hungarian composer and pianist, and Dmitri Shostakovich was
a Russian composer and pianist.

105. RICE : RISOTTO :: (**a. couscous**, b. quinoa, c. barley, d. bulgur) : TANGINE
(**a**) A wheat-based grain called couscous is the base for the Moroccan dish called
tangine, and arborio rice is the base for the Italian dish called risotto.

106. WAVE : TSUNAMI :: BREEZE : (a. typhoon, b. hurricane, **c. gale**, d. tornado)
(**c**) A gale is an extremely strong wind, and a tsunami is an extremely strong wave.

107. ARCHAEOLOGY : CULTURE :: HERPETOLOGY : (a. disease, b. stone, c. blood,
d. reptiles)
(**d**) Archaeology is the study of old cultures, and herpetology is the study of reptiles.

108. ERNEST LAWRENCE : ALBERT EINSTEIN :: CYCLOTRON : (a. calculus, b. black
holes, **c. photoelectric effect**, d. gamma rays)
(**c**) Ernest Lawrence won the Nobel Prize for the cyclotron, and Albert Einstein won
the Nobel Prize for the photoelectric effect.

109. TELEVISION : RADIO :: PHILO : (**a. Guglielmo**, b. Enrico, c. Niels, d. Erin)
(**a**) Philo Farnsworth invented the television, and Guglielmo Marconi invented the
radio.

110. EXTRA : TRANS :: BEYOND : (**a. across**, b. under, c. drag, d. avert)
(**a**) *Extra–* is a prefix meaning beyond, while *trans–* is a prefix meaning across.

111. (a. saltarello, b. courante, c. mambo, **d. samba**) : DUPLE METER :: SARABANDE :
TRIPLE METER
(**d**) The samba is an Afro-Brazilian dance in duple meter (two beats per measure), and
the sarabande is a Spanish Baroque dance in triple meter (three beats per measure).

112. WINNIPESAUKEE : (a. New York, b. Massachusetts, c. Ohio, **d. New Hampshire**) ::
KISSIMMEE : FLORIDA
(**d**) Lake Winnipesaukee is located in New Hampshire, and Lake Kissimmee is located
in Florida.

113. BHAGAVAD GITA : (a. Islam, **b. Hinduism**, c. Confucianism, d. Taoism) :: TORAH :
JUDAISM
(**b**) The Bhagavad Gita is a sacred book of Hinduism, and the Torah is the sacred
book of Judaism.

114. NILE RIVER : MEDITERRANEAN SEA :: YELLOW RIVER : (**a. Yellow Sea**, b. East
China Sea, c. North Sea, d. Sea of Japan)
(**a**) The mouth of the Nile River is the Mediterranean Sea, and the mouth of the
Yellow River is the Yellow Sea.

115. LEE : SHERMAN :: (a. Gettysburg, **b. Fredericksburg**, c. Vicksburg, d. Petersburg) :
SIEGE OF ATLANTA
(**b**) Robert E. Lee was the victorious general at the Battle of Fredericksburg, and
William Tecumseh Sherman was the victorious general of the Siege of Atlanta.

116. (**a. Pavlov**, b. Adler, c. Hegel, d. Erickson) : SKINNER :: CLASSICAL
CONDITIONING : OPERANT CONDITIONING
(**a**) Ivan Pavlov's most famous theory is that of classical conditioning, and B. F.
Skinner's most famous theory is that of operant conditioning.

117. DONATELLO : RAPHAEL :: (a. drawing, **b. sculpture**, c. architecture, d. engraving) :
PAINTING
(**b**) Donatello was an important Renaissance sculptor, and Raphael was an eminent
Renaissance painter.

118. SONAR : ACRONYM :: KAYAK : (a. oxymoron, **b. palindrome**, c. portmanteau,
d. alliteration)
(**b**) *Sonar* is an acronym (a word made up of the first letters of other words), and
kayak is a palindrome (a word spelled the same forward and backward).

119. TRISKAIDEKA– : (a. 3, **b. 13**, c. 30, d. 300) :: HENDECA– : 11
(**b**) *Triskaideka–* is the Greek numerical prefix for 13, and *hendeca–* is the Greek
numerical prefix for 11.

120. (a. Cassatt, b. Caillebotte, c. Van Gogh, **d. Gauguin**) : TAHITI :: CÉZANNE : MONT
SAINTE-VICTOIRE
(**d**) Tahiti was a favorite location and subject for Paul Gauguin, much as Paul Cézanne
repeatedly painted Mont Sainte-Victoire.